Keelhauled

Unsportsmanlike Conduct and the America's Cup

DOUG RIGGS

STANFORD MARITIME LIMITED

LONDON

DEDICATION

This book is lovingly dedicated to my wife Mary, who inspired my best, tolerated my worst, and endured many lonely hours.

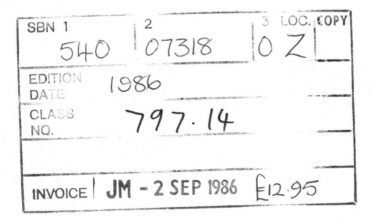

SBN 1	2	3 LOC. COPY
540	07318	0 Z
EDITION DATE	1986	
CLASS NO.	797.14	
INVOICE	JM – 2 SEP 1986	£12·95

STANFORD MARITIME LIMITED

Member Company of The George Philip Group
12-14 Long Acre, London WC2E 9LP

First published in Great Britain 1986
Copyright © 1986 The Providence Journal Company
Originally published in the United States by Seven Seas Press, Inc., Newport, Rhode Island

Printed in the United States by R.R. Donnelley & Sons, Harrisonburg, Virginia

ISBN 0 504 07318 0

ACKNOWLEDGEMENTS

My first thanks go to my employers at the Providence Journal-Bulletin, for putting me where the action was in the summer of '83, then for their patience as the "instant book" they proposed evolved and stretched to more than two years. Especially to Chuck Hauser, Jim Wyman, Joel Rawson, Chips Quinn and Dave Gray. And a special thanks to Joyce Fabizak and the rest of the Journal's Newport bureau staff, for keeping the Cup files up-to-date and tolerating my extended stay. And to Dave Philips, for sharing his vast knowledge.

Next, to my editor, Jim Gilbert, for his patience, enthusiasm and his countless and invariably perceptive comments and suggestions.

To the staff of Redwood Library, the Mystic Seaport Library, and Sohei Hohri, New York Yacht Club librarian, for their research help, and to Dorsey Milot, Susan Marshall and Leslie Ehman of the America II syndicate for sharing their extensive clip file on 1987 Cup contenders. And to the dozens of Cup veterans, named and unnamed, who took the time to answer my questions and share their thoughts.

Of the 50-odd books and articles I read about the Cup, I found the following especially helpful: "The Lawson History of The America's Cup," by Thomas Lawson and Winfield M. Thompson. 1902. Privately printed in Boston; "Defending the America's Cup," edited by Robert W. Carrick and Stanley Z. Rosenfeld. 1969. Alfred A. Knopf, New York; "America's Cup Book," by John Rousmaniere. 1983. W.W. Norton & Co., New York, London; "America's Cup Fever," by Bob Bavier. 1980. Ziff-Davis Publishing Co., New York; "No Excuse to Lose," by Dennis Conner, as told to John Rousmaniere. 1978. Norton, New York; "Ben Lexcen, the Man, the Keel and the Cup," by Bruce Stannard. 1984. Faber and Faber Ltd., London; "The Triumph of Australia II," by Bruce Stannard. 1983. Lansdowne, Sydney; "Trials, Canada 1 and the 1983 America's Cup," by Jeff Boyd and Doug Hunter. 1984. MacMillan of Canada, Toronto; "Upset: Australia Wins the America's Cup," by Michael Levitt and Barbara Lloyd. 1983. A Nautical Quarterly book. Workman Publishing, New York; "Born to Win," by John Bertrand as told to Patrick Robinson. 1985. William Morrow & Co., New York; "The Grand Gesture," by Roger Vaughan. 1975. Little-Brown, Boston; "Ted Turner, the Man Behind the Mouth," by Roger Vaughan. 1978. Sail Books, Boston.

My thanks to these authors and others who have gone before, with the understanding that they should not be held responsible for any errors I may have committed.

Last of all, because most of all, my thanks and deep appreciation to my wife Mary, for her inspiration, suggestions, support and endurance. Without her, I would not have dared.

CONTENTS

INTRODUCTION

The America's Cup was deeded to the New York Yacht Club in 1857 as a perpetual challenge cup "for friendly competition between foreign countries." It became the most sought-after, most elusive, most expensive and most prestigious trophy in the world. But by the time the Australians finally snatched it away in 1983, the once-gentlemanly event it symbolized resembled a back-alley brawl more than a sporting contest, and the spirit of friendly competition was in tatters.

What happened? That question kept tugging at me as I began work on what was intended to be little more than an account of the 1983 races. The search for answers led back to *America*'s victory in 1851, forward to the next match in 1987, and to this book.

My first impulse, frankly, was to set the record straight on the summer of '83 — a record I had helped to write in a small way as a member of the Providence Journal-Bulletin's team covering the match.

Don't misunderstand: Our coverage was as good as anyone's and better than most. But no member of the America's Cup press corps had anything like a complete picture until after the races were over. On the one hand, we were faced with the New York Yacht Club's obsessive secrecy and deep suspicion of journalists, which grew more impenetrable as things started going badly for the defense. On the other, none of us could even begin to guess the extent to which we were being brazenly manipulated by the Australians.

But beyond that, as one who was seeing a Cup match at close range for the first time, I was struck by its sheer magnitude and intensity. Naively, I had expected a yacht race; but this was more like war, with a relatively insignificant naval component. Had it always been like this? Or was 1983 an aberration?

The answer is no, to both questions. But to understand that, you'll have to start at the beginning, in 1851, and work your way forward. Or you may want to start where I did, in 1983, then go back to the first race.

Either way, don't look for heroes or villains. You may find a few here and there, but they're beside the point. America's Cup campaigns, by and large, have been mounted by men of extraordinary ambition and average virtue. In 1983, as in 1870 when the New Yorkers defended the Cup for the first time, they and the challengers tried to play by the rules as they saw them. It is the perception of those rules, and our capacity to deal with the outside forces that influence them, that has changed.

For me, that is the real significance of the America's Cup — what it says about us and our rules and the things that shape them. The daily papers provide a running boxscore of the modern malaise in sports, the betting scandals, recruiting violations, payoffs, fixes, drugs and all the rest. Are these isolated evils, or signs of strain brought on by unbridled growth and a general deterioration of sporting values? Are the people who commit them spoilers or victims?

We tend to think of yacht racing as above all that, simpler and more pristine than professional football or even the Olympics, certainly in an entirely different category than auto racing or boxing. But in yachting as in other sports, professionalism, commercialism, corporate-style organization and media hype, to name just the most obvious modern seductions, have begun altering the event in unforeseen ways.

Nowhere are these influences more visible than in the America's Cup. The New York Yacht Club's 132-year winning streak, longest in sports history, provides an unparalleled yardstick for measuring their impact. And perhaps, as we look toward Australia's first defense in 1987, for gauging whether "friendly competition between foreign countries" is still possible on an America's Cup course anywhere in the world.

Prologue

At 3 in the afternoon on September 12, 1983, the phone rang in James Michael's temporary home in Newport, Rhode Island. Robert W. McCullough, chairman of the New York Yacht Club's America's Cup Committee, was on the other end. He had bad news: Alan Bond, head of the Australia II syndicate, had refused to sign the committee's three-page "certificate of compliance."

Six days earlier, *Australia II* had won the right to challenge for the America's Cup. But the NYYC was almost certain the Australians had violated the rules to get there. The committee was especially suspicious about the legality of her secret winged keel and some of her components, including her mast. The 10-point "certificate" Michael drafted was intended as a formal denial of those allegations. If Bond refused to sign, the committee could cite that as reason enough to disqualify his boat.

But time was drawing terribly short. The races were set to start the following day and the captain's meeting was scheduled for 5 p.m. The club's leaders had just two hours to decide whether to act on their convictions, or let the Australians race. Everyone knew *Australia II* was faster than the defender. The club's 132-year domination of the America's Cup, the longest winning streak in the history of sports, hung in the balance.

Michael, the committee's legal counsel, thought the tough decision had already been made.

"Well, all right, Bob," he said on the phone. "You will recall that I said if we were going to make the decision to require these written assurances of the Australians, we must also agree that if they refuse then they do not qualify as a challenger — which everyone agreed to. So where does that leave us? Are we prepared to go forward on that basis?"

"No, I don't think so," McCullough said. "I think we'll let them go ahead and sail anyhow." Michael argued vehemently.

"Well, why don't you come on down to the dock. The commodore and all the officers are here and some of the people on the committee. We'll have a meeting and decide what to do," McCullough answered.

On that almost casual basis several key members of the embattled
NYYC assembled for what proved to be one of the most fateful meetings in its history. Like so many actions the club took that summer,
the meeting was held in private and not disclosed until weeks later.

In lonely isolation they wrestled with their a moral dilemma.
Should they fulfill their obligation as trustees of the Cup by
disqualifying *Australia II*, knowing they had no tangible proof and
knowing a firestorm of criticism was sure to follow? Or should they
bow to the public perception of sportsmanship and let the match
continue, knowing they would very likely lose their precious trophy to
an illegal challenger?

When they emerged 45 minutes later, the fate of the Cup had been
decided. The Australians' stonewalling and manipulation of the press
and public opinion, aided substantially by the NYYC's bungled
detective work, had succeeded. The club would race *Australia II.*

With grim faces, Michael and McCullough arrived together at
Marble House for the 5 p.m. captain's meeting. As they went through
the doors, Michael was handed a telegram. The message, from an
American supplier, confirmed that the Aussies were using an illegal
U.S.-designed mast. Michael handed it to McCullough as they
entered the meeting room. McCullough glanced at it, then simply put
it in his pocket. Time had run out.

Marble House, one of the grandest of Newport's grand mansions,
was once the home of Harold S. "Mike" Vanderbilt, the skipper who
defended the America's Cup during the J-boat era of the 1930s — the
high-water mark of gentlemanly sportsmanship in America's Cup
racing.

If Vanderbilt's ghost was looking on as McCullough pocketed that
incriminating telegram, it is hard to know whether it was with
approval or dismay. Certainly Vanderbilt, a former NYYC commodore, would have sympathized with his successors over their dilemma.

But he and his era were long gone. Their once-genteel sporting
event had become a brutal test of professional skills on the water, a
bitter and back-stabbing street fight on shore. And on the eve of the
match in which they lost the Cup, hardly anyone in America
sympathized with the New York Yacht Club or its leaders.

They had fallen victim to a no-holds-barred assault on their trophy,
their sportsmanship and their honor as gentlemen. They had tried to
play a 20th-century game with 19th-century rules, and they had
failed.

But whose failure was it, really?

PART ONE

The Rise

1851-1937

1
AMERICA AND THE
NOBLE DEED

The year was 1850. America was at the height of her national adolescence, that heady period of geographical, industrial and psychological expansion that preceeded, and in part provoked, the Civil War a decade later. She had just taken Texas, New Mexico and California in a brief and profitable little war with Mexico and had begun to nail down her manifest destiny with railroad spikes — 7,000 miles of track in the last 10 years alone. A booming economy and a steady stream of American inventions, ranging from the telegraph to safety pins, had confirmed Capitalism and Progress as the true secular religions.

The Industrial Revolution had been building to a full head of steam since the beginning of the century, and those who owned the engines — steamboats, locomotives, factory steam power — had amassed huge fortunes. Now the sons and grandsons of these industrious and generally respected men (the phrase "robber baron" would not enter the language for another generation) had leisure and wealth enough to seek a new outlet for the competitive drive inherited from their more single-minded forebears. Many of them found it in sports and games. Even those not endowed with the skill or hardihood to play an active part could, and did, wager on the outcomes. Fortunes equal to the combined lifetime earnings of a dozen mill workers were ventured on the speed of a horse or a boat.

Such was the fertile ground upon which in the autumn of 1850 fell the invitation, perhaps merely a suggestion, from an English merchant to several New York businessmen: Great Britain would be holding an International Exhibition the following year. Many British yacht clubs would be holding regattas. Why don't some of you chaps send over one of your famous New York pilot boats next summer, to test their mettle against our fast schooners?

Organized yacht racing was still in its infancy in America but was finding interest among the wealthiest of the new leisure class. Not only was it inherently elitist, expensive and satisfyingly ostentatious, it also bore a direct relationship to the source of many of the great fortunes of the day, based as they were on commerce carried under sail. The first known yacht club in America was formed in Boston in 1835, but was disbanded two years later. The one formed in New York in 1844, the New York Yacht Club (NYYC), would endure.

England, the kindly but domineering old mother country, chose precisely the right moment to offer her strapping offspring a rite of passage, a chance to join the grownups at one of their most exclusive games. In fact, it must have been an irresistible proposition on both sides of the Atlantic. The Yanks, for their part, had reason to think they might beat the Brits in their home waters. Like most occupations in that unregulated era, piloting in New York was highly competitive; the first pilot to hail an incoming ship got the job of directing her through the harbor. With that incentive, their boats had grown sleeker and faster until they gained a worldwide reputation.

The British must have taken more than a sporting interest in those tales from New York. Innovations in ship design were as important to the Victorians as advances in electronic circuitry are today. Yankee clippers already dominated the tea trade between Britain and China. If Britannia hoped to continue ruling the waves, it might behoove her to take a firsthand look at those new colonial boats.

The letter from that unknown English merchant was shown to John Cox Stevens, commodore of the NYYC and one of the city's leading sportsmen. It could hardly have reached a more appropriate recipient. It was Stevens, grandson of a member of the Continental Congress and son of a colonel in the Revolutionary War, who had founded the club six years earlier, along with eight fellow yachtsmen. Not only was he its first and only commodore, the original clubhouse was built on the grounds of his estate in Hoboken, New Jersey. (His father, Col. John Stevens, owned Hoboken. All of it. The elder Stevens moved on from waging Revolutionary war to inventing the steam screw propeller and generally making a fortune in steamboating. He bought the land that was to become Hoboken, which had been expropriated from a Tory sympathizer. Then he and his four sons, John Cox, James, Edwin and Robert, built a town, amusement park and seaport on the site.)

The Stevens brothers also were fascinated, and enriched, by steam navigation, to which they made significant contributions. It was Edwin who founded the Stevens Institute of Technology in Hoboken, where more than a century later designers of America's Cup defenders tested their ideas in one of the country's first towing tanks. John Cox Stevens had other interests as well: yachting, horse racing, cricket (which he introduced to America) and a fondness for betting large sums of money on the outcome of any of those endeavors.

Not surprisingly, he seized upon the yacht racing suggestion. But he and the small syndicate he formed for the purpose (including Stevens and his brother Edwin, George L. Schuyler, John K. Beekman Finlay and Hamilton Wilkes, NYYC members all, joined informally by James Hamilton, third son of Alexander Hamilton), decided to carry it a step further: They would build a new vessel, finer and faster than any pilot boat, specifically to trounce the British. The details would be arranged primarily by Stevens and Schuyler.

SHREWD MEN

Schuyler and Stevens were the first in a long line of shrewd businessmen associated with the America's Cup. Perhaps they were the shrewdest since, as far as is known, they are the only ones ever to turn a profit on the deal. Like John Cox Stevens, George Schuyler, grandson of a Revolutionary War general and heir to a major fortune, developed steamship lines. Unlike him, he also wrote history. That was fortunate, for it was Schuyler, at 39 the youngest syndicate member, who outlived all the others and therefore was called upon many years later to help shape the future history of the Cup, as we shall see.

They selected William H. Brown to build the new yacht at his yard on the Manhattan side of the East River. Brown was chosen chiefly because his 30-year-old house designer, George Steers, had turned out the fastest pilot boats in New York as well as some highly successful racing yachts for the Stevens brothers. Steers had achieved his early and immoderate success in the usual way: by ignoring the conventional wisdom of his elders. The conventional wisdom, inherited from England, was that a ship should have a "cod's head and a mackerel's tail" — i.e., a rounded bow and pointed stern. Steers gradually turned that concept back to front in successive designs, each faster than the last. His plan for the Stevens syndicate would be the most radical yet, a 170-ton schooner, 90 feet from stem to stern, with a sharply pointed bow and rounded stern whose transom, keel and masts would all be sharply raked. Nothing would be spared on the interior finishings, which included elegant saloons finished in carved rosewood, polished American walnut and green silk velvet. She would be named *America*.

When the work was well advanced, in March of 1851, Stevens received a cordial letter from the Earl of Wilton, commodore of the Royal Yacht Squadron in London. The commodore had gotten wind of the Yankees' plans and was taking the opportunity to invite them to avail themselves of his club's hospitality while they were in British waters. There was no mention of races or wagers, but that aspect of the venture was understood by both sides, as Stevens' equally cordial reply made clear:

New York, March 26th, 1851
My Lord, — I take the earliest opportunity offered to convey to the gentlemen of the Royal Yacht Squadron, and to yourself, the expression of our warmest thanks for your invitation to visit the Club House at Cowes. Some four or five friends and myself have a yacht on the stocks which we hope to launch in the course of two or three weeks. Should she answer the sanguine expectations of her builder and fulfill the stipulations he has made, we propose to avail ourselves of your friendly bidding and take with good grace the sound thrashing we are likely to get by venturing our longshore craft on your rough waters. I fear the energy and experience of your persevering yachtsmen will prove an overmatch for the industry and skill of their aspiring competitors....

John C. Stevens,
Commodore New York Yacht Club

Stevens' uncharacteristic deference owed more to gamesmanship than trepidation, as the terms of the agreement under which *America* was built make clear. One of the "stipulations" to which William Brown agreed in order to get the contract was that *America* would prove faster than any vessel of her tonnage, American or British, or the syndicate could refuse her and owe nothing! Not only that, the judge of whether she met the conditions was to be none other than Hamilton Wilkes, a member of the syndicate, though not an owner.

It was one of the most generous guarantees any shipbuilder has ever made, before or since. Whether it was freely offered or won after prolonged negotiation is a matter of conjecture. And, although the letter of acceptance implies the proposal was the subject of considerable deliberation within the syndicate because the price ($30,000) was high, it is dated the same day as the proposal itself, November 15, and presumably was executed during the same sitting.

To his credit, having complained about the price, Schuyler did praise Brown for the "liberal and sportsmanlike character of the whole offer" and accepted it, with the stipulation that the yacht be ready for trials by April 1, 1951.

It is rare for a yacht to be completed on time, and *America* was no exception. As April 1 dawned, she was still on the ways. The following day Schuyler wrote to Brown agreeing to a one-month extension, providing he meet certain other conditions that gave the syndicate the right to refuse her if she were beaten by any vessel in England, regardless of size. Brown's reaction to this further test of his "liberal and sportsmanlike character" went unrecorded. But the next turn of the screw might have rattled a saint:

He missed the May 1 deadline by two days. Soon after launching on the 3rd, *America* was sailed against *Maria*, a sloop owned by Stevens on which he had lavished $100,000 to make her probably the fastest yacht in the United States. Accounts differ as to the results, but it is certain *Maria* beat *America* in at least some of the trials in the smooth water around Sandy Hook. No one was dismayed by the result, however. *Maria* was known to be superb in sheltered waters, but no match for *America* in the rougher seas she would encounter abroad. The tests were inconclusive at best. Furthermore, *America* beat every other vessel sent against her.

Nonetheless, Brown had not met the deadline. On May 24, Schuyler wrote a new proposal. The unanticipated delays left no time for further trials before the schooner had to sail for England. Therefore, the syndicate would agree to accept her forthwith, providing Brown would agree to a new price: $20,000.

Just how much of a loss that meant for Brown is unknown. Even though he had produced a remarkably fast vessel in a remarkably short time, he had not fulfilled the contract. He was left with a choice between signing the new proposal or losing his buyer. He signed.

AMERICA MAKES WAVES

Under the command of Capt. Dick Brown, a renowned pilot boat skipper, *America* made the crossing from New York to Le Havre, France, in 20 days, having passed every vessel in sight. There she was provisioned and fitted out for the contests to come while the Stevens brothers and James Hamilton, who had crossed by steamer, enjoyed a brief sojourn in Paris. If there remained any doubt in their minds that their adventure had international implications, it was dispelled in Paris when a number of Americans approached them to warn against testing their unproven yacht against the English. Horace Greeley, editor of the New York Tribune — the same Horace Greeley who urged America's youth to go west — warned his friend Hamilton: "The eyes of the world are upon you. You will be beaten and the country will be abused."

Undeterred, *America's* backers sailed aboard her to the Solent, the channel that separates the Isle of Wight from the mainland. On the evening of July 31, they anchored about six miles below Cowes, home of the Royal Yacht Squadron.

The next morning, as *America* prepared to get under way, *Lavrock*, one of the newest and fastest of the English cutters, came gliding down to "escort" her up the channel. There was no doubt as to her real intentions: It was a nautical version of the gunfighter and the marshal facing each other on a dusty street. A crowd gathered on shore. Commodore Stevens described the scene in an after-dinner speech two months later:

"They saw we could not escape, for the *Lavrock* stuck to us, sometimes lying-to and sometimes tacking round us, evidently showing she had no intention of quitting us. We were loaded with extra sails, with beef and pork and bread enough for an East India voyage, and were four or five inches too deep in the water. We got up our sails with heavy hearts; the wind had increased to a five- or six-knot breeze, and after waiting until we were ashamed to wait longer, we let her go about 200 yards, and then started in her wake.

"I have seen and been engaged in many exciting trials at sea and on shore ... without feeling one-hundredth part of the responsibility and ... trepidation I felt at the thought of being beaten by the *Lavrock* in this eventful trial. During the first five minutes not a sound was heard save, perhaps, the beating of our anxious hearts or the slight ripple of the water upon her (*America*'s) swordlike stem. The captain was crouched down upon the floor of the cockpit, his seemingly unconscious hand upon the tiller, with his stern, unaltering gaze upon the vessel ahead. The men were motionless as statues, their eager eyes fastened upon the *Lavrock* with a fixedness and intensity that seemed almost supernatural.... It could not and did not last long. We worked quickly and surely to windward of her wake. The crisis was past and some dozen of deep-drawn sighs proved that the agony was over."

America arrived at Cowes a quarter of a mile or more ahead of *Lavrock*, where her owners were greeted warmly by Lord Wilton and several other yachtsmen.

If there had been any conflict in Stevens' mind between his gambling and sporting instincts, they aren't apparent in the speech quoted above. Clearly he worried more about losing this informal test than he did about tipping his hand before any bets were placed. Perhaps he had no idea just how much faster his yacht would prove to be. Or perhaps, like the marshal with his courage and honor on the line, he had no choice. In any case, *America's* showing sent shock waves through the yachting establishment and thwarted Stevens' hopes of finding willing wagerers. The agitation among them, said the London Times, was like that which "the appearance of a sparrowhawk in the horizon creates among a flock of woodpigeons or skylarks."

The Times would have even less complimentary things to say about the manliness of English yachtsmen as Commodore Stevens' repeated offers to race for wagers of various amounts were greeted with thundering silence. By the second week of August he was offering to race "any cutter, schooner, or vessel of any other rig of the Royal Yacht Squadron, relinquishing any advantage which your rule admits is due to a schooner from a cutter..." for any prize ranging from a cup of limited value to a purse of up to 10,000 guineas. (That translated to about $50,000, a huge sum in those days — more than twice the cost of the American syndicate's entire campaign, in fact. For a modern equivalent, imagine Alan Bond, head of the Australian syndicate that won the America's Cup in 1983, offering to bet $10 million on a single race between his *Australia II* and any boat of roughly comparable size the NYYC might select, 12-meter or not.)

Barred from one regatta on a technicality, and failing to enter another because of a delay in receiving an acceptance, *America* showed up on the courses anyway. In both cases she started miles behind the participants and passed them all before they reached the finish. Finally, on August 16, despairing of arranging an individual match, Stevens accepted an invitation from Lord Wilton to enter the Royal Yacht Squadron's annual regatta on August 22. It would be open "to all rigs and nations," though in fact *America* was the only foreign vessel entered. The course would be approximately 53 miles around the Isle of Wight. The prize was a bottomless, ornate silver ewer, 27 inches tall and weighing 134 ounces. It was called the Hundred Guinea Cup because that's what the London firm of R. and S. Gerard was paid for it earlier that year.

CONSOLATION PRIZE

After that was arranged, Stevens' general challenge for a match race finally got a positive response. Robert Stephenson, M.P., ventured 100 guineas cash that his 100-ton schooner *Titania* could beat *America* on a 40-mile course. He did so reportedly more to uphold the honor of British yachtsmen, who had just received another blistering dressing down for their timidity from the London Times, than from any hope of winning. Their race was set for August 28.

There is some speculation that Stevens, who viewed the regatta and the chance to win an ugly silver ewer on the 22nd as a sort of consolation prize, would not have entered it had the match with *Titania* been arranged earlier. Even The London Illustrated News, which carried the most complete account of the regatta, described it as "a sort of trial heat" before the "great international contest" that would take place six days later between *Titania* and *America*.

But the News also noted that, once word got around that *America* was entered in the Cowes regatta, "the most intense interest was manifested by all classes, from the highest to the humblest, who have thronged in such masses this season to the Isle of Wight." The London Times correspondent at Cowes reported people knocking on doors long after midnight the night before the race, looking in vain for a place to sleep. The betting, he said, was heavily of the opinion that "the Yankee" would win.

Eighteen yachts were entered, but only 15 started: eight cutters and seven schooners, including *America*. Despite great differences in size and rigs (the smallest cutter weighed 47 tons, the largest schooner 392), no time allowances were given.

When the starting gun sounded at 10 a.m., *America* was slow getting under way. In the past she had tended to overrun her anchor and slew around, so the crew kept her sails lowered while the anchor was hoisted, then raised them. But within the first 90 minutes, with a freshening breeze, she had overtaken and passed all her rivals. *America*, the Times reported, "flew like the wind, leaping over, not against, the water.... The way her sails were set evinced superiority in the cutting which our makers would barely allow; but, certain it is, that while the jibs and mainsails of her antagonists were 'bellied out,' her canvas was as flat as a sheet of paper. No foam, but rather a water-jet, rose from her bows.... While the cutters were threshing through the water, sending the spray over their bows, and the schooners were wet up to the foot of the foremast, the *America* was dry as a bone."

Three of the yachts dropped out with various problems. *America*'s only mishap was the loss of her jib boom off Sandown Bay, which may have been an advantage. Captain Brown, in his usual crusty manner, remarked he was "damned glad it was gone," as he never liked to carry a flying jib to windward, anyway. She finished at 8:37 p.m., somewhere between eight and 24 minutes ahead of her nearest rival, the 47-ton *Aurora*, smallest yacht in the fleet. (The accounts vary; time-keeping was a less exacting occupation in those days, apparently.) Spectators cheered and a band played "Yankee Doodle" as she crossed the line.

There was a protest, from the owner of the *Brilliant*: *America*, along with a few other competitors, had gone inside the Nab Light, saving a couple of miles. The race committee dismissed the protest, noting that one set of instructions specified rounding the light while another set, the one given to *America*'s captain, was silent on the subject. There were no further objections and the Hundred Guinea Cup, henceforward to be known as the America's Cup, was bestowed upon the Yankees from New York.

RUMORS OF CHEATING

It had been a pleasant little venture for the New Yorkers all the way around. They were given the utmost hospitality after they won, including a visit from Queen Victoria, who inspected the yacht from stem to stern and charmed her owners. Six days after the victory at Cowes, *America* met *Titania* as planned, and beat her by almost an hour, as expected. The owners collected the 100-guinea wager. Four days later they sold *America* to an Irish peer for the equivalent of

$25,000. After deducting the original cost of the yacht, plus $3,750 in expenses, that left a profit of $1,750; and the Cup, worth $500.

But there were foreshadowings of future events, when the pursuit of the Cup would become far less sportsmanlike. *America*'s performance had so startled some British yachtsmen, for example, that rumors of cheating arose, specifically, the suspicion that she carried a concealed propeller. No less a personage than the Marquis of Anglesey, known as "the father of British yachting," came aboard soon after the race to look for himself. It was the Marquis who had uttered a sentence, on first sighting *America* just after she beat *Lavrock* up the Solent, that would be heard again in the years to come: "If she is right, then we must all be wrong." Now he stomped his way across the deck on his peg leg (his own had been blown off by a cannon at Waterloo), and leaned so far over the rail to look for the alleged propeller that Commodore Stevens had to grasp his good leg to keep him from pitching overboard.

The rumor was finally dispelled when *America* was hauled out to repair some damage caused by grounding, and a number of Britain's most respected boat builders came down to gaze at her private parts, hitherto concealed by water. Unlike the Australian Cup contender 132 years later, nothing out of the ordinary was found. But it was again left to the Marquis of Anglesey, having regained his equilibrium if not his composure, to sum up the general consternation of British yachtsmen as he took another long look at *America*'s sharp bow and rounded stern: "I've learned one thing," he said. "I've been sailing my yacht stern foremost for the last 20 years."

America, in fact, was what we have since come to call a "breakthrough" yacht, an innovative design that so outclasses the competition as to influence yacht building from then onward — or at least until the next breakthrough. Not only was her hull superior, so were her sails. They were made of machine-woven cotton duck, vastly better than the loose-woven flax canvas English sails, which had to be doused with water to keep their shape. Although no one could have predicted it at the time, the United States was destined to remain one technological step ahead of her challengers for more than a century.

Beyond that, the Cup was won by skillful sailing, hard bargaining, and a syndicate of tough-minded, shrewd and dictatorial men who were prepared to sacrifice vast sums of money and any sentimental impulses in pursuit of the goal. John Cox Stevens' attempt at gamesmanship — the letter in which he tried to convince the British he saw little chance of winning — failed to elicit the hoped-for wagers. But it set a precedent that would lead eventually to full-scale psychological warfare.

America's race generated some nationalistic mythology, too, foreshadowing the fact that the America's Cup, almost from the start, would be seen as more than just a race between yacht clubs, but rather a contest between nations. One of the minor legends, unproven, is that "Old Dick" Brown, *America*'s taciturn captain, asked Prince Albert when he visited the yacht to wipe off his feet before going below. When the consort hesitated, Brown reportedly said, "I know who you are, but you'll have to wipe your feet." (If the story is true, it is one more foreshadowing: In the summer of 1983, the year the NYYC finally relinquished its hold on the America's Cup, Peter deSavary, the flamboyant head of the British syndicate, asked Prince Andrew to take off his shoes before stepping aboard deSavary's private luxury yacht *Kalizma*. The prince meekly obeyed.)

But the most enduring myth is that Queen Victoria, watching the race from the royal yacht *Victoria and Albert*, asked her signalman as they approached the finish, "Which is first?"

"The *America*, Mam," he answered.

"And which is second?"

"Ah, Your Majesty, there is no second."

The evidence from correspondents on the scene suggests that the Queen, along with many other observers, had left the course long before such an exchange would have been possible. But the phrase "there is no second" would forever be linked with the Cup.

As for the *America* herself, she embarked upon a curious career that included service as a racing yacht, a pleasure craft, a blockade runner for the Confederacy, then, after being sunk and recovered by Union forces, a blockader for the North. After the war, she became a training ship for the U.S. Naval Academy. She was destined to be restored in the early 1940s, but World War II halted those efforts. Her life ended rather ignominiously on March 28, 1942, when the roof of the shed in which she had been stored at the Naval Academy in Annapolis collapsed during a freak blizzard.

FRIENDLY COMPETITION

The Cup that bears her name has had far more solicitous care — but not at first. After returning to the States, *America*'s owners

debated what to do with it. There was some talk of melting it down to
make medallions for each member of the syndicate. Instead, it was
passed from one owner to another for a time. There's a story,
undocumented, that it had been banished to a closet in the Manhattan
mansion of John Cox Stevens. There it became badly tarnished and
was almost tossed out with the trash by a new maid.

Eventually, on July 8, 1857, the remaining members of the original
America syndicate decided to donate the Cup to the NYYC as a perpetual challenge trophy. They wrote a simple and sportsmanlike deed
of gift, blissfully ignorant of the thousands of man-hours that would
later be spent revising, interpreting or bending their straightforward
words to gain an advantage:

> *Any organized yacht club of any foreign country shall always*
> *be entitled through any one or more of its members, to claim the*
> *right of sailing a match for this cup with any yacht or other vessel*
> *of not less than thirty or more than three hundred tons, measured*
> *by the custom-house rule of the country to which the vessel*
> *belongs.*
>
> *The parties desiring to sail for the cup may make any match*
> *with the yacht club in possession of the same that may be*
> *determined upon by mutual consent; but, in case of disagreement*
> *as to terms, the match shall be sailed over the usual course for the*
> *annual regatta of the yacht club in possession of the cup, and sub-*
> *ject to its rules and sailing regulations — the challenging party*
> *being bound to give six months' notice in writing, fixing the day*
> *they wish to start. This notice to embrace the length, custom-*
> *house measurement, rig and name of the vessel.*
>
> *It is to be distinctly understood that the Cup is to be the prop-*
> *erty of the club, and not of the members thereof, or owners of the*
> *vessels winning it in a match; and that the condition of keeping it*
> *open to be sailed for by yacht clubs of all foreign countries upon*
> *the terms above laid down, shall forever attach to it, thus making*
> *it perpetually a challenge cup for friendly competition between*
> *foreign countries.*

The deed would survive intact for several years. The Cup would
last even longer. But the spirit of friendly competition was in trouble
almost from the start.

2

NEW YORK
RULES THE WAVES

On July 21, 1857, the New York Yacht Club sent foreign yacht clubs an announcement of its new Cup, and invited "spirited contest for the championship," promising "a liberal, hearty welcome and the strictest of fair play." Before anyone put that promise to the test, America nearly dismembered itself in a bloody and searing Civil War that banished all thoughts of yacht racing.

1870: FIRST CHALLENGE
Finally, in 1868, after the war-related strains in Anglo-American relations had eased, an Englishman came forward. He was James Ashbury, whose father, a wheelwright, made a fortune by inventing a railway carriage. Like many other wealthy men of little or no social standing who would follow him, Ashbury saw the challenge as an avenue to social status and a possible political career. He yearned for a seat in Parliament.

He was determined to take charge of the negotiations from the start, offering a complicated, multi-race challenge between his yacht *Cambria* and the best of the NYYC fleet, culminating in a race for the Cup. He also proposed his own race conditions, quite different from those practiced by the New Yorkers.

In response, the NYYC first pointed out that challenges had to be made by clubs, not individuals. That was remedied: The Royal Thames Yacht Club would sponsor. (Presumably Ashbury, as a mere businessman of no great pedigree, was not eligible for membership in the stuffy Royal Yacht Squadron — as Sir Thomas Lipton was not,

13

many years later.) Then the NYYC pointedly reminded Ashbury that the deed of gift allowed a match to be arranged "by mutual consent," but if negotiations failed, it would be run according to the rules of the club holding the Cup. The New Yorkers weren't about to let a challenger dictate terms.

The correspondence became protracted; the proposed race was pushed from 1869 to 1870. Both sides were jockeying for advantage and their positions owed far more to that than to sportsmanship, logic, or even common sense:

The deed of gift clearly stated that the Cup should be challenged for and defended in a match — i.e., a race between two vessels. On the other hand, there appears to have been a strong feeling on the part of the NYYC that anyone who hoped to wrest the Cup would bloody well have to face the same odds *America* had faced in winning the thing in the first place. Therefore it followed that if a "match" were arranged, Ashbury's challenger would have to face the entire NYYC fleet of some 30 yachts, or at least as many of them as chose to race. That was only fair, wasn't it? The club's vote on the one-against-the-fleet condition was eighteen-to-one, with only Commodore Henry G. Stebbins opposed.

Ashbury's position was that the 1851 race had no bearing on the proposed contest. The deed of gift had wiped the slate clean and set forth new conditions. Furthermore, even if one accepted the club's premise, along with its peculiar definition of the word "match," the logic was faulty: *America* had taken part in a regatta in which 15 vessels raced individually for a prize, each with an equal chance of winning. That was a far cry from the proposed contest, in which one challenger would face any number of defenders who might, if they chose, act in concert against him.

The two positions were never clearly spelled out in the convoluted correspondence, probably because on other issues (see below) the club chose to cite the deed as authority, whereas Ashbury found it convenient to regard the 1851 race as precedent. Indeed, it may be that Ashbury wasn't even aware of the club's intention before he sailed for New York, where the final agreement was hammered out at closer range.

As if that weren't enough, the club also insisted on two other conditions. The first was that the match be raced on the club's infamous "inside course" off Staten Island. This was roughly 38 miles, from

Robbins Reef through the Narrows to Southwest Spit Buoy, around Sandy Hook Lightship and back — a tortuous course with strong currents, dangerous sand bars and heavy traffic. Like the 1851 course around the Isle of Wight, it strongly favored local knowledge. Ashbury urged a fairer test in open water, but dropped the issue without much of a fuss.

On the second, however, he dug in his heels, at least briefly. That was the club's intention to allow centerboard yachts to sail against the challenger. Centerboarders, or "skimming dishes" as the British contemptuously called them, were then common in the shoal waters of New York Harbor and other American ports, but were banned by the Royal Yacht Squadron on the grounds that they were unseaworthy and unfairly fast. A centerboard is a movable keel; when lifted it decreases a boat's draft and its water resistance, thus increasing its speed, especially running downwind. Centerboarders are inherently unstable, and, at least back in the late nineteenth century, were certainly not up to a transatlantic run. Challengers had to sail to New York, so they had no chance to use them.

"The cup having been won at Cowes, under the rules of the Royal Yacht Squadron, it thereby follows that no centre-board vessel can compete against the *Cambria* in this particular race," Ashbury asserted.

The club's negotiators replied that this logic didn't follow at all: The conditions of the 1851 race had nothing to do with future races, which would be governed by the deed of gift. But then they asserted that because the deed specified the "match" be subject to the Cup-holder's rules and sailing instructions, they could not exclude any yacht duly qualified to sail under the rules of the NYYC. Not only would centerboarders be allowed, they had no power to prevent any qualified boat from lining up at the starting line. (That was about as close as the club would get in trying to reconcile its multi-defender plans with the deed of gift.)

The record is silent as to Ashbury's response; chances are his exact words would have been regarded as unprintable in the Victorian era. But we know he conceded on all points, for on August 8, 1870, his *Cambria* lined up with 17 other boats, Americans all, at the start of the NYYC's inside course.

The race attracted great interest, part of it no doubt generated by the appearance of the renowned *America* as one of the defenders. She was then the property of the U.S. Naval Academy and manned by midshipmen. Some of the financial institutions on Wall Street and Broad Street closed so their employees could see the race. One reporter counted 58 steamers, some carrying 3,000 passengers.

Most of the defenders were smaller and more maneuverable than the 248-ton *Cambria*, which gave them an advantage on that crowded course. Many of them were centerboarders. In fact the winner was the centerboarder *Magic*, one of the smallest of the fleet. *America* came in fourth. *Cambria* was eighth, tenth on corrected time. (Time allowances were in effect during the first several challenges, calculated according to a set formula to compensate for inequalities in size and design.)

On the first leg, *Cambria* had been put about several times while on starboard tack by boats on port tack, despite the basic rule of racing that gives a boat on starboard tack right of way. Ashbury later claimed he had been fouled by another entrant, *Tarolinta*, which forced *Cambria* about and may have damaged her head gear, resulting in her foretopmast being carried away later in the race. But he made no protest at the time. (The club later pointedly distributed copies of the yacht racing rules to its members.)

Whatever his private thoughts, Ashbury and *Cambria* remained in American waters for more than a month, racing (he lost more than he won), joining the NYYC in its annual cruise to Newport, entertaining President Ulysses S. Grant at breakfast aboard *Cambria*, and generally, so it seemed, cementing relations between the Colonies and the Mother Country.

1871: ASHBURY RETURNS

The defeat must have gotten his blood up, however. While still in America he ordered a new vessel from Michael Ratsey of Cowes, on the Isle of Wight. He named it *Livonia*, after a province in Russia in which he had made money building railroads. *Livonia* incorporated many of the design characteristics of the American schooners, including sails of American cotton with a total area of 18,153 square feet, the greatest sail-spread ever carried by a Cup challenger.

At a dinner given him in his native Manchester that December, Ashbury remarked that "the best of feeling exists among Americans with regard to England." But he made it clear in private conversations with friends that he didn't reciprocate, at least not as far as the NYYC was concerned. He told them he would no longer give the deed of gift "an equitable, sportsmanlike interpretation" in the discussions about his second challenge. Then he took a step that can be seen in hindsight as fateful — if not pivotal — in the history of the America's Cup: He consulted his lawyers.

With their help in the winter of 1870-71, Ashbury again urged upon the NYYC the unfairness of racing against a fleet. The club, which had received a few unflattering comments from fair-minded yachtsmen on that point, sought the opinion of George L. Schuyler, surviving member of the *America* syndicate. Schuyler replied: "I think that any candid person will admit that when the owners of the *America* sat down to write their letter of gift to the NYYC, they could hardly be expected to dwell upon an elaborate definition of their interpretation of the word 'match,' as distinguished from a 'sweepstakes' or regatta; nor would he think it very likely that any contestant for the cup, under conditions named by them, should be subjected to a trial, such as they themselves had considered unfair and unsportsmanlike.

"It seems to me that the present ruling of the club (one challenger vs. a fleet of defenders) renders the *America*'s trophy useless as 'a Challenge Cup,' and that for all sporting purposes it might as well be laid aside as family plate."

This scornful gust must have shivered a few timbers in the NYYC's committee rooms. In any event, the club changed course: On March 24, 1871, it resolved "that we sail one or more representative vessels, against the same number of foreign challenging vessels."

Having won on that point (or so it seemed), Ashbury renewed his demands that centerboarders be excluded and that a different course be chosen — one that didn't give such an advantage to local knowledge. Then, once again, he tried to put his personal stamp on the affair with a strange proposal: He held membership in no fewer than 12 different yacht clubs, he said, and wished to represent all of them. Therefore, he proposed a series of up to 12 races, the first yacht to win 7 out of 12 being declared the winner. He would sail under the burgee of a different club each day, and if he won the Cup it would go to the club whose colors he was flying in the final race.

The NYYC waited until Ashbury arrived in New York in early October. Then it fired off an answer so scornful ("The deed of gift of the cup carefully guards against any such sharp practice," it said in part) that Ashbury responded with an even more extreme proposition:

"My ultimatum is that all 12 races must be sailed, not only as a matter of right, but as I think, as an act of courtesy and consideration to me; seeing that the masts of *Livonia* were reduced to cross the Atlantic, as yet the sails are unbent, the trim of the vessel as a consequence requires to be found, and it will take at least 4 or 5 races to get *Livonia*'s exact time. A decision to reduce the 12 races will result in *Livonia*'s at once returning to England without any race, either public or private; or, I may have to consider whether I am not under the circumstances quite justified in exercising my rights, by giving you notice that as you decline 12 races, 7 out of 12 to win, I have no alternative but to act strictly up to the deed of trust by which you hold the cup, viz., by sailing the 12 races on behalf of as many clubs against your champion vessel — keel boat or centre-board, as you may select; and the first race *Livonia* won I should in that case formally and officially claim the cup on behalf of the club whose flag I sailed under."

There was a kind of rough justice in this quixotic proposition: By giving himself a 12-to-1 advantage he would be merely redressing the odds of the previous race, when he faced 17 yachts. Needless to say, the New Yorkers didn't see it that way.

After further "ultimatums" on both sides, during which Ashbury more than once threatened to sail home without a race, or sail around the course alone and claim the Cup by default, he finally gave up. Remarking that it was getting too cold to sail — it was now well into October — he agreed to the following: The Cup would be decided by a seven-race series, four races to win, three on the inside course, three on an outside course preferred by Ashbury. The seventh race, if necessary, would be raced on the outside course. Ashbury would represent the Royal Harwich Yacht Club only. Centerboarders would be allowed.

On the face of it, the conditions were a genuine if grudging compromise. But the New Yorkers, having agreed to a one-on-one match, had kept an ace up their sleeve: They would select four boats to defend the Cup, reserving the right to choose which of the four to send against *Livonia* on the morning of each race. By fielding four yachts of differing sailing characteristics, they were able to pick the one best suited to the weather conditons on a particular day. None of the club's negotiators regarded this as "sharp practice," apparently.

Ashbury protested, but less vigorously than on the other points in dispute, proposing only that if the club intended to send four boats against him he should be allowed to face each of them, three races each, on dates set in advance. Ultimately, he gave in on that, too. He still yearned for a seat in Parliament and the yacht club was adamant that this was its last offer. If he declined it, he faced the unthinkable prospect of returning to the voters without even having raced.

The committee named *Columbia, Sappho, Dauntless* and *Palmer* as its stable of defenders. *Columbia*, a centerboarder which drew only six feet with the board up, was specially designed for light and moderate breezes. As the first contest, on October 16, was to be sailed in a light northwesterly, the committee named her its defender. The race was a rout: *Columbia* by 27:04 corrected time. It was witnessed by a large crowd.

The second race was October 18. *Columbia* was chosen again, despite a freshening breeze from the southwest, which rose to a moderate gale after backing to west-northwest, turning the outside course into two reaches rather than the leeward-windward legs agreed upon. *Columbia* won by 10:33 corrected time.

That race was notable chiefly for a protest lodged by Ashbury — the first formal protest by a challenger — which had strong echoes of the one lodged against *America* in 1851: The sailing instructions were silent on the question of which way to round the turning mark. Franklin Osgood, owner of *Columbia*, asked the committee for instructions. The committee replied that the mark could be turned "as you please." It did not see fit, however, to pass that clarification on to Ashbury. In England, according to Ashbury, the rule was that when no instructions are given you must leave all marks on the starboard hand. That required a risky and time-consuming jibe at the mark, which *Livonia*'s captain performed. *Columbia*, meanwhile, merely tacked around, gaining time, distance, and the favored windward side on his opponent.

The committee ruled the protest "could not be entertained," as Ashbury should have known the rules make the method of rounding optional in the absence of instructions. The English rule Ashbury cited applied only to fleet races, not matches, it said. Ashbury declined, in writing, to accept the decision. There followed what Cup historian Jerrold Kelley described as "a rattling newspaper skirmish all along the line, which, while settling nothing, irritated right-thinking men, who finding what they called logic unavailing, simply viewed the discussion from a national standpoint."

In its official report, the NYYC's America's Cup Committee described the race in two brief sentences, then devoted more than a page to Mr. Ashbury's protest: "The committee regrets to be obliged to report Mr. Ashbury's dissatisfaction with their decision in this race," it began. This was followed by a long discussion of the *America*'s two races 20 years earlier, which seemed to establish a precedent in favor of the club's present position.

Then, as a parting shot, the committee took the first step down a long, unfortunate road that led more or less directly to the debacle in Newport 112 years later:

"The committee have dwelt at some length on this matter because, although by the rules of this club there is no appeal from their decision, Mr. Ashbury not only declined to accept it as final, but made it the foundation of communications to them through the press, which were of a disagreeable character generally, threatening to appeal to tribunals unknown to this club for redress against what he deemed unjust treatment. The friendly relations which from an early period in its history have existed between the club and the Royal Harwich of England, have induced the committee to take no notice of the communications referred to, presuming they would not be indorsed (sic) by the club, which, in other respects, Mr. Ashbury has represented in so spirited manner, and they are on that account not incorporated in this report."

Perhaps the paragraph's haughty tone owed something to the stuffier writing style of the day, as well as exasperation over Ashbury's intransigence. But there's no mistaking the underlying message: The NYYC will entertain no appeals from its decisions, and certainly not through the press or at the bar of public opinion. We take no notice of the rabble's rantings, the club seemed to be saying, and are confident that our fellow yachtsmen across the sea will understand fully, being gentlemen like ourselves.

The New Yorkers had started digging a figurative moat around their club house, one that would widen and deepen in the years ahead.

For the third race, the committee planned to enter one of the other three boats, but each was out of commission for various reasons. So *Columbia*, whose crew had done nothing to prepare her, was pressed into service again. Her sailing master, Nelson Comstock, was out of action; his brother Andrew was pressed into service, along with members of the *Dauntless* crew. Also, there was a lot of "amateur talent" aboard — a factor later cited in her loss.

Columbia's race, in a fresh southwesterly, was a sailor's nightmare. She lost three minutes at the start. She carried too much sail for the conditions. Her fore-gafftopsail split. Her flying jib stay went by the board. Her steering gear broke under severe strain caused by failure to reef the mainsail. The crew desperately hacked open the wheel housing with axes and improvised a tiller. Then the maintopmast staysail parted. At that point she gave up, lowered her main, and limped in 15:10 behind *Livonia*, which suffered no mishaps. Not only was this the first win by a challenger, the winning time remains the largest margin of victory by a challenger in America's Cup history.

For the fourth race the committee chose *Sappho*, which won in a walk by 30:21. It was *Sappho* again in the fifth and final race, by 25:27.

As far as the yacht club was concerned, the score was 4-1 and that was that. But Ashbury wasn't satisfied. On his scorecard he should have won the second race on a protest, making it 3-2. He announced that he would be at the line the next two days, October 24 and 25, for races six and seven. On October 24, he sailed against *Dauntless* in a private race. *Dauntless* won by 10:31, but Ashbury claimed victory because he went over the course alone as far as the committee was concerned. On October 25 the weather was so bad the mark-boat couldn't go out. Ashbury claimed another victory. By his figuring, which was inventive to say the least, he had won the Cup, 4-3. Needless to say, the club disagreed and the Cup remained in place.

Back in England, Ashbury wrote a long letter to the New Yorkers in which he reviewed his claims, accused them of "unfair and unsportsmanlike proceedings," and remarked that he would bring legal counsel with him if he ever challenged again. The club made no reply, other than acknowledging receipt of the letter, which it tabled indefinitely. It also voted to return three trophies Ashbury had placed in the hands of James Gordon Bennett, the club's commodore, to be sailed for by NYYC yachts.

Ashbury then wrote a pamphlet, renewing the attack. The club felt aggrieved enough to respond directly to the Royal Harwich:

"We are accustomed to hold that there are certain acts which a gentleman cannot commit. Whatever the cause, Mr. Ashbury evidently thinks otherwise, and with apparent unconsciousness that it ought to give offense, he seems to look behind every action for an unworthy motive, and seek in every explanation evidences of concealment and want of candor."

Ashbury finally got his seat in Parliament. He raced *Livonia* for a time, and eventually emigrated to New Zealand where he became a sheep farmer. His first challenger, *Cambria*, ended up as a coal freighter plying between Swansea, Wales, and Cork.

1876: CANADA ENTERS THE BREACH

Five years passed — five years of stony silence from the British Isles; the Ashbury episode had not gone down well over there. The ill feeling was such that members of the NYYC began to wonder if anyone would ever challenge again. Finally, in 1876, someone did — but not from Britain. The third (and five years later the fourth) challenges for the America's Cup came from Canada, of all places.

If the New Yorkers were startled by the source, they recovered quickly. They needed a challenger, any challenger, to remove the sour taste left in everyone's mouth by the second Ashbury match, and they proved to be gracious hosts. In fact they readily granted concessions steadfastly denied to Ashbury five years earlier. It would be pleasant to conclude, as some Cup historians have, that this new spirit arose spontaneously from sober reflection upon their past behavior and a maturing appreciation of their responsibilities under the deed of gift. Perhaps. But other circumstances may have contributed:

It was America's centennial year, a time for celebration and good fellowship. Bickering with the neighbors would be unseemly. Furthermore, the club had fallen on hard times after the financial panic of 1873; there was some talk of giving up its station on Staten Island and heaving-to to wait for better times. A new challenge would revive the membership, which in fact kicked in handsomely to put the club back on an even keel. Also, in welcome contrast to Ashbury, the Canadians proved to be accommodating guests. Like Sir Thomas Lipton a generation later, they came to New York without demands, without suspicions — and without lawyers.

But when all that is said, one other factor may have been decisive: The Canadians were no threat. Their boat, not to put too fine a point on it, was a real dog.

She was the *Countess of Dufferin*, a centerboard schooner of 221 tons, designed and built by Capt. Alexander Cuthbert of Cobourg, Ontario. When she reached New York, the yachting writers were merciless: Why, she was nothing but a fresh-water boat built to race on the Great Lakes! they sputtered in a tone that suggested bringing her to New York was like entering a draft horse in the Kentucky Derby. And she was a scruffy sort of fresh-water boat at that, with a hull "as rough as a nutmeg grater" and sails that "set like a purser's shirt on a handspike."

The NYYC readily agreed to three races, one on the inside course, one outside, and the third, if necessary, to be determined by lot. After some initial hesitation it also agreed, by an 11-5 vote, that it would name a single defender, in advance. The keepers of the Cup had finally exorcised the ghost of *America*'s race against a fleet and were beginning to chart their own course, with the deed as compass.

The club chose as defender the schooner *Madeleine*, a converted sloop. She, too, was a centerboarder, but as graceful and trim as her opponent was ragged. She won the first race by nearly 10 minutes and the second by more than 26. To add further humiliation, the yacht club, in a burst of Centennial Year sentiment had permitted the aging *America* to sail the course also, though unofficially — and even she came in more than 19 minutes ahead of Cuthbert's *Countess*.

After the match, Cuthbert hoped to bring his hopelessly outclassed schooner up to snuff by making alterations in New York, then challenge again the following summer. But financial difficulties, and some differences among her owners, persisted. As a final indignity, the *Countess of Dufferin* missed the NYYC's annual cruise because she had been impounded at the behest of various creditors. One story has Cuthbert slipping her lines in the dead of night and sailing her back north. But the more prosaic version — that she was released after sale of one of her owners' shares — is probably the correct one. Later she was sold and ended up back in fresh water, in the Chicago Yacht Club fleet, where she led her class for many years.

1881: CUTHBERT'S FLOATING EMBARRASSMENT
Cuthbert came back in 1881 — this time as challenger in his own right — with another boat of his own design and construction, a sloop named *Atalanta*. (The *Countess of Dufferin* proved to be the last schooner to challenge for the Cup; *Atalanta* was the first of the sloops and at 70 feet the smallest challenger until 1958.) The challenging

club was the obscure Bay of Quinte Yacht Club of Belleville, Ontario, of which Cuthbert was a member.

When he again questioned whether he would be facing one defender or a fleet, the club's America's Cup Committee sought the advice of its flag officers. They reaffirmed the 1876 position in favor of a single defender, with the following statement:

"In our opinion every opportunity should be offered for a most impartial contest for the America's Cup. In this view we sincerely trust that the interpretation of the deed of gift may be so liberal and sportsmanlike as to be beyond cavil."

Liberal and sportsmanlike it was, but not beyond cavil. For once, indeed perhaps for the only time in its long stewardship of the Cup, the club found itself out in front of the press and public opinion in the matter of sporting ethics. Jerome E. Brooks in his 1958 history, "The $30,000,000 Cup," wrote, "other yachtsmen and most of the press" felt the challenger should be forced to face a fleet. That may be an exaggeration, but clearly some observers felt the Cup's stewards had gone too far. One contemporary journalist, quoted anonymously by Herbert L. Stone and William H. Taylor in their "The America's Cup Races," also published in 1958, put it this way:

"We view the making of this match to sail a single yacht against the challenger as conceding advantages to which no challenging party is entitled, either by the equities of sporting law or conditions named in the deed of trust. This historic emblem is no prize-fighter's belt. It was won by sailing against the fleet par excellence of the world....

"It is an axiom in sport that 'a good match is won when made,' and really our yachting friends, guardians of the America's Cup, do not shine as matchmakers."

(This may seem a startling reversal to modern readers, accustomed as we are to hearing the NYYC roundly abused for the opposite behavior. One of the ironies surrounding the Cup is that the more concessions the club made through the years, the louder grew the accusations of poor sportsmanship, rules-bending and cheating. The myth grew, nurtured by frustrated challengers and a suspicious press, until it clung to the Cup like barnacles. Toward the end of its reign, the club had ceded nearly all of its inherent advantages, including some very legitimate ones. But not until after it lost the Cup would it again be criticized for giving away the store, and even then it was a minority view.)

Cuthbert apparently felt he would do better mounting his own challenge. He was mistaken. Underfunded and built in haste, *Atalanta* never came close to her proper racing trim. She was launched September 17, woefully late. The yachting season in New York would be over in less than a month, and a voyage down the St. Lawrence would take too long. Cuthbert, a resourceful and determined man, hit upon an ingenious albeit undignified time-saver: He proceeded to Oswego, New York, where, at the entrance to the canal connecting with the Erie, the *Atalanta*'s crew of four professional seamen unshipped her rigging and spars and shifted her ballast to one side, so she would list enough to pass through the locks. (Upright, she was 16 inches too wide in the beam.) Then she was towed to Albany by mules, still listing, bumping and scraping against the sides, before she could be refitted and sailed down the Hudson to New York.

One can imagine the strangled comments from the depths of the NYYC's leather chairs when the news arrived: "Mules? You say she was towed by MULES??" Nevertheless, the club was most lenient, agreeing to push the race into early November. That tolerance may have owed something to a consciousness of the farcical elements in its own campaign:

Never having faced a sloop before, the club looked around for a fast one to send against her. There was an embarrassing shortage. The *Arrow*, owned by Ross Winans of Baltimore, was judged the fastest sloop in America, but Winans didn't belong to the club. While debating the wisdom of buying her, the officers got an offer from her builder, David Kirby, to build an even faster one for them. (Whether they also debated the simpler solution of conferring membership upon Winans is not recorded.)

Kirby's offer was accepted and in due course the new sloop *Pocahontas* slid down the ways, the first yacht built specifically to defend the America's Cup. The club tried her against three other candidates, *Hildegard, Gracie* and *Mischief*, in a series of three races. Unfortunately, she proved to be disastrously slow and was promptly retired, but not before earning the nickname "Pokey".

It came down to a choice between *Gracie* and *Mischief*. *Mischief* was the first would-be defender with an iron hull, and the first to be designed "scientifically," her lines taken from a drawing board rather than from a model whittled by hand. *Gracie* was faster, but she would have had to concede eight minutes in time allowance to the challenger, whereas *Mischief* would spot her only three. *Mischief* was selected largely on that account, despite the embarrassing fact that her owner, Joseph R. Busk, though a bona fide member of the NYYC, was an Englishman! (Not surprisingly, anguished howls arose from *Gracie*'s owners, but to no avail. In an epic "I-told-you-so" gesture, they would go on to complete the farce by bringing *Gracie* to the start of each Cup race, crossing the line 10 minutes behind *Mischief* — and beating her to the finish both days.)

Meanwhile Cuthbert and his crew worked furiously to get their floating embarrassment into some sort of racing trim, but they ran out of money and time. When *Atalanta* came to the line November 9, her hull was still rough, her reworked sails looked baggy, and most of her crew were amateur fresh-water sailors from the Bay of Quinte Club. In the first race, held on the inside course in a strong, gusty wind, she seemed in such imminent danger of capsizing that the club assigned its tug to stay close to her, to rescue her crew. She lost by more than 31 minutes. The next day she lost the second and deciding race by almost 42 minutes.

If anything, the yachting writers were even more caustic this time. New York's principal sporting journal, The Spirit of the Times, commented:

"The race Wednesday, if race it can be called, amounts to this: *Mischief*, a tried and proved sloop, confessedly one of the fastest in the world, thoroughly fitted out and equipped, fully manned, and magnificently handled, distanced the *Atalanta*, a new yacht, hastily built, totally untried, and miserably equipped, with sails that misfitted like a Chatham Street suit of clothes, and bungled around the course by an alleged crew, who would have been overmatched in trying to handle a canal boat anchored in a fog."

If anyone expected Cuthbert to hitch up his mules and slink back up the Hudson, he was disappointed. He confessed puzzlement over *Atalanta*'s poor showing and declared he planned to make alterations, if necessary, and challenge again the following spring.

Cuthbert, who was said to have entered his challengers as a way of promoting his boatbuilding business, seemed oblivious to the comic aspects of his campaigns, and the public derision that attended them. But the NYYC, which by then had come to regard the Cup as a sacred trust, was not. Mules, indeed! And what, pray tell, would that man come up with next spring? Something would have to be done.

What the club did, in a carefully orchestrated move of doubtful legitimacy, was formally hand the Cup back to George Schuyler, the remaining member of *America*'s syndicate, with the understanding that he would convey it back to the club by means of a new deed. That was accomplished early in 1882.

The new document contained the following basic changes: 1. Only a single yacht could be named defender. 2. Challenges would be accepted only from clubs that had their annual regattas on the sea, or an arm of the sea. 3. Challenging vessels had to reach the port where the races were scheduled under sail and on their own bottoms. 4. No defeated challenger could challenge again until another challenger, or two years, had intervened.

That first provision reflected Schuyler's strong conviction and merely ratified what had by then become custom. The second, third and fourth, however, were aimed more or less directly across the bows of Cuthbert's 20-mule-team contender. The following spring he raised *Atalanta*'s anchor (a tedious process as she didn't have a windlass) and sailed back to Lake Ontario, this time by sea and the St. Lawrence. The Canadian clubs on the Great Lakes raised a fuss over the "arm of the sea" clause, which excluded them, but no one else offered any objections. Thereafter the Canadians maintained a silence that would last for more than a century. The New Yorkers, much pleased over their "improved" deed of gift, sat back to await a worthier challenge.

1885: THE CLUB CALLS FOR HELP

They got it — or rather them — on February 26, 1885. The fourth and fifth challenges were written simultaneously by J. Beavor Webb, an English yacht designer who saw an opportunity to show off two of his latest cutters, a new breed of racing yacht then on the ascendency in Britain. His proposal was that his first entry, *Genesta*, race between August 20 and September 1, and if she were beaten his second, *Galatea,* be allowed to challenge before September 17. Webb challenged on behalf of Sir Richard Sutton, owner of *Genesta*, representing the Royal Yacht Squadron, and Lt. William Henn, R.N. (retired), owner of *Galatea*, representing the Royal Northern Yacht Club.

The New York club promptly accepted the *Genesta* challenge, later provisionally accepting that of *Galatea*. But it postponed the latter until the following year — assuming, of course, that the club still held the Cup.

Negotiations over conditions of the *Genesta* challenge went smoothly, with Schuyler acting as referee on points of difference, which were few and trifling. The match would consist of three races, over a compromise course: One race on the infamous inside course, another over a triangular course in open water, the third a 20-mile windward-leeward course off Sandy Hook.

The negotiations lasted several months, but were marked throughout by cordiality and good sportsmanship. The NYYC's evenhandedness was all the more impressive given its well-founded perception that the Cup was in danger. In 1881, a cutter named *Madge* had been brought over from Scotland on the deck of a steamer, had entered eight races and won seven of them. When the challenge came from *Genesta*, another cutter, American yachtsmen worried that they had no sloop capable of beating her.

The NYYC then took another pivotal step: It asked for help. It sent a circular to all U.S. yacht clubs, announcing trials for the upcoming race. They would be open to any single-mast vessel of at least 60-foot waterline belonging to "any duly organized yacht club in the United States, with the condition that any vessel taking part therein shall be subject to selection by the committee in charge as the representative of the NYYC in the coming races for the America's cup."

Doubtless the club rationalized its plea on the grounds that the Cup truly had become a national symbol of yachting supremacy, and ought to be defended accordingly. But the New Yorkers had swallowed their pride, which then as now was a large mouthful. Anyone looking for another motive — desperation — would find more than a hint of it in the circular's last sentence, which urged anyone interested to get in touch with the committee "as soon as possible."

Immediately, a syndicate was organized in Boston to build such a yacht, the *Puritan*, which was launched May 26, 1885. She was entered as an Eastern Yacht Club vessel. One can just imagine the glee with which "The Eastern" of Marblehead, an old but junior rival of the NYYC, condescended to help the New Yorkers in their hour of need.

They also seemed determined that their entry would outshine as well as outsail anything their rivals had ever built. The *Puritan*, according to a contemporary description, had a main cabin finished in mahogany and pine, two mahogany sideboards, large lounges, a ladies' cabin "beautifully furnished with every convenience," and two staterooms. She also boasted below a room for the captain and two for the mates, plus a roomy galley, lavatory and forecastle with bunks for a crew of 18. With all that excess baggage, it seems a wonder she could race at all. But she beat out three other contenders and was chosen as the defender.

The Bostonians were not about to let anyone forget whose yacht she was, either. She went onto the NYYC list under the name of Edward Burgess, her designer, and flew his pennant throughout the trials and Cup races. Burgess was not a member of the New York club, but Gen. Charles J. Paine, who managed the boat, was. She was entered for the races under his name. That was enough to comply with the letter of the deed, but ended for all time the pleasant fiction — which the framers of the deed probably intended to be fact — that the America's Cup was a trophy to be challenged for by one yacht club against another.

The challenges had been individual affairs from the beginning: Ashbury offered to race on behalf of any or all of a dozen clubs. Cuthbert's challenges came from two different clubs, and now Webb was entering his two designs; the involvement of the clubs to which their owners happened to belong was a mere formality.

Meanwhile, defenses had been all-NYYC productions. The club seemed capable of defending the Cup by doing little more than appointing a committee for the purpose. But now the first true America's Cup defense syndicate had been formed, by men who owed little or no allegiance to the club whose Cup they hoped to defend. From this point forward the potential always existed for conflict over control of the defense.

But the full realization of that potential remained in the future. The match of 1885 was notable for something else entirely: good sportsmanship.

In the first race, *Genesta* was fouled by *Puritan*. As the boats converged before the start, with *Genesta* on starboard tack and thus with the right-of-way, *Puritan*'s sailing master misjudged his time and distance, failing to tack away before the boats collided. *Genesta*'s bowsprit was driven through *Puritan*'s mainsail.

After some deliberation, the race committee ruled *Puritan* out and informed Sir Richard Sutton, *Genesta*'s owner, that he could have the race if he would merely sail over the course alone. Whereupon Sir Richard replied, "We are very much obliged to you, but we don't want it in that way. We want a race; we don't want a walkover." The committee, needless to say, was happy to accept that sporting gesture.

This was, beyond a doubt, the high point of chivalry in the entire history of the Cup — not that there was ever much competition for that distinction. *Puritan*'s owners, for their part, offered to pay for all repairs to *Genesta*. Sir Richard declined.

Puritan went on to win the first complete race, held on the inside course, by 16:19 corrected time. The race was marked by flukey winds, troublesome tides and far more excitement than the final time indicated, as the cutter frequently threatened to close the gap. In the second race, *Genesta* was actually ahead at the first mark by 2:06. After a close, exciting race, during which only a few seconds separated the boats near the finish, *Puritan* took advantage of a better angle toward the line and put on a burst of speed, crossing 1:38 ahead on corrected time (2:09 elapsed time).

The closeness of the races and Sir Richard's gallantry revived public interest in the Cup, restoring the prestige that had been eroded by the Canadian challenges. Sir Richard was made an honorary member of the NYYC and good relations between English and American yachtsmen, strained by the Ashbury affair, were fully restored.

1886: MOTHER HENN'S MENAGERIE

On October 22, 1885, the club formally accepted the *Galatea* challenge of Lt. William Henn, the conditions being much the same as for the *Genesta* challenge. Gen. Charles J. Paine placed an order with Burgess for another vessel, an "improved *Puritan*." She was named *Mayflower*, and after some initial faltering, she did indeed surpass *Puritan*, which served as a trial horse. After two trial races, in which she beat *Puritan, Priscilla* and *Atlantic*, the America's Cup Committee chose her to defend.

Genesta had been a graceful, even elegant vessel, with a frame of steel and oak planking, the first such composite to sail for the Cup. She had been opulent enough in her interior furnishings as well — but no match for *Galatea* in that respect.

To the modern Cup-watcher, accustomed to stripped-out 12-meter boats in which every unnecessary pound has been jettisoned, *Galatea* seems simply astounding: She was built of steel and appeared formidable enough from the deck up. But below she looked more like a Victorian mansion than a racing yacht, with lots of heavy tables, mirrors, paintings, leopard-skin rugs, potted palms and a fireplace in the saloon. In effect, she WAS a mansion. Her owners, Lieutenant Henn and his wife, lived aboard.

Henn had retired from the Royal Navy at the age of 28, determined to spend the rest of his life sailing for pleasure. He married a like-minded lady of means, who supplied the money for *Galatea* and obviously had more than a little to say about her furnishings, not to mention the passenger manifest, which included a remarkable menagerie of pets — dogs, cats, a racoon and a monkey named Peggy. Peggy, according to one press report, would help the crew make and lower sail, pulling on a halyard like a trained sailor. And when *Galatea* pulled ahead in a race, she would run out on the bowsprit and jump up and down.

Not surprisingly, that didn't happen very often. *Galatea* entered 15 races during her first season, 1885, and failed to win a single one. When her designer decided to enter her as an America's Cup challenger anyway, one gets the impression that Henn didn't so much embrace the idea as go along with it. His alleged tune-ups in New York Harbor were so lackadaisical (he carried only small working sails and towed his dinghy) that some members of the press suspected he was deliberately holding back, to lull the defenders into a false sense of security. These reports contributed to a great public interest in the race; the course was jammed with spectators before the first gun.

They were disappointed. *Mayflower* won the first race by 12:02, corrected time, the second (during which Henn, who was ill, relinquished the helm) by 29:09. Henn, like Sir Richard Sutton before him, took his defeat gracefully. He was well liked and regarded as a genial sailor, but not much of a racer.

1887: FIRST SECRET DESIGN

The next challenge came in 1887 from Scotland. It was issued by a syndicate headed by James Bell, vice commodore of the Royal Clyde Yacht Club. Their designer was George L. Watson, regarded as the ablest British designer at the time. Watson, who had been in America the year before, studying the best U.S. yachts, thought he could combine the best features of American sloops and English cutters, and come up with an unbeatable design.

The letter announcing an intention to challenge was actually sent the previous year, shortly after the *Galatea-Mayflower* race. It amounted to a friendly, informal announcement of interest, and an attempt to arrive at an amicable agreement in leisurely fashion, with a formal challenge to follow in time to schedule the races in September, 1887. The NYYC, however, responded rather haughtily with a letter saying when the challenge arrived "in proper form" it would be considered. The response included a copy of the second deed of gift. Perhaps, after Lt. Henn and his wife and monkey, it wanted no more challengers inclined toward a leisurely informality.

The Scottish syndicate tried again to reach some understanding, at least about the size of the boats, so neither side would be outbuilt. That failed. So they went ahead on their own. Perhaps it was this frosty treatment that led them to take full advantage of the deed, building their boat under tight security and delaying their challenge until March, just under the six-month deadline — which forced the New Yorkers to hustle in building a defender.

The challenger, named *Thistle*, was built by D. & W. Henderson at Patrick on the Clyde and launched April 26, 1887, amid utmost secrecy. Like the Australian challenger of nearly 100 years later, she was covered with canvas. That naturally piqued considerable press interest, which reached a crescendo after Watson began to plant false leads, passing off the plans of other vessels he had designed as those of *Thistle*. Shortly after her arrival here, one of the New York newspapers hired a diver to go down and have a look at her hull. But the water was very muddy and when the result was published as a drawing it was so wildly inaccurate that Bell remarked the paper's owner would feel like shooting the diver when *Thistle*'s real form was revealed.

Heightening the suspense was the knowledge that the British rating system, which had imposed a penalty on width of beam and led to extremely deep, narrow designs called "plank on edge," had been abolished the year before. Watson was free to design a hull much closer to the Americans', or strike out in search of a breakthrough design. All this had the same effect in 1887 as similar circumstances had in 1983: The New Yorkers got nervous.

When Paine and Burgess announced they would build still another boat, the club breathed a collective sigh of relief. So great was the eminence of the Paine/Burgess team by that time that no one else even attempted to build a defender. The result was *Volunteer*, a steel-hulled sloop, built in the incredible time of 66 days. Because of the haste her finish was very rough, but she lived up to expectations under Capt. Henry Clayton Haff ("Hank Haff"), a veteran yachtsman from Long Island. *Volunteer*'s first races were an unbroken string of victories. She beat *Mayflower* and *Puritan* with ease.

However, *Thistle* was doing just as well across the Atlantic. She easily beat *Genesta* and won 11 first prizes in 15 races, against the pick of English yachts. The challengers had high hopes when she sailed across the Atlantic under Capt. John Barr, as able a skipper as Scotland could produce, it was said. When the syndicate members arrived later by steamer, they brought bagpipers with them, and a supply of Scotch, which they declared they would drink from the America's Cup — apparently unaware that it had no bottom.

The defender trials were pro forma. Only *Mayflower* opposed *Volunteer*, and was beaten in the first complete race by more than 16 minutes. That was enough for the committee: *Volunteer* was named the same day.

Paine, incidentally, was not to be outdone by the Scots in the canny tricks department. While practicing one day before the match, he noticed *Thistle* keeping pace just outside the course. The wind was increasing, but rather than lower the topsail he ordered it to be deliberately luffed through some heavy gusts, hoping Watson would conclude *Volunteer* was unusually stable and would add ballast to his own boat to match her. That's just what he did, and it slowed *Thistle* markedly.

On September 22, *Volunteer* and *Thistle* were officially measured and it was found *Thistle*'s waterline was 86.46 feet, as opposed to the 85 feet reported by the designer. This should have been regarded as a petty concern, a discrepancy easily adjusted by means of time allowance. But the NYYC, probably because of the secrecy and suspicion that had surrounded *Thistle* from the outset and possibly because they were afraid of losing, chose to regard it as a "great discrepancy" that raised a question as to whether *Thistle* should be allowed to race.

After much discussion, it was decided, once again, to submit the question to George Schuyler, then 76 years old. Schuyler ruled, in effect, that the discrepancy was significant, it gave the challenger a decided advantage, but it was unintentional: *Thistle's* owner, Schuyler said, had relied upon "remarkably inaccurate" information from his designer, and should not be held responsible. Therefore, *Thistle* should not be disqualified.

After all that, the races themselves were an anticlimax. A huge fleet of spectators jammed the inside course for the first one, making maneuvering difficult. They saw not a race but a procession. *Volunteer* won by 19:23 corrected time. *Thistle's* owners were so perplexed by her showing that they ordered her bottom swept to see if any foreign object was causing drag. They found nothing and in the second race, *Volunteer* won by 11:48 corrected time, and that was that. The bagpipers remained silent. There is no record of what happened to the Scotch.

The New Yorkers were much relieved at the outcome. They had kept their Cup and no one was terribly upset. But they were about to embark upon an episode far pricklier than a Scottish *Thistle*.

3
DUNRAVEN TARNISHES THE CUP

A full generation had passed since the New York Yacht Club assumed possession of the America's Cup. Perhaps to its own surprise, it had survived seven challenges. The partnership between club and Cup was becoming an institution.

Thistle had thrown a scare at the New Yorkers, however. By waiting until the last minute to reveal the basic outlines of their challenger, the Scots had given them only six months to design, build and try out their defender. That was too close for comfort. And then yet another member of the Royal Clyde Yacht Club had come forward on the very day of the final race against *Thistle*, asking for a match the following summer.

Perhaps for all of these reasons the club decided to call a halt in order to catch its breath and review the deed. What with Ashbury's lawyers, the Henns' monkey, Cuthbert's mules and the Scots' secrecy, there were ample indications that America's Cup challengers were an unpredictable and contentious lot who would need plenty of reining in. And what if one of these people actually won the thing?

'AN ACT TO PREVENT YACHT RACING'
A committee was appointed to revise the deed, in consultation with the only surviving grantor, George Schuyler. The club told the would-be challenger, a Scot named Charles Sweet then living in New York, that Cup competition was temporarily closed for repairs.

But when the new deed emerged less than a month later, Sweet took one look and promptly withdrew his challenge, by means of a formal letter from the Royal Clyde Yacht Club and without comment: He held membership in both the New York and Royal Clyde clubs and probably didn't want to offend the former by speaking his mind.

Others were less reticent. Editorial comment on both sides of the Atlantic was swift and severe: Forest and Stream, an American journal covering yachting, called the new deed "An Act to Prevent Yacht Racing." British condemnation was even more scathing.

The New Yorkers were aghast. They thought they had merely closed a few loopholes and tidied up some language, thus assuring the deed and the event would survive if and when they lost the Cup. What was all the fuss about?

Part of the fuss was over the tone. George Schuyler signed it, but it was clear it had been drafted by a lawyer. It was more than five times as long as the 1857 original and, in the words of Cup historian Jerome E. Brooks, "read like a mortgage."

"Because of it," Brooks wrote in "The $30,000,000 Cup," "the Cup seemed no longer to be a trophy designed for 'friendly competition.' It seemed to have lost what, essentially, it had long represented: the irrepressible elements of the wind and the sea and the fellowship of sport for its own sake. Learned counsel had done a restrictive, formalizing job. In order to get the Cup now, challengers had to navigate cautiously through 'parties of the first and second part' and equivalent hazards."

But most of the criticism was directed against the content, especially the change inspired by the Thistle challenge: Henceforth, challengers would have to give ten months' notice rather than six. Furthermore, along with such notice, they would have to submit the name, rig and following dimensions of the challenging vessel: Load waterline length, beam at load waterline, extreme beam, and draught. Once announced, these dimensions could not be exceeded.

Another provision abolished time allowances, which had been used up to then to adjust for inequalities owing to differences in the boats' dimensions. It didn't take the critics long to see a link between that and the ten-months-notice clause: Knowing well in advance what they had to beat, the New Yorkers could practically guarantee themselves a faster boat by simply making it bigger — without penalty. Or if both boats were built to the maximum limits in the deed (90 feet), the defenders could make theirs lighter, therefore faster, because they wouldn't have to weather a transatlantic trip under sail. Nor could a challenger respond: His boat would be fixed and unalterable ten months in advance, whereas the defenders still didn't even have to identify theirs until the morning of the first race.

George Schuyler, the Solomon of the America's Cup, vigorously defended the deed he had signed. The defending club, he said, had a right to some idea of what class of boat it would be facing, and the dimensions required would not provide enough information to give them an unfair advantage: "I deny most emphatically that giving the dimensions asked for will reveal the lines of a vessel, and I do not believe any yacht designer will say it will." He cited *Volunteer* and *Mayflower* as examples of boats almost identical in those dimensions, yet very different in lines.

His defense was silent on the effect of abolishing time allowances, however. Whether that was a rare example of disingenuousness on his part, or whether he and the others involved simply hadn't foreseen the unfair advantage the combined clauses would give the club, is a matter for conjecture. It is known that subsequently the club never insisted on learning more than the waterline length in advance, and almost routinely waived the ten-month's-notice rule.

Schuyler said he had regarded that clause as of minor importance when he reviewed the new deed. The important change, he said, was the one that provided that all races would be sailed on "ocean courses, free from headlands" and "practicable in all parts for vessels of 22 feet draught of water."

That finally abolished the club's notoriously unfair "inside course," the tortuous and increasingly traffic-clogged course through the Narrows. The strong tides and shifting shoals in that stretch of water put such a premium on local knowledge that, in the opinion of more than one challenger, it did not permit a fair test of relative boat speed. But the clause also ruled out the equally unfair courses in the Clyde, with its headlands, or the Solent, with its sand bars. The NYYC made no secret of the fact that it was also protecting its own interests should the New Yorkers find themselves in the role of challenger.

Two other new clauses were written with that possibility in mind: Centerboarders (still frowned upon in England) would "always" be allowed to compete for the Cup, and any challenging yacht club that won it would have to agree, in writing, to abide by all provisions of the deed before taking it over. The NYYC was trying to set conditions for all time.

The whole thing was hedged about with a thicket of legalisms and required deep study. Some students emerged declaring it was designed to protect the rights of challengers, and was a step in the right direction. But most foreigners thought they saw the devious hand of unsportsmanlike men trying desperately to strengthen their grasp on the trophy — *their* trophy — by fair means or foul.

The Yacht Racing Association, to which many European yacht clubs belonged, proclaimed: "The terms of the new Deed of Gift are such that foreign vessels are unable to challenge." Forest and Stream pointed out that any change in the deed was probably illegal to begin with. The club had received the Cup in trust and was legally powerless to alter the terms without due process of law — a good point, but one which failed to provoke a legal challenge. The article concluded by voicing a question that would continue to be raised in the future:

"The whole future of international racing was, and still is, in our opinion, centered on the question whether the America's cup as a perpetual challenge trophy for international competition is the common property of all existing yacht clubs, to be raced for on fair terms, or whether it is in effect the private property of the New York Yacht Club, the privilege of competing for it being accorded foreign clubs as a favor and not as a right."

The London Field, which reflected the general British view, editorialized:

"To prevent any other club tinkering the conditions in a similar way, the club which may win the cup will have to covenant that the present unsportsmanlike conditions shall not be altered. Copies of the conditions have been sent to British and foreign yacht clubs, with a letter to the secretary very similar to the one issued thirty years ago. The letter, after recommending enthusiasm on the part of the contestants, winds up with the declaration that any races for the cup will be conducted on strictly fair terms by the New York Yacht Club; but if the club is to be the sole judge of 'fair terms,' we do not think they will inspire enthusiasm."

Six months later, in response to a request for clarification from the Royal London Yacht Club, the NYYC backed down. Whether it realized the folly (intentional or otherwise) of its deed, or was merely feeling the heat is impossible to guess. Discussions within the club's meeting rooms, then as now, were as confidential as those within the highest levels of government — and less often leaked. What did emerge was a resolution pointing out that the "mutual consent" clause would allow the parties to ignore most of the new clauses, and stating that the terms under which the past three challenges had been raced were satisfactory. A challenge under the same terms would be accepted. But with the "positive understanding" that any challenger who won the Cup would be required to hold it under the full terms of the new deed, which the club regarded as "in the interest of all parties, and the terms of which are distinct, fair, and sportsmanlike."

Of course they were nothing of the sort, a fact the club tacitly acknowledged by agreeing to ignore most of them. It was, to say the least, an awkward stance. Perhaps the logic was that, having decided to retain the "mutual consent" clause, the framers felt the need to stake out highly favorable conditions for themselves, knowing they would be eroded by subsequent negotiations.

All that is sheer speculation, however. No meaningful explanations were voiced at the time. Potential challengers were left with an indigestible deed and the distinct impression that the NYYC was prepared to cut a deal, even while insisting upon the virtue and immutability of an obviously one-sided document.

ENTER LORD DUNRAVEN

Chances are this confusing situation would have sorted itself out eventually, given a reasonable challenger and some dispassionate discussions. But, instead, fate sent Windham Thomas Wyndham-Quin, fourth Earl of Dunraven.

Lord Dunraven's first challenge was received on March 19, 1889, from the Royal Yacht Squadron. He named his yacht, *Valkyrie,* and gave its dimensions. The challenge was accepted three weeks later and a seven-member committee was appointed to arrange details, with instructions to insist that the Royal Yacht Squadron agree to abide by the deed if it won the Cup.

This the RYS refused to do, and on June 27, 1889 it announced by letter that it was "unable to confirm the challenge" with that condition. The NYYC replied that the RYS appeared to have overlooked the mutual consent clause, which meant it would not have to insist upon conditions it regarded as unsportsmanlike if it won the Cup. It suggested that other differences could be ironed out through

further discussion. It wasn't until the following year, however, that
Lord Dunraven expressed his personal views, in a letter to the
chairman of the arrangements committee in New York.

The Earl of Dunraven's early life reflected the troubles that still af-
flict his Irish homeland. His father, a convert to Catholicism, packed
him off to school in Rome rather than having him associate with his
mother, a Protestant. This early conflict bred in him "an obstinate resistance," according to one of his biographers, which followed him
through a restless life that included big-game hunting in America,
spiritualism, writing (he was a war correspondent for the Daily
Telegraph during the British and Abyssinian War) and politics,
among other things. He confessed (or boasted) that he was not highly
regarded in his party, the Liberals, because of his independent,
"cross-bench mind." He chaired a committee in the House of Lords
to reform workhouses at the same time he was racing expensive
cutters.

It is not surprising, therefore, that he had some contrary opinions
on the new deed. He objected to the change from six months to ten
months notice, as it "would lead to much inconvenience," and to the
stipulation that a challenger must furnish his boat's exact dimensions,
on the grounds that this would give the defenders too great an
advantage. Furthermore, "It might be impossible to find a vessel's
proper trim without exceeding the calculated dimensions."

The mutual consent clause, he asserted, was ambiguous at best,
and would place any club successfully challenging for the Cup in the
following ridiculous position: "It would be liable to have to accept a
challenge under circumstances which it considered more unfavorable
to the challenger than those under which it challenged. It would have
to solemnly declare for itself, and on the part of all other clubs, that
the cup, if won, should be held under, and subject to the full terms of
the deed of gift of October 24, 1887; and at the same time, it would be
obliged to make an equally solemn declaration that it considered
those terms unfair, and that it would never adhere to them. Such a
position would not, I think, commend itself to yacht clubs over here."

It may be assumed Dunraven did not endear himself by this
exercise in reductio ad absurdum, and chances are the New Yorkers
were just as pleased he had bowed out. But they were not to escape. In
November of 1892, after more than two years had passed, they
received another challenge — from Dunraven again. He named

Valkyrie II, 85 feet load-waterline, designed by George L. Watson. After some correspondence terms of the race were worked out, the new deed being all but forgotten in the process.

The load-waterline measurement would be the only dimension required. It could be exceeded, but by no more than 2%; any excess would receive a double penalty in calculating time allowance. The defender could be no more than 2% longer than the challenger, any excess counting double. The winner would be determined by three out of five races. If the Royal Yacht Squadron won, it agreed to hold the Cup "subject to challenge under precisely similar terms as those contained in this challenge, provided always that such club shall not refuse any challenge according to the conditions laid down in the deed of 1887." In short, the RYS was spared the necessity of insisting on the terms of the odious deed if it held the Cup, whereas the New York club could invoke it as challenger.

Edward Burgess, the naturalist turned yacht designer who had designed the previous three Cup defenders (and thereby heightened the rivalry between his club, the Eastern Yacht Club, and the NYYC), had died in the summer of 1891, at the age of 42. It was said he succumbed to typhoid brought on by overwork; he had produced the lines of 137 vessels in seven years. When the NYYC looked for a successor it soon came to Nathaniel Greene Herreshoff of Bristol, Rhode Island, whose career seemed to have been genetically ordained: His grandfather, Frederick Herreshoff, was a Prussian engineer who married Sarah Brown, daughter of John Brown, the leading ship owner in Rhode Island.

THE WIZARD OF BRISTOL

Nathaniel, who got his technical education at the Massachusetts Institute of Technology, began work at the Corliss Engine Works in Providence. He then joined his brother, John B. Herreshoff, in building launches and small steamers in Bristol. John, though blind, invented engines and boilers, which laid the foundation of the Herreshoff Manufacturing Company. Their first success with yachts was in the early 1870s when they produced several small catamarans and sloops. Herreshoff, who would come to be known as "the Wizard of Bristol," was destined to have a greater impact on the Cup than any other designer, at least until the modern era. He designed and built six Cup defenders from 1893 to 1920.

Presumably it was only his unparalleled success that caused the keepers of the Cup to knock six times on his door; by all accounts he was not an easy man to work with. The story is told that in 1904 Kaiser Wilhelm, the German emperor, placed an order for a Herreshoff schooner, then made the mistake of demanding a design alteration. Herreshoff refused, explained why, and sat back to await a letter indicating the emperor had withdrawn his demand. Getting none, he simply dropped the project. The emperor was astounded, but his subsequent overtures had no effect.

He was painfully shy in social situations but a real tyrant in his work, which in truth was his whole life. In her biography of the Herreshoffs, "Let the Best Boat Win," Constance Buel Burnett described his first (and last) real vacation, which he took with great reluctance only because of exhaustion. He sailed for Europe to visit relatives aboard a German liner, *Goethe*. His diary entry for the first day provides some insights into his view of life:

"Steamer left dock at 2h.40m. Passed Castle Garden at 2-55. Engine 46 rev. Passed S.W. Spit at 4h.5m. Engine 50 rev." He numbered the passengers, recounted the menu for dinner (without comment), then turned in at 8 p.m., after the following entries: "...wind W.N.W. strong, sea beginning to make up but ship quite steady. Engine 52 rev. Thermometer in state room 45 degrees."

When he returned to his native Bristol, it was with a sense of relief and a disinclination to wander far from the security of his familiar steam gauges and drawing board ever again.

Meanwhile, two years into the Gay Nineties, the NYYC was flourishing. It counted several of the world's richest men among its members. Nor were they at all reluctant to spend their money, especially on ostentatious displays such as their yachts — and the summer "cottages" they built in Newport. Probably it was that impulse toward conspicuous consumption — and perhaps rivalry with Boston's Eastern Yacht Club — rather than fear of losing the Cup, that led to the commissioning of not one but two potential defenders from Herreshoff's drawing board. To give some idea of the rarified level at which the Cup game was played in those days, the 17 club members involved in both syndicates included two Morgans (J.P. and E.D.), two Belmonts and three Vanderbilts.

The yachts were *Vigilant*, a centerboarder, and *Colonia*, a keel boat. Boston, meantime, produced two radical boats, *Jubilee* and

Pilgrim; both had fin keels, which had been tried on smaller craft but were an unknown quantity in 90-footers. In the first trial race among the four, which attracted much interest because of their innovations and the New York-Boston rivalry, both Boston boats proved too weak for the prevailing brisk wind and had to retire because of broken gear.

The race between *Colonia* and *Vigilant* was noteworthy for being the first dead heat recorded in trial races. *Colonia*'s time allowance was 14 seconds, the exact margin by which she was beaten by *Vigilant* in elapsed time. *Vigilant* won the second and third races and was immediately selected. It was said *Colonia*'s principal fault was that her fin keel wasn't deep enough. It was rumored that her draft was limited by the depth of water in the slip at the Herreshoff yard: Launching a deeper vessel would have required dredging, which the thrifty Yankee was reluctant to do.

Valkyrie II, somewhat deeper than *Vigilant* although slightly smaller in other dimensions, arrived September 22, 1893, and was soon touted as a formidable challenger. Dunraven made a similar impression in New York society. He was widely imitated by the young men of the day. When he appeared on the street wearing a brown shoe on one foot and a felt slipper on the other — the result of a painful gout attack — many of his followers adopted the same footgear. He did not endear himself to his 35-man crew, however; he imposed curfews, supervised their diets and fed them a noxious tonic called a "Valkyrie cocktail."

In their first attempt at a race, *Valkyrie* gave the New Yorkers a scare. She rounded the outer mark 26:20 ahead of *Vigilant* in a drifting match, which was called off when the wind died completely. The first full race was held in a moderate breeze, and *Vigilant* won by 5:48, corrected time. In the second, she won by 10:35.

The third race fell on Friday, October 13. Despite the ominous date, it was a corker. *Valkyrie* narrowly led up to and around the first mark, both yachts boiling along in a brisk wind. On the run home, both crowded on canvas; *Valkyrie*'s spinnaker ripped. A second one, too light for conditions, was run up. It, too, ripped. By the time a third was hoisted, *Vigilant* had passed her. *Vigilant* won by a scant 40 seconds corrected time. The defense had held again.

Dunraven proved to be a sore loser. He complained that the races had not been a fair test under the wind conditions. He grumbled about interference from steamers. He said *Valkyrie* was out of trim and too light in order to keep her within the stipulated 85-foot waterline: "We need not have been so sacrificing, for *Vigilant* was practically 87 feet long, and we should have increased the length of our boat." When it came to the torn spinnakers, there was just a hint of possible sabotage: "This was very unfortunate for us, and it was very singular, too. In fact I have never known it to happen in England."

But these were mere oratorical zephyrs compared to the storm to come.

DUNRAVEN CHARGES FRAUD

Dunraven challenged again, in October of 1894. He suggested races along the lines of the previous match, slightly modified. The challenge was again through the Royal Yacht Squadron, which renewed its opposition to strictly maintaining the deed if it should win. Feelings on that issue were still running strong. The RYS said they didn't really want the Cup anyway; if they won, they would be happy with the victory and the New Yorkers could keep the bloody thing. The New York club, doubtless aghast at such blasphemy, replied firmly that the RYS could not reject custody if it won. The challenging club grudgingly accepted its potential burden.

The Herreshoff hegemony firmly established by then, only one boat was built to defend. It was ordered by a syndicate consisting of William K. Vanderbilt, E.D. Morgan and C. Oliver Iselin, millionaires all. *Defender* was launched by Herreshoff June 29, 1895. Utmost secrecy surrounded her, the first — but not the last — time a defender was so cloaked. Apparently that was due more to Herreshoff's reclusive nature and deep mistrust of the press than to any imagined advantage.

She was a sloop with a fin keel, the first non-centerboarder to defend the Cup, and a cutter in everything but name. She was built of bronze, steel and aluminum, lightness being the chief aim. The use of aluminum plates reportedly saved about 17 tons dead weight, but the combination of metals proved disastrous: She had to be scrapped less than six years later, the victim of corrosion in her hull caused by galvanic action, an effect Herreshoff apparently had not foreseen. She also had to be handled gingerly throughout her racing career, lest the mast, under severe strain, put a hole in her bottom. But she was fast.

Dunraven's *Valkyrie III* was designed by George L. Watson as a light-weather racer. At 26.2 feet, her beam was the widest ever seen in a Cup match. She looked a lot like *Defender*, and indeed the two were more evenly matched than any previous contenders, in both design and performance.·

In the negotiations over race conditions, particular attention was paid to measurement. The yachts were to be measured "with all weights on board to be carried in a race," and a clause was added that required remeasurement whenever a yacht underwent any modification that changed its waterline length. Such measurements were to be final "and not subject to protest by either party."

Dunraven apparently came to New York believing the load waterline points would be marked on the hull. He also made a strange request of the America's Cup Committee. On September 6, 1895, the day before the first race, he wrote that the committee should "take every precaution that the vessels sail on their measured load waterline length," in view of the possibility that "alterations" might be made "without the owner's knowledge, and without possibility of detection."

Dunraven probably had gotten wind of some unfounded rumors being whispered around the docks at that time, dark rumors about juggled ballast on a boat formerly controlled by Iselin, head of the *Defender* syndicate. If the New Yorkers took offense at his suggestion, they gave no sign. They appointed a special committee to mark the load waterline of both boats, but because *Valkyrie* had already been measured and could not be brought back before the first race, neither was marked beforehand.

In the first race, *Defender* beat *Valkyrie* by 8:49 corrected time in light wind and a lumpy sea, conditions that put the challenger, with her broad beam, at a disadvantage.

It wasn't revealed until some weeks after the series that, just before the race, Dunraven levelled a charge against the NYYC's syndicate that would later erupt and reverberate for years: He told the club's representative aboard *Valkyrie*, Latham A. Fish, that in his opinion *Defender* had sailed the race three or four feet beyond her given waterline length. Dunraven said he believed the change had been made without the knowledge of *Defender*'s owners, "but that it must be corrected or he would discontinue racing," according to the committee's subsequent report. He asked for a remeasurement. There could be only one interpretation of Dunraven's words: Someone had illegally added ballast to give *Defender* an edge. In short, the NYYC or its representatives had cheated.

From today's perspective, such a charge might seem less than earth-shaking, little more than the standard background noise in an America's Cup summer. But in 1895 the Cup was still an emblem of the highest sporting traditions; even the slightest imputation of fraud became the gravest affront to personal honor.

The committees Fish reported to kept quiet about it, preferring for reasons they later explained to regard it as a call for a remeasurement only, which they granted the following day. Only a 1/8-inch difference was found in *Defender*, 1/16 inch in *Valkyrie III*. If anyone thought that would settle the matter, he was mistaken.

Most people watching the second race were ignorant of all this, but the race itself gave them plenty to talk about. As the yachts maneuvered for the start, a large steamer, the *City of Yorktown*, blundered into their path. *Defender* went astern and to leeward of her, *Valkyrie* by her bow. Then their courses converged, with *Defender*, to leeward, having the right of way. *Valkyrie*, in order not to cross the line before the gun, bore off toward *Defender*. Capt. Edward Sycamore luffed *Valkyrie* at the last minute to avoid collision, but it was too late. A shackle on the end of her main boom caught in *Defender*'s starboard topmast shroud. The shroud sprang out of the spreader and *Defender*'s topmast sagged to leeward. *Defender* immediately ran up a protest flag, which the committee answered with a pennant. *Valkyrie*, rather than return and report to the committee as the rules and common courtesy prescribe (she was clearly in the wrong), continued for the line.

A little more than a minute later, *Defender* also crossed the line, while the crew made repairs. She was unable to carry her full sail load to windward, however, and lost ground to the challenger. She made up more than a minute and a half on the last two legs, but still crossed 47 seconds behind on corrected time.

When C. Oliver Iselin presented his written protest on behalf of *Defender* on September 10, Dunraven replied that *Defender* had luffed into *Valkyrie* after establishing an overlap, and was to blame for the foul. He also said *Valkyrie* barely managed to clear the committee boat. This was starkly refuted by photographs taken at the start, which showed *Valkyrie* luffing and having plenty of room to clear the committee boat. The committee ruled in favor of *Defender*, giving it the win.

Iselin offered to resail the race, but Dunraven, somewhat petulantly, declined. Many people thought the committee should have ordered the race resailed, but the committee explained that it felt it should order a rematch only when neither party was at fault, as in the case of fog.

That evening Dunraven wrote the committee that "with great reluctance" he must inform them that he would not race under the same conditions again, i.e., the crowding of the spectator boats, which hampered his maneuverability and visibility, produced a heavy, sloppy wash, and even endangered the lives of his crew. He acknowledged the committee had done everything it could to prevent overcrowding. But he reminded them he had recommended sailing off Marblehead rather than New York, and they had refused.

Dunraven's concern was understandable. The year before his previous challenger, *Valkyrie II*, had been sunk after a collision during a race in the Clyde, when struck amidships by *Satanita*, which had luffed up sharply to avoid sinking a spectator boat that got in the way. *Valkyrie*, with Dunraven at the helm, sank within three minutes. Everyone was rescued, but one sailor died of injuries a short time later.

The club named a special committee to consult with the Earl the next day. Dunraven said he would sail, but only if the Cup committee agreed it would declare the race void if either boat was interferred with. The committee had no such authority, so it ordered the regatta committee to proceed with preparations for the next race the following day, September 12. Dunraven had no way of knowing whether his demand would be honored.

On the 12th, the excursion boats were much better behaved; the starting line was clearer than it had been in years. The press was reporting that Dunraven was on the verge of quitting, and the steamer captains were anxious not to give him an excuse.

Nonetheless, as *Valkyrie* approached the starting area that morning, it was obvious something was wrong. She came out under jib and mainsail only, without making any of the normal pre-race preparations. When the preparatory gun fired, she made no move to gain position on her opponent, who crossed the line 24 seconds after the starting gun. *Valkyrie* followed, moving slowly, about a minute and a half later. As soon as she crossed, she came about. Down came her racing pennant and up went the burgee of the NYYC, of which Dunraven was an honorary member. Then she picked up her tug and was towed back to port, leaving *Defender* to sail the course alone.

Dunraven had quit!

He went first to Newport, where he met several previously scheduled social engagements. While there he refused to talk about the match. Then he sailed home across the Atlantic, both sides of which were bristling with editorial censure. Many people who followed the races, then as since, were ignorant of the rules on which the controversy turned. But they knew a quitter when they saw one.

On October 24, the America's Cup Committee made its report to the NYYC, in which Dunraven's protest about *Defender*'s waterline was published for the first time. The committee downplayed it and it got little attention in the press. But a little more than two weeks later cabled reports from London revealed that Dunraven had published his version in the London Field.

In that account, the imputation of fraud was unmistakable. Among other things, Dunraven said if the Cup committee had stationed representatives aboard each yacht immediately after the first race as he had requested, to stay there until each could be remeasured, overnight if necessary, his charge that *Defender* lay some four inches deeper and at least a foot longer than her measurements would have been proved or disproved.

That wasn't quite as blunt as saying the *Defender* people had juggled their ballast illegally under cover of darkness — adding new ballast before the race, then removing it before the remeasurement — but it came close enough to cause C. Oliver Iselin, managing owner of *Defender*, to write a blistering letter to the NYYC, dated November 18, 1895:

Lord Dunraven, he wrote, "knew perfectly well, as every gentleman knows," that there could be no innocent explanation for the changes in *Defender*'s trim that he claimed to have observed.

"I consider myself, therefore, as standing before the world solemnly charged by Lord Dunraven with an offense as base as possibly could be imputed to a sportsman and a gentleman, and which I indignantly resent and repel, and more than that: with having betrayed the confidence of my associates in the ownership of the *Defender*, the trust placed in me by the New York Yacht Club, and the good name of my country, whose reputation for fair play was in volved in the contest."

When all this got into the newspapers, it provoked a great public outcry against his Lordship, who had not only quit when behind but had waited until he was back home and safely beyond reach before publicizing his scurrilous charges. The general outrage extended even to the New York Stock Exchange. When James D. Smith, a broker and former NYYC commodore, appeared on the floor he was cheered. Trading halted by tacit consent for half an hour while speeches were made, all suggesting that Dunraven was a thoroughgoing rotter.

REPUDIATION

The club promptly appointed a committee of investigation, which asked Dunraven to return to New York. The Earl agreed. The committee also wrote to the Royal Yacht Squadron, asking if such charges had been formally placed before it, and what it planned to do about them. The reply was a bit frosty: The whole problem, which resulted from the NYYC's failure to comply with Dunraven's request for guards, was none of the Squadron's affair, but a personal matter between Dunraven and the New York club. The RYS had no intention of interfering.

To the charge that he had fled home before publishing his accusations, Dunraven replied in a speech that he never would have done so at all if the NYYC hadn't released them first, after he had returned to England. Then, he said, he felt he had to make his position clear. He also said he had accused no one, but simply put forth his observations.

Meanwhile, the America's Cup Committee rebutted Dunraven's charges. The club denied he had ever asked or suggested that a watch be placed on both vessels until measured. Furthermore, his charge of fraud should have been made formally, in writing. It also contended he should have signalled a protest before the last race. At the time, the Cup committee regarded Dunraven's charge as "absurd and preposterous," and therefore determined to treat it as a call for remeasurement, "and to disregard all imputations of fraud; and by so doing to force upon the accuser the issue either to support his charge and protest against the treatment by the committee, or to drop the subject and go on with the match." As Dunraven chose the latter course, the committee regarded that as tantamount to a withdrawal of the charges.

The formal inquiry finally began on December 27, 1895, in the model room of the clubhouse, then on Madison Avenue. When Dunraven arrived in New York, he was placed under police protection, but it wasn't needed for very long. Following the same pattern he had established on the race course, he left in the middle of the hearing, after only one day, pleading pressing business at home. Throughout his brief appearance, Dunraven repeatedly shied away from calling what happened a deliberate fraud. But when pressed he agreed that was the unmistakable implication.

The facts uncovered at the hearing can be briefly stated. Dunraven based his charge on two observations: He and others had seen ballast in the form of lead pigs being carried aboard *Defender* from her tender the night before the race, and on the morning of the race a bobstay bolt and drainage hole that Dunraven had observed earlier a few inches above *Defender*'s waterline had disappeared, indicating she was riding lower in the water.

Testimony brought out the fact that the lead pigs placed aboard *Defender* that night had been removed from her earlier, to be cut in half so they could be properly stowed. No new ballast had been introduced. As for the bobstay bolt and bilge pipe, both were supposed to be underwater when the boat was properly trimmed, but could have been exposed by a slight listing of the vessel to starboard, which might have been caused a variety of ways.

In its report to the club the committee reviewed the case as follows:

"The fraud that is involved in the charge thus made, if it is found to be true, is a very grave one, utterly destructive to the reputation of all who should appear to have been concerned in it, and especially odious under the circumstances of a friendly contest between citizens of different countries, exciting international interest, and supposed to be conducted by gentlemen, upon a high plane of honor and mutual confidence." Dunraven's charge, however, "had its origin in mistake," and had been "completely disproved." Furthermore, Dunraven should never have made such an accusation on evidence "so slight, so extremely liable to mistake."

It concluded with an expression of generosity and confidence it had been given little reason to feel:

"And the committee are not willing to doubt, that if Lord Dunraven had remained present throughout the investigation, so as to have heard all the evidence that was introduced, he would of his own motion have withdrawn a charge that was so plainly founded upon mistake, and that has been so unfortunate in the publicity it has attained, and the feeling to which it has given rise."

The Earl was pilloried in the press on both sides of the Atlantic. One London journal summarized British sentiment as follows: "Lord Dunraven has blundered in taste, and the New York committee have let him down in generous and chivalrous fashion."

People who had not seen the Earl at close range expected him to apologize. He did not. After waiting for three weeks, the NYYC asked for his resignation as an honorary member. Dunraven, who had renewed his charges and tried to rebut the committee's evidence in correspondence with club members, mailed a letter of resignation in which he said in effect he didn't want to belong to a club that didn't want him. But that didn't reach the club until after its meeting of Feb. 27, 1896. At that meeting, the members passed a resolution taking a stronger stance:

"We deem it to be among the unquestioned rules which regulate the intercourse of gentlemen that when one finds that he has been led by mistake to cast unjust imputations upon the character of another, he should promptly make such reparation as remains in his power by acknowledging his error, withdrawing the imputations and expressing his regret.

"Such reparation to Mr. Iselin and his associates the Earl of Dunraven, after full opportunity, has failed to make....

"It further appears that in print and in public speech Lord Dunraven has sought to justify the making of the charge by numerous misrepresentations of fact. He has been forced, however, to admit the untruth of most of them, yet he stubbornly refuses to retract the injurious inferences drawn from them....

"Lord Dunraven, by this course, has forfeited the high esteem which led to his election as an honorary member of this club, therefore:

"Resolved, That the privileges of honorary membership heretofore extended to the Earl of Dunraven are hereby withdrawn, and that his name be removed from the list of honorary members of the club."

According to Cup historian Winfield M. Thompson, the resolution was read and passed, by a 39-1 vote, "with much evidence of earnestness and enthusiasm."

The Earl of Dunraven would not be heard from again. His name was stricken from the rolls, but it would live in memory long after those of other challengers had been forgotten.

4
LIPTON RESTORES
ITS LUSTER

In a just world, no odium would have attached to the NYYC once Dunraven's charges were proved groundless. But in the real world an accusation, once made, often outlives its refutation — especially when people are predisposed to suspect the worst. The club's latest revision of its deed had created just such a climate, which the unrepentant Earl exploited for a time by continuing to assert his original charges. As they had after the second Ashbury match, the New Yorkers wondered if the unpleasantness would lead to a general boycott of their Cup.

They had reason for concern. Two British challenges were issued in 1895, after the match but before Dunraven's expulsion. Both were later withdrawn. One was from Charles Day Rose, a Canadian-born banker and horse-fancier but no yachtsman, representing the Royal Victoria Yacht Club. When the NYYC accepted it, Dunraven sent up a howl. He found it "offensive" that the NYYC would accept a challenge from "an American" because the U.S. yachting press had seen it as "a mark of censure upon me and a vindication of the action of the Cup committee." Rose promptly withdrew, citing "the general impression that my challenge might be construed as an expression of opinion on the result of the last race."

The other challenge, from Sir George Newnes, owner of the Strand Magazine and Tit-Bits, died aborning. His club, the Royal London Yacht Club, refused to forward his challenge the following year, on the grounds that it had already gone on record as being opposed to the third deed of gift, which it regarded as "inimical to the sport of yacht races."

1899: 'SIR TEA' COMES FORWARD

The New York club tried to recruit a challenger; by one account, some of its members even offered to finance one. But for three years none materialized. Finally, on August 6, 1898, a challenge was sent by the Royal Ulster Yacht Club on behalf of one of its members, a Scottish-born businessman residing in Ireland whose name was virtually unknown in yachting circles, but familiar to tea-drinkers around the world: Sir Thomas Johnstone Lipton.

As it turned out, the long, anxious wait was worth it. If the NYYC had sent detailed specifications to some cosmic central casting office, it could hardly have come up with a better antidote to the bombastic Earl. Lipton, whose genial countenance still beams forth daily from millions of boxes of Lipton tea, was Dunraven's exact opposite in every important respect. He was a Horatio Alger hero, born into poverty, rising to fame and fortune through honest toil, never forgetting his roots, a man of exemplary character and regular in his habits. Above all, he would prove to be the two things the New Yorkers desired most in their challengers: a keen competitor and gracious loser.

It was as if fate, having regretted her cruelty in sending Dunraven to New York, had relented and was doing her best to make amends. It wasn't fate alone, however. Lipton, no yachtsman, explained later that he had acquired a deep affection for ordinary Americans at an early age, when he spent a few years there as a common laborer. He was distressed at their vilification by Dunraven's partisans in England, and hoped to help restore good relations.

When his challenge reached New York, the club accepted with alacrity, declaring it "most agreeable" and promising that the RUYC planning committee would be warmly welcomed. That warmth was more than reciprocated; the negotiations were brief (less than 24 hours) and friendly. Sir Thomas' representatives demanded little and conceded much, and he was generally regarded as a fine sport.

The conditions established were much like those governing the Dunraven series, with some added provisions inspired by it, having to do with measuring and marking the boats. Lipton's vessel would be *Shamrock*, a cutter with a load waterline of 89.5 feet designed by William Fife Jr. and built on the Thames near London. Her underbody plating would be manganese bronze, her topsides of aluminum alloy over steel frames. She would be finished and

launched the following summer and the races would be held more
than a year from the date of the agreement, in October of 1899. With
this agreement, the NYYC ushered in the longest (1899-1930) and
by far the pleasantest association with any challenger in the history of
the America's Cup.

When Sir Thomas arrived in New York the following summer, the
press made much of his rags-to-riches story and Americans at large
took him to heart. After all, despite his knighthood (conferred upon
him after he had made a large contribution to a royal charity during
Queen Victoria's Jubilee year), he was more "American" than most
members of the stuffy old NYYC.

He was born in 1850 of Irish peasant stock in Glasgow, Scotland,
where his parents had fled during the potato famine. His father found
work as a timekeeper in a mill and later opened a small grocery store.
The family's income was meager and young Thomas, his formal
education over at age 10, emigrated to America five years later.
There his informal education began — on the docks in New York, in
the tobacco fields of North Carolina, and several points in between,
where he worked at a variety of menial jobs, traveled much, made
several lifelong friends, and kept his eyes and ears wide open.

After three restless years, he landed a job in Manhattan, in the grocery section of a department store. What he saw and heard there
taught him the value of that most American contribution to the field
of merchandising: advertising. When he returned to his father's tiny
store at the age of 19, he brought with him a barrel of flour and a
rocking chair for his mother (whom he idolized throughout her life), a
small nest egg, and some large dreams.

He used what he had learned in the States to increase his father's
business. When that succeeded he tried to convince his parents to expand. He ran into stiff Irish resistance, but within two years, at the
age of 21, he had his own store and was off and running. He made
some canny purchases, and exploited them to the hilt. He advertised
his ham and bacon, for example, by buying two enormous pigs, tying
ribbons to their tails, and parading them through the streets of
Glasgow wearing signboards that said, "I'm going to Lipton's, the
best shop in town for Irish bacon."

This and other stunts got into the papers (often with a little nudge
from Lipton), which meant free publicity. Lipton didn't invent
advertising, but he did invent the modern promotional campaign, and

it served him well. Within nine years he owned 20 stores. Although his name is associated with tea today, by the time he threw his hat into the America's Cup ring he was presiding over an international business conglomerate that included hundreds of stores, tea plantations in Ceylon, and stockyards in Omaha and Chicago. None of his interests had even the slightest connection with yacht racing.

Lipton had never been a yachtsman, had never even stood behind a helm. His involvement grew out of his friendship with England's most illustrious yachting enthusiast, Edward, Prince of Wales, as well as his desire to set things right after Dunraven's rampages.

A man of splendid virtues — he didn't smoke, drink, or tell off-color stories — Sir Thomas was not devoid of vanity. He entertained lavishly in his sprawling mansion in Osidge Park outside London, described as a "hideous house" filled with trophies and in such bad taste that it came to be called "Sausage Park." It was an epithet that Sir Thomas, whose pretentions toward good taste began and ended with tea and ham, found amusing. He took great pride in his success and delighted in contrasting his first entry to Manhattan, as a passenger in steerage, with his later triumphant returns.

A FORMIDABLE DEFENSE

Arrayed against him in this first challenge was perhaps the most potent defense syndicate ever formed. Just three men, but among them they controlled a significant fraction of America's wealth: J. Pierpont Morgan, Edwin D. Morgan, and C. Oliver Iselin. J.P. Morgan, commodore of the NYYC, had just made a gift to the club of $200,000 worth of property on West 44th Street in Manhattan, on which it would build its new clubhouse, the one it occupies today. But that was from petty cash. At the time he was the most powerful banker in the world, and one of its richest men.

They gave Herreshoff an order for a defender, to be known as *Columbia*. Iselin, unscathed by Dunraven's attack, would be managing owner. Both sides had unlimited wealth at their disposal, which was just as well; costs had grown considerably since the introduction of bronze and other expensive metals, and it was guessed that each vessel cost about $250,000 to build, fit out and sail for a year — though later estimates had Lipton spending twice that before the summer was over.

As with *Defender*, Herreshoff operated in great secrecy, or tried to. But before long it was known that *Columbia* was to be an improved version of *Defender*, plated with bronze, with nickle-steel frames. Morgan, at his own expense, practically rebuilt *Defender* to sail against her as a trial horse. *Columbia* was in the charge of Capt. Charles Barr and carried a crew from Deer Isle, Maine, a popular recruiting ground. In a series of trial races on Narragansett Bay, *Columbia* proved her superiority.

Shamrock was launched June 24, 1899. After the measurement, *Columbia* gave her a huge 6:31 time allowance. As had become the usual pattern, the experts declared *Shamrock* would have been a worthy opponent of *Defender*, but in *Columbia* American technology had advanced just that one step further. It would be enough.

For the first time, the U.S. government got involved in the race — a tacit acknowledgement that the America's Cup was truly an international event. Empowered by an act of Congress, six revenue cutters and six torpedo boats were sent to patrol the spectator fleet, later augmented by six tugs for the press corps, two steam-yachts and a naval militia yacht. As a result, there was no overcrowding.

Bad weather kept the boats from finishing a race for an unprecedented 13 days. When they finally did, on October 16, *Columbia* crossed the finish line 10:08 ahead on corrected time.

In the second race, *Columbia* was leading when *Shamrock* lost her topmast and retired. The negotiating committee had anticipated such an event. Deciding that the Cup should be a challenge of supremacy in design and construction as well as sailing skill, it had included a provision that if a boat were forced to retire because of a breakdown, the remaining vessel would be required to sail the course alone and accept the victory. *Columbia* did so.

That provision may seem unduly harsh, but it was regarded as a necessary safety measure at the time. There had been an increasing tendency for challengers and defenders alike to carry more sail than their rigging could safely stand, in an effort to squeeze out more speed. When the wind blew, they were vulnerable to dismasting — an event no one who lived through would care to repeat. Unless some penalty were imposed for breakdowns, it was felt, the trend would continue until someone was killed.

The third and final race was held in a strong wind. The challenger led in an exciting contest almost to the first mark. But *Columbia* then took over and finished 6:34 ahead to hold the Cup.

Sir Thomas seemed not at all displeased at the result. For an entire summer he had been the center of attention in the city he had loved since the age of 15. Now, at 49, he had reestablished cordial relations between his native and adopted countries. And his U.S. tea sales were soaring. Of course he would try again, he announced, to general applause.

1901: THE LAWSON EPISODE

Lipton announced his second challenge on October 2, 1900, suggesting the races be held the following August, under the same conditions as the first match. He commissioned a second yacht, *Shamrock II*, this time from George Watson, who had designed *Thistle* and the two *Valkeries*. The NYYC had two candidates for the defense, *Columbia*, the 1899 defender, and *Constitution*, a new Herreshoff design.

While these preparations were under way, word reached New York that a yacht was being prepared in Boston with the intention of crashing their exclusive little party. Aptly named *Independence*, she was being built by a maverick stockbroker, Thomas W. Lawson. Thus began one of the strangest controversies in the history of the Cup — a highly personal one, despite the general long-standing rivalry between New York and Boston yachtsmen.

Lawson had the soul of a riverboat gambler. In those days, long before the Securities and Exchange Commission, it was easier to gain and lose huge fortunes in the stock market, and Lawson did both repeatedly. By 1901, he was a multimillionaire, riding high on a very fast and slippery track.

The details of his stock-market escapades are lost to history, but reportedly he had been thwarted in some of his riskier dealings by the more sober-sided tycoons of Wall Street, who had a vested interest in maintaining a less volatile investment climate. Chief among them was J. Pierpont Morgan, former commodore of the NYYC and head of the *Columbia* syndicate. By commissioning *Independence* from B.B. Crowninshield, a Boston designer, and announcing his intent to enter her in the Cup trials, Lawson was merely adding a naval component to a battle already joined on a different front.

As in his stock manipulations, he had no intention of playing by the unwritten rules — one of which was that the yacht selected to defend would have to represent the NYYC. Lawson was not a member and declared he had no intention of becoming one. He took the position that nothing in the deed of gift or subsequent race conditions barred an outsider from competing for the honor of defending the Cup, which was, after all, a national trophy rather than the property of a single yacht club.

That was debatable, as it had been from the beginning and would continue to be throughout the NYYC's 132-year reign. Lawson, of course, made sure the yachting writers heard his side. Meanwhile, the club reacted as it normally did in the face of such an attack: with private formality and public silence. Public opinion was soon heavily in Lawson's favor. It was a pattern that would be repeated many times, reaching its apotheosis in 1983.

Commodore Lewis Cass Ledyard, a Wall Street lawyer, and several other emissaries from the club tried to resolve matters in a sensible way. In a series of painfully polite messages they pointed out to Lawson that he need not join the club to participate. All he had to do was sell or charter his vessel to a member, temporarily, and it could race. When Lawson seemed to miss the point, the club was even more explicit: Look here, it said in effect, all you've got to do is agree to sail under the club's burgee. Give a member titular charge of her, and you can retain ownership, remain aboard, and even sail her yourself.

Lawson somehow interpreted that to mean "no American other than a member of the New York Yacht Club has a right to take part in the defense of an international cup, rightly named America's and belonging to all Americans." Ledyard finally grew exasperated and broke off the correspondence, charging "willful misconstruction" on Lawson's part. He was right, but most of the press saw it through Lawson's eyes and the battle continued.

Fortunately for the NYYC, Lawson's disingenuous campaign included another "misconstruction," not at all willful: *Independence* herself.

She was basically an enormous (140-foot) racing "scow" with a very flat body, a huge sail spread, a deep fin keel and a balanced rudder with which she was nevertheless almost impossible to steer. After she was launched in May at the Atlantic Works, East Boston, her first trials looked promising. The Newport Yacht Racing Association thereupon intervened in the New York-Boston dispute by arranging a series of races between *Independence* and the two New York boats, to be held off Newport starting July 6. The test, according to Lawson, at least, was eagerly awaited "by the whole country."

To say her performance in the first race was embarrassing would be an understatement. *Independence* was so sluggish the race committee quit timing her at the first mark. *Columbia* came in first, 9:49 ahead of *Constitution* on corrected time. The spectators waited for *Independence* for a while, but when she finally wallowed across partisans called Lawson's entry "a fresh-water lumber-broker" and worse.

She did little better in the second race, coming in more than an hour behind the winner, *Constitution*. It was during that race that the yachting reporters began to suspect what Lawson and her crew already knew: *Independence* had sprung some leaks in the hard pounding she encountered under tow around Cape Cod and was carrying tons of water. She lost two more races before being laid up for repairs. They didn't help: *Independence* steered erratically, was still leaking, and "her bow took one angle of heel while her stern took another, through weakness of construction," according to Lawson himself. She never won a race and was taken back to Boston, where on September 3, three months to the day after her first trial, she was decommissioned and shortly thereafter broken up.

Lawson carried on his feud through a different medium, however. In 1902, libraries and yacht clubs around the country began receiving copies of something called "The Lawson History of the America's Cup," a 402-page, richly bound limited edition that purported to be a history of the first 50 years. Lawson paid for all 3,000 copies himself.

The book is remarkable in that the first 273 pages — written by Winfield M. Thompson, a yachting historian commissioned by Lawson — constitute the most comprehensive, accurate and objective record of those years ever written, an indispensable resource for future Cup historians. The remaining pages, written by Lawson, are devoted to a long-winded and highly partisan description of the entire *Independence* episode, including the lengthiest, most wide-ranging and probably the most vicious attack on the NYYC ever printed. Like graffiti on a public monument, Lawson's shirt-tail diatribe gained more public attention than it deserves. We will return to it in a later chapter, when we look at the NYYC's public image and how that affected yachting history.

THE CLUB BARRS THE DOOR

Constitution, owned by a syndicate headed by Vice Commodore August Belmont, proved an expensive failure. She was launched,

under darkness, on May 6, 1901. Herreshoff attempted to veil her —
just as ineffectively — and in the same secrecy that surrounded
Vigilant, Defender and *Columbia*. Her lines resembled those of
Columbia and *Defender*, but she incorporated some novel construction techniques in her framing and spars. When she sailed against *Columbia* in the trials, a number of weaknesses were discovered; after
only two complete races, the selection committee gave *Columbia* the
nod.

Constitution was the first real setback for Herreshoff, but her
defeats were judged to have been caused at least as much by poor
management and poor rigging as inherent structural defects. The
timidity of her skipper, Capt. Uriah Rhodes, came in for pointed criticism. Capt. Charlie Barr on *Columbia* almost always got the better
start and frequently bluffed *Constitution* out of her rights using
tactics that ranged from intimidating to downright illegal. The
consensus was that Rhodes, who apparently had orders from the
owners not to risk collision, should have called Barr's bluffs.

There were those, including Herreshoff, who maintained *Constitution* was the faster boat. The two faced each other 18 times that summer before the trials, and each won nine races. It was only Barr's ag-
gressiveness that kept the older boat in the running, they said. Indeed,
although *Columbia* was ahead in all three official trial races, the
score stood at 1-1 when she was selected: One race was called when
the wind died and another, the last one, was awarded to *Constitution*
when Barr fouled her. Thus it was that Barr earned the curious distinction of fouling out and being selected as defender on the same day
— a telling example of the way the NYYC resolved the inevitable
conflicts between its roles as impartial steward and very partial
defender of the Cup.

Meanwhile, *Shamrock II* was having troubles of her own, including
a spectacular dismasting with King Edward VII aboard. (The king, it
was reported, was sitting at the top of the companionway when the
whole rig suddenly collapsed and went overboard. He calmly asked if
anyone was hurt, then lit another cigar.)

Shamrock II was notable as the first Cup challenger designed as a
result of tank-testing. Her designer spent nine months testing eleven
different paraffin models and 60 different modifications. Sir Thomas
described her in glowing terms as a breakthrough design "likely to
have a very important effect on the future of yacht-designing." In

fact, she looked little different from other bronze-hulled boats of the period, and once launched had difficulty beating the first *Shamrock* around the course.

When she finally met *Columbia* in the first race for the America's Cup on September 28, *Shamrock II* got off to an early lead but *Columbia* eventually passed and crossed the line ahead by 1:20, corrected time. In their next meeting, *Shamrock* was ahead when the race was called for lack of wind. In the real second race, the wind conditions were perfect, there were no accidents, no glaring errors — and *Shamrock* lost by 3:35, corrected time. The third race proved to be the closest ever in Cup competition, with the challenger coming in first by two seconds, but losing on time allowance by 41 seconds.

Sir Thomas expressed keen disappointment, declaring that Watson had done a fine job, but Herreshoff's design was better. Watson seemed to share that view. The first naval architect to design a Cup challenger with the help of a test tank, he also became the first (though hardly the last) to disparage the results. He caustically remarked that he wished Nat Herreshoff, who drew his lines directly from wooden models he carved by hand, had also had the use of a tank. (Another naval architect put the whole thing into perspective: "The trouble with the tests seems to be that Watson did not have the model of *Columbia* to test also.")

Many Americans shared Lipton's disappointment. "Sir Tea" was such a charming fellow, they wished he had won. They were heartened when Lipton cheerfully vowed to return, then sailed home to Sausage Park, where he doubtless alternated between brooding among his trophies and smiling over his scrapbooks — there would be 84 of them by the time he died — which recorded his social triumphs abroad at least as faithfully as his racing failures.

1903: LIPTON TRIES AGAIN

Shamrock II was still in America, having been laid up in the Erie Basin for the winter. In view of that, and the fact that she'd come so close to winning, Sir Thomas thought it would be a fine thing to challenge for another match the following year. But the club turned him down, standing on the provision of the new deed that barred a challenger's return until two years or another challenge had intervened.

The New Yorkers probably just wanted a rest, but the editorial writers were unwilling to give them one. One noted critic, William P.

Stephens of New York, fired off a letter to The Yachtsman in which he pointed out that the club could simply waive that clause if it wished, as it had quietly waived many provisions in the past when it suited them. For example, when it accepted challenges in 1893, 1895, 1899 and 1900, each without 10 months' notice and without exact dimensions being given, and again when it allowed both *Shamrock* and *Shamrock II* to be towed most of the way across the Atlantic, rather than arriving here under sail, as the deed specified. In short, the club stuck by the letter of the deed when it wished and cited the "mutual agreement" clause when it didn't. Stephens referred to the deed as "a mixture of bad sportsmanship, bad law and bad English, made in a hurry by a little clique." The NYYC, as usual, made no reply.

Lipton must have been disappointed at this delay. Whatever the motives for his first challenge, he was no longer content just to be on the scene; he had caught the fever and was out to win. He accepted the ruling cheerfully, however, vowing to resubmit a challenge when enough time had elapsed, unless someone beat him to it.

There was little chance of that, as both sides knew full well. Challenging for the Cup had become an increasingly less attractive prospect among most yachtsmen. The days of William Henn and his potted palms were long gone. A modern Cup contender had to lay out a small fortune for a highly specialized, stripped-down new boat that would be of no earthly use for any other purpose once the races were over — and indeed were so lightly built that few of them survived more than a season or two. Furthermore, the New Yorkers seemed to have a stranglehold on the thing. As the 20th century dawned, it was apparent that only multimillionaires and incurable optimists would bother. Fortunately, Lipton was both.

After waiting the required time, he sent a challenge for the summer of 1903, along with a gracious letter: "In thus desiring an opportunity of making a third attempt to obtain possession of the America's Cup, I hope I may not be deemed importunate or unduly covetous of the precious trophy so long and so securely held in trust by the New York Yacht Club." The conditions were arrived at quickly and amicably.

Sir Thomas had taken advantage of the interval to commission a third contender, *Shamrock III*, designed by William Fife, who had drawn the first *Shamrock*. Meanwhile, another blue-ribbon syndicate (this time including a Rockefeller and a Vanderbilt) was formed for the defense. It quickly agreed to commission another boat from

Herreshoff, to be named *Reliance*. The Wizard of Bristol set to work under his usual tight security — probably out of sheer Yankee cussedness as much as anything else.

Herreshoff's attitude toward the press is illustrated by this conversation with a reporter from Boston, as quoted by Brooks in "The $30,000,000 Cup." It was in April, just before *Reliance* was launched:

"What do you think of the *Reliance*, Mr. Herreshoff?"
"I have nothing to say."
"Will she beat the *Constitution*?"
Yankee silence.
"What is your opinion of *Shamrock III*?"
Continued silence.
"Good day, Mr. Herreshoff."
"Good day, sir." He walked away a pace, then turned. "Now please do not make this interview long. Do not print any more information than I have given you."

Reliance was the largest defender ever built, before or since — 144 feet overall, with more than 16,000 square feet of sail on her single steel mast, more than twice the sail area of the 1886 racers. She was the most extreme example of the style Herreshoff had introduced with his first defender, *Vigilant* — which yacht historian Winfield Thompson had described as "the prototype of a vicious kind of yacht, whose existence has been more a curse than a blessing to the sport of yacht racing."

The Herreshoff line, unlike their predecessors, made no compromises when it came to speed. Their plating was too thin, their sail area too large and their overhangs too extreme to be seaworthy. The enormous overhangs were a particular abomination to yachting purists, as they had no purpose other than to beat the 90-foot waterline limit imposed by the deed of gift. When a Herreshoff boat heeled in a breeze, the overhangs — the portions of the bow and stern above the waterline — dipped into the water, adding many feet to the sailing waterline and hence to the boat's speed.

Reliance was built to heel in a breeze of just five to seven knots, whereupon her incredible 54 feet of overhangs extended her effective waterline from just under 90 feet to 130 feet. That gave her a theoretical hull speed of 15 knots. But her leeward rail would go under in any breeze over 12 knots. She was, as William Stevens put it, "perhaps the most wonderful and useless racing machine known to yachting."

Shamrock III had been built along roughly the same lines, but was smaller and less extreme. Also slower. She lost her first two races by 9 minutes and 3:16, respectively, then suffered the indignity of steering so far off her course in heavy fog in the third that her captain didn't even try to finish.

For the first time, Sir Thomas seemed genuinely discouraged as he faced reporters:

"It is the greatest disappointment of my life," he said. "What can I do? I have tried my best.... They tell me that I have a beautiful boat. I don't want a beautiful boat. What I want is a boat to lift the Cup — a *Reliance*. Give me a homely boat, the homeliest boat that was ever designed, if she be like *Reliance*."

1920: A REAL THREAT

His wish would not be granted; *Reliance* was the last of her breed. Ironically, her designer, Nathaniel Herreshoff, was a key member of the committee that drafted the new rule that would make her type obsolete. This was the so-called Universal Measurement Rule, which proved to be universal in name only. It took displacement into account as well as waterline length, and penalized excessive sail area and overhangs, thus bringing yacht design back to a safer and more seaworthy course. It was adopted by the NYYC in 1903, modified in 1905.

However, during two conferences in London in 1906, to which American yachting representatives were invited but did not attend, another set of rules, the International Rule of Yacht Measurement, was adopted by the British and most European clubs. These, too, were designed to produce sounder, more seaworthy boats. But the two measurement formulas differed enough that a yacht built to race for the Cup under the Universal Rule could not race in Britain without taking heavy penalties. (Although the International Rule was accepted in America in 1929, the largest classes of boats were still excluded. Thus challengers were forced to build under the Universal Rule, which prevailed only in America, until the NYYC switched to 12-meter boats in 1956.)

Sir Thomas Lipton, having waited to see if this situation would sort itself out, forwarded a challenge in 1907 in which he agreed to follow the Universal Rule. He asked in return only that the club stipulate its defender would not exceed the dimensions of his proposed challenger.

As it had in the past, and would again, the club stood on principle at the expense of courtesy and good sportsmanship: It said no. It cited the deed, which allowed it to build up to 90 feet. And although it had adopted the Universal Rule for all its regular races, it held that only the deed of gift should govern the Cup. J. Pierpont Morgan declared the Cup should be raced for by "the fastest and most powerful vessels that can be produced."

Cup historians Herbert L. Stone and William H. Taylor suggest the club's cool response may have owed partly to a feeling that Sir Thomas had had enough chances, that it was time for a fresh face. It's also reasonable to conjecture that they were hoping for someone more patrician, like themselves, and less beloved by the masses. It must have galled them then, as it would three-quarters of a century later, that so many Americans were rooting for the other side.

If so, they waited in vain.

Finally, in 1912, he challenged again, naming a boat of 75 feet waterline. He asked the club to stipulate that its defender would be no larger. Again the club cited the deed, insisting on its right to build up to 90 feet. The following year, an exasperated Sir Thomas made his challenge unconditional. This the club accepted — then promptly agreed to limit itself to precisely what Lipton had asked for the year before, a defender 75 feet on the waterline and built to the Universal Rule. Having successfully asserted its rights under the deed, the club came out exactly where it might have started — after a considerable loss of time and good will.

World War I broke out as Sir Thomas was towing *Shamrock IV* across the Atlantic. She was dry-docked for the duration and the match was not held until 1920, when Sir Thomas was 70. Then, the only disagreement in the negotiations was over the site of the races. The New Yorkers wanted to move them to the less congested waters off Newport, Rhode Island. But Sir Thomas, who enjoyed the attention he never failed to receive in New York, demurred. The club dropped its suggestion.

For the defense, three boats were built by different syndicates: *Resolute* by Herreshoff and two boats by Boston naval architects new to the Cup game, William Gardner's *Vanitie* and George Owen's *Defiance*. Once again Herreshoff's genius prevailed. *Resolute*, commissioned by a syndicate headed by Cornelius Vanderbilt, was selected.

The 1920 series is notable as marking the end of the professional era; for the first time the helmsmen and nearly the entire afterguards of both boats were amateurs. Charles Francis Adams of Boston, later Secretary of the Navy under President Hoover, took the defender's helm, while William P. Burton, who enjoyed considerable renown as a brilliant tactician, was asked to steer by Lipton.

In the case of *Shamrock IV,* the transition was not entirely smooth. Burton insisted on having his wife as timekeeper, despite strong feelings about women on board, especially among the tough Essex fishermen who made up the professional crew. Also, the crew was disgruntled because he had forbidden them to brew tea during a race — not even Lipton tea! Then Burton crossed the line early in the first race. This caused no loss of time because the rules then in force provided for a two-minute grace period, during which he was able to go around and cross again. But it was an embarrassment nonetheless, which led to much criticism by those ignorant of the fact that false starts were common. Finally, there were too many conflicting suggestions among the afterguard during the race, which led Sir Thomas to replace one of them, the boat's designer, Charles Nicholson.

Shamrock won the first race, after *Resolute* lost her main due to improper handling of a winch while well ahead, and her afterguard decided to retire — the first time a defender had ever dropped out of a Cup race. The decision was roundly criticized later, as she could have continued with her topsail, jibs and spinnaker. She probably would have stayed in the race had her crew known that *Shamrock* was having serious troubles with her own rigging and was in danger of losing her mast in the stiff breeze.

Indeed, aboard *Shamrock* there had been talk of retiring, until they saw *Resolute* in trouble. They kept her going, well eased up, but not until after a lengthy debate over whether to cross the finish line. They finally decided to do so. The hesitancy was a matter of sportsmanship — not wanting to accept a win from a crippled boat that had them beaten before her accident. Sir Thomas generously offered to resail the race, but the committee refused, the conditions of the race being the same as for the *Columbia* series.

Lipton's magnanimity was rewarded in the second race, which

Burton won by superior sailing in light, baffling winds despite a torn balloon jib which was replaced with a small, light sail. The winning margin was 2:26, corrected time. Sir Thomas danced a combination jig and fling and proclaimed himself "the happiest man in the world," a sentiment shared by most of the spectator fleet, whose sympathies were squarely with the challenger. In the entire history of the Cup there had been 33 races in 13 matches, and this was the first time a challenger had beaten a defender by outsailing her. Furthermore, the score was now 2-0. One more win with three races to go, and the Auld Mug would be his at last!

The third race was unique in that both boats covered the course in precisely the same time: *Shamrock* started 19 seconds before *Resolute*, and crossed the line exactly 19 seconds ahead — but lost the race due to *Resolute*'s heavy time allowance of more than 6 minutes. The score was 2-1 in favor of the challenger.

In the fourth, *Resolute* came in almost 10 minutes ahead on corrected time. That made it 2-2, with the final race to decide.

On the scheduled morning, droves of spectators came out. Business took a back seat to the race, and calls came in to city desks from all over the country demanding news. There hadn't been such excitement in a long time — nor would there be again until many years later. But the wind failed to show that day, and the next. On the third day, the wind rose to 25-30 knots and the committee cancelled the race, much to the disgust of yachtsmen generally, who groused that things had reached a pretty pass when a mere gale would keep two such towering racing boats in harbor. Even Sir Thomas reportedly exploded in front of the committee, but later relented and said they were correct. (His skipper, after all, had agreed to the postponement.)

After all that, the actual final race was an enormous letdown. *Resolute* got the best of the light and flukey winds — *Shamrock* was becalmed for a time — and came in ahead by nearly 20 minutes, corrected time. The Cup was safe once again, after the narrowest escape yet.

This time, when reporters asked Sir Thomas if he would come back, he hesitated and said he didn't know. He would return, but not until 10 years later, at the age of 80, when his fifth and final challenge would mark the end of one era and the beginning of another.

5
THE J-BOATS:
THE CUP'S FINEST HOUR

The yachting world, like the world in general, seemed more relaxed in the decade after the Great War, more determined to enjoy itself. Yacht racing was still a rich man's game in the Roaring Twenties, but no longer confined to the very rich, and no longer mainly a spectator sport. Wealthy men who once contented themselves with watching professionals sail their boats to victory or defeat learned it was far more fun to get behind the wheel. The era of the amateur skipper was at hand.

As in other sports, amateurism brought a higher level of sportsmanship. Paid captains were rewarded for winning races, period. Now that the men who made the rules and arranged the matches also did the sailing — and had to face each other at the club-house bar when the race was over — there was more emphasis on fair play. Efforts were made to rid yachting of the excesses and inequities of the past.

At the top of this evolving sport, the America's Cup was about to enter its brief Golden Age, otherwise known as the J-Boat era. It was a happy conjunction of majestic boats, technological advances, sportsmanlike conduct, and some close and exciting races. Above all, the NYYC finally seemed determined to give challengers an even break.

It lasted only seven years. Only three matches were held, in 1930, 1934 and 1937. Only 10 J-boats were ever built. It was a magnificent flowering, but its roots were shallow, planted in the rocky soil of the Great Depression. By the time the winds of war once again blew the

Cup contenders back to port, their day was over, like the gargantuan dinosaurs that ultimately gave way to smaller, sprightlier mammals. When Cup racing resumed many years later, it was on a diminished scale and steering a far different course.

1930: LIPTON'S LAST

It is ironical that this new era was launched by a challenge from the oldest participant in America's Cup history. Sir Thomas Lipton had already celebrated his 80th birthday when he made his fifth and final attempt to lift the Cup. Thirty-one years had passed since his first challenge, a record of persistence that may never be surpassed. In 1930, he faced Harold S. Vanderbilt, whose uncle and father had backed the defenders that preceded Lipton's first challenge. The boats built for the defense were designed not by Lipton's contemporaries, Edward Burgess, Charles Paine and Nathaniel Herreshoff, but by their sons. Sir Thomas had outlived an entire America's Cup generation!

No one knows precisely why he waited nine years after his 1920 effort; his autobiography is silent on the subject. Perhaps, as several historians have suggested, he was waiting for some rules changes that would give him a better chance of winning. That happened in 1927, when the International Yacht Racing Union and the North American Yacht Racing Union, which had been founded only two years earlier, met to hammer out a set of measurement rules and racing regulations that would bring sanity and uniformity to their sport. Several helpful changes were adopted and put into effect the following season. The one that reportedly inspired Sir Thomas to reenter the fray was the rule that large yachts had to meet Lloyd's construction specifications: Henceforth, defenders as well as challengers would have to be built strong enough to withstand an Atlantic crossing, taking away the unfair speed advantage Americans had always enjoyed through lighter construction.

It also was agreed that the International Rule would govern on both sides of the Atlantic, but only for boats rated up to 14.5 meters. American yachtsmen preferred to stick to the Universal Rule for their larger yachts because it allowed designers more freedom to experiment than the more restrictive International Rule. "We look towards progress in design," commented Junius Morgan of the NYYC. "The Europeans seem to wish to crystallize design with a view to retaining the racing life of a boat for the longest period of time." A cynic might point out that the real reason could have been just the reverse: Adopting the International Rule would have rendered the Americans' big boats obsolete.

In any case, the NYYC did not commit itself to either rule for America's Cup matches. When Sir Thomas submitted his challenge in May of 1929, he assumed the club would stand by its old position that only the deed should govern and the old measurement rules would apply. He was pleasantly surprised, therefore, when the club's negotiators suggested the boats be built under the Universal Rule, to the top rating of either the J or K Class, and that the races be held without time allowances, the winner of four out of seven races to take the Cup.

That was almost exactly what Lipton had asked for last time around, and he readily agreed. He chose the larger J Class, which meant a waterline length of 75 to 87 feet. He also agreed, though less eagerly, to the club's suggestion that the races be held off Newport, Rhode Island, far from the growing traffic congestion and pollution around Sandy Hook — as well as the shoreside distractions Sir Thomas loved so well.

The J boats got their name from the Universal Rule's alphabetic size classification. The J Class was one step below the largest sloops, the I Class, of which none were then being built or raced.

We tend to think of the Js as a step down from previous America's Cup contenders, but in fact they were longer, heavier and far more costly than most of their predecessors. All of them were larger than the 1920 contenders, *Shamrock IV* and *Resolute,* in every dimension except beam and sail area. The 1937 racers, *Endeavour II* and *Ranger*, were the heaviest Cup boats since the second race in 1871.

The impression that they were smaller derived mainly from their smaller and totally different sail plan, which closely resembled what we see on 12-meters today. This was the so-called Bermuda or Marconi rig, in which the gaff mainsail and topsail of the past was replaced by a single, tall, triangular main on a huge mast. (The latter name was bestowed because the tall mast, heavily stayed at the sides, resembled the towers and guy lines on Marconi wireless stations then beginning to dot the landscape.) Despite the fact that a J's sail area was generally about half that of the older Cup boats, the new shape was so much more efficient, in conjunction with other changes permitted by the new rule, that the Js actually were faster than their larger predecessors.

Lipton's boat — *Shamrock V*, of course — was a centerboard cutter, 77 feet on the load waterline, designed by Charles Nicholson. She was constructed of steel, teak, pine, mahogany, elm and spruce, with 78 tons of lead in her keel, and was regarded as the loveliest *Shamrock* of them all.

The NYYC formed two syndicates for the defense, but encouraged others as well, with the result that for the first time since the 1893 match four potential defenders were built. They were *Enterprise*, designed by W. Starling Burgess (Edward Burgess' son), *Whirlwind* by L. Francis Herreshoff (Nathaniel's son), *Yankee* by Frank Paine (Charles' son), and *Weetamoe* by Clinton Crane, who somehow managed to get a commission even though his father, as far as we know, never designed a Cup contender.

It is estimated that the four boats combined cost well over $3,000,000 — a staggering sum in that Depression year, even for the multimillionaires who formed the syndicates. *Enterprise* alone cost around a million dollars — maybe a bit more after Burgess and her skipper, Harold Vanderbilt, finished fooling around with her.

Both were inveterate tinkerers. Together they developed a boat and a system of sailing that was 50 years ahead of its time — a combination of state-of-the-art technology and by-the-numbers organization that would not be seen again until Dennis Conner brought *Freedom* to the line in 1980.

Although the syndicate that built *Enterprise* was headed by Winthrop Aldrich, Harold Vanderbilt (known as "Mike" to almost everyone) was her skipper and manager. He was clearly a man with an orderly but inventive mind, a maker of rules. He invented contract bridge, reduced a helmsman's task in arriving at the starting line just as the gun goes off to a mathematical formula (the term "Vanderbilt start" is still used), and devised many sailing rules still in use.

Not surprisingly, he organized his crew like a geared machine. Each position was given a number. Crewman were issued jerseys with the number of their position printed on them, and when orders were given, numbers, not names, were called out. The afterguard, too, was assigned specialized tasks. Vanderbilt steered at starts and upwind and someone else steered off the wind. His sail-trimmer, Sherman Hoyt, steered when the wind was light — or when Vanderbilt needed a break to calm his nerves.

Vanderbilt wrote two books about his 1930 and 1934 campaigns: "Enterprise" and "On the Wind's Highway." Aside from an occasional sentimental flight, both are devoted almost entirely to equipment and tactics. Readers looking for personal insights must search elsewhere.

Starling Burgess probably would have been more fun to know. He was a published poet, notorious for reciting Swinburne while standing on his head — no hands. He said the blood rushing to his brain helped his comprehension and gave the words the proper melancholy tone. But above all else he was a mechanical genius. He dropped out of Harvard to serve as a gunner's mate in the Spanish-American War. Before he returned, he had invented a new type of machine gun. Educated as a naval architect, he opened a shipyard in Marblehead, Massachusetts in 1905, but then turned to aviation. He built the first plane to fly in New England in 1910, opened the first licensed airplane company in the United States, and a year later built the first true seaplane. After building warplanes for England during World War I, he went into partnership with Frank Paine as a yacht designer. Many of his innovations can be traced directly to his knowledge of aerodynamics, the first — but not the last — time knowledge of one medium was used in the other.

When he got the commission for *Enterprise*, he started the way 12-meter designers begin today: He towed models through a test tank, tested sails in a wind tunnel, and performed structural tests at the Bureau of Standards. Before he decided how long she should be, he checked records of wind velocities off Newport in September, going back 20 years. (He concluded that she should have a relatively short 80-foot waterline. That turned out to be dead wrong, but she won anyway.)

Before he was finished he had a boat crammed with gadgets, inventions, and exotic new materials. She had not one but two centerboards, for sailing on and off the wind, and her stripped-down hull held some two-dozen winches below decks. (They were operated by eight men, called the "Black Gang," who never saw daylight during a race.) She had a shunt dynamometer to measure strains on headstays and backstays, a strain gauge to measure the degree of compression on the leeward side of the mast... but no toilet! Anything that didn't contribute directly to speed and maneuverability was simply discarded. The crew had to manage without the latter amenity as best they could, presumably by the numbers.

Her mast, the first big one made of duralumin, was one of her major innovations. It was lighter than standard wooden masts of that height by about a ton — too light to satisfy some safety-minded yachtsmen — giving the boat an enormous advantage in stability. Her other remarkable new feature was her "Park Avenue" boom, so-called because it was wide enough on top (four feet) for two men to walk abreast. That wide top was fitted with transverse slides so the foot of the sail could slide from side to side and could thus assume its natural aerodynamic shape on either tack.

This sort of gadgetry sounds commonplace today, but it was all a bit of a wonder in 1930, and a bane to the yachting purists, who called Burgess' creation "a mechanical yacht" and a "box of clockwork." They must have been heartened by the first several trial races, in which *Enterprise* was consistently beaten by the other NYYC boat, *Weetamoe*. But Burgess and Vanderbilt kept tinkering with the boat and the crew, experimenting right through the August trials.

Vanderbilt was a perfectionist who left nothing to chance. He had an inventory of 50 sails, more even than some of the recent 12-meter contenders, and tested every one thoroughly. He was also a shrewd psychologist. One of his tricks was to order the mainsail removed at the end of every race day, even if it was likely to be the logical choice for the next day's race. Each main weighed more than a ton and it was backbreaking work to haul it down, carry it ashore, and bend it on again the next morning. But he knew what he was doing: If a main was already in place, there was always the temptation to go ahead and use it, even when another might be a shade better for that day's wind velocity.

Little by little, their tinkering paid off; Vanderbilt's well-trained crew, talented afterguard and exceptional helmsmanship did the rest. *Enterprise* started winning. On August 27 she was selected to defend.

Shamrock V was no mechanical boat — and as it turned out, no match for *Enterprise*. The experts declared her badly rigged and badly handled throughout. She lost the first race by 2:52 and the second by 9:34. In the third race, her main halyard parted and the mainsail fell. The damage was too great to be repaired immediately, and she was towed back to her dock. Vanderbilt sailed the course alone and claimed the victory.

Many Americans, either ignorant of Cup tradition or blinded by their affection for Sir Thomas, thought that was poor sportsmanship — which it was not. The fact is, an interesting metamorphosis had taken place in American sporting sensibilities, as yachting historian Alfred Loomis pointed out:

"In 1920 the defender's main halliard let go and *Shamrock IV* sailed on to win a race. America criticized the crippled defender for not trying to finish. In 1930 *Shamrock V*'s main halliard parted and the defender sailed on to win a race. Her action was, in the eyes of many Americans, an infernal outrage. Thus, in sixty years of defending the Cup, inconsistency had become a virtue and sportsmanship was exalted. In the first race of 1870 we would have said such a mishap to the challenger served him good and right for attempting to steal our Cup."

The conditions for the next series, in 1934, settled the matter — or so it was thought: If one vessel were disabled, the other would be required to sail around and accept the win.

In the fourth and final race, *Enterprise* got a favorable wind shift at the start and jumped out to a 9:10 lead at the weather mark. She coasted home under reduced sail on the final two legs, allowing *Shamrock* to reduce her deficit to 5:44 at the finish.

The 1930 series ended, as so many others had, in a clean sweep. But it was a bittersweet victory, at best. Sir Thomas Lipton had tried so hard for so long and had been such a good sport, and now he was 80 years old and in failing health. And he had lost again. As Vanderbilt himself wrote in his diary as he neared the finish of that final race:

"Our hour of triumph, our hour of victory, is all but at hand but it is so tempered with sadness that it is almost hollow."

Sir Thomas added to the general pathos by sounding utterly disconsolate as he greeted sympathizers. "I canna' win. I canna' win," he said over and over again. Will Rogers suggested everyone send a dollar to a Lipton Cup Fund, c/o New York's Mayor Walker, to buy "Sir Tea" a consolation cup. Within a week, $16,000 had poured in and Tiffany's produced a masterpiece in 18-carat gold. When Sir Thomas picked it up in November, he was deeply touched — and promised to try again. But he died, quite suddenly, within a year.

He left many valuable legacies, not the least of which was the sportsmanship displayed by both sides during and after the 1930 series.

For the first time since it was introduced in the 1887 match, the secrecy that always shrouded construction of Cup boats was completely abandoned in 1930. As an article in Rudder commented, this was "practically unheard of in the history of this big race, and it certainly seems to indicate an improvement in sportsmanship."

The friendliest of relations prevailed between challengers and defenders. Not only did they socialize on shore, on one occasion Vanderbilt invited members of *Shamrock*'s afterguard out for a tune-up sail before the races began. Meanwhile the competing designers, Nicholson and Burgess, exchanged the lines and sail plans of their boats and freely discussed their relative merits. Persons unfamiliar with America's Cup history might find nothing exceptional in any of that, but in more recent times such open-handedness would be regarded as little short of treason. Indeed, the NYYC banned Ted Turner, the 1977 defender, from two trial races in 1980 for his "serious indiscretion" in having the Australians' designer, Ben Lexcen, aboard *Courageous* during a race against *Freedom*.

Even the stuffy old Royal Yacht Squadron, which had denied membership to Sir Thomas many years earlier, relented after his final defeat and admitted him. The club's traditional class barriers, which excluded mere "tradesmen," had finally been lowered, even if ever so slightly. Lipton accepted graciously, but never set foot in the clubhouse.

Sir Thomas Lipton should not be given complete credit for this new spirit. Other factors were at work as well, notably the fact that yachting, in an interesting and healthy reversal of the normal progression, was evolving from a mainly professional to a mainly amateur sport. And as its horizons broadened to the middle class, yachting magazines and organizations sprang up to promulgate its more sportsmanlike self-image. But he deserves a lot of it. As Alfred Loomis wrote:

"The amiable tea-vending Sir Thomas Lipton bridged a generation in which American sportsmanship reached maturity and wondered why it had been such a nauseating infant.... He helped us lift Cup racing from the level of a barroom brawl and establish it as a contest between architects, legislators and sportsman-sailors."

1934: A CLOSE SHAVE

The next series, four years later, was an eventful one. Not only did the NYYC come within an ace of losing the Cup, the fourth race involved a controversy that threatened for a time to destroy Lipton's 31 years of fence-mending, his almost single-handed revival of "friendly competition between foreign nations."

The 15th challenge came from Thomas Octave Murdoch Sopwith, the second aviator to pursue the Cup and a man of at least as much complexity as his name. His first introduction to American waters came in 1912, when he fell into the ocean off Coney Island while barnstorming as a stunt flier. Another time he made news by buzzing the statue of William Penn atop Philadelphia's City Hall. Later he raced motorboats before he got heavily involved in building Sopwith Camels for Britain in World War I. When he took up sailing, he went at it with a will, winning the English 12-Meter Championships four years running, 1927-30. After Lipton's death, he bought *Shamrock V*, raced her for a while, then challenged for the Cup in 1933. His club was the Royal Yacht Squadron.

After the usual negotiations, the terms were announced in February, 1934. They called for a four-out-of-seven series off Newport, the conditions being much the same as for the 1930 series. The NYYC made one major concession, however: For the first time it agreed to let the challenging club substitute another yacht if Sopwith's new boat wasn't up to snuff.

The club had made other concessions earlier which also affected the series. Reacting to criticisms of Vanderbilt's mechanical boat, the New Yorkers and British yachting authorities had held a conference on J boats at which they agreed to outlaw most below-decks winches, require heavier masts, and provide living quarters for the crew. These changes spelled death to *Enterprise*, which was consigned to a junk dealer. Her controversial mast ended up supporting the radio tower of the Rhode Island State Police barracks at Scituate.

Sopwith's J boat, a centerboarder 83 feet on the waterline, was called *Endeavour*. She was designed by Charles Nicholson, designer of the last two *Shamrock*s. The defender was *Rainbow*, similar in size and general lines. Again her designer was Starling Burgess with Mike Vanderbilt as skipper/manager. Much was made of the fact that she cost "only" $400,000. She used much of *Enterprise*'s equipment and even borrowed sails. Doubtless this was more a bow to public opinion in that year of deep economic depression than actual hardship within the syndicate, which included four Vanderbilts!

Once again Mike Vanderbilt did not win selection easily. In the trials, he faced his previous competitors *Weetamoe* and *Yankee,* both revamped to meet the new rules. *Rainbow* lost repeatedly to the latter, which was steered by Charles Francis Adams. But again Vanderbilt and Burgess tinkered with the ballast and sails incessantly, rigged a "bendy" boom that shaped the sail even better than the Park Avenue boom, and made other improvements. Eventually she began to win.

She also had a lucky break: The selection committee was about to choose *Yankee* when she had to drop out of a race with a rigging failure. Then *Rainbow* beat *Yankee* in light air. In the next race, *Yankee*'s jib split, costing her a minute and a half for repairs, but she gained quickly after that. *Rainbow* crossed the line in first place — by one second — and was promptly selected. There were bitter feelings aboard *Yankee.* Charles Adams broke down and wept. But the selection committee stuck by its guns. *Yankee* might have been the faster boat, but Vanderbilt seemed the better sailor and manager.

Sopwith's first protest — a mild one — had to do with cabin fittings. *Rainbow* may have followed the letter of the new regulations, he said, but not the spirit. Compared to his boat, she was a stripped-out shell. The NYYC race committee took a look below decks, said Sopwith had a point, and gave him permission to remove furniture and fittings from his vessel also — including Sopwith's bathtub!

If that dispute caused any tension, it was doubtless eased when American yachtsman Gerald Lambert put his converted J boat *Vanitie* at Sopwith's disposal, to use as a trial horse while tuning up off Newport. This was an unprecedented gesture of sportsmanship which apparently had the approval of both the NYYC and Mike Vanderbilt, though both were already very worried about *Endeavour*'s speed. (As we will see, the climate that permitted it didn't last. In 1970, when it had far less cause for worry, the club was critical of Ted Turner for allowing his 12-meter *American Eagle* to be used as a trial horse by the Australian challengers.)

The first race began with another sporting gesture unknown in modern times. Sopwith had trouble getting his mainsail up in rough seas before the start. The NYYC's race committee, without authorization and contrary to the conditions of the match, called a

15-minute postponement to let the challenger sort things out.

In his book, "On the Wind's Highway," Vanderbilt expressed some irritation over the decision — especially as *Rainbow* suffered a gear problem of her own later in the same race which might have cost her the victory. Cup tradition and the rules were clearly on his side; by rights the committee should not have intervened. "But visualize the storm of protest that would have arisen in the press!" he wrote. "I am glad the Race Committee saved me the necessity of making a difficult decision." Later, the committee acknowledged that had the same problem befallen the defender, they would not have dared postpone the start. If the club had bent the rules to favor its defenders in the past, now it was bending them in the opposite direction, to the satisfaction of almost everyone.

After the postponement the boats started within a second of each other and *Endeavour* was ahead when *Rainbow*'s inner spinnaker boom lift parted, sending the spinnaker pole crashing to the deck.

It took about a minute to repair. Chances are Sopwith would have won anyway. *Endeavour* crossed the line 2:09 in front. In the second race, Sopwith won the start and stayed ahead throughout. *Rainbow* gained on the last leg, but still lost by 51 seconds.

For only the second time in Cup history (the first was in 1920) the score was 2-0 in favor of the challenger. By then Sopwith was a two-to-one favorite to win two more races and take the Cup. The NYYC began to get nervous.

So did Mike Vanderbilt. He was a brilliant organizer and manager and a pretty fair sailor, but he was inclined to feel the pressure in tense moments. In one 1930 trial race, for example, after some vigorous pre-start maneuvering and with two minutes to go before the gun, Vanderbilt got so flustered he thought he was steering the boat toward the line when in fact he was heading directly away from it!

Normally that sort of susceptability would weigh heavily against success in an uphill struggle, but in 1934 it probably saved the Cup. Vanderbilt, you see, had a backup system. His name was Sherman Hoyt.

Hoyt, a shrewd tactician, had various duties aboard *Rainbow,* one of which was relief helmsman. Now, in the third race with Vanderbilt at the wheel and Sopwith ahead by 6:21 at the final mark, the situation looked hopeless. Ten minutes after rounding the mark, Vanderbilt, thoroughly discouraged, handed the helm over to Hoyt. "See if

you can make the darned thing go," he said, and went below to eat
lunch and settle his nerves.

Vanderbilt recalled his thoughts at that moment in "On the Wind's
Highway":

"As far as I was concerned, the America's Cup was on its way back
to England. Three down and one to go against a faster boat was a little too much. Perhaps it would be a good thing for the sport to have
the Cup cross the Atlantic — many argued that it had been in the
possession of the New York Yacht Club too long — still I hated to go
down in history as the first skipper to lose it."

Meanwhile, back at the helm, Hoyt was about to gamble — why
not? He had noticed that Sopwith almost always tried to keep his opponent covered, regardless of the mark. In a desperate tactic, even
though *Rainbow* was able to fetch the finish line (which neither boat
could see), Hoyt luffed well past *Endeavour*'s weather, hoping the
challenger would follow suit to cover. He did. Hoyt wrote in his
"Memoirs:"

"The bluff came off! Tommy tacked... right into a calm patch. Immediately I bore away and sailed right through *Endeavour*'s lee."
Endeavour came about four times while *Rainbow* fetched the line
without a single tack. That fatal tack cost Sopwith the race, and possibly the Cup. The score now stood at 2-1 in favor of the challenger.

It was in the fourth race that two incidents occurred that
threatened to cause the greatest unpleasantness since Dunraven. The
first was during the pre-start maneuvering, when there was a near-
collision. Each skipper believed the other was to blame. Neither
hoisted a protest flag immediately. The second happened just after
both rounded the first mark, with Sopwith in the lead. When
Rainbow rounded, she came out on *Endeavour*'s weather side.
Sopwith then luffed to force his opponent to give way, as the rules
permit.

Vanderbilt, however, held his course. He had a firm grip on the ru-
lebook, which included the perplexing dictum that a leeward boat
"within risk of collision range" had to be in a position when she luffed
to strike the other boat forward of the amidship shrouds if both held
course. Vanderbilt was sure Sopwith had begun his luff too late, but
assumed he would hold the luff long enough to decide where, in fact,
the point of collision might be if she continued. Sopwith, however,
bore away when the boats were, a.) 90 feet apart (Vanderbilt's

version) or, b.) in imminent danger of collision (Sopwith's version). In any case, the maneuver slowed the challenger, whereas *Rainbow* was able to hold course and speed.

Sopwith felt Vanderbilt should have given way. He hoisted a protest flag — the first by a challenger in America's Cup history — but not until two hours later, when he drew near the committee boat at the finish line. By one account, he and his afterguard took that long to make up their minds what to do. By another, he asked the NYYC observer aboard *Endeavour* if he should hoist a protest flag immediately, or wait until he was closer to the committee boat as was the British custom. The club's representative said he thought it would be okay to wait, so he did.

Vanderbilt went on to win by 1:15. That would have made it 2-2, but Sopwith was convinced he would win the protest, which incorporated both incidents. One can imagine his shock when the race committee, 24 hours later, announced it would not hear the protest. When he heard the reason, he was downright furious: The racing rules clearly state that a protest flag must be flown "promptly" after the incident being protested, the committee explained. Sopwith's flag had gone up three hours after the first incident, two hours after the second. At that critical juncture in America's Cup history, the race committee was standing on a technicality that every experienced yachtsman knew was more often ignored than not!

Press condemnation was swift, severe and virtually unanimous. It was this incident that prompted the classic headline: "Britannia Rules the Waves, but America Waives the Rules." Even Vanderbilt expressed his dismay that Sopwith wasn't going to have his day in court. Sopwith himself showed admirable restraint under the circumstances. First he declared he was "bitterly disappointed at his treatment in Newport," and vowed he would never challenge again. But then he lapsed into a discreet silence and muzzled his designer, Nicholson, who had promised to "blow the lid off" when he got back to England. ("Reports were that his comments on the result were too lurid for reproduction in cold type," according to the Providence Journal's yachting writer, Jeff Davis. This was the same Nicholson who had been sent ashore by Lipton when his heated arguments over tactics distracted the other members of *Shamrock*'s afterguard.)

It wasn't until about two months later that the committee issued a report in which it explained its real reasoning: The first incident had taken place in full view of the committee. In the members' judgment, Sopwith had been clearly at fault; photographic evidence later supported that conclusion. Therefore, the committee would have had to disqualify *Endeavour* on the first count, making the second one moot.

In sidestepping the protest rather than ruling against the challenger, committee members apparently felt they were continuing their efforts to avoid unpleasantness. They were dead wrong.

By all contemporary reports, the committee was composed of honorable and sportsmanlike gentlemen. The irony is that, in 1934 as in 1983, had the club been represented by men of a more devious turn of mind, they probably would have foreseen the effects of their misplaced discretion — which effects they merely compounded by their silence when the storm broke. They did not, and they caught unshirted hell. Nonetheless, their ruling stood. There was no appeal.

It was another indication (if any were needed) that public relations was not the club's long suit. In retrospect, the whole episode should have provided a clear presentiment of events in 1983, when the NYYC finally lost its Cup after a series of remarkably similar miscalculations.

That incident seemed to take the starch out of Sopwith. Or perhaps it was a new spinnaker, borrowed from *Yankee* before the fourth race, that turned the tide for Vanderbilt. In any case, he won the fifth race decisively by 4:01.

The sixth race, which involved another protest at the start (later withdrawn by both sides), was an almost eerie repetition of the third — at least according to Hoyt's account in his "Memoirs." Once again Sopwith seemed to have it in the bag. Again Vanderbilt got nervous, turned the wheel over to Hoyt, and went below. Hoyt again gambled that Sopwith would cover blindly. He set a course that would take them both away from the line, and Sopwith foolishly followed suit. The maneuvering (and a lucky wind shift) gave *Rainbow* the better angle to the line, which she crossed 55 seconds in front. The Cup was safe, after one of the closest calls in its history.

The experts agreed that Sopwith had the faster boat, but Vanderbilt and his crew were the better sailors. As a footnote to this eventful series, Sopwith may have lost in part because he stood on principle before the racing even started: Just before *Endeavour* was to leave for America, his professional crew struck for higher wages, figuring they had him over a barrel. Sopwith, feeling their demands were unjustified, refused to give in. He put out a call for amateur sailors, who responded by the score and eventually made up more than half his crew. They were among the best but hadn't trained together long enough, and had not been toughened. Their uncalloused hands bled before the series was over from hauling on the ropes, and that may have been a factor in the boat's relatively slow sail-handling.

1937: END OF THE GOLDEN AGE

Bitter feelings over the protest incident lingered for a time, especially in Britain. Charles Nicholson, no longer muzzled, charged in Yachting World that *Rainbow* had increased her speed by illegally adding ballast, and that if the weight of her crew had been figured, she would have had to sacrifice some sail area. Nicholson, like Dunraven before him, took pains not to implicate individuals or committees. It was the fault, he said, of the "autocratic control by a few persons in the New York Yacht Club." Sopwith, he said, had thought that both design and racing rules had been violated by the club in the match.

Fortunately, all this was smoothed over when it was shown there were honest differences between British and American methods of measuring freeboard. Experts from both countries convened on the matter, agreed nothing untoward had been done, and changed the rules to prevent such discrepancies in the future.

In 1936, Sopwith challenged again, through the Royal Yacht Squadron. The NYYC accepted, and generously agreed to let Sopwith enter *Endeavour* again if his new design, *Endeavour II*, proved inferior. Races would be in July and August, 1937, under the rules of the previous match.

Clearly a new defender would have to be built. The Depression was now at its height, however, and ready cash was scarce, even within the august clubhouse on West 44th Street. Finally, after the designers agreed to cut their fees and the Bath (Maine) Iron Works offered to build her at cost, Mike Vanderbilt decided to go it alone, underwriting all expenses himself. That inspired the following doggerel:

> *My mast is duralumin, but it's costlier than gilt,*
> *The wind that fills my riggin' is a million dollar breeze.*
> *From my bowsprit to my topsail, I am wholly Vander-built*
> *And I only go a-sailing in the most exclusive seas.*

The nations mourn the income tax, for bread the countries cry.
But whistle the Endeavour *out, and run the pennants up —*
Three quarter million dollars will be racing in July
For a mid-Victorian trophy, for a silver-plated cup.
                                        "Redbook," July, 1937

Vanderbilt called in two designers, the aging Starling Burgess and a young man named Olin Stephens, about whom more — much more — would be heard later. Each of them made two models and all four were tested in the tank at the Stevens Institute before one was chosen. It was agreed between them that they would keep secret whose model was chosen, and it was one of those rare America's Cup secrets that actually was kept. Even Vanderbilt didn't know. It wasn't until 20 years later, after Burgess had died and Stephens had been credited with the design, that he revealed it had been Burgess'.

The new boat, named *Ranger,* was built to the J Class maximum waterline, 87 feet. She was all steel with a welded hull and incorporated further advances, including an arrangement of two booms that allowed the boat to jibe without collapsing the enormous spinnaker, which saved about three minutes. The NYYC race committee, however, without any protest or encouragement from Sopwith, declared the new boom illegal. The relevant rule stated that a spinnaker could not be set without a boom; Vanderbilt's was not attached for only a moment during the maneuver, but that was enough. He appealed the decision, but was overruled. (The rule was later discarded.)

Ranger was a huge, powerful and, by the nautical esthete of the day, not a very pretty yacht. But she was fast. When Nicholson saw her out of water for the first time, he declared her the most revolutionary boat in the past 50 years. She was blunt in the bow, flat in the stern, flying a huge cloud of canvas, including a spinnaker of 18,000 square feet — greater than the entire measured sail area (which doesn't include spinnakers) of most previous Cup contenders and about *10 times* the sail area of a modern 12-meter!

During her tow around Cape Cod from the Maine works, she encountered rough weather and lost her mast and most of her rigging. With the first informal trial races less than two weeks away, that was a potential disaster. However, in another display of sportsmanship that uniquely marked the J-boat era, the owners of Vanderbilt's

The schooner *America* under full sail in 1893. After bringing home the Cup that bears her name, she was sold to an Irish peer for $5,000 more than she cost to build. Even after expenses, the *America* showed a profit — the only America's Cup yacht ever to make that claim. *America*'s career included duty as a racing and cruising yacht, as a Confederate blockade runner and finally as a training ship at the U.S. Naval Academy. (Rosenfeld Collection, Mystic Seaport Museum)

The construction contract for *America*. Never since has any America's Cup builder or designer had such confidence in his work. William Brown, *America*'s builder, guaranteed his creation would be the fastest yacht in the U.S. or England or he would release the owners from their contract. (Rosenfeld Collection, Mystic Seaport Museum)

Galatea in 1886, the sixth British challenger. Even though soundly thrashed more than 30 years before by the innovative *America*, the British were still unable to field a competitive boat. Unlike U.S. boats, *Galatea* was a gentleman's yacht designed to sail comfortably across oceans. Down below,

Galatea gave Lt. and Mrs. William Henn all the amenities of home, including a fireplace, potted plants, leopard-skin rugs and a menagerie of pets — a dog, a cat, a raccoon and a monkey. (Rosenfeld Collection, Mystic Seaport Museum)

YACHTING—1872.

Clearly, the America's Cup in the late 19th century had not yet been embraced by mainstream Americans as anything but a curious pasttime for the mighty and the lofty, as shown in this 1871 spoof in "Harper's Weekly." (Mystic Seaport Museum)

Lord Dunraven (center, in bowler hat) cried "foul" in 1895, touching off the first of many international
embroglios centering on the America's Cup. (Rosenfeld Collection, Mystic Seaport Museum)

THE YACHTING FEVER IN NEW YORK: EXCURSION STEAMERS WHICH FOLLOW THE RACING

Reclusive, enigmatic Nathanael Herreshoff dominated America's Cup yacht design from 1893 to 1920. He raised secrecy to an artform, including launching his hulls under cloak of darkness. Few good photographs exist of Herreshoff. The large photo above is a rare shot from the Iselin collection at the Mystic Seaport Museum. Most likely he is aboard C. Oliver Iselin's *Columbia*.

VOL. 41 NO.1041   SEPTEMBER 28 1901.   PRICE 10 CENTS

Judge

ENTERED AT THE POST OFFICE AT NEW YORK AS SECOND CLASS MATTER COPYRIGHT 1901 BY JUDGE COMPANY. TITLE REGISTERED AS A TRADE MARK.

FIND THE CUP.

Unc'e Sam (to John Bull)—''Well, John, there is one good thing about the yacht races—whichever wins, we have the Cup between us!''

Capt. Hank Itoff (above) at the helm of *Defender* in 1899. Most of the pre-World War II America's Cup yachts were sailed and skippered by professional crew. Amateurism was never an issue; in fact, many early America's Cup yacht owners rarely stepped foot aboard their boats. *Ranger*'s interior (below), reflected the class structure that separated crew and owners. By 1901, as evidenced on the cover of "Judge," the America's Cup had become an important symbol in the national consciousness. (Providence Journal)

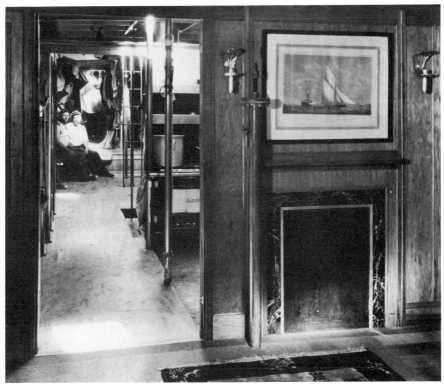

AN ENGLISH PROVERB ILLUSTRATED.
"THERE IS MANY A SLIP 'TWIXT THE CUP AND THE LIP (TON)."

The affable, popular Sir Thomas Lipton reestablished America's Cup sporting tradition following Lord Dunraven's bellicose challenges. Shortly after this photograph was taken in 1920, defender *Resolute*'s halyard parted, sending her mainsail to the deck. Under new rules, *Shamrock IV* finished the course for the win, where in the past the sporting tradition was to resail the race. The America's Cup had become too important an institution — and the bone of too much contention — to allow mere traditions to rule. (Judge: Mystic Seaport Museum; *Shamrock IV:* Providence Journal)

In this 1920 photo, likely taken aboard his motor yacht *Erin*, "Sir Tea" plays host to numerous notables, including (second and third from right) Rose and Joseph Kennedy. (Rosenfeld Collection, Mystic Seaport Museum)

T.O.M. Sopwith aboard *Endeavor* with his wife. Sopwith, an adventurer and pioneer aviator (of Sopwith Camel fame), was the first of many owners who would take the helm, making the America's Cup a more personal sort of challenge. (Rosenfeld Collection, Mystic Seaport Museum)

(Left to right) Roderick Stephens, Olin Stephens, Prof. Zenas Bliss, Mrs. and Mr. Harold Vanderbilt and Arthur Knapp were "Mike" Vanderbilt's braintrust aboard *Ranger* in 1937. Hard work and assembling the right team were Vanderbilt's keys to successive America's Cup victories in 1934 and 1937, a formula others would raise to militaristic levels in the years following World War II. (Rosenfeld Collection, Mystic Seaport Museum)

A pre-1983, state of the art 12-meter sailboat (Providence Journal)

What the 11 man crew does:

The AFTERGUARD:
The afterguard handles running backstays during maneuvers.

HELMSMAN:
The skipper of the boat; makes all sailing decisions.

NAVIGATOR:
Plots the position of the boat on the course, observes wind, sea and current conditions; operates the on-board computer systems.

TACTICIAN:
Plans strategy, observes competition and advises on maneuvers.

MAINSAIL TRIMMER:
Advises on sails, operates hydraulic systems.

FOXHOLE MAN:
Located in the cockpit. Clears jib when tacking and mans the foredeck

TAILERS:
Trim the genoa jib.

GRINDERS:
Handle the coffee-grinder winches: two go forward to help with pole and sails, and two pass sails up from below

How to measure a 12 Meter

It's actually a 28.44 meter.

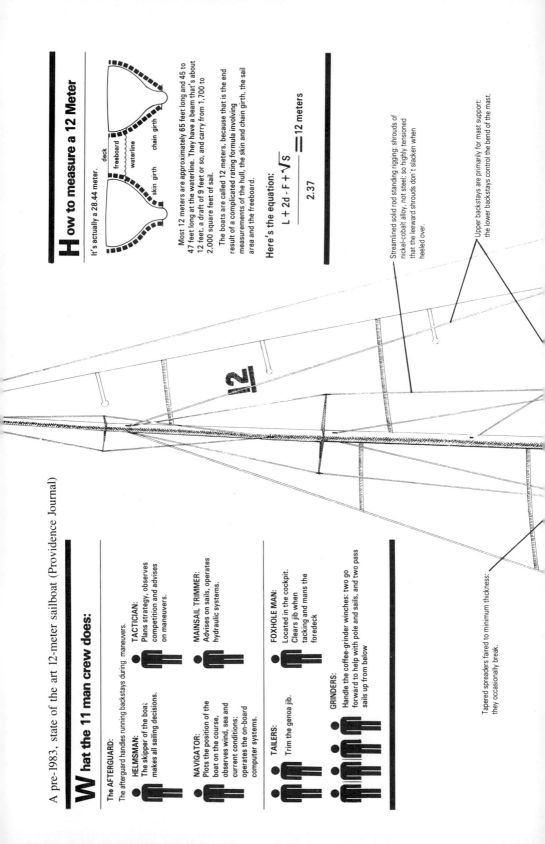

deck
freeboard
waterline
skin girth   chain girth
skin girth   chain girth

Most 12 meters are approximately 65 feet long and 45 to 47 feet long at the waterline. They have a beam that's about 12 feet, a draft of 9 feet or so, and carry from 1,700 to 2,000 square feet of sail.

The boats are called 12 meters, because that is the end result of a complicated rating formula involving measurements of the hull, the skin and chain girth, the sail area and the freeboard.

Here's the equation:

$$\frac{L + 2d - F + \sqrt{S}}{2.37} = 12 \text{ meters}$$

Streamlined solid rod standing rigging: shrouds of nickel-cobalt alloy, not steel; so highly tensioned that the leeward shrouds don't slacken when heeled over.

Upper backstays are primarily for mast support; the lower backstays control the bend of the mast.

Tapered spreaders faired to minimum thickness; they occasionally break.

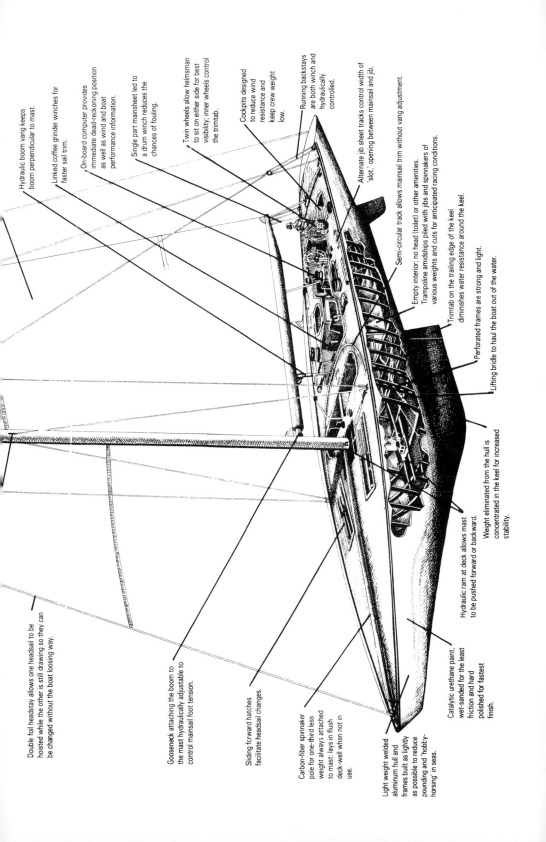

Hydraulic boom vang keeps boom perpendicular to mast.

Linked coffee grinder winches for faster sail trim.

On-board computer provides immediate dead-reckoning position as well as wind and boat performance information.

Single part mainsheet led to a drum winch reduces the chances of fouling.

Twin wheels allow helmsman to sit on either side for best visibility; inner wheels control the trimtab.

Cockpits designed to reduce wind resistance and keep crew weight low.

Running backstays are both winch and hydraulically controlled.

Alternate jib sheet tracks control width of 'slot,' opening between mainsail and jib.

Semi-circular track allows mainsail trim without vang adjustment.

Empty interior: no head (toilet) or other amenities. Trampoline amidships piled with jibs and spinnakers of various weights and cuts for anticipated racing conditions.

Trimtab on the trailing edge of the keel diminishes water resistance around the keel.

Perforated frames are strong and light.

Lifting bridle to haul the boat out of the water.

Weight eliminated from the hull is concentrated in the keel for increased stability.

Hydraulic ram at deck allows mast to be pushed forward or backward.

Catalytic urethane paint, wet-sanded for the least friction and hard polished for fastest finish.

Light weight welded aluminum hull and frames built as lightly as possible to reduce pounding and 'hobby-horsing' in seas.

Carbon-fiber spinnaker pole for one-third less weight always attached to mast: lays in flush deck-well when not in use.

Sliding forward hatches facilitate headsail changes.

Gooseneck attaching the boom to the mast hydraulically adjustable to control mainsail foot tension.

Double foil headstay allows one headsail to be hoisted while the other is still drawing so they can be changed without the boat loosing way.

Sir Frank Packer was the first Australian challenger for the America's Cup. Like others who would follow him in the modern era, Sir Frank was a brash and outspoken self-made man. (Rosenfeld Collection, Mystic Seaport Museum)

competitors for the defense, Gerald Lambert (*Yankee*) and Chandler Hovey, who had bought *Rainbow*, offered him whatever spare equipment they had, and volunteered to postpone the start of the preliminary races by four days.

With their help, repairs were made quickly, whereupon *Ranger* promptly beat the others in four straight races, won all the observation trial matches, and was selected after just one race, against *Yankee*, in the final trials. (She made two attempts to race *Rainbow*, both cancelled because of a lack of wind. But the committee had seen enough.)

After its fright in the previous match (and the controversy), the NYYC was doubtless ready for an easy win, and that's just what it got. *Ranger*, which would prove to be one of the four "super boats" in America's Cup history *(Reliance, Ranger, Intrepid* and *Australia II)*, was unbeatable. In the first race, *Endeavour II* lost by an embarrassing 17 minutes. She did even worse in the second, and was then hauled out to see if a lobster pot or something else was dragging along her bottom. (It was clean.) Her record in the next two races was better, but she lost four straight.

Even more pleasing to the New Yorkers perhaps was the fact that Sopwith pronounced it a fair contest and had no complaints. "It had been a most pleasant series of races, devoid of ill feeling, bickering and unpleasant incidents," Vanderbilt wrote in "On the Wind's Highway." But he had a premonition of things to come:

"Was *Ranger* so good that she has killed the class and dampened the ardor of others? Have I inadvertently killed the thing I love?"

In a concluding paragraph, an uncharacteristic attempt at lyricism, he wrote of the five J boats sailing that season:

"As they have come out of the distance, so shall they go into the distance. The fair wind, their never weary white wings, carry them on — On the Wind's Highway, 'homeward bound for orders' — on, to destiny."

As it turned out, their destiny was to be broken up and melted down for scrap metal, then reincarnated as tanks, guns and bullets for a larger and uglier international contest, World War II. Thus ended the Golden Age.

PART TWO

The Decline

1958-1980

The J boats, and the sheltered world of elegance and privilege that nurtured them, were simply swept away by the second great war. For a while it appeared the America's Cup itself might become a relic of that vanished age. A dozen years after the last J-boat challenge, four years after Hiroshima and Nagasaki, it was removed from the vaults at Tiffany's to the NYYC's landlocked clubhouse at 37 West 44th Street. A special wrench was used to secure it to an oaken table in the crypt-like Trophy Room. The wrench was placed in the club's safe, along with the deed of gift.

But in 1956 the deed was taken out, dusted off, and amended with the blessings of the Supreme Court of the State of New York: Henceforth, the matches could be raced in 12-meter boats. And with that the modern era was born, an era so distinctly different from the past it was almost as if a century of Cup challenges had never happened.

At first, during the 1960s, the differences seemed trivial — a matter of adjusting to smaller boats, smaller bank accounts, learning to play the same game with new toys. But during the 1970s the America's Cup took on a life of its own, steering an uncharted course away from the placid straits of gentlemanly sport into the shark-infested waters of corporate intrigue.

By 1980, it was being sucked into an ever-widening whirlpool of commercial tie-ins, tax write-offs, media campaigns, high-tech design, corporate espionage, litigation and psychological warfare. For the keepers of the Holy Grail and the sailors who defended it, it had become one long, exhausting, deadly serious grind, the only object of which was to hold the Cup. Emil Mosbacher, the NYYC's 1984-85 commodore, put it best: "We had a tiger by the tail."

Thus far, we have looked at the matches individually and in order. The chronology will blur somewhat from here on, however, as we focus more directly on those changes, and on three men who dealt with them in different ways during the decade before the fall: Alan Bond, who exploited them; Ted Turner, who resisted them, and Dennis Conner, who tried to master them.

6
THE EMPIRE STRIKES OUT

After the war, the problem was apathy. No one seemed to care much about the America's Cup anymore. In 1948, DeCoursey Fales, commodore of the NYYC, and John Illingworth, commodore of England's Royal Ocean Racing Club, agreed the races should be resumed in smaller ocean-racing yachts, about 45 feet at the waterline. But despite their leader's enthusiasm, the New Yorkers turned thumbs down on any move toward smaller boats. Their post-Edwardian world may have been diminished by events beyond their control — but shrink the boats? Belittle the Cup? Never!

By the 1950s it had become apparent, even within that bastion, that the deafening silence from abroad might be prolonged indefinitely. Racing boats with 65-foot waterlines, the minimum specified by the deed, were as extinct as dinosaurs and no one was eager to revive them.

"Probably the time had come to take the Cup, put it in a case somewhere, and say, 'This is a piece of our history. Let's go on to something else,' " Mosbacher reflected some 35 years later. "A number of the members thought about it," he said. "I know I did."

Commodore Mosbacher is better known as Bus Mosbacher, the defending skipper in 1962 and 1967 and one of the all-time great 12-meter sailors — a bit of personal history that would not have occurred if it hadn't been for one of his predecessors, Commodore Henry Sears (1955-56). It was Sears' tireless negotiation and persuasion that led his club and England's Royal Yacht Squadron to agree on 12-meters as the new America's Cup standard.

The deed was amended by changing the minimum waterline from 65 feet to 44 feet, and abolishing the provision that challengers must sail to the contest on their own bottoms. It was signed December 17, 1956. The Royal Yacht Squadron responded within six months, challenging the New Yorkers to a match in 1958. It had been 21 years between races, the longest hiatus in Cup history. Many things had changed, many others had been forgotten. The first task was to revive the 12-meter class.

There's a popular impression that the 12s were brand new, developed specifically to race for the America's Cup. In fact, in 1957 they were exactly 50 years old. The original 12-meter boat was built in 1907, a year after adoption of the International Rule, which defined classes in terms of their rating in meters. About 100 had been built since then, mostly in Europe. More than half were still afloat, though almost all had been converted for cruising. But none had been built since the war and the fact is, before they were given a new lease by the amended deed, they were in danger of following the J boats into yacht-racing's out basket.

The NYYC had only one at its disposal, the wooden-hulled *Vim*, designed by Olin Stephens for the prescient Harold Vanderbilt in 1939. It had been laid up in 1940 after two highly successful seasons of racing in England and America. Stephens was the only living American naval architect who had ever drawn a 12-meter.

1958: A GENTLEMANLY ROUT

Although the British had been racing 12s before Stephens was born, they were even less prepared for the modern era. The first thing they did was form a syndicate of gentlemen whose names are redolent of Empire: Hugh Goodson (chairman), Lt.-Col. A.W. Acland, H.A. Andreae, Lord Camrose, B. Currie, Group Capt. Loel Guiness, Maj. H.W. Hall, Sir Peter Hoare, Maj. R.N. Macdonald-Buchanan, Lord Runciman, C. Wainman, and Sir John Wardlaw-Milne. One yachting writer described them as "a group of kindly, elegant, elderly British gentry, whose sense of loyalty and gallantry was infinitely superior to their sense of competition and their critical understanding of boat speed."

They asked four of England's best designers to work up two designs and models each, one of which could be as radical as desired within the rule, from which they would choose one after tank-testing. The eight resulting models were towed in the Saunders-Roe Experimental Tank. After a mere 41 hours of testing, the model submitted by David Boyd, a Scot, was deemed the fastest and was chosen. His boat would be named *Sceptre*.

In retrospect, the whole procedure was a disaster. The British tested nine models (they threw in the lines of a pre-war 12-meter for good measure) for a total of 41 hours; the Americans, meanwhile, used the tank at the Stevens Institute of Technology for an entire year in testing the three defense candidates. The defenders used the tank as a research tool, the challengers as a referee. Furthermore, the British results were misleading. All the models were designed for a brisk breeze (a mistake in itself), but the tank had no wave-making machine. So when they were towed it was under conditions that simulated a strong wind and flat water. The results pointed toward Boyd's second model, which had rounded forward sections — instant death in the confused, choppy seas off Newport.

Meanwhile, Commodore Henry Sears was struggling to put together a syndicate of NYYC members. He hadn't wanted to get involved at all, but the embarrassing fact was that no one was eager to build a defender. As Sears said at the time, he "would have looked awfully damned silly to have sponsored a challenge and then have no boat to defend." So he lined up Briggs Cunningham, Gerald Lambert and Vincent Astor among others. They commissioned Olin Stephens to design a new 12, to be named *Columbia*. They were getting a late start. Worse yet, for the first time in its history, the club had trouble lining up enough financial backing. All progress halted at one point, whereupon the New Yorkers put out another call for help.

As had happened back in 1885, when the club issued a similar SOS for different reasons, a member of its arch-rival, the Eastern Yacht Club, was only too eager to lend a hand. This time there were personal reasons as well.

The volunteer was Chandler Hovey, a retired stockbroker in Boston, the same Chandler Hovey who had backed *Yankee* in the 1934 trials. That was probably the faster boat that year, but the selection committee picked Mike Vanderbilt's *Rainbow* instead, after she beat a crippled *Yankee* — by one second. "I was irked," Hovey recalled 30 years later, "so in 1957 when I heard the New York Yacht Club syndicate was getting a little wobbly, and they called me, I decided to build a Twelve." He commissioned it from designer C.

Raymond Hunt, who also sailed as a member of her afterguard. No doubt with malice aforethought, he named her *Easterner*. It must have sharpened the 78-year-old Hovey's appetite for the trials even further to know that his old opponent, Mike Vanderbilt, 74, was on the New York selection committee.

If Hovey's motives were competitive, his racing style was not. *Easterner* was run very much as a family effort. His two sons alternated as helmsman, son-in-law Sherman Morss navigated, daughter "Sis" was a member of the crew, and two grandsons were added for the preliminary trials. As Carleton Mitchell put it in his book, "Summer of the Twelves," it was "something like getting up from a picnic table to take on the Chicago Bears." Sportswriters began referring to the boat as the "Covey of Hoveys." Hovey himself said, "We have always sailed informally as a family.... We always lived aboard and never took our racing too seriously, but we had a lot of fun." The Hoveys would have been an ideal defender against Lt. and Mrs. William Henn's 1886 challenger, *Galatea*, with its potted palms, leopard skins and pet monkey.

The call for help flushed out another volunteer, closer to home. He was Henry Mercer, a longtime member of the NYYC who had not been approached by the Sears syndicate, possibly because he was not a racing man. Marcer was a shipping tycoon who had known Sir Thomas Lipton in the '30s, and who had vowed he would back a Cup contender if he ever got the chance. He commissioned a boat from designer Phil Rhodes, giving him total responsibility and assuring him in advance that he wouldn't complain if she lost — a model agreement, at least from the designer's point of view. The boat did lose that year, but would be heard from again. Her name was *Weatherly*.

Meanwhile, John Matthews, another shipping magnate, had bought *Vim* in 1951. He took out the small engine he had installed, lined up an afterguard that included Bus Mosbacher and Ted Hood, who also would be heard from again, and entered her.

There was a lot of rivalry among the crews, all of it, at this early stage of the 12-meter era, good-natured. Arthur Knapp Jr., who had crewed aboard *Ranger* in 1937 and was *Weatherly*'s helmsman, reportedly had slipped and fallen overboard the day before *Weatherly* arrived in Newport. When she came in, she passed close by *Columbia* — whose crew had lined up on deck wearing orange life jackets as if ready to perform a rescue. Later, *Columbia*'s navigator discovered a wooden box with a glass front on the bulkhead near his station. Across the top it said, "In Emergency, Break Glass." Inside was copy of Arthur Knapp's book, "Race Your Boat Right."

Weatherly and *Easterner* were eliminated first, leaving two Olin Stephens designs in the trials. Surprisingly — shockingly — the 19-year-old *Vim* outdistanced *Columbia* consistently in the early going, and wasn't far behind at the end. The races between those two were hailed as the most exciting in the Cup's history. *Vim*'s performance was a tribute to her helmsman, Bus Mosbacher. *Columbia* was the faster boat right along, and she proved it as soon as her crew got its act together, first under helmsman Cornelius Shields, 63, then under Briggs Cunningham when Shields was benched by his doctor. She was selected after taking four of the last six races.

Meanwhile, the challengers were struggling just to bring a boat to the line. After *Sceptre*'s inauspicious birth in the waveless test tank, things really started to go downhill. Her managers decided none of her deck crew should be over 30 — which eliminated anyone with 12-meter experience to start with. Her final crew wasn't selected until June 23, giving them precious little time for training, let alone tuning the boat. According to an article by Maitland Edey in Life magazine, her management needed some basic training of their own:

"When the navigator asked for a Fathometer, they gaped at him. This is an instrument for measuring the depth of water.... The value of such an instrument in fog is obvious. But no Fathometer was provided for *Sceptre* until she arrived in the U.S. and it was seen that the other 12s were so equipped. A couple of the experts even insisted that *Sceptre* would not need a compass in closed-course racing. 'You can stay with the other boat,' they told the navigator.

" 'You're assuming we'll always be behind?' he asked. A compass was provided."

They trained against *Evaine,* a pre-war 12-meter that had been badly beaten in the past by *Vim.* They fell into the same error that many more sophisticated campaigns would commit in later years: They spent all their energy on the new boat and neglected her trial horse, with the result that the new one looked better than she was. She proved only marginally faster than *Evaine* at that. When the implications of that awful truth hit home, there was talk of abandoning the challenge even before crossing the ocean. But stiff upper lips prevailed and over she went. That probably was a mistake.

In Newport the British had the use of another pre-war 12, *Gleam*, but whether that helped or hurt is an open question. *Gleam*, which had been converted for cruising, was so far off the pace that *Sceptre*'s crew had to drag warps, fenders and buckets behind her to keep from running away, and that threw off her maneuverability. One of *Gleam*'s problems was that she had an engine; dragging the prop through the water slowed her down. Finally they hit on the obvious solution: They turned the engine on. From then on *Gleam* was able to keep pace with *Sceptre*, but as far as tuning up went the British might have done almost as well against a cabin cruiser.

The first race was September 20. Fifteen minutes after it began the end was obvious to all: *Sceptre* just didn't have it. *Columbia* won four straight by margins of seven to almost 12 minutes, and a great many members of the NYYC were kicking themselves for having gone to all that trouble and expense when *Vim* could have held the Cup just as easily.

The New York Herald Tribune commented on the last race: "It is a spectacle calculated to make the tea break at a cricket test seem wildly exciting." The first three hadn't been any better. President Eisenhower watched the first from a destroyer, but left before it ended to play golf.

At the final press conference, both crews noted the series had been free of controversy, at least. "It was a lot of fun, not as grim as I thought it would be," said Briggs Cunningham, *Columbia*'s helmsman. British syndicate chairman Hugh Goodson, his upper lip stiffer than ever, said, "We are very glad the America's Cup has ended on a happy note for everyone but us."

Then both crews went off to have dinner together and toast each other's health.

1964: TRADITIONS OF EMPIRE

The British planned another challenge for 1962, but they were beaten to it by the Australians (see next chapter). When they did come back in 1964, the results were even worse — so dismal, in fact, they didn't try again for 16 years.

The 1964 challenge was organized, if that's the word, by Anthony Boyden, a 35-year-old business tycoon who had been involved with 12-meters for years. In fairness, it should be noted that his timing was thrown off, first by the Aussies, whose challenge caught everyone by surprise, and then the NYYC. The New Yorkers had strongly implied, though not promised, that they would accept a British challenge for 1963. That was good enough for Boyden, whose preparations were well advanced when his club, the Royal Thames, cabled its formal challenge after the 1962 match. New York decided it needed a rest. It said no.

For a time this promised to develop into one of those classic America's Cup bruhahas. Boyden hinted he might launch a legal challenge, on the dubious grounds that the club had no power under the deed of gift to turn down a challenge. The New Yorkers protested they weren't turning anyone down, they just wanted a postponement until 1964. Eventually the windy arguments moderated to the "We said...you said" level, and a 1964 challenge was issued and accepted. But the delays had thrown off some of Boyden's planning.

None of this explains why he went back to David Boyd, designer of the miserable *Sceptre*. The theory apparently was that Boyd would have learned a lot from his previous mistakes. From that somewhat restricted point of view, *Sceptre* had been a magnificent learning experience.

One lesson he learned was to do his tank-testing in America, at the Stevens Institute where Olin Stephens tested *Columbia*. He got there just in time, before a December, 1962, resolution by the NYYC that banned challengers from using American equipment or facilities. But once again either the tank lied to him, or he asked the wrong questions. His 1964 design, *Sovereign,* proved to be little better than *Sceptre.*

Boyden had expected to have at least one other new 12-meter to tune up against, but the syndicate that was to build it folded before it began work. Although the British had more time than they expected, there was no rush to form another. The London Times, as it had in 1851, chided British yachtsmen, saying it would be little short of a national disgrace if no one else came forward. Eventually two tossed their watchcaps into the ring. They were the brothers Frank and John Livingstone, millionaire Australian sheep farmers, who had been planning a challenge and already had a design in the works.

But they had waited too long. By the time they decided to go ahead, they couldn't find a builder who would promise delivery. All they could do was finance the construction of a duplicate of *Sovereign* from the same yard, Alexander Robertson's, which would take less time. They named her *Kurrewa V* and found Owen Aisher, who was willing to form a separate organization to manage her. Aisher, who had been active in Britain's post-war pursuit of the Cup, announced the boats would compete against each other, and the best would challenge for the Cup. Whether that's what Boyden had in mind when he went looking for a trial horse is a moot point. In trial races off Newport, *Sovereign* came out on top, though not by much. As far as advancing British yacht design went, the competition was a little like kissing your sister.

Meanwhile, Boyden named Peter Scott as helmsman. Scott, as British yachting historian Ian Dear wrote in "The America's Cup, an Illustrated History," was "the kind of brilliant amateur all-rounder which Britain excels at producing. Not only an Olympic helmsman, he was a noted explorer, champion glider pilot, painter, author, naturalist — and a naval hero who won the DSC, while commanding a patrol boat during the Second World War.... But unfortunately, racing in the America's Cup is not for the all-round genius but for the man who can do one thing and one thing only: maximize his boat's speed through the water — and this Scott did not appear to do."

Scott was a top dinghy helmsman, but he had had little or no match-racing experience. Dr. Robin Wallace, a Newport, Rhode Island pediatrician and yachtsman who came to this country with his father in 1964 when the latter was physician for the *Sovereign* crew and has been heavily involved with the America's Cup ever since, had a first-hand view of the results:

"I remember Peter Scott was absolutely baffled," Wallace said. "I remember him saying, 'Why do the boats keep going around in circles? What are they doing? Why don't they try to go to the line?' That was in the early days of pre-race maneuvering."

Scott's father was the Antarctic explorer Robert Falcon Scott, the quintessentially British heroic figure who overcame great obstacles and hardships (many created by his own stubborness) in his failed attempt to beat Amundsen to the South Pole, then perished on the return trip. Robert Scott, against advice, tried to use tractors and ponies, which were no match for Amundsen's dog teams and skis. His son, valuing muscles over skill, recruited rugby players to help him win the America's Cup, with more or less the same results. It will not diminish the father's genuine heroism to note that both were magnificent failures in the finest British tradition.

Two new boats were built for the defense, *American Eagle*, designed by A.E. Luders Jr., who had improved *Weatherly* in 1962, and *Constellation*, by Olin Stephens. Pierre S. Du Pont III, of the chemical fortune, was chief backer of *American Eagle*. The Constellation syndicate was headed by Eric Ridder, a successful publisher, and Walter Gubelmann, heir to a fortune from office machines.

Nefertiti, built for the 1962 campaign, was back with Ted Hood at the helm; *Easterner* and her covey of Hoveys returned for a third go, and *Columbia*, the 1958 defender, arrived from the West Coast. (She had been bought by Pat Dougan and sailed by Briggs Cunningham and Lowell North, among others — Californians all. This was the first time, but hardly the last, that West Coast sailors would have a role to play in the event.) But from the start the contest was between the new boats, *Eagle* and *Constellation*.

The psychological warfare was just a little more advanced this year, if that's the word: "Beat the Bird" bumper stickers began to appear in Newport, answered by rolls of toilet paper printed with: "Prevent Constipation."

Ridder started steering *Constellation* himself. She did badly. In one race, which he barely won against the hopelessly outclassed *Nefertiti*, Ridder actually made contact with the committee boat. On the tow in, the afterguard held the usual post-mortem. Ridder ended it by saying, "By the way, Bob (Bavier) will start against *Eagle* tomorrow." The crew was mainly silent but someone, Bavier doesn't recall who, murmured, "Good man, Eric."

She did far better then, and the syndicate asked Bavier, a yachting writer and editor as well as an expert sailor, to take over permanently, with Ridder as titular skipper. After Bavier got assurances from Ridder that he would in fact be in charge, he agreed. It was the first time a syndicate had replaced a skipper because he wasn't producing. It would not be the last. But never would it be done with more grace.

Eagle's skipper, Bill Cox, was a superb manager who excelled at preparing the boat, but Bavier was considered the better tactician. After a grueling set of trial races, *Constellation* won the dubious honor of being selected to demolish the unfortunate *Sovereign*.

For the first time, the match was held on the Olympic course. The old courses alternated between straight windward-leeward courses one day, a triangle the next. The Olympic course, in effect, combined the two, with an extra windward leg thrown in. It was the same length overall, 24 miles, but its six legs put more of a premium on tactics and skill and made for more exciting races. There was also a suspicion that the NYYC chose it because it involved more windward work. The Australians had proved too fast downwind for comfort two years earlier. Besides, the crucial last leg would now be into the wind, where the leading boat has the tactical advantage. In the past, that almost always was an American boat.

The series was a walk-over, to no one's great surprise. But the winning times were stunning, even to the Americans: 5:34, 20:24, 6:33 and 15:40. Bavier's margin in the second race was the largest since *Mayflower* beat *Galatea* in 1886. *Sovereign*'s overall performance was twice as bad as that of the hapless *Sceptre* in 1958. In the final race, with *Constellation* way ahead and approaching the line, Bavier asked Eric Ridder to take the helm. He refused. Bavier insisted, but he still declined, leaving the honor to Bavier alone.

Once again, the New Yorkers were quietly fuming over the waste of time and money. Olin Stephens summed up the general reaction as follows: "It's too bad for all of us who have put so much into it — we've put in so much that there isn't a contest left."

As for the losers, Ian Dear had this comment: "Britain ... is a sporting nation *nonpareille*, but, unfortunately for her, sportsmanship really has nothing to do with the America's Cup...." That missed the mark in 1964, though it would have hit the bull's eye in almost any of the later matches: The Americans were every bit as sportsmanlike in 1958 and 1964 as the British. Yachting commentator Norris Hoyt came closer in his book, "Twelve-Meter Challenges for the America's Cup:"

"The challenge was in the best tradition of empire, and it lost against modern management."

The sun was setting on the British America's Cup efforts, at least for the foreseeable future. And that was a pity, because had they learned organization from the Americans, and had the Americans absorbed some of their nobler "traditions of empire," we might have seen some glorious matches. Meanwhile, the Australians had come to town with some traditions uniquely their own. One of them was to keep coming back until they won the bloody Cup.

7

THE AUSSIE ASSAULT: 'ALCOHOL AND DELUSIONS OF GRANDEUR'

When the Australians came to Newport in 1962, the effect was galvanizing. It was as if a bunch of boisterous fraternity brothers, from a school no one had ever heard of, had crashed a very exclusive, very traditional and rather dull tea party. The perennial guest of honor was miffed, the host was apprehensive, but everyone else was grateful for the diversion.

Within hours, so it seemed, these brash newcomers had completely captivated the town, from the society matrons on Bellevue Avenue to the pub-keepers on Lower Thames Street. They were so very down-to-earth, so charmingly oblivious to the stuffy nonsense that surrounded the Cup, so — American. All they wanted to do was make friends, lift a few beers, get on with the regatta, win the thing, and take it home.

The British, however, were not amused. The Royal Sydney Yacht Squadron had announced as early as October, 1959, that it was planning a challenge for 1962, to be headed by publishing mogul Frank Packer. But the Londoners either weren't listening or didn't take Packer seriously. A member of the Royal Thames Yacht Club was actually on his way to New York to deliver *its* 1962 challenge when Packer, getting wind of it, cabled a formal challenge ahead of him. The New Yorkers promptly accepted it. The British, who had come to think of challenges as their exclusive prerogative, sent up a howl.

There was quite a triangular trade in cablegrams for the next few months, London to New York to Sydney. The British first tried to get the Aussies to back down, then agree to a Commonwealth challenge in which both countries would vie for the right to challenge. Packer was firm. "Maybe we won't do any better," he told the Brits, "but every now and again you have to give the young fellow in the family his head."

The Duke of Edinburgh got involved at one point, pushing the idea of a coordinated challenge. In May, 1960, a member of the Sydney syndicate, Bill Northam, was in London when he got an invitation from the Royal Thames to attend a meeting. His letter to Packer describing that session has become a classic in Australian yachting circles:

"I walked into the room and there were twenty blokes, mostly Lords and Earls, and at the head of the table the old cobber the Duke. I don't mind telling you I started to feel nervous, as nobody told me he was to be present. However, he left his chair despite the stony stares at me and walked over and shook me by hand and said he was glad I could attend and I sat down at the opposite end of the large table like a shag on a rock, facing HRH at the other end.

"The meeting opened as per the agenda enclosed and for a long time I looked at a lot of necks, nobody even troubling to look my way, and I chipped in when HRH asked me whether we had changed our minds with regard to elimination tests and I swear you could have heard a pin drop when I took it upon myself to say NO and believe me he really grinned and asked why not. I explained that it was in my opinion too late to alter. Owen Aisher (a big shot) and Lord Craigmyle surprised me by saying 'hear, hear'. Then we got cracking.

"He directed more questions at me than anyone in the room and I swear that at the finish I had 95 per cent on our side and it was unanimous that Australia was the logical challenger and we had all their good wishes and definite offers to help.... Apparently I saved a sticky meeting and we all had lunch and a few snorts and everyone was happy and I finished up in a corner with HRH and we had a long friendly yarn."

Clearly, the America's Cup would never be quite the same again. Part of the difference was Frank Packer. Like Rupert Murdoch a generation later, he was a brash, domineering owner of an Australian publishing empire, the Australian Consolidated Press, and a man who liked to keep things stirred up. He was known for firing his editors almost at whim; those who survived referred to his domain as "Packerstan," but always behind his back. Packer himself was inclined to be more forthright. When Queen Elizabeth visited Australia in 1954, Packer was sitting beside her on a reviewing stand. He leaned over and said, "You are costing us a lot of money, but we are very glad to see you here."

When an American reporter asked him what had inspired his Cup challenge, Sir Frank (the Queen had forgiven him by then) replied with unprecedented candor: "Alcohol and delusions of grandeur."

He made several shrewd moves, the shrewdest of which was hiring Alan Payne, 38, the country's only fulltime naval architect, to design his challenger. Another was chartering *Vim* for four years, to use for crew training and as an example for Payne, there being a distinct shortage of 12-meters in Australia. (Some said John Matthews, *Vim*'s owner, allowed her to go to the enemy because of his pique over being passed over in 1958. He turned over his $42,000 fee to a Catholic parish in Rhode Island for its parochial school building fund.)

Payne made a few shrewd moves of his own. First he talked the NYYC into giving him permission to use the testing tank at the Stevens Institute in Hoboken. Then he got permission to use American Dacron for his sails. Both the tank and the sailcloth were better than anything in Australia, or anywhere outside of America. Later, after trying a variety of winches, he used American-made Barients. Also, the extrusions from which the challenger's masts were made were fashioned in the United States, as was one of her booms.

After being built in complete secrecy, Payne's creation was unveiled February 28. She was named *Gretel*, after the late Lady Packer. No one knew it at the time, but she would prove to be faster than the defender, both in the tank and on the water.

The Americans were taking the challenge seriously right from the start, however. Paul V. Shields, senior partner in a Wall Street brokerage, had bought *Columbia* in 1960 for about $150,000. When the Aussies challenged, he turned her over to Cornelius Shields, his brother. Corny's son, Cornelius ("Glit") Shields Jr., 28, was named skipper. Meanwhile, Henry Mercer did some drastic surgery on *Weatherly* (two feet were sliced from her stern, a new keel and 1,000 pounds ballast were added) and asked Bus Mosbacher to steer her. Mosbacher, a meticulous man, made further changes to get rid of excess weight and move the remainder as low as possible: One pound aloft was worth 10 below to the boat's stability. He tossed out every unneeded fitting from the cockpit and cabin — even a pipe rack left by his predecessor, Arthur Knapp.

Easterner was still a hopeful, but still a family affair, despite earnest entreaties from young go-getters who yearned to get behind her wheel.

Late in the game, when no one undertook to build a new boat, Boston management consultant E. Ross Anderson commissioned one from Ted Hood, a Marblehead sailmaker and designer of cruising boats. Hood and Britton Chance Jr., a young man in his employ, designed *Nefertiti* in two months. She was a radical design, beamier and with a larger foretriangle than the 1958 crop. She proved to be okay in heavy weather but definitely slower than the others in light going.

Easterner and *Columbia* just didn't have it and were eliminated after six races. Then *Nefertiti*, with Hood steering, was beaten by *Weatherly* 4-1 in the finals and *Weatherly* got the nod. Ironically, both *Weatherly* and the challenger, *Gretel*, were using sails or sail cloth supplied by Hood.

While the defenders were sorting things out, Sir Frank, true to his nature, was keeping them stirred up in the Australian camp. Instead of racing, he put his people through exhausting drills. At one point, the crew was testing a bewildering inventory of 85 sails. And he didn't name his final skipper or crew until the last minute, leaving them no time to train together as a unit. Jock Sturrock won the skipper's role, but he knew he would have little authority off the boat. Then, on the very morning of the first race, Packer replaced his navigator with someone who had no knowledge of Newport waters.

That race, on a Saturday, was delayed by the crowding of an estimated 2500 spectator boats (including a destroyer carrying President John F. Kennedy) — more than twice as many as witnessed the first 12-meter race in 1958. When it was over, Mosbacher crossed the line 3:43 in front, thanks in part to an error by *Gretel 's* navigator-for-a-day. (Packer replaced him with someone else for the next race, an assistant helmsman.)

In the second race, *Gretel* started from behind but began a tacking duel and gained, until *Weatherly* broke it off and maintained only a loose cover. (Mosbacher knew better than to mix it up with the Aussies if he could avoid it. *Gretel* had a huskier crew, and a Payne-designed device to link two "coffee grinder" winches together, so four men could haul in a sheet rather than two.) Then, on a downwind leg sailed under spinnakers in a 25-knot wind with *Weatherly* only slightly ahead, Mosbacher's crew was startled to hear a banshee-like scream from the other boat. Next it was rushing past them as if they were dead in the water! *Gretel* had caught a series of huge rollers just right and surfed into the lead. *Weatherly*'s afterguy parted at almost the same moment, and that was the race: *Gretel* by 47 seconds.

It was the first win by a challenger since 1934. Australians and their partisans, who included many Americans, celebrated until dawn at a waterfront bar. It was one of the biggest and certainly most raucus celebrations Newporters had ever seen.

It was all downhill for them from then on, however. Mosbacher won the third, in light air, as well as the fourth and fifth, by superior tactics or better luck, although he won the fourth by only 26 seconds - - the closest time yet in a Cup race. Like Sopwith in 1934, Sturrock probably lost that one because he got sucked into covering Mosbacher when ahead, and lost his advantage.

It had been a close match, especially for a first-time challenger — probably a lot closer than Mosbacher had expected. Some of his crew had reason to expect even worse, however. Models of both *Gretel* and *Weatherly* had been tested at the Stevens Institute, which gave the people there a chance for direct comparison. Their verdict: *Gretel* had the faster hull. Some of *Weatherly's* crew got the discouraging word early but decided not to tell their skipper until after the series.

Sir Frank said he felt the races had been well run and eminently fair. "We weren't beaten by the conditions," he said, "the Americans were just too good for us." After the last one, both crews ended up at the Cameo Bar on Pelham Street, which the Aussies had made their unofficial home away from home. Probably for the first time in that predominantly Irish Catholic neighborhood, choruses of "Waltzing Matilda" were heard long into the night. It wouldn't be the last.

The following day, a *Gretel* crewman was married to a girl from back home in St. Spyridon's Greek Orthodox Church on Thames Street. The Mosbachers gave the reception.

Many years later, Mosbacher was asked whether the arrival of the Australians had an immediate impact on the defenders, as it clearly had on the spectators. He started by using almost the identical words one hears Australians use in speaking of members of the NYYC: So many of them are "great guys and fun to be with." And yet....

"It was different, probably more competitive in some ways. A friend of mine who had known Packer for many years warned me that he would be a strong, try-anything kind of guy; if you slapped his wrist, he would say, 'Jolly good try, what?' and go on to the next thing. And they did try things.... In the very first race they did something that was clearly against the rules. But rather than protest — we'd won the race anyway — I came in and I spoke to Alan Payne about it, and they stopped doing it. They put their afterguy over the side and then had all their crew stand on it. That's an outrigger, and that's clearly against the rules, then and now. They're always trying...."

1967: 'ONLY A GAME?'

They tried again in 1967. The New Yorkers were pleased to receive another Australian challenge, especially after the British fiasco of 1964 (see previous chapter). But they knew by then the Australians would take advantage of any soft spots in the rules or conditions of the race. In retrospect, they had been overly generous with the persuasive Alan Payne and the wily Sir Frank in 1962. They almost had been beaten by a hull designed in an American tank, with American sails and American extrusions. So they tightened up their interpretation of the deed shortly after the 1962 races: Henceforth, defenders and challengers alike would have to confine themselves to equipment, sails and design research available in their own countries.

That caused some grumbling, both at home and abroad. On the surface, the new resolution looked even-handed enough, but the catch was that American technology was way ahead of anyone else's. The provision practically guaranteed the defenders faster boats. But what could you expect, the critics said, from a club that for more than a century had simply changed the rules whenever it came close to losing?

The New Yorkers didn't deny they had a technological edge. In fact, the defenders had been one step ahead ever since 1851, when *America* won the Cup with a new hull design and superior sail cloth. But, they argued, we didn't get that advantage by changing the rules, we earned it by a lot of hard work. The America's Cup was always intended to be emblematic of national superiority in design and construction as well as sailing skill. We aren't changing any rules. We're simply saying we were too accommodating last time, the other fellow took advantage, and we aren't going to let it happen again. If you want the Cup, you can have it by beating us at our own game — but not with our own equipment, for heaven's sake!

But the 1962 resolution contained a "grandfather clause": It applied only to new boats. When Sir Frank ran that through his resourceful mind, it came out "loophole." He handed in a challenge immediately after the 1964 races, then announced he planned to "repair" *Gretel*'s hull. By that he meant Alan Payne would completely redesign the boat below the waterline, while he kept everything above the deck intact — including those lovely Dacron sails from his American "grandfather." The "repairs" were so extensive, the shipwrights who did the work declared it would have been easier to start from scratch.

Meanwhile, another Australian syndicate came forward with a challenge of its own. It was headed by Emil Christensen, a retired ice cream tycoon who had scooped up a couple of Packerstan refugees: Warwick Hood, Alan Payne's former assistant, and Jock Sturrock, skipper. They named their boat *Dame Pattie* after the wife of the Australian prime minister, Dame Pattie Menzies. Christensen also had help from sailmaker Jan Pearce, Ted Hood's representative in Australia, who had learned his trade cutting defenders' sails at the Hood loft in Marblehead, Massachusetts. Nothing in the rules could prevent that sort of cross-fertilization, which would become more troublesome to the defenders as time went on.

But not this year. This was the year of *Intrepid*, the first breakthrough design since the 12-meter era began and the benchmark for every successful 12-meter to follow until 1983. Olin Stephens, who was beginning to rival the legendary Nat Herreshoff as the premier designer of Cup defenders, had been given enough time, money and encouragement to experiment, and he did just that. After running tank tests on an unprecedented 35 variations, he drew a boat that the yachting purists declared ugly — a sure tipoff that he had either a real dog or the next champion in its class.

He reduced the size of the keel to lessen wetted surface, and put the rudder far aft of the keel. To reduce the resulting tendency to sideslip, he attached a flap (later called a "trim tab") to the keel's trailing edge. By turning it to leeward, he could get added lift and better stability. For the first time, all the winches were placed below deck level, to give the helmsman better visibility, bring the weight lower, and make room for one more change — lowering the boom almost to deck level.

Stephens and his brother Rod, who designed the sails and rigging, did that on the advice of aerodynamics experts and Halsey Herreshoff (Nat's grandson, who was on his way to a measure of Cup fame himself). Herreshoff had made a study of the aerodynamics involved while teaching at MIT. The research suggested that a lowered boom would create an "end plate effect" that would improve upwind power. It did. (If Herreshoff or someone else had turned that knowledge upside down and pondered the effect of an end plate in the water, on the bottom of a keel, the Cup might still be in New York!)

The Intrepid syndicate was put together by William Strawbridge, a wealthy yachtsman who got involved in the *American Eagle* campaign in 1964 and then, like so many, couldn't kick the habit. Neither could Bus Mosbacher. He resisted for weeks — his father was ill and he had business commitments — before finally consenting to take the helm again. Strawbridge put together a small but well-heeled syndicate (Mike Vanderbilt, 83, was a member) which eventually spent around a million dollars on the campaign. *Intrepid* may not have looked like a million dollars, but she sure sailed like it. Mosbacher easily outclassed all the old boats competing for defense honors, *Constellation, American Eagle* and *Columbia*. Nineteen trial races were completed and *Intrepid* won 18 of them. Her one loss was due to a navigation error.

Mosbacher, who was known to lose as much as seven pounds during a race from sheer nervous tension, should have been more relaxed that summer than he was in 1962. If anything, he was more uptight. "Sometimes at night I walked up and down in my bedroom saying, 'It's only a game; it's only a sport. It's only a game.' " he recalled. A large part of the reason was the fact that, while the competition on the water may not have been as intense, it was getting tougher on shore:

"One of the first really strong protests or problems I had with the Australians was in '67, when we measured the boats," Mosbacher said. "Everything was fine, and we went out sailing. When we came in that afternoon at the dock at 5 o'clock, someone brought me a copy of the newspaper and an interview with Warwick Hood (*Dame Pattie*'s designer) that accused us of cheating! Well, that was the first blast I was aware of of the kind of onslaught that went from there on, in increasing intensity, through '83. And there wasn't a word of truth in it! Not an iota. And he'd been standing right there; if he'd had any question or complaint or protest or anything, he could have said it. But that wasn't the point. The point was to get newspaper ink. And some very obliging (journalists) were happy to give it to him."

Intrepid's crew was at least partly responsible for that dust-up. They didn't want the Australians to figure out how many winches they had, or to notice *Intrepid*'s lowered boom, because they might have copied it even at that late date. So they arranged a diversionary tactic when the two sides first inspected each other's boats. They removed most of *Intrepid*'s winches (along with many of the halyards) before the measurement, replacing some of them with clamps. The Aussies complained, whereupon the Americans put them all back — including some they would later discard. It worked. Not only were the Aussies confused about the final number of winches, they had been completely distracted from the boom. It was all perfectly within the rules, but sneaky. And it prompted Hood's comment about cheating.

What infuriated Mosbacher was the fact that Hood and the Aussie skipper, Jock Sturrock, whom Mosbacher regarded as a friend, hadn't said anything at the time, but then lodged a protest and complained in the press — a tactic that would be raised to an art form in later challenges. Eventually the matter was resolved. Everyone agreed no one had cheated.

Mosbacher had other causes for concern early in the summer, including the fact that *Intrepid* lost her mast twice during the trials. That problem was traced to the spreaders and repaired. Then there was the news from Australia: Sturrock, who ran a far tighter ship than Packer, had steered *Dame Pattie* to 11 victories in 13 races with the redesigned *Gretel*. In the end, *Dame Pattie* was shipped to Newport, *Gretel* stayed home. Once there, however, her campaign suffered from a shortage of money and the absence of a trial horse. It sagged visibly even before the match.

The races were enlivened (they needed it) by the threat of a hurricane (it didn't materialize) and what could have been the first-ever collision between a Cup defender and a helicopter.

That was during the third race. A small catboat had somehow wandered onto the course, despite the usually highly efficient efforts of the U.S. Coast Guard boats assigned to keep it clear. A Coast Guard helicopter was sent to chase it away, but the downdraft from the chopper capsized the boat instead. So the copter crew lowered a line to fish the boat's occupants out of the water. All this took place directly in the path *Intrepid* was sailing, which she was reluctant to leave because she was on the layline for the windward mark.

Mosbacher recalled the incident in one of several interviews with the *Intrepid* team published in "Defending the America's Cup," by Robert W. Carrick and Stanley Rosenfeld:

"We got closer and closer and could see there was a boat. I kept hoping that the progress of the rescue was such that the chopper would be up and out of the way before we got there, but as we came closer, it was obvious that either she wasn't going to move out of the way or wasn't able to, so at the last minute I swung to leeward of the helicopter.

"I'd never been in a helicopter, but I assumed that it took off into the wind like an airplane. I thought that if I swung around under her stern I would be in pretty good shape. As we got there and eased off, we forgot to let go our backstay. The mainsail could have been badly ripped or even broken the boom.

"We swung to go under her stern and she did start to take off, but she started going backwards. This brought her much closer than I had any idea she would come and as she backed down on us we were all scared to death."

Mosbacher's crew won that race as they had the first two, going away. By then even Australia's partisans in Newport, of whom there were many, were calling their boat by a new name: "Damn Pity." When it was all over, *Intrepid* had beaten the *Dame* by margins ranging from 3:36 to nearly 6 minutes. *Dame Pattie* wasn't the dog she was said to be. *Intrepid* and Mosbacher were simply the best boat-and-skipper combination ever to that point, and maybe since.

1970: ENTER MULTIPLE CHALLENGES

Packer and his roistering crew had lost again. But for Packer and others, it was becoming obvious the Cup itself was not the only prize to be gained from participating in the event. Despite the lopsided results in '64 and '67, the America's Cup was front-page news again for the first time in 40 years, and not just in Sir Frank's newspapers. For the kind of men who had always challenged — restless, self-made men whose egos and bank accounts demanded new worlds to conquer —the switch to 12-meter yachts had made the prospect more affordable. The publicity made it irresistible.

It was a symbiotic relationship. The press, as always, hungered for eccentric characters, controversy, and if all else failed, some exciting races. In 1970, it got all three.

The NYYC, feeling the financial and emotional strain of defending the longest winning streak in sports against what seemed an almost continual assault, had announced it would not defend more than once every three years. When it accepted challenges for 1970 immediately after the '67 race, four countries were standing in line — Britain, Greece, France and Australia. Greece and Britain pulled out, however, leaving two strong-willed men to face each other in the first formal challenge trials off Newport.

Sir Frank was back with a new boat, *Gretel II*, but when the season opened, all eyes were on the newcomer: Baron Marcel Bich, onetime door-to-door housewares salesman who made a fortune with his 19-cent Bic ballpoint pen. Then he followed a well-worn path in the Cup's history: Having gained fame and fortune, he yearned for class. So he bought his title and took up yachting.

Not one to do anything by halves — he was always spending more money than he made, he confessed — Bich watched the 1967 Cup races, then bought his first 12-meter, *Kurrewa V*, as a present for his children. (He had nine of them, almost a full crew.) That led to an attack of Cup fever. In rapid succession, he bought *Sovereign*, then *Constellation*, the 1964 winner. He tried to buy *Intrepid*, but her owners wisely refused.

He still needed a new boat. Americans built the best 12-meters in the world, he knew, but that would be against the rules. No problem. He commissioned Britton Chance Jr., who had worked on Ted Hood's *Nefertiti*, to draw him a fast Twelve. It was named *Chancegger* after its designer and Swiss builder, Herman Egger. When Bich took delivery, he turned it over to his own designer, Frenchman Andre Mauric, for inspiration and profound study.

Mauric studied well. When Bich's 1970 challenger, *France*, emerged from his drawing board, it incorporated all the latest elements of American design. He couldn't use American sailcloth or titanium for the mast, however. That was partly responsible for her undoing. Bich handled the rest.

Baron Bich's arrival in Newport was more like an invasion. He brought most of his armada, along with a number of support boats, some 60 sailors, two chefs and a great deal of the best French wine.

He spent an awful lot of money, an estimated $4 million, much of it wasted according to more experienced hands. He ran his campaign with an engaging but fatal blend of baronial autocracy and Gallic unpredictability. No one in Newport could overrule him. No one seemed disposed even to contradict him as his crew rosters changed more rapidly than French governments before De Gaulle. He tried out two helmsmen during the trials, then took over the wheel himself in the fourth (and final) race.

That race has become something of a Newport classic. Dressed in formal white yachting attire, complete with white gloves, the Baron steered into a thickening fog. When he emerged 42 minutes after the Aussies crossed the finish line, it was at the end of a tow, heading back to port. He insisted he had NOT gotten lost; it was just that with the fog and crowding spectator boats, the conditions were little short of impossible. When he reached the dock, he was damp and hopping mad because the race committee hadn't cancelled the race. (It probably should have.) On the walk back, he punched a French TV cameraman. He was even madder later, when the papers said he had gotten lost, and that he had "abandoned" the race — a word which, translated into French, has unsportsmanlike connotations. He said he had been "dishonored" by the challengers' race committee and vowed he would never set foot or sail in Newport again. But he did, in 1974, '77 and '80. He lost again each time, extravagantly.

The Australian challenger was a new design commissioned by Sir Frank from Alan Payne. Reports from Australia were that she had done poorly in tune-up races against the original *Gretel*. That might have been a smokescreen sent up by the sly Sir Frank to conceal the fact that he had produced one of the fastest 12-meters yet. Her performance was hard to judge, though. She beat *France* easily in the trials, but Payne kept making major changes in her right up to the start of the Cup match itself.

Packer seemed to have learned a few things. This time, he announced his skipper before they left home: James Hardy, a winemaker aptly nicknamed "Gentleman Jim." He also did away with the monotonous drills for the crew. Instead, he raced *Gretel II* against *American Eagle*, which he had chartered from Ted Turner, the Atlanta television station owner from whom much more would be heard later on. Turner had tried to enter *Eagle* in the defender trials but was told he was too late.

For the defense, Olin Stephens built a new boat, *Valiant*, larger and heavier than her predecessors and with all but one winch below decks. She was commissioned by Robert McCullough, NYYC vice commodore, and was considered the heir apparent to the defender's throne that year, before being knocked off by a pretender. The other new boat, *Heritage*, like Alexander Cuthbert's Canadian challenger *Atalanta* 90 years earlier, was a one-man project. She was owned, designed, built, rigged and sailed by Charley Morgan, a sailmaker and boatbuilder from St. Petersburg, Florida. And she proved to be almost as quixotic an entry as *Atalanta* had been.

The old boats were *Intrepid* and *Weatherly*, the 1962 defender, whose ostensible purpose in 1970 was to provide a four-boat defenders' series so two match races could be held every day. When she actually held her own against the other three in the early going, people started worrying about the strength of the whole field.

But the boat to beat turned out to be *Intrepid*, the 1967 defender, which had been so radically altered by Brit Chance as to be virtually a new Twelve. She was almost two feet longer and heavier than her 1967 form. Opinion was, and remains, divided as to whether Chance's modifications made her slower, faster or left her speed unchanged.

Syndicate manager Bill Strawbridge brought back many of her original backers for a second go. Bus Mosbacher was tending to his duties as President Nixon's chief of protocol that year, so Strawbridge turned to William Ficker of California, nicknamed "Mr. Clean," the completely bald *Columbia* helmsman during the 1967 trials and former Star World champion.

After *Heritage* and *Weatherly* were eliminated, *Intrepid* beat out *Valiant* (6-1) to become the only boat since *Columbia* (1901) to defend twice. *Valiant* proved to be Olin Stephens' only failure.

AN INTERNATIONAL INCIDENT

The controversies of 1970 began with a toilet and ended with a disputed foul that caused the biggest row since Dunraven. Before it died down, Packer threatened to take his complaint to the New York Supreme Court. There was talk of breaking off diplomatic relations between Australia and the U.S., even withdrawing the Aussie troops from Vietnam.

The toilet protest was over the fact that the door had been removed from *Intrepid*'s head — one of several weight-saving moves by the Americans. Packer regarded that as a violation of the spirit and letter of the International Rule, which still required at least minimal cruising accommodations even though no one in his right mind would cruise in one of those stripped-down racing machines. After some discussion, the door was replaced.

Chances are Packer never would have protested such a small point if he hadn't gotten his back up over what the Australians saw as a far more serious violation. *Intrepid* had been fitted with plastic fairing sheets on either side of her rudder, in effect extending her hull a foot or more beyond the rudder post. The Americans argued that the waterline measurement should be taken from the rudder post forward, ignoring the fairing sheets. The Australians argued they should be included. If they were, *Intrepid* would exceed the 12-meter measurement rule and the sheets would have to be removed before she could race.

Clearly the fairing sheets were a "rule-cheating" device, a means of extending the water flow and thereby making *Intrepid* a faster boat. But did they extend the hull?

In those days, there was only one official measurer — a NYYC man. He decided the fairing sheets were not an integral part of the hull and could be left where they were. The Australians were livid. They wrote a letter of complaint to the NYYC's America's Cup Committee. Committee members came to the dock, took a look, called for a slight modification, and left the fairing sheets intact.

According to yachting writer Jeff Spranger, who was then covering the races for the Newport Daily News, it was that incident that provoked Packer's famous remark: "An Australian skipper complaining to the New York Yacht Club committee is like a man complaining to his mother-in-law about his wife."

Spranger says this dispute didn't get the publicity it deserved, partly because it was a rather technical question and partly because neither the Americans nor Australians were willing to talk about it. He said it deserved far more attention because it was that incident, rather than the more celebrated protest a few days later, that ignited the Australians' deep resentment toward the NYYC — a resentment they harbored through successive campaigns under different leadership, right through the summer of '83.

From the Australians' point of view, in fact, their tainted victory in 1983 was only poetic justice: The Americans had done the same things in 1970. They had built a secret underwater device of questionable legality that increased their boat speed, they kept it under wraps until it was too late for the Aussies to copy it, and they successfully rebuffed all attempts to challenge it. And the Americans had a clearly unfair advantage the Aussies didn't have 13 years later: All disputes were settled by members of the NYYC itself!

Spranger says the Australians' outrage prompted the first of two incidents on the race course. During the maneuvering before the start of the first race, the Aussies "went hunting" for the American boat, deliberately steering a collision course in hope of prompting a foul. Ficker twice altered course; each time Hardy altered his accordingly. Finally, as collision seemed imminent, it was Hardy who tacked away.

Both boats ran up protest flags. Then *Gretel II* had a disastrous race; her crew managed to get a wrap in their spinnaker, then lost a man overboard. She lost by almost six minutes.

She fared no better in the protest room. The NYYC race committee ruled there had been no rules infringement and disallowed both protests. The committee also said it was bending over backwards to be fair — by which it apparently meant, to avoid ruling against the Australians. The Aussies were indignant nonetheless. "We left the protest meeting like little boys who have just been lectured by their schoolmaster," Hardy remarked. They suggested they should have maintained course, forced a collision, and won the protest. (In fact, they almost certainly would have lost: A boat on starboard tack cannot, under the rules, continually alter course to force a boat on port tack to give way.)

It had been 36 years between protests, the last one having been in 1934 when Sopwith protested Vanderbilt for failure to respond to a luff. The next protest came five days later, at the start of the next race. And it was a momentous one.

Both boats were heading toward the committee boat end of the starting line on starboard tack. Ficker tried to squeeze between *Gretel II* (steered at the start by Martin Visser) and the committee boat. Visser headed up, as he thought he had the right to do, to close the gap. Just after the starting gun *Gretel*'s bow struck *Intrepid*'s port side with enough force to break off a false bow onto *Intrepid*'s deck. Because all this happened right beside the committee boat, its members had a ringside seat.

Intrepid shot ahead in the light air; *Gretel* had been luffing up so long she was virtually stopped. But with Hardy steering again, *Gretel* soon gained and passed the defender on the run. Ficker was hampered because his regular tactician, Steve van Dyck, had suffered a violent reaction to a bee sting and had to be evacuated by helicopter just before the start. *Gretel* went on to win the race by 1:07.

The protest hearing the following morning was a classic confrontation, a clash of cultures as much as a judicial proceeding. On one side were the blunt, aggressive Aussies, the outsiders from Down Under who believed they were in the right and expected to be railroaded. On the other the smooth-talking, lawyerly Bill Ficker, an architect by profession, with a polished presentation including photographs, drawings, and frequent references to the rule book. Presiding was race committee chairman B. Devereux Barker III, whose unsmiling formality and unbending approach — indeed, his very name — were calculated to instill an almost atavistic mistrust in the average Aussie breast. Not to mention the fact that all the committee members belonged to the club against whose boat their protest was lodged.

Under those conditions, it was unlikely the Australians would ever forgive or forget if the decision went against them, regardless of the merits. It did, and they didn't.

The committee members doubtless would have given anything to avoid a ruling, just as they had ducked one five days earlier. But they really had no choice. A collision had occurred, in full view of the committee, and the Australians were clearly in the wrong. The Aussies claimed *Intrepid* had been guilty of barging, or reaching down on the other yacht at the start, which is illegal. However, aerial photos confirmed what the committee members had already seen for themselves: *Gretel II* had luffed up after the starting gun, trying to force *Intrepid* off her tack, and that simply isn't allowed. If she had maintained her original course, there would have been no collision and *Intrepid* would have had room enough to squeeze between her and the committee boat. The *Gretel II* protest was denied, the *Intrepid* protest upheld, leaving the score 2-0 in favor of the defender.

The Australians simply didn't know the rules. Martin Visser reportedly had to borrow a rule book from a journalist to take to the hearing. Years later, Barker, the committee chairman, recalled "how astounded we on the committee were at the Australians' very primitive knowledge of the racing rules. Here at the very highest level of international competition ... were men with a 'junior program' knowledge.... Bill Ficker tore them apart at the hearings."

But after studying the rule book the Aussies, rather than acknowledge error, carried the fight on in the press. Here was an arena Sir Frank knew well, and the NYYC seemed not to want to know at all. Many if not most of the journalists in Newport that summer, as in every recent Cup summer, had a rudimentary knowledge of the racing rules and a low threshold for complexities and ambiguities. Sir Frank knew just how to play them. Give them a lively quote, a show of indignation, and the headline is yours. "Gretel Robbed" was a typical example, in an Australian paper.

The New Yorkers, as usual, maintained a dignified silence, which others construed as guilt. All this was taking place at the height of the strong anti-war, anti-Establishment movement in the United States and elsewhere. And there were, and are, few organizations in America quite so thoroughly Establishment as the NYYC.

The general public, of course, knew nothing about the finer points of the rules and cared even less. All they knew is what they read in the papers: Those fun-loving, down-home Aussies, the underdogs, were being railroaded by a kangaroo court set up by those stuffed-shirt New York yachties. The race committee alone got more than 500 telegrams, almost all condemnatory. One letter-writer said the whole thing wouldn't have happened if the committee boat hadn't gotten in the way! Even the U.S. ambassador to Australia, who should have known better, issued a public apology for the club's actions.

Robert Bavier in his book, "America's Cup Fever," wrote that Bill Fesq, *Gretel II* navigator, privately acknowledged to him at the time that the committee had been correct, and promised to say so publicly once the series was over. But he never did.

Bavier also described a conversation aboard the America's Cup Committee boat, after another race had been sailed but before the series was over. Bavier was president of the North American Yacht Racing Union, and they — the committee members and a number of former commodores — called him over to ask his opinion in that capacity: Should they cancel the second race and order it resailed, even though they agreed with the race committee's decision? Bavier said no, that the committee had made the only possible decision under the rules, and a reversal would make a mockery of enforcement. The committee agreed.

"I mention this only to demonstrate how far the New York Yacht Club bent over backwards in the interest of being fair and impartial,"

Bavier wrote, "(and to) offset all the unwarranted vilification the club had received from a number of bleeding hearts who knew nothing about what really had happened or the pertinent rule which governed the situation."

After that second race, the rest should have been anticlimax, but it wasn't. In the third, Ficker forced *Gretel II* over the line early to gain the start, then held on for the win despite Hardy's efforts to break through. The Aussies won the fourth race, after Ficker took a chance on the winds, failed to cover, and lost the gamble. *Intrepid* got hit by a wind shift and *Gretel II* slipped over the line in front.

In the fifth race, the Aussies were out front by 10 lengths when Ficker started a tacking duel, in which he gained and finally broke through. In the final beat, *Intrepid* got a favorable wind shift and sailed home easily to hold the Cup, 4-1.

Aside from the disastrous first race, the winning times were all under two minutes. It was the closest call since 1934. If the Aussies had known the rules, and realized how fast their boat was and sailed accordingly, the score might have been reversed.

One result of the protest was the NYYC's decision that henceforward an international jury would hear protests, with no members representing either defender or challenger — a change it should have made much earlier. Most impartial yachting authorities believe the decisions rendered by the various NYYC race committees through 1970, when they doubled as protest committees, had been fair. When they erred, it had been on the side of the challenger. But that unnecessary conflict of interest, tolerated for a century by the British (who had tolerated far worse), left the club open to precisely the charges that erupted after the protest hearing.

By abolishing it, the New Yorkers went about as far as they could go toward removing even the appearance of favoritism. Only one conflict remained, the inherent one between the club's roles as impartial steward and highly partisan defender of the Cup. That one had been imposed by the deed of gift in 1857 and seemed inescapable.

For a century, since the first challenge in 1870, the NYYC had been slowly, sometimes grudgingly, ridding itself of the unfair advantages that dual position made possible. In 1970 the pendulum began to swing in the opposite direction. Beginning in 1974, it would be pushed along an accelerating arc by the most determined challenger the club had ever encountered.

8
BONDAGE

When the Royal Perth Yacht Club submitted a challenge on behalf of Alan Bond after the 1970 series, it was one of eight clubs vying for the honor, an unprecedented onslaught. Thanks in part to Bond's countrymen, Sir Frank Packer and his roistering crews, the Cup had regained its pre-war popularity, and then some. Never again would the NYYC have to worry about apathy.

As things turned out, it didn't have to worry about the consequences of this potential mob scene, either — not yet. The challenges came from five countries, Britain, Canada, Australia (two clubs), France (three clubs) and Italy. But America's Cup campaigns since the 12-meter era began had become far more sophisticated, technologically complex, time-consuming and costly. In constant dollars, the switch to 12-meters had reduced the cost of Cup racing dramatically. But those dollars were much harder to find. The days when people like Harold Vanderbilt could reach into their own pockets for a few million dollars to mount a campaign were over. And the budgets were shooting up. The average expense was roughly $3 million per syndicate — more than triple the budgets of 1964. After adding it all up, six of the eight clubs quietly withdrew, leaving only one each from France and Australia.

Meanwhile, the match was postponed from 1973 to 1974 because the NYYC decided to allow aluminum hulls and the syndicates needed more time to develop them. Despite that breathing room, the 1974 campaign was a vexing and contentious one for almost everyone. Sir Frank Packer was spared that, at least. He submitted a challenge for 1973, but withdrew it when the match was postponed. He died before it was held.

The French challenge was mounted by Baron Bich, who had gained control of his temper but little else. He angered his own countrymen by appointing Paul Elvstrom, the brilliant but erratic Danish Olympic champion, as helmsman and gave him complete charge of the campaign. Elvstrom apparently had little faith in French seamanship. Before long it looked as if the French entry would be designed by a Dane, built by a Swiss, and crewed by Norwegians, Danes and Swedes. Then Elvstrom was held responsible for the sinking of the Baron's 1970 challenger, *France*, in a North Sea gale. When reports began to circulate that he tended to suffer mental breakdowns at tense moments, it was the last straw.

Bich excused Elvstrom from further trials, then told his builder, Herman Egger, to stop work on the new boat. He sent the salvaged *France* to Newport instead with a young French helmsman, Jean-Marie Le Guillou. But the wind had left his sails. The 1974 campaign was just for practice. *France* went down for the third time, 4-0, at the hands of the Australians in the challenger trials.

If Bich seemed to attract trouble, his Australian counterpart created it. At 36, Alan Bond was the youngest challenger ever, and by far the feistiest. Like many who went before him, Bond had worked himself up the hard way. He and his parents emigrated to Australia from England when he was 13. By his own testimony, he was a precocious child, bored by school; he left at the age of 14 to become a $6-a-week sign painter and handyman. Then he bought a bit of property, sold it at a profit, then another, and pretty soon he was in the real estate business. By 1974, he headed a sprawling business conglomerate based in Perth, Western Australia, and had a personal fortune estimated at $80 million.

Unlike those others, however, he was not at all interested in using his challenge as a stepping stone into the ranks of the privileged class. He wanted to beat them, and knock the stuffing out of their shirts in the process.

"It's all very well for the 'old money' people in London and New York to look down their noses at my challenge," he said. "They're the very people who wouldn't hesitate to change the rules if they thought it might help them. The good old days when gentlemen could say, 'Jolly good show, sir, well done' are gone forever. America's Cup racing is far too competitive for that sort of sentimental nonsense today."

That kind of blunt talk wasn't likely to endear Mr. Bond to

members of the NYYC — especially because some of his barbs were
so damnably accurate. Those days WERE gone, and it was no good
blaming Alan Bond or Frank Packer or anyone else. The 'old money'
people just didn't have enough of it anymore. Blame the war or the
Depression or income taxes.

But if they had wanted to blame someone for Bond's presence in
Newport, they would have had to point the finger, curiously enough,
at one of their own most stalwart members, Victor Romagna:

FATEFUL ENCOUNTER

The story of how Bond first decided to go after the Cup is almost
too pat to be believed, but it's true. In 1970, he and his designer, Bob
Miller, were at Robert Derecktor's shipyard in New York, looking
after the preparation of Bond's 58-foot *Apollo*, which he was entering
in that year's Newport-Bermuda Race. By fate, *Valiant*, one of the
new America's Cup contenders that year, was in a nearby slip.

Bond had never seen a 12-meter before. Curious, he went over for a
closer look, peering down into her big, open cockpit. Romagna, who
was destined to be a member of the club's America's Cup Committee
the year Alan Bond won the Cup, happened to be aboard at the time.
As Miller later told Australian yachting writer Bruce Stannard in
"Ben Lexcen, the Man, the Keel, " Romagna was upset:

"He snapped Bondy's head off. He said, 'How would you like me to
come shove my face in your living-room window?' Well, that really
got Bondy mad. He said something like, 'What is that bloody thing
anyway?' I explained to him that it was a 12-meter boat, an
America's Cup boat, and he asked me, 'What's the America's Cup?' I
told him and he said, 'Right, you design me one of those 12-meters
and we'll come back here and win their bloody America's Cup.' I
didn't think he was serious, but he was. When we got back to
Australia he got his sailing master to ring me up to confirm (it)."

Bond had another motive as well. He may not have been the first to
cash in on his challenge — American sales of Lipton tea and Bic pens
were brisk, thank you — but he was certainly the first to brag about
it. "Anyone who considers that racing for the Cup isn't a business
proposition is a bloody fool. There can be no other justification for
spending six million dollars on the Australian challenge unless the return is going to involve more than just an ornate silver pitcher. Let's
see what they say about commercialism and sportsmanship after we
win."

Specifically, Bond used his first challenge to promote investment in Yanchep Sun City, his $200-million, 20,000-acre coastal development project 35 miles north of Perth. The development, dubbed "Yanchep Fly City" by those who experienced its most prevalent life form, was a barren landscape of sand and rocks that Bond was turning into a vacation resort, with a giant marina. When the time came to take publicity photos, the onetime sign painter ordered vast portions of the landscape spray-painted green, to look like grass. Then he started billing it as the site of the 1977 America's Cup match. All of his 1974 Cup challenge costs were written off as advertising expense.

Some observers describe Bond as a latter-day Sir Thomas Lipton — a comparison that probably amuses the former but certainly would have horrified the latter. Lipton was a consummate showman, constantly in search of new and unusual ways to advertise his products. On the other hand, he had a genuine reverence for the "Auld Mug" and its Corinthian traditions, unsullied by the taint of commercialism. He made a great point of seeing to it that his challenges never were linked directly to his business enterprises.

But of course that linkage was there anyway, and Sir Thomas knew it. Lipton, his challenges and his principal product were so inextricably bound that to promote one was to promote them all. When he brought his huge steam yacht *Erin* to New York, he turned one of her cabins over to the press — fully equipped with typewriters, telephones and other amenities.

A lifelong bachelor who doted on his mother, he nevertheless frequently surrounded himself with beautiful women, at least when press cameras were in evidence. During his *Shamrock IV* challenge he once appeared at her Manhattan shipyard with a bevy of models from a local dressmaker's, causing a temporary halt to all work. With several photograhers in train, he led them through the yard, up and down ladders, and finally aboard *Shamrock*, where he posed at the helm. It was, said Sherman Hoyt in his "Memoirs," the only time he ever saw Sir Thomas aboard one of his challengers!

The gentle-hearted and deferential Lipton was a name-dropper, a man of enormous personal vanity, but to describe him as an egotist would be too harsh. Few words would be too harsh, on the other hand, to describe Alan Bond's effect on members of the NYYC, especially once he started telling them what the America's Cup is all about:

"A great deal of nonsense is spoken and written about the

America's Cup being purely a sporting contest," he said. "The Americans certainly aren't sporting about it. They have always defended the Cup with big company money. Of course it's a sporting challenge, but to suggest that it is nothing more than a sporting challenge is absolute rubbish."

That wasn't strictly true, of course. More often than not during the Cup's long history defenses were mounted by individuals of vast wealth. But if corporate America hadn't been directly involved in the past, it would be soon enough. Bond, who hadn't even heard of the Cup before 1970, was a better prophet than historian, and he set out to show the world how it is done. To make sure the message got across, he commissioned a book about the 1974 campaign, and budgeted $150,000 for a documentary.

His publicists had plenty of material to work with right from the start. Bond started firing salvos across the NYYC's bow more than a year before the match. He said he would protest even before the races if the defenders were allowed to use a Kevlar mainsail, one of the new and exotic sail cloth materials then being developed. In the fall of 1973, he learned that another designer had sold a story to Australian and American yachting magazines purporting to describe Bond's top-secret challenger, *Southern Cross.* He threatened to sue both publications. He also vowed to protest any American boat that incorporated any of her innovations.

He warned the New Yorkers that he would be bringing his own lawyer to Newport, and a videotape camera crew to record any infractions. The club, he was telling the world, was not to be trusted.

Whether he actually believed that himself may never be known. The fallout from the 1970 protest was still reverberating in Australia, but Bond was close enough to some of the central actors in that drama (Jim Hardy was his skipper, for example) to have gotten a more balanced view. On the other hand, it provided a splendid object lesson on the power of the press to rally nationalistic fervor behind a challenger — especially in Australia, where the home-team sympathies of both the media and its audience were (and are) more easily enlisted than in America. In the end, it didn't matter whether Bond believed what he was saying, or even whether the reporters believed it, as long as the people back home got a chance to read it.

TWO MAVERICKS

Bond passed over his country's only experienced 12-meter design ers, Alan Payne and Warwick Hood, on the grounds they had produced losers. Instead, he stuck with Bob Miller, who had designed Bond's highly successful *Apollo* and whom Bond regarded as a genius. Miller had worked his way into the small circle of Australia's top naval architects from a starting point far humbler than Bond's. As an infant, he had been carted about the Australian bush by his itinerant parents. He was left more-or-less on his own at an early age. Neither Bond nor Miller had much of a formal education. Both were gamblers who enjoyed operating outside the conventional rules. Both had a healthy contempt for pomposity. And both had tempers, which occasionally flared up at each other.

They formed a lasting alliance and in 1983 they won the biggest gamble of their lives. By then, through a process as mysterious and eccentric as the man himself, Miller had changed his name to Ben Lexcen, the name under which he designed the boat that won the America's Cup.

There are several versions of the name change. One of his favorites goes something like this:

He started his design career in Sydney with a man named Craig Whitworth, forming a partnership known as Miller & Whitworth. When that came unglued sometime during the early 1970s, Miller wanted a new identity. Not just any old name, something unique. So he asked a friend with access to a Reader's Digest computer bank to find him a new one, a name no one else had. The computer tapped out six names, Miller chose one, and thus Ben Lexcen sprang full-blown from the modern conjurer's mysterious black box.

Lexcen's America's Cup career began in 1974 when he designed *Southern Cross.* Predictably, she was a radical 12-meter, at 70 feet overall the longest yet, with very narrow forward sections, a keel that swept back sharply to a narrow base and a rudder shaped like the bottom part of a tiger shark's tail. She proved superior to both *Gretels* (which Bond had bought), though only marginally faster than *Gretel II.* That was good enough to demolish the hapless *France.* But the defender was another story.

Bond celebrated his victory in the trials with a bit of petulance — or loyalty to his team, or a demand for equal treatment, take your pick. After the last race between *Southern Cross* and *France*, he refused to sit at the press conference under a row of five Rolex clocks, set for five different time zones. Rolex had donated the clocks and given watches to the crew members of each contender, in exchange for the free publicity it got by having its name prominently displayed in front of the TV cameras. Bond had asked the company for watches for the crew of his trial horse, *Gretel II*, as well, but the company representative had turned him down. The conference was delayed for 15 minutes while workmen took the Rolex sign down. Rolex later relented and the *Gretel II* men got their watches.

MORE BLUSTERING

After a contentious summer (see following chapters), *Courageous* was named defender, one of the best and hardiest contenders ever built. She would be modified many times, defend the Cup twice, and even be resurrected as a 1987 challenger.

The original *Courageous* syndicate was formed by William J. Strawbridge and several other veterans of the two *Intrepid* defenses. They lined up Sparkman & Stephens to make the design and signed Bill Ficker as skipper. With that patrimony, she was touted as the next champion even before she was born. But the gestation period proved difficult.

The first indication of trouble came after the 1973 Arab-Israeli War and resulting oil embargo. Strawbridge asked the club to postpone the match for a year, on the grounds that something as frivolous as an America's Cup race would be "inappropriate" in a time of distress caused by the energy crisis. The club deliberated, then denied the request. It would carry on, even if it had to reduce the number of attendant powerboats.

That decision was not made quickly enough to head off a blast from Bond, who knew the defenders were lagging well behind his own campaign. Talk of postponement on humanitarian grounds, he said, was a cynical move by the NYYC to gain more time.

He may have had a point, though he chose the wrong target. A few days later, the *Courageous* syndicate announced it was abandoning the effort, and it became clear its temporizing had had little to do with social conscience and a lot to do with the fact that contributions, like the oil reserves, were drying up. The syndicate had raised only $600,000 at that point. Two major *Courageous* backers had pulled out because of the oil crisis and its effect on their pocketbooks.

By then, other potential defenders were in the field, including the seven-year-old *Intrepid* and a radical new design, *Mariner*. But their syndicates were having troubles of their own, as we shall see.

Courageous looked like the best hope — if they could get her to the starting line. NYYC representatives met with syndicate members and urged them to continue. They agreed and the campaign resumed after a 10-day break. But meanwhile, Ficker, an architect, had taken on some new projects for the summer and was no longer available.

Late in the year, the syndicate was reorganized with Robert McCullough, the NYYC's vice commodore, as manager. McCullough got other club members to open their wallets and recruited Bob Bavier, skipper of the 1964 defender, to take the helm. Still later, with *Courageous* and *Intrepid* tied four-all in the final trials, McCullough fired Bavier and installed Ted Hood behind the wheel. Hood promptly won the next race and *Courageous* was selected.

McCullough had already recruited a hot 31-year-old Californian as helmsman for the starts, after the young man's original boat, *Mariner*, was dropped by the selection committee. He was an America's Cup newcomer, but his reputation for aggressive starts had preceded him. His name was Dennis Conner. Alan Bond couldn't resist meddling. He issued a press statement, the gist of which was that the Aussies were "apprehensive and concerned."

"We are fearful that fouling and striking tactics will be introduced to America's Cup starts," he said. "We deplore this approach which is degrading to the dignity and prestige of the America's Cup as one of the world's most important sporting events and we are most concerned that this style of racing could be condoned by the NYYC.... Apart from the unsportsmanlike nature of this approach, there is a definite element of danger to the safety of the crews and boats by adoption of rodeo tactics afloat."

When asked if he had communicated his concerns to either the NYYC or the Courageous syndicate before issuing his press statement, Bond blandly said, "Our approach to them is through public opinion."

Attentive listeners might have questioned his solicitude for sportsmanship, given his previous comments. "Australian yachtsmen generally lack the killer instinct that the American defenders have in plenty," he told his crew earlier. "We will cultivate the American approach for the 1974 challenge."

Yachtsmen knew his "concern" was phony anyway: He and his crew would be delighted if their opponents engaged in "fouling and striking tactics," which would lead to disqualification and a win for the Aussies. But Bond didn't care what the establishment thought. He was playing for the galleries, and the galleries, by and large, loved every vituperative minute of it.

After all that, the Cup races themselves were, once again, an anticlimax — to the surprise of almost everyone. *Courageous* swept the series four straight. The margins were 4:54, 1:11, 5:27 and 7:19.

A number of people felt it had been closer than the scores indicate, however. Dennis Conner, for one, thought *Southern Cross* could have won the first two races, and if she had perhaps Alan Bond would not have made several abrupt switches in crew, sails and gear, which only added to her problems in the third and fourth races.

"Gentleman Jim" Hardy (later Sir James), the Aussie skipper, supplied one of the few light moments during that irritating summer. Someone asked him how he had slept after the first race.

"Like a baby," he replied. "Woke up every two hours and cried."

Before the start of the second race, the two boats almost collided. Both raised protest flags. The next day Dennis Conner found himself facing Bond's lawyer, as well as the opposing crew, in the committee room — another new wrinkle on the America's Cup scene.

Legal intervention didn't help — not this time. Both protests were disallowed. Many observers believed *Southern Cross* had clearly committed a foul, and that the international protest committee, like the NYYC committees in previous matches, had done the politic thing rather than give Bond more to bluster about.

Bond promised to come back, and he did. But it was a far different Alan Bond who returned to Newport in 1977 and '80, a more subdued, thoughtful, even sportsmanlike Alan Bond.

"We just brought one boat this time, and all we want to do is win some races," he said at the start of the 1977 campaign. "Last time we were here to promote Yanchep. We achieved that purpose (he sold it to the Japanese, in fact), and now we're here to sail.... I'll enjoy it much more this time. There was too much tension before. And we didn't think we could lose!"

Some attributed his mellower approach to rumors of financial difficulties involving one of his companies, and the fact his campaign was operating on a drastically reduced budget — a mere $1.4 million, of which he put up $750,000 himself, as opposed to his huge expenditures in 1974. (Estimates ranged up to $9 million.) In any case, by the time *Australia* made it into the match itself in

September, the syndicate had run out of money. Frantic calls were placed to 150 companies in Western Australia. The syndicate was looking for an additional $220,000 just to complete the match and get *Australia* shipped home.

Another possible explanation is that his pared-down campaign was deliberate, that after 1974 Bond had decided it would take several more trips to Newport to learn the game well enough to win. There was no point in spending a great deal of money or nervous energy on what was essentially a training mission. According to that scenario, *Australia* ran out of money because he hadn't budgeted beyond the August trials.

But these speculations aside, he was showing us a new side of his personality, and it went down well (though it merited fewer headlines). When asked in 1977 why he wanted to win the Cup, his answer was worthy of a Thomas Lipton or a Harold Vanderbilt: "There is a great fascination about competing for and winning such an old sporting event that has never been won by anyone but the Americans. It's like climbing a great mountain." When asked again in 1980, he replied: "You always hear it can't be done. But in my heart I *know* it *can* be done. So, I have to try. Money has nothing to do with it. All the money in the world can't win the Cup."

But money was never far from Bond's mind. According to Australian journalist Bruce Stannard, 1980 was also the year he used his America's Cup contacts — international bankers he met in Newport — to borrow the $37.5 million he needed to purchase Australia's natural gas producer, Santos. No one in Australia had been willing to loan that much on what they saw as a risky investment. By 1983, Santos was worth $450 million. Looked at that way, Bond's decade-long, $16-million investment in the Cup netted him a tidy $400-million profit!

He spent a mere $1.5 million or so on the 1980 Cup campaign, however — well off the pace of the American defenders, whose spending was climbing toward the $3-million mark. But again it was enough to get him into the match and gain still more experience.

When he came back in 1983, he had a $6-million budget, a two-boat campaign, and he told his crew this would be the last assault, win or lose. The training period was over. And as the world soon learned, the old Alan Bond had returned.

9
CORPORATE AMERICA TAKES THE HELM

"This America's Cup business is . . . rough, tough, and nasty, like a corporation."   — *George Hinman, 1974*

The America's Cup became big business in the 1970s. The transformation of this onetime sporting event into a corporate enterprise followed two separate but collateral routes: 1. As costs escalated beyond the means of individual yachtsmen or yacht clubs, businessmen and corporations who had little or no connection with the sport became its sponsors; 2. The growing complexity and intensity of modern campaigns forced the challenge and defense syndicates to become mini-corporations themselves, independent of their sponsoring clubs.

When that power shift was accomplished, the days of amateur Cup racing were over, and those of sportsmanship were numbered. The win-at-all-costs, no-excuse-to-lose philosophy was in the saddle and riding hard, and nobody held the reins.

CUP DEFENDERS, INC.

It was William Strawbridge who said it first, back in 1967 when he was manager of the *Intrepid* syndicate:

"My sense of responsibility to the New York Yacht Club was not all that great," he confessed. "I figured they should be darn glad we were there. That isn't the way they like to look at it, but it was the syndicate that was putting on the show."

His comment, quoted in "Defending the America's Cup," was less a declaration of independence than a statement of fact. America's Cup syndicates are as old as the Cup itself, but for most of the event's first 100 years they were small, clubby groups, generally formed from within the challenging and defending clubs. When America's Cup racing was reborn in 1958 after a 21-year hiatus, however, it entered a different world. Yacht designers were fooling around with aluminum hulls, new and exotic sailcloth, computer programs and a host of other space-age gadgets and methods.

Not only were these developments beyond the ken of the average yacht club member, they were also beyond his means. The days of fabulously wealthy men like Harold Vanderbilt, who could mount a defense, steer his boat to victory and pay the bills out of his hip pocket, were over. By the 1970s, not even the most resourceful yacht club could mount a Cup campaign from its membership alone.

Americans, meanwhile, were raising the art of corporate problem-solving to new and dazzling heights. When the first 12-meter race was held, the "military-industrial complex" was building basketball-sized Earth satellites. Eleven years later it sent a man to the moon. By then the defense of the America's Cup was becoming a corporate enterprise as surely, and as inevitably, as the exploration of space.

The elements of the corporate campaign came to include public fund-raising and commercial sponsorship, professional management, task-oriented divisions of responsibility, sophisticated research and development, exhaustive training, and a ruthless willingness to sacrifice individuals in favor of the transcendent goal. And it worked; corporate America held the Cup for more than a decade. But in the process it transformed the event from a yacht race into a technological crash program.

The change held other implications as well, less visible and never fully examined at the time. Without anyone willing it, without the slightest evil intent, the amateur sportsmen who built the corporate campaigns of the 1970s were creating a Frankenstein monster — all body and no soul — that would turn on them in the 1980s.

Consider first the matter of goals. Yacht clubs, as the framers of the original deed of gift knew well, are founded to promote yachting's best and most sportsmanlike ideals. Trophies, even the America's Cup, are incidental. A yacht club's reputation derives more from the way its members conduct themselves than from the size of its trophy case.

The priorities of an independent syndicate, by its nature if not by intent, are precisely the reverse. It has only one reason for existence — to win — and owes allegiance only to itself and its backers. As long as it remains under the control of an individual or a small group of people of unquestioned sportsmanship, such as Strawbridge, that doesn't matter. But when syndicates grow into mini-corporations, the key element of personal control begins to slip.

In law, corporations are accorded human status. But they do not behave like humans. If unchecked, they take on personalities of their own, independent of their creators, responding ruthlessly to their own imperatives. The biggest corporate imperative is to survive, grow and prosper, and in sports that means winning. When the corporate campaign grew to the point that its collective goal transcended those of its human constituents, sportsmanship was in trouble.

Then there's the matter of responsibility. A yacht club is responsible to its sport as well as to its members, who generally share that dedication. Until 1983, the NYYC had the additional responsibility as trustee of the Cup, under the deed of gift. By comparison, a modern corporate syndicate must reach out to a more diverse constituency — individuals and corporations — to survive, many of whom have no direct connection with the sport. They share the syndicate's primary goal, victory, but little else.

Furthermore, the genius of the corporation is that it creates a collective responsibility. No one person can be held accountable for its actions. An individual might think twice before taking a hard step, such as firing a skipper or issuing a false press release. But when a committee votes, there is no recourse — and no blame. The mere existence of a corporation legitimizes behavior that would be unacceptable in a human being. We saw that at work in the 1970s, when skippers were fired by committee, and in 1983, when both the challenging and defending syndicates did things that would have been cause for censure, or worse, had they been ordered by an individual club member in more innocent times.

Finally, there's the matter of performance. Yacht clubs generally are composed of gentlemen and amateurs who sail and race for the fun of it. Syndicates demand winners.

The corporate campaigns of the 1970s called forth a new breed of competitor, better suited to carry out the win-at-all-costs mission than were the gentlemen sailors of an earlier era. These were tough-minded, pragmatic men from every walk of life chosen for the task on the basis of only one criterion — that they sailed supremely well. They were amateurs in the strict formalistic sense that they were not directly paid for racing, but their skills, their methods and goals were thoroughly professional. Many of them were connected with the marine industry and would reap financial rewards from their participation, as we shall see. In some cases, as with sailmakers Lowell North and Ted Hood in 1977, their competition on the course was an extension of their business rivalry on shore.

In 1983, the financial considerations that flow from success or failure on the race course played a role in the war of psychological intimidation that accompanies every Cup race. *Australia II* had just lost the fourth race and was trailing *Liberty* 3-1. At the press conference, John Bertrand, *Australia II*'s skipper, ran into John Marshall, *Liberty*'s sail trimmer. Bertrand was in charge of North Sails' loft in Melbourne. Marshall was head of North Sails in America, and thus Bertrand's boss. Bertrand was due to take over North's entire Australian operation in Sydney, but had not yet signed the papers. Marshall turned to Bertrand's wife and said, "John should have signed that North Sails contract."

Two of the best sailors of the era, Ted Turner and Dennis Conner, had no direct economic connection with the boating industry. They had very different styles and methods, as we shall see. But they shared one characteristic that became the essential mark of an America's Cup winner: They were fanatics, yacht-racing junkies, driven hard by some inner need to excel; men who would sacrifice almost anything to stand behind the helm of a winner. They and other skippers of the 1970s lifted the campaigns to new levels of skill and aggression. Neither fit the NYYC's rather stuffy image of a yachting gentleman, and it is doubtful either would have sought, or gained, admission if it weren't for the Cup.

1974: THE DEFENDERS GO PUBLIC

This new intensity in America's Cup racing didn't happen overnight. Some of its elements were in place when the modern era began, if not earlier, and the whole picture is evolving still. But if you want a starting point, pick 1974, when Alan Bond dismissed a century of Cup traditions as "sentimental nonsense" and faced the Americans with a thoroughly businesslike campaign. The America's

Cup began to get serious.

It was also the year the corporate approach to personnel management made its first appearance on the Cup scene. One of the rules of the corporate campaign is that good men sometimes must be sacrificed for the sake of the cause. In 1974, one of the three defense syndicate managers and three of the four defending skippers on the scene when the summer began either stepped down or were pushed aside during the course of the campaign. In the case of two of the skippers, as we shall see in the next chapter, it was a hard push.

Meanwhile, the syndicates developed a voracious appetite for funds which could no longer be met from private individuals. First they turned to the general public. Eventually, and perhaps appropriately, they went to their structural and spiritual counterparts in the business world. By that time, even the NYYC was forced to acknowledge the new order. The America's Cup had become a business and there was no turning back.

Four boats came to Newport for the defense in 1974, *Courageous*, *Intrepid*, *Mariner* and *Valiant*. William Strawbridge, manager of the highly successful *Intrepid* campaigns of 1967 and 1970, was the first to announce he was forming a syndicate, and as is often the case the campaign with the earliest start had the longest run. His new boat, *Courageous*, was named defender and went on to hold the Cup.

George Hinman, the former NYYC commodore who had chartered the aged *Weatherly* in 1970 with no real hope of winning, was next to declare, with *Mariner,* a radical new design by Britton Chance. His syndicate entered *Valiant* as well, but the old Sparkman & Stephens boat was never really more than a trial horse for the new one.

Finally Gerry Driscoll, a boat designer and yachtsman in San Diego, announced his bid early in 1973. Driscoll was among a number of people who felt the original *Intrepid* had been a near-perfect design and that the modifications made by Chance had slowed her down. So he bought her, shipped her to his yard, rebuilt the hull more or less along the original Sparkman & Stephens lines, and entered her in her third campaign.

But it was a nonstarter, the California International Sailing Foundation, that may have had the most lasting impact on defense campaigns from then on. Before it abandoned its plans to mount a defense, the foundation received a ruling from the Internal Revenue

Service that gave it tax-exempt status: Contributors could deduct donations from their income taxes.

Hinman and Driscoll both took note of the ruling and availed themselves of it through similar foundations, the Kings Point Fund of the Kings Point (New York) Merchant Marine Academy and the Seattle Sailing Foundation, respectively. Henceforth, most defense syndicates would be formed, nominally at least, by these and other tax-exempt groups. They would own the boats, accept contributions, and retain any leftover cash and equipment after the campaigns to further their charitable goals — generally teaching young people to sail.

This device gave syndicates something to sell potential backers besides satisfaction, and they started selling hard. The result was a profound change in the image of America's Cup defenses. The contrast between the financing of *Intrepid*'s first campaign and her last is a striking illustration.

William Strawbridge's 1967 effort was backed by a highly select and harmonious group of only seven individuals who met the campaign's initial $700,000 budget out of their own pockets. Strawbridge, who recruited them himself, reflected on that process in "Defending the America's Cup:"

"It took about eight months to put it all together because we had to be careful how we made our approaches. It wasn't like raising money for a charity, where you walked in hat in hand and said it's tax deductible. You had to find someone that was involved and not just a casual observer.... We wanted to keep it small because the people who had been in the *Eagle* and *Constellation* syndicates (in 1964) had very little satisfaction out of them. The big boys felt the little boys were getting all the say and vice versa. Both these syndicates appeared to have been unhappy situations. We were very careful about whom we asked because we didn't want anyone in the syndicate who would try to take over the organization and running of the boat. We turned down two or three people for just that reason."

Under Gerry Driscoll's management, *Intrepid*'s 1974 budget was only a little higher, $750,000, and once again a syndicate of well-heeled yachtsmen was formed. But this time the Seattle Sailing Foundation also hired a professional marketing man named Dick Friel to go after individual contributions from ordinary folks. He arranged speeches at Rotary clubs, ordered *Intrepid* T-shirts and bumper stickers, organized spaghetti-and-meatball suppers and launched an advertising campaign. *Intrepid* was a sentimental favorite by this time, and the fact that she was a West Coast entry made her even more popular wherever the Eastern Establishment was held in contempt — which in the early 1970s meant just about anywhere west of the Holland Tunnel.

Friel's techniques brought in more than 2,000 contributions, ranging from $15,000 down to nickles and dimes. He described it as the first successful public subscription drive in Cup history. "This campaign has all the aspects of a mini-corporation," he said.

Strawbridge, meanwhile, retained happy memories of his '67 and '70 campaigns, the latter being much like the first. When he launched his fund-raising effort for *Courageous* in 1974, he elected to forego the tax windfall, declaring it "inappropriate". Later, the 1973 oil crisis and a plunging stock market nearly shut down his campaign while the *Mariner* group was within sight of its $1,000,000 goal. *Courageous* was the last defender to sail without a tax exemption. For better or worse, the days of the privately mounted campaign were over.

Olin Stephens, for one, thinks it was for the worse. Looking back many years later from his hilltop retirement home in Putney, Vermont, far from the ocean and those hectic campaigns (five of the six defenders from 1958 through 1980 were his), the dean of America's Cup designers saw tax exemption as "the worst thing that ever happened to the America's Cup."

He confesses to a personal ambivalence: On the one hand, the increased flow of dollars enabled him and other naval architects to spend more time and money on computers, tank tests and the like. On the other, it was a disaster for the sport:

"Now the people who are running the show and sailing the boats are acting for other people rather than themselves, and I think that lowers the level of sportsmanship a great deal. Any skipper who is do-ing it for an organization that is supported by a lot of money, a lot of hopes of a lot of different people, is going to take a no-excuse-to-lose attitude, which is wrong.... I think sports should be either completely professional or completely amateur. This borderline presents a lot of problems."

Some of those problems developed quickly.

1977: ENTER THE CORPORATE SPONSORS

The next step in the marketing of the America's Cup was corporate sponsorship, and it wasn't long in coming. Oddly enough, it was a first-time challenger from Sweden that showed the way, during the very next match in 1977. Others had had corporate help in the past. Even the autocratic Australian Alan Bond signed up a tobacco company and an aluminum manufacturer as co-sponsors in 1974. But most sponsors had merely contributed goods and services in exchange for free publicity. The Swedes were the first to go for the cash in a big way.

The Royal Goteburg Yacht Club syndicate told its countrymen the Cup challenge would be a splendid opportunity to show off Sweden's industry and culture as well as its yachting skill. The response was impressive. Volvo spearheaded the $2-million campaign, but no fewer than 64 corporations were involved in one way or another. The syndicate rented three Newport mansions (one just for visiting executives and VIPs), ran a three-day Export Exhibition in Newport, and staged concerts with Swedish musicians there and elsewhere around the United States, each presented by a different corporate sponsor. Sweden's King Carl Gustaf was the patron of what amounted to the first national challenge in America's Cup history.

The NYYC, meanwhile, was sailing against the tide on a different tack.

Public interest in the America's Cup was at an all-time high in 1977, at least for the modern era — higher even than the previous peak in 1962, when the Aussies arrived on the scene. Newport during an America's Cup was THE trendy place to be. The odor of money hung in the air like a damp June fog. For marketing men and merchants, the whole summer-long event was a juicy plum waiting to be picked.

The marketeers' first tactic was infiltration. Wave after wave, Cup summer after Cup summer they came, a growing flood tide of T-shirts, coffee mugs, postcards, ashtrays and the like, each bearing an America's Cup decal. By 1977, the town seemed buried in the stuff. One reporter set out to see if he could dress himself from head to foot in America's Cup souvenirs, and succeeded within minutes.

The New Yorkers, predictably, viewed all this with distaste — and perhaps a touch of envy. Here were all these merchants, God knows who from God knows where, cashing in on *their* Cup and *their* event while they had to dig into their own pockets to pay the bills — an estimated $200,000 to $300,000 just to run the races, never mind mount a defense. And some of the stuff those people were peddling, with the name of *their* trophy on it, was pure junk!

The club couldn't do much about it, but it did what it could. It registered the phrase "America's Cup" and the Cup symbol as trademarks. Then, in the spring of 1977, club representatives came to Newport to display a line of "approved" souvenirs to local merchants. The club expected a one-percent cut of the sales prices in exchange for use of its trademarks, the merchants were told, but it would make no effort to enforce that, nor to restrict sales of unauthorized stuff of reasonable quality. The real purpose was to try to exercise some control.

"A lot of people were using the name, and not always in good taste," Commodore Robert McCullough told a Newport County Chamber of Commerce meeting. "We decided we'd better get on top of it.... Last time we were here somebody was selling America's Cup foul weather gear. The damn stuff leaked like hell." As Emil "Bus" Mosbacher explained, if you don't act to protect your copyright when it is infringed, you lose title to it. By going through the motions of policing it, the club was preserving it in case it needed to fight a truly horrendous misuse later on. "You didn't want to walk down the street and see the America's Cup on the seat of everyone's pants," he remarked.

But it was one of those awkward predicaments the NYYC seems to have a genius for walking into. To try to stem the rising tide of objectionable mementoes, it registered the name of the Cup. To preserve its enforcement rights it had to exercise them, which meant selling trademarked goods. But the only goods the merchants cared to try to sell were precisely the ones that had been selling like hotcakes before — ashtrays, mugs, T-shirts, etc. Thus, while Swedish industrialists were picking up orders for Volvos and sharing their country's cultural heritage with people all over America, the NYYC found itself hawking cheap souvenirs to the shopkeepers of Newport — in the name of protecting the purity of the America's Cup!

It was a small but telling example of the club's fatal inability, after more than a century of private campaigns, to operate effectively in the public arena.

1980: PAN AM NAMES A BOAT

Commercial sponsorship is one issue (professionalism is another) that the sport of yachting has never resolved. Like deviant sexual behavior, for decades it was simply understood that one did not engage in it. Those who did were not invited into polite society. But by the late 1970s, the NYYC, American yachting's politest society, no longer possessed the means to uphold its Corinthian traditions and defend its precious Cup at the same time. When push came to shove, it chose the latter.

The push came from the Swedes in 1977. The shove came three years later, from American shipping and tobacco heir Russell Long, 24, the youngest man ever to launch a campaign. Long had little 12-meter experience but had grown up in other boats, including the 80-foot *Ondine*, raced with distinction by his father, Sumner A. Long. Russell was a child of the new era, however, a Harvard graduate with a degree in psychology. In 1980, he judged the psychological moment had arrived.

His campaign, he announced, would be backed by Pan American Airlines and Bacardi Rum, among other contributors. When he explained himself to the press, he sounded almost defensive:

"We're breaking with tradition in having commercial sponsorship, but we feel it may as well be us as anyone," he said. "We feel we can do it the right way." He pegged the campaign cost at close to $2 million. "It's gotten so tremendously expensive. It's come to the point where you just don't have any more $100,000 people."

The camel's nose was under the tent. When Long's new boat was launched, more than the nose was visible.

Long's syndicate had kept the boat's name secret right up to the christening ceremony, though word had leaked out that "Eagle" was preferred. But when the time came, lo and behold, it was *Clipper* — a not-so-subtle reminder of the "Pan Am Clippers" being flown by her major sponsor. Mysteriously, a red-and-white painting of an American eagle shared space on the transom with the white lettering. It turned out the syndicate had worked out a last-minute deal with Pan Am: the sponsor kicked in some extra dollars, a sign painter was hastily summoned the night before, and the name was changed. There hadn't been time to remove America's national symbol, but that was done later.

It also turned out that *Clipper* carried a spinnaker, during practice races only, emblazoned with a colorful ad for Bacardi Rum. Both the NYYC and the United States Yacht Racing Union, which polices the rules governing yacht racing in America, had given the name and the sail their sanctions, if not their blessings. One of the rules prohibited any name that "specifically" refers to a corporation. Another barred advertising during an official race. But as Commodore Henry H. Anderson said, there wasn't much the club could do about it any other time.

"I think the future of the America's Cup rests in the hands of corporate sponsors, and I'm very happy the NYYC realizes this, or I think the future defenses would be in jeopardy," Long said.

Elsewhere in Newport, the smell of money was beginning to mingle with the faint odor of hypocrisy.

Robert McCullough, chairman of the yacht club's America's Cup Committee in 1980 as well as in 1983, was saying in July that the club frowns on such things as the use of a Pan Am name for one of its contenders. "We don't like anything controversial," he said. "We don't like borderline things. We're that conservative. It's kind of like being a little bit pregnant. Pretty soon you're in trouble."

But even as he spoke, the club was raking in fees of $15,000 each from 15 companies it had named "official sponsors" of the races, a designation that allowed them to tout their products as "the official (whatever) of the America's Cup," and was collecting royalties, up to 10 percent, on souvenirs bearing its trademarks.

Gary Jobson, who makes a living primarily by talking, writing and teaching sailing, was among those who pointed out the club's inconsistency. And that led Jobson, who was Ted Turner's tactician aboard *Courageous* that year, into a discussion of professionalism, as reported in a Providence Journal-Bulletin story by Katherine Gregg.

Jobson defined a professional as "someone who gets paid directly to compete or is rewarded financially for winning," which made the America's Cup still a solidly amateur event in his mind. "I can assure you that it's costing me plenty to sail on *Courageous* for the summer," he said. "Will there be rewards later? Perhaps for some there will be. But I don't believe anyone does it for that. I certainly don't."

As Gregg pointed out, Jobson's face was beaming forth that summer from a Michelob beer ad that read:

"A Michelob toast to the America's Cup challengers and defenders, with a special salute to Gary Jobson, Michelob's sailing advisor.

"Michelob offers you an autographed copy of 'How to Sail,' the new book by Gary Jobson. Send $6.95, check or money order, to...."

The Swedes meanwhile, who had gotten a head start, seemed to be coming to better terms with the commercial campaign. They had fewer backers in 1980, just 30 corporations who chipped in at least $50,000 each, with Volvo again the biggest. The crew all wore white T-shirts that said "I love my Volvo." But according to a spokesman, they had learned to place more distance between sponsors and crew. In 1977, he said, the crew had to have their pictures taken wearing sponsors' clothes, and perform other promotional chores. These non-sailing duties were dropped in 1980.

1983: CASHING IN

One afternoon midway through Newport's summer of '83, Bob Entin was relaxing aboard his 57-foot replica of a 1790 topsail schooner, the *Compass Rose*, at Bowen's Wharf. A friend came along, shouldered his way through the crowd of camera-toting tourists admiring the boat, and remarked that the tide was much higher than usual. Entin looked over the side and saw that the waterline had indeed reached a new height against the pilings. Then he looked around at the crowd.

"It isn't the tide," he concluded. "The island is sinking."

It wasn't of course, but there were times during the summer when the crush imposed strains of almost geological proportions. The Chamber of Commerce estimated four million tourists visited the City-by-the-Sea (pop. 30,000) during the year, the vast majority of them in the summer months. That worked out to 133 tourists for every man, woman and child who calls Newport home. They were estimated to have left behind upwards of $100 million in exchange for America's Cup T-shirts, mugs, decals, lodging (up to $165 a night), Australian beer, Canadian ale, French champagne, Italian wine and British gin, along with such thoroughly American souvenirs as small bottles of water scooped from the America's Cup course ($1.95 each). They spent untold millions on bus tours, harbor tours, historic tours, mansion tours, corn plasters and parking fines. Some even boarded boats to go out and see the races.

In 1983 the challengers and defenders combined spent a staggering $50 million in pursuit of the Cup. Much of that money came from corporate sponsorship. The America's Cup had not only moved off the sports pages into the news sections and onto network news broadcasts, it was showing up in the ads as well. Meanwhile, the docks in Newport were beginning to resemble the infield at the Daytona Speedway. Corporate names and logos were everywhere, on bulkheads, on deck mats, on equipment, even on the crew members themselves, who reaped a bonanza of clothing, wristwatches, shoes, etc., from dozens of sponsors. International corporations were hoisting their sales and racing for America's cash in a big way.

The challengers were still far ahead in this competition, though the Americans were catching up. The Italians, first-time contenders in 1983, did it best.

Their $5-million campaign was organized by the Yacht Club Costa Smeralda in Sardinia, part of a resort development so plush it publishes its own magazine, in full color. The development's founder and the president of the club, as well as prime mover behind the challenge, was none other than Karim el-Husseini, Shah, His Highness the Aga Khan, 49th hereditary Imam (leader) of 15 million Shia Imami Ismaili Muslims, direct descendant of the Prophet Mohammed, and one of the world's richest men. (At his wedding, the guests threw pearls instead of rice.)

Despite that formidable leadership, the Italians also sought corporate backing. Unlike the other syndicates, they didn't have to look far. The presidents or chairmen of 12 of their 18 major corporate sponsors were already members of the yacht club. That helped, of course, as did the appeal to nationalism. The Italians have a proud yachting tradition, but had never before ventured to Newport. They wanted to make an impressive showing. But according to Gianfranco Alberini, commodore of Costa Smeralda, most of the 18 corporations signed up for the usual reason — because they saw it as good business, a chance to get international exposure, expand their American markets, and associate themselves with a prestigious event.

Alberini said it took a little persuasion, at first. But when the corporations learned about the intense media coverage the Cup received, they signed up quickly. In fact, the corporate sponsors underwrote the campaign's entire budget. In return, the syndicate gave them what they wanted. In Newport, they rented a building on Bowen's Wharf that they turned into the Italian Pavilion, a kind of trade mart where such sponsors as Agusta (helicopters), Alitalia (the national airline) Cinzano (wine) and Mario Valentino (fashions) could advertise their services or sell their wares. They also rented a mansion overlooking

Cliff Walk, renamed it "Casa Italia," and entertained there frequently, imaginatively, and with the same gentle grace that inspired them to name their boat *Azzurra* (after the azure waters of the Mediterranean) while other contenders were named *Challenge, Victory* and the like.

Each of the 18 backers took its turn as host, entertaining clients and potential customers as well as people associated with the Cup. If there were commercial overtones, the sell was invariably as soft as a Mediterranean breeze.

At one party, a "barbecue" held by an Italian helicopter manufacturer, guests were greeted with Italian champagne, Mediterranean musicians, and a slip of paper that told them when their flight aboard one of two helicopters would leave the front lawn for the race course. While waiting, they were invited to stroll the lawns, play croquet, sample hors d'oeuvres from heaping silver trays, listen to the lilting music and generally make themselves at ease. After all the guests had returned from their 20-minute flights, where they had a bird's-eye view of *Azzurra* losing what proved to be her last race, the barbecue was served: a sumptuous repast of Mediterranean-style vegetables, beef and swordfish shish-kabobs, salads, casseroles, fanciful desserts and more wine, all served on linen-covered tables beneath a flower-bedecked tent by smiling waiters and waitresses in full livery.

No one else approached the Italian standard, but every other campaign had at least some corporate sponsorship in 1983. Even the NYYC, which held its nose when it took the plunge in 1977, had upped the ante. This time, it lined up 25 "official" sponsors, each donating $30,000, to defray the cost of mounting the races. Meanwhile, the defense syndicates were beating the bushes looking for sponsors of their own.

All this made for strange bedfellows. The Freedom campaign signed up a shoe company, for example, that was a direct competitor of one of the club's sponsors. Dennis Conner posed for a Jeep Wagoneer ad, and the manager of his campaign, Edward du Moulin — a former vice president of Bache and Company, stock brokers — found himself posing in an ad for E.F. Hutton.

That ad, incidentally, involved two full days of filming the crew aboard one of the boats — time spent away from training. Du Moulin, sitting in the trailer (donated by Airstream) that served as the campaign's dockside office, recalled those 48 hours with resignation, but no regrets. Corporate sponsors accounted for only 10 percent of the syndicate's budget, he said, but they were essential.

The scramble for corporate cash has altered and distorted the campaigns in other ways. Corporations like to back winners. That single, stark reality has prevented more yacht racing than it encourages. Cup campaigners have been unwilling to test themselves against the competition before the actual trials. If they won, it might give them an edge in reaping the corporate bonanza. But if they lost, it could be disaster. So they either don't race at all or — like the Italians' *Azzurra* syndicate and the NYYC's *America II* syndicate tuning up for the 1987 series off Fremantle, Australia — they agree to race but not to disclose the results. Then each side is able to tell its backers they got the best of it.

How much can ride on a single practice race? In "Born to Win," John Bertrand quoted a conversation he had with Alan Bond before the last race of the Advance Australia Cup in March, 1983. America's Cup contenders *Australia II* and *Challenge 12* were going head-to-head in their only formal race in home waters before packing up and heading to Newport. The score was tied, 3-3. Bond called Bertrand from Brisbane: "Now hold on, John, bullshit apart, this is getting serious," he said. "I estimate that this last race is worth a million dollars to me, one way or the other, in corporate sponsorship."

P.S.: *Australia II* won.

Contrary to predictions, corporate support reached new heights when the Cup moved to Australia in 1983, despite the problems of distance and that country's relatively small consumer base. And as we shall see, the issues of commercialism and control were becoming even pricklier.

The issues involved in the win-at-all-costs corporate-style campaign came to a head even sooner.

10
TED TURNER: LAST OF THE HAPPY WARRIORS

He set a regal cap on his famous victory, in the true style of the outrageous character we all know him to be. In the middle of the post-match press conference, he collapsed, heroically drunk, with an empty bottle of rum still gripped in his fist.

It was a display of gloriously drunken joy. And, of course, it was frowned upon by the committee of the New York Yacht Club.... Rather than frowning, they should have installed a brass commemorative plaque in the place where Turner fell, for this was without doubt the last gesture of carefree amateur reckless-ness that would ever be seen in the America's Cup.

(from "Born to Win," by John Bertrand and Patrick Robinson 1985; William Morrow & Co., N.Y.)

Ted Turner's Cup career spanned three challenges, 1974, 1977 and 1980, probably the most fateful period in the entire history of the America's Cup. The trophy itself was relatively safe, but the nature of the competition hung in the balance. Would it continue as an amateur sport or become a quasi-professional grind? Would defenses remain earnest but clubby affairs, or would they become corporate crash programs, calling upon resources and motivations far beyond the gentlemanly restraints of "friendly competition"? Were the repercussions of the growing win-at-all-costs mentality acceptable?

It's safe to say none of these questions was on Turner's mind in

1974. Thoughtful yachtsmen were just beginning to pose them, and he is not a reflective man. All he wanted to do was win some races; let somebody else worry about the rest of that crap. But it was Turner, however unwittingly, who upheld some of the best traditions of the America's Cup in the 1970s — sometimes against the active resistance of the NYYC. And ironically, it was Turner who helped turn the Cup into an on-and-off-the-water media event, one of the developments that would destroy many of those same traditions.

CAPTAIN OUTRAGEOUS

The NYYC would have preferred almost anyone else as its champion. Robert E. (Ted) Turner III may have mellowed somewhat now that he is in the spotlight as a giant of the communications industry. But in those days he was loud, crude, vulgar and outrageous, a braggart, a public drunk, a public womanizer and sometimes a public nuisance. He was also straightforward, totally unaffected, unpredictable, enthusiastic, and engagingly frank about his foibles. And he was the people's choice. In short, he was everything the NYYC was not.

He fancies himself another Rhett Butler, the swashbuckling iconoclast in Margaret Mitchell's Civil War novel "Gone with the Wind." He even named one of his sons Rhett.

After being thrown out of Brown University in 1960 (they didn't allow women in dormatory rooms in those days), he went to work at his father's Atlanta-based billboard and advertising business. Three years later his father, ill and heavily in debt, abruptly sold out and then shot himself. Ted had a choice: Let the sale go through, which would give him enough money to spend the next several years sailing, or block it and take over the failing business at the age of 24. Ted Turner, never one to think small or take the easy way out, chose the latter.

Now, as anyone who watches the evening news knows, he owns a multimillion-dollar cable-TV station, baseball and basketball teams in Atlanta, and he's still running on a fast, slippery and sharply rising track. When he tried to take over CBS in 1985, a lot of people at the network and elsewhere got very nervous — not because it looked as if he had any chance at all, but simply because he had done the impossible so often it was becoming routine.

His sailing career followed the same script. As described in Roger Vaughan's excellent chronical of the Mariner syndicate's losing effort in 1974, "The Grand Gesture," Turner followed his own dictum:

"You have to go where the hot stuff is and get whipped." With no big boat experience at all — he had never even crewed for anyone — he chartered *Scylla*, a Block Island 40 owned by sailmaker Charles Ulmer, and took her south for the start of the Southern Ocean Racing Circuit.

That was in October, 1964, with a bunch of small-boat sailors as crew. "It was the damnest four days of my life," one of them, Irwin Mazo, recalled. There were storms, the radio and much of the gear was broken, she ran aground, there was a galley fire that almost got out of control.... "Give me a million bucks and I wouldn't go to sea with Turner again," said Mazo, who remained Turner's friend and accountant, two relationships in which the sailing could be equally harrowing.

That first SORC was a disaster, as was his second outing with *Scylla*, the Montego Bay race, in which he ran short of food and water, got lost, and finally turned back. But the fever had struck; Turner went looking for a fast boat to buy. He settled on a Cal 40, *Vamp X*. Then he did the unthinkable: He entered her in the SORC the following year — and won. By the biggest margin ever. He and his small-boat sailors from inland Atlanta, in a stock boat, had won a race on their second time out that remains the lifetime goal of serious ocean racers! Now he was hooked.

In 1969, several victories and near-disasters later, he bought *American Eagle*, the unsuccessful 1964 Cup contender that had been converted for ocean racing by her Canadian owner. Twelve-meter boats are not designed for ocean work, even when converted. Nonetheless, as oldtimers shook their heads, he entered a transatlantic race, finishing third. Then he decided to have a go at the World Ocean Racing Championship, an insane event consisting of 18 races held in various spots around the world. To qualify, you had to sail in seven races within three years. So, 12 hours after landfall in Cork, Ireland, *Eagle* was sailing for the northern tip of Denmark, where the Skaw race would begin in 10 days.

As it happened, the 5.5 World Championship — a class in which Turner had excelled in the past — was to start in Sandham, Sweden, two days after the Skaw race began. Turner wanted to win both, so he chartered a plane to pick him up at the Skaw finish line, 290 miles from the start, two days later. Not surprisingly, *American Eagle* was still racing in the Skaw when the 5.5 World start loomed. Turner calmly announced to his amazed crew that he and the 5.5 sailors aboard would be leaving the boat at the next mark, 12 miles out to sea. He would row ashore, call the pilot, get picked up and be at the start of the 5.5 just in time to hop aboard his chartered boat. He got the rubber dinghy on deck, inflated it, and had oars at the ready before his crew talked him out of it. It took a lot of talking.

In 1970, after an even more hectic racing schedule, he was given the prestigious Martini and Rossi Yachtsman of the Year award, beating out Bill Ficker, who had just defended the America's Cup in four straight races. That particular award is voted by yachting writers and editors. If it had been up to the NYYC, Turner wouldn't have had a prayer. He had had the temerity to bring *American Eagle* to Newport earlier that year and sail her, under a Confederate flag, as a trial horse for the Australians' *Gretel II*!

That was an unusual move, though not unprecedented. In 1934, American yachtsman Gerald Lambert loaned his converted J boat *Vanitie* to the British challenger, T.O.M. Sopwith, for the same purpose. Then, it was generally viewed as a sportsmanlike act. It is a measure of the distance the Cup had already strayed from its goal of "friendly competition" by 1970 that Turner was criticized for giving aid and comfort to the enemy.

Turner figures he spent approximately $1 million in the decade of racing leading up to his first Cup venture, perhaps $20,000 a year on plane tickets alone. Clearly Turner, more than any other Cup contender before or since, was (and is) a driven man. He once attributed that to a latent inferiority complex — a rare personal insight for a man who seems more familiar to us saying things like, "If I just had some humility, I'd be perfect."

He was handed a large dose of humility in 1974, but it didn't take.

1974: DISASTER

Ted Turner was 35 years old in 1974. By then he had sailed more miles in a 12-meter boat than any man alive. He had just won his second Yachtsman of the Year award when he got a call from George Hinman, who had commissioned a new 12-meter from Britton Chance and was planning to enter her in the defense trials for the America's Cup. Would Ted take the helm? Certainly.

It was, in fact, Hinman's third call. The first two were to Bus Mosbacher and Buddy Melges, the 1972 Soling Olympic gold medal winner. Both turned him down because of business commitments.

Turner's racing record had made him a logical choice from the start, but the problem was he had alienated a number of people , including members of the NYCC, with his off-the-water indiscretions.

Hinman called people who had sailed with Turner and was reassured. "Terrible Ted" was basically a good guy with a big mouth, they said. And a hell of a sailor. Hinman signed him up.

That posed a dilemma for the NYYC. Turner had applied for membership, and had been turned down. A skipper didn't HAVE to be a member, but it would be embarrassing, to say the least, to have the club's most precious relic defended by someone it had excluded. On the other hand, if Turner were brought into the fold, the members could count on being embarrassed sooner or later, simply because Ted was Ted.

The club faced two things it feared above all: losing the Cup and being embarrassed in public. But when the chips were down, it had always chosen the second over the first. Turner was elected a member in December of 1973, six months before the trials. He had been sped by Hinman, who wanted him at his helm, and Bob Bavier, who ironically soon after was selected to skipper Turner's chief rival, *Courageous.*

Hinman's new boat was *Mariner,* which turned out to be the single greatest design disaster in the modern Cup era. Not only was she slow, her design failure led to a paralysing skepticism about test-tank results and design innovations generally. Brit Chance had come up with a revolutionary, chopped-off bustle rather than the usual tapered stern. It looked peculiar, but tank tests had shown it would "fool" the water into thinking the hull was longer than it really was. But the water wasn't fooled. In fact, the drag-inducing turbulence at her stern reportedly made enough racket to be heard over the outboard motor on a boat following her.

Chance and Turner were never friendly. Chance, the aloof, superior, patrician designer with a sardonic view of life, was precisely the sort of person Turner needed to needle, and the transparent failure of his design provided an excellent opportunity. It didn't help that Chance didn't think much of Turner's sailing ability and had tried to block his selection. (Chance later said he had tried for a breakthrough design because he figured that was their only hope, with Turner at the helm.)

Their bickering was prolonged and very public, with Turner

predictably getting in the best shots. Referring to *Mariner's* squared-off stern sections, Turner said, "Brit, do you know why there are no fish with square tails? Because all the pointed-tail fish caught them and ate them." He walked a few paces away, then turned around and said,"Damn, Brit, even shit is tapered at both ends!" Chance, against all evidence, continued to assert the problem was the way Turner handled her, not the boat itself.

Mariner was sent back to Derecktor's Shipyard in Mamaroneck for a major overhaul which took almost a month, thereby missing most of the July trials. While she was gone, Turner steered the syndicate's other boat, the old *Valiant*, which though entered in the trials was never more than a trial horse for *Mariner*. His performance was erratic. When *Mariner* finally returned, George Hinman went back to *Valiant's* helm, but stepped aside a few days later. His replacement was *Mariner's* tactician, the only man Turner recruited who hadn't sailed with him previously: Dennis Conner, the cool and aggressive hotshot from the West Coast.

It was clear in the next few days that Hinman was testing Turner against Conner, a contest that would assume far more importance the next time it took place, in 1980. Turner, apparently rattled by this challenge to his authority, fouled Conner several times at the starting line. On August 14, at 4:30 a.m., Hinman made up his mind. Conner would replace Turner at the helm of *Mariner*. (Looking at both men's later careers, one might conclude the way to assure Cup champions is to make sure each serves his apprenticeship on a real dog.)

"There was no question a change had to be made," Hinman told Roger Vaughan later. "Ted did a great job in many areas this summer. His contribution was substantial. But he is an extrovert, he is temperamental, and he wasn't working out on the boat."

Turner took it hard, but it didn't show. Conner asked some of his crew to stay with the boat. When they resisted, Turner told them to do what they were told or they would never sail with him again. Then he transferred his gear to *Valiant* and started talking about making a comeback with her, which convinced no one. When Conner clobbered him at the start of their first race after the change, Turner complimented him sincerely, later gave him a gift inscribed, "To Dennis, a good friend and a great helmsman." Conner responded, "Turner is the hero of this summer. No question about it."

Mariner, with a new bustle and new skipper, still wouldn't go. She and *Valiant* were eliminated the same day, August 20.

Conner's Cup summer wasn't over, however. The *Courageous* syndicate was having problems, too, and invited him aboard as starting helmsman. His job was to win the start, then turn the helm over to skipper Bob Bavier. Then, 10 days later, Bavier got the ax. He was replaced by Ted Hood, the taciturn Marblehead sailmaker and yacht designer who had been involved in three previous Cup matches. Hood had replaced Jack Sutphen as tactician and relief helmsman three weeks earlier. Conner remained aboard as starting helmsman. It was reaching the point where Cup-watchers needed a scorecard, and a big eraser on their pencils.

Bavier's firing came when *Courageous* and the come-from-behind *Intrepid* were locked in a 4-4 tie in the final trials. Everyone assumed, correctly, that the next race would settle it as far as the NYYC's selection committee was concerned. Ironically, Bavier, then the editor of Yachting magazine and one of the sport's true statesmen, had been involved in one of the very few firings of a defender's skipper to date, having replaced Eric Ridder aboard *Constellation* in 1964. Now the shoe was on the other foot, and it hurt.

In his book, "America's Cup Fever," Bavier wrote he was feeling pretty good as he walked down to the dock the morning of August 31, despite some obvious reasons for gloom: After winning four straight races against *Intrepid* he had lost three straight. Bavier blamed himself for some bad decisions. He said one reason for his optimism that morning was that he and his afterguard, Halsey Herreshoff and Ted Hood, had figured out the night before how to solve some communication and decision-making problems — each of them had been deferring too much to the others at critical moments. All agreed they would do better from then on.

"Thus buoyed up (he wrote), and encouraged also by the conviction that *Courageous* was now a slight bit faster than *Intrepid*, I felt surprisingly confident as I strode down the dock. Half way to *Courageous* was the imposing figure of Bob McCullough, head of our syndicate. He was all alone and apparently waiting for me. He didn't look happy. As I drew near, he stepped forward to meet me and with only a perfunctory 'Good morning, Bob,' instead of his customary hearty greeting, he then blurted out the fateful words — 'The syndicate has had a meeting and we feel you should get off the boat.' Those might not have been the exact words but they were close.

"Suddenly it wasn't such a sparkling day."

Bavier asked if it had been discussed with Herreshoff and Hood, and was told it had been and that they agreed with the decision. Furthermore, they knew it was coming the night before, even as they conferred with Bavier over their new strategy.

"If I had still had any questions about whether or not a firm decison had been made, it was dispelled when Bob showed me a neatly typed press release," Bavier wrote. "It commenced with the statement that Bob and I had been friends since we were kids, and that the previous evening we had had a long discussion about what was best for *Courageous*, and I had volunteered to get off and turn her over to Ted Hood. It had some other statements which made me look good. The rub was that aside from the statement of our being longtime friends (we still are) there was not a shred of truth to it...."

For the first time on an America's Cup dock, one of the more devious corporate tools, the phony press release, was being used to cover up one of the more distressing facts of the corporate campaign: A decent man was being fired, for the good of the Cup.

To his credit, Bavier refused to go along with it. He told McCullough, "When they ask me, I'll tell them I was kicked off." And he did, without rancor and with his best wishes for the syndicate's success. In later campaigns, it would become far more difficult for the press to sort out what really happened.

Bavier's daughters, meanwhile, had already left in a friend's boat to watch their Dad take on *Intrepid*. Bavier said he would never forget the look on their faces when they spotted him watching the race from the tender, instead. What made it even more agonizing was the fact that the wind never came up enough to permit a race that day. When it was held, Hood won and *Courageous* was selected. She went on to win the Cup with ease.

Of the four boats that entered the trials that year, only *Intrepid* was steered by the same skipper the entire summer. Probably it is no coincidence that her helmsman, Gerry Driscoll, was also the founder and head of her syndicate. (Driscoll presumably had learned some lessons from his 1967 experience, when he was designated helmsman for the revamped *Columbia*, but left after a crew dispute.)

John Bertrand reflected on the 1974 series in "Born to Win" as follows:

"Now there was a hard, relentless streak.... When sports competitions take such a turn toward cold professionalism, they never return to what they were. And people become the victims, the debris all along the path to glory."

1977: TRIUMPH

That was not to be Ted Turner's fate, however. He had gone where the hot stuff is and gotten whipped, and in 1977 he was back. The usual Turner game plan. He tried to buy *Courageous* in 1974, but the Kings Point Fund syndicate gave it to Ted Hood instead. Hood asked an old friend and benefactor, Alfred Lee Loomis, to manage his syndicate. He and Loomis planned to build a new boat and use *Courageous* as a trial horse. If she proved faster than the new boat, Hood would get her.

But who would steer *Courageous?* Dennis Conner was mentioned, but Loomis regarded him as too aggressive for his own good at the starting line. Besides, he wanted a hefty financial contribution too, and Conner was not a wealthy man. He called Turner.

Turner, who had learned some lessons in 1974, said no thanks, not on those terms. He came back with some terms of his own: He would raise *Courageous'* basic campaign expenses. The syndicate would enter her in the trials as an equal partner to the new boat, not a trial horse, and Turner would stay at her helm. Loomis could fire him, but only if an intermediary, a wealthy Texan named Perry Bass whom both men respected, agreed.

There was one other detail, as set forth in Roger Vaughan's Turner biography, "Ted Turner, the Man Behind the Mouth:" Loomis expected Turner to use Hood sails exclusively.

Turner said in that case, count him out. He wanted to be free to use sails from Lowell North, and he didn't like the idea of using the Cup to further anyone's business. "It would be nice to have one amateur out there who wasn't part of the factory team, who was doing it like it had always been done," Turner told Loomis. Loomis grudgingly acquiesced.

The professional rivalry between Hood and North, the two premier sailmakers of the day, had spilled over onto the America's Cup course in 1974, when Hood's sails were used almost exclusively aboard *Courageous*, North's almost exclusively aboard *Intrepid*. This rivalry illustrated the problems that arise when sailors have a vested commercial interest in decisions they make on the race course.

Just before the first race between *Courageous* and *Southern Cross*,

Robert McCullough, manager of the *Courageous* syndicate, thought his skipper had chosen the wrong mainsail for the conditions. He got on the radio and ordered Hood to lower the main, a Hood sail, and raise another, a North product. Hood refused. Dennis Conner, who was on the radio relaying Hood's words to McCullough, wrote in "No Excuse to Lose" that Hood's last words were, "You tell Bob that I'm the skipper and we're going with what we have up." Opinion remains divided on whether this insubordination was a crass business decision, or a case of the skipper's right to select his sails.

But their big confrontation came in 1977 when North on *Enterprise* and Hood on *Independence* went head-to-head in the trials. It was assumed at the start that one of them would be named defender, go on to win the Cup, and reap huge financial rewards. (If Hood won, the fruits of victory would be twice as sweet: He also designed his boat.)

North, president of North Sails in San Diego, got involved when Andy McGowan, a key member of *Intrepid*'s 1974 crew, decided to have another go with a new boat. Joined by Edward du Moulin, who became syndicate manager, he recruited many of the old *Intrepid* crew, then bought *Intrepid* herself as a trial horse.

They commissioned *Enterprise* from Olin Stephens and decided to use North sails again, as they had on *Intrepid* in the last campaign. But this time they went one step further by naming North himself to the helm. *Intrepid* would be their counterpart to the other syndicate's *Courageous*: a full-fledged contender as well as trial horse, skippered once again by Gerry Driscoll. As it turned out, *Enterprise* consistently beat *Intrepid* in early races. Eventually the syndicate decided it couldn't afford to ship her east, and she was put up for sale.

So the stage was set for a commercial contest between the world's top sailmakers, with Turner thrown in for comic relief. But a funny thing happened on the way to the sail-off: Turner began winning! He beat Hood consistently in early tune-up races off Marblehead, and when *Enterprise* was shipped east and joined the fray, he kept on winning. At the end of the June trials it was *Courageous* 7-1, *Enterprise* 5-3, and *Independence* a miserable 0-8.

Yachting writers started speculating about the consternation within the patrician ranks of the NYYC. One of them declared the selection committee would sooner wear motorcycle boots and blue jeans on the course than select Terrible Ted to defend their Cup.

"We chuckled over that," said Commodore McCullough — the same Bob McCullough who had tried unsuccessfully to smooth over Bavier's ouster in 1974, speaking now for the club. "If we did have a problem with Turner," he told Roger Vaughan, "we would have told the syndicate to get another man."

If they had gone looking for an excuse to do so, they would have had quite a thick dossier to choose from. For one thing, Turner was then in the middle of a one-year suspension for flouting the rules of another sport, baseball. He had bought the Atlanta Braves in January, 1976, for a reported $10,000,000. Commissioner Bowie Kuhn suspended him just one year and four days later. The proximate cause was Turner's indiscretion in announcing his interest in signing a player who was not yet a free agent, which is strictly forbidden. During the ensuing legal battle, Turner promised to give Kuhn's lawyer a knuckle sandwich.

Kuhn might also have been offended by some of Turner's promotional gimmicks. Ted once dressed as a jockey and raced an ostrich around the field before a game. Another time he and Phillies reliever Tug McGraw pushed a baseball around the base paths with their noses. (Turner won.)

Mostly it was his mouth that got him into trouble, though. During a speech at an awards meeting of the National Sportscasters and Sportswriters Association in North Carolina, he got onto the subject of why he disliked sports agent Jerry Kapstein: "After all, you should have some reason to dislike a guy besides the fact he wears a full-length fur coat and is a Jew," he said.

During the Cup summer, he was escorted out of Newport's ultra-exclusive Reading Room for bellowing, and he had to write a letter of apology after making some suggestive remarks about a female guest during a party at the equally posh Bailey's Beach.

"If he *is* selected," said Don MacNamara, a former Cup helmsman who had opposed Turner's admission to the club, "he will be the first skipper in the history of the Cup to appear on the starting line wearing a muzzle."

The fact is, the NYYC had no real options. Ted Turner, the Mouth of the South, had the press and the public eating out of his hand. If the club denied him the selection because of his off-the-water antics — the same antics that had made him something of a national folk-hero — they would never live it down, and they knew it.

Turner faced another problem, closer to home, in the personage of syndicate manager Lee Loomis. Alfred Lee Loomis Jr., 63, ran a tight ship along the rather stuffy lines of his investment banking business. He chose to live apart from the crew during the summer of '77, but he attended dinner with them at Conley Hall, and insisted they wear coats and ties. He kept the press off the *Courageous* dock, which was like depriving Turner of oxygen. He confessed he was uncomfortable around people with long hair.

That was precisely the sort of pomposity Turner loved to prick, and he went at it with a will. The deferential treatment he had accorded the 1974 syndicate boss, George Hinman, was gone. Loomis was aboard *Courageous* one day before the June trials, Vaughan relates, all 6'4", 230 pounds of him, sitting in the stern. Turner wanted him to move forward, but Loomis didn't budge.

"Hey! Now I know why you named your boat *Northern Light*," Turner said in a voice the whole crew could hear.

"Why?" asked Loomis.

"Because you're the Big Loom!"

The nickname stuck.

Turner said Loomis tried to fire him several times; Loomis says it was only once. But the friction was palpable, and upsetting. Aside from their wildly divergent personalities, there was also the fact that Loomis clearly wanted Hood to defend the Cup, which led to exactly the kinds of conflicts that would swirl around *Courageous* again six years later. (See next section.) Loomis and Hood had been close friends for 20 years. "I'm backing Ted Hood, not a boat, and I'll stick with him to the finish," he told McCullough in 1976.

Regardless of his sympathies, Loomis insisted he took an even-handed approach to the two boats when Turner started winning. Loomis said it was Turner who suggested he spend more time on Hood's boat, because Hood needed more help at that point. "Don't let Ted (Turner) sell you the story he was a poor boy being plotted against," Loomis told Vaughan. "Part of his act is to be the underdog."

It didn't look like an act in July. Turner hit a slump and the other two began to catch up. Part of the problem was that *Courageous* needed new sails. The new Hood sails were going to Hood's boat, and North wouldn't sell him any at all. It was then that a private feud Turner and Lowell North had been carrying on all summer began to go public.

Turner said North had promised in 1976 to make some sails for *Courageous*, and that North had reneged. North acknowledged his promise, but said his syndicate meantime had banned issuing North sails to its competitors. He said he and Turner had agreed to let the syndicates sort it out, and when the sorting out process didn't go his way, Turner reneged on *that* agreement. At the height of the dispute, Turner called North "a no-good liar." North didn't fight back until the end.

The racing was very close, and confusing, as the July trials ended. But then Turner got hot again and signs of strain appeared among the other two crews. Lowell North was fired as skipper on August 23, replaced by tactician Malin Burnham. Halsey Herreshoff was named tactician. *Enterprise* stood 2-5 in the final trials at that point, and North had been criticized repeatedly for tactical errors. North took it well: "I've made mistakes and when you're behind you've got to make a change," he said.

On the same day, the Independence syndicate (3-4 in the final trials) replaced tactician Scott Perry with Steve Van Dyke, a veteran of four Cup defenses.

There were no changes on Turner's boat.

Independence was eliminated August 29. Turner looked on as the selection committee made the time-honored trip to Hood's dock to give him the news. There were tears of compassion in his eyes. *Enterprise* was excused the following day, and Turner was in.

That same day, Alan Bond's *Australia* beat out *Sverige* to become the challenger, after a close series of elimination races in which Baron Bich's *France I* and "the other" Australian boat, Gordon Ingate's *Gretel II*, had been the first to fall.

'PEOPLE LOVE ME'

There is a long and honorable America's Cup tradition that when the defender is selected, the defeated syndicates and crews rally behind the winner, offering moral and material assistance for the battle ahead. That didn't happen in 1977. When *Australia* was selected, members of the *Enterprise* crew came over to share in the Aussies' victory celebration. Some of them shouted they'd like to see Turner's head at the NYYC — a reference to the oft-quoted remark that if the Cup ever left the club, it would be replaced by the head of the skipper who lost it.

North let fly with some almost treasonable comments in the press: "I wouldn't mind going to Australia," he said. He added that he didn't plan on helping the Aussies, but "at this point, I can't feel strongly about seeing Ted Turner win." He said his attitude was based on Turner's summer-long attacks, but he also noted that *Australia* was using North sails, made by a North loft in Sydney. Hood, meanwhile, pitched in and helped Turner prepare for the match against *Australia*, which would begin in two weeks.

For Ted Turner, it was a heady fortnight. From an also-ran three years ago, he had emerged a hero — better yet, a folk hero.

"People love me, all over the place, they really do. I can communicate on all levels," he told Roger Vaughan in July, and now the evidence was all around him. He had taken on the Eastern Establishment, the professional sailmakers, the NYYC, and he had beaten them all! And the people, his kind of people, were there by the hundreds of thousands. He chartered a plane to bring his entire Atlanta Braves team up to Newport at one point, but most of his fans rolled into town on their own. To an extent, they were a different kind of crowd from past Cup galleries. Vast numbers of them couldn't tell port from starboard and didn't care; they just wanted to get a glimpse of Captain Outrageous in full flight.

"It was horrible, the pits. You know, they were the ones with the white belts, the white shoes, and no money. They usually got chowder and didn't tip," complained a waitress at the Black Pearl, one of Newport's established restaurants. That was probably unfair. Turner's charisma extended up and down the social spectrum. It stopped somewhere short of the upper echelons of the NYYC, however.

Commodore Mosbacher, who served as chief of protocol in the Nixon administration, is a diplomatic man. When asked to assess the impact of Ted Turner on the America's Cup, he sighed.

"I'm not sure I should comment on it," he said. "Certainly he brought a lot of color to it. He was quotable, good source material for the morning headlines, so in that way he brought color and a certain — uh — attention. His Braves fans got interested in the America's Cup."

The NYYC expected twice as many spectator boats for the first race as had witnessed the 1974 series. For the first time, the national TV networks were taking an active interest. Reporters were tripping over each other on the docks. Turner didn't merely bask in all this, he bathed in it.

"There will never be a time in my life as good as this time. I can't believe all this is really happening to me. I'm so hot I just tell my guys to stand by me with their umbrellas turned upside down to catch the stuff that falls off me and onto them," he told UPI's Terry Anzur.

"When I come back next time I won't change anything on *Courageous* or the crew. We're fast. We're perfect. She's the most perfect 12-meter that ever sailed and I can't think of anything I could do to be any better.

"My biggest problem now is to keep from getting a big head. You don't think I have one, do you?"

It was that outrageously uninhibited, almost naive, childlike adoration of self, followed by the quick phrase that lets you know he can recognize his folly but can't help himself, that either charmed or repelled people. But there was a childlike vindictiveness, too, as when he acknowledged to Anzur that he had been trying to rattle Lowell North all summer:

"The highest I ever scored on an IQ test was 128 and I figured that North was about a 148, and since I spotted him 20 points I knew I had to use guile and cunning. I didn't just eliminate Lowell North, I destroyed him. He left here a broken, bitter man. I'm three times the man he is."

The match itself, as usual, was expected to be something of an anti-climax and it was. But it was close all the way. Turner won in four straight, by margins of 1:48, 1:03, 2:32 and 2:25. The Australians confessed they made a poor choice of sails in the first two races. It was generally conceded Turner had sailed a faultless series, with a big assist from his tactician, Gary Jobson, who played the wind shifts to perfection.

But Ted Turner would be forever remembered less for the way he won his victory than the way he celebrated it.

He had had a few beers even before the boat docked. When it approached, he was in the bow, a cigar tilted jauntily upward in an FDR pose, feet apart, his trademark denim engineer's cap at a jaunty angle. He bowed to left and right, doffing the cap. At the dock he imbibed, depending on which eyewitness account you believe, champagne, rum, aquavit, or all three. Then his crew rushed him and threw him into the water.

Eventually everyone got dunked, Americans and Aussies alike.

Only Lee Loomis, who had been among the first to board *Courageous*, was left standing; Turner's crew had plotted their revenge against their remote, autocratic manager with consummate cunning. Finally, after waiting in vain to be tossed in, Loomis jumped off the dock.

It was a poignant moment for him, and for the NYYC. The People's Choice had triumphed, leaving the Old Guard to make whatever lonely adjustments they could. As if to underline the point, the inebriated Turner grabbed a fire hose and aimed it straight at the NYYC's committee boat.

His legs were getting a little wobbly by then. He had to be escorted to the press conference at the National Guard Armory on Thames Street by two Newport policemen. Someone placed two bottles of aquavit in front of him at the table on the stage. Someone else, perhaps a NYYC official mindful of the TV cameras, placed them under the table. Turner reached for one of them, discovered it missing, then slowly disappeared from his seat only to emerge moments later with the bottles in hand and a silly grin on his face.

When his time came to speak, his brotherly love had reached global proportions. "I never loved sailing against good friends any more than the Aussies," he said. "I love 'em. They are the best of the best. The best of the best...." When he paused, Gary Jobson shoved a note in front of him. When he focused on it, he thanked the NYYC, Bob McCullough, "and the crew of *Courageous*, my crew...." His crew, as if on signal, rushed the stage, grabbed their leader, and carried him on their shoulders amid applause and laughter, off to oblivion.

"We, too, would like to thank the crew of *Courageous*," said Bill Ficker, the obviously relieved moderator.

Turner had already decided on a return. In fact, the day after he was selected defender, he had made a secret trip to the Maritime Academy at King's Point to talk to them about securing *Courageous* for himself in 1980 — a move that outraged Loomis ("complete disloyalty," he called it when he found out).

But 1980 was a different story. Dennis Conner, who had likened Turner's bravado to that of a Confederate cavalry officer leading his troops into battle, had finally been given a command of his own. Turner was still aboard the same old horse, still charging ahead. But this time he faced a Sherman tank.

11
DENNIS CONNER AND THE ENDLESS CAMPAIGN

When Turner came back to Newport in 1980 with the same boat and crew, everyone expected him to do it all over again — the headlines, the jokes, the verbal jousting, the adoring crowds, the tough, hard-fought races and the champagne corks popping at the end. But the fire was gone from the belly.

Turner once said he was driven by the need to prove himself "in increasing circles of competition." He had reached yachting's outermost circle three years earlier. His Atlanta TV station thrived on reruns, but its owner did not. Besides, he was preoccupied with launching his Cable News Network (CNN), which went on the air June 1, just about the time he and his competitors showed up in Newport.

But above all, Turner insisted on regarding the America's Cup as a yacht race, not a grueling, two-year, win-at-all-costs professional campaign. When he was beaten it was by a man who knew better and whose assault on the Cup would change the tenor of the event, perhaps for all time.

KING OF THE SPACE INVADERS
Conner's campaign, like so many modern American upheavals, was born in California, his native state. The son of a commercial fisherman, he grew up within half a block of the San Diego Yacht Club and hung around it the way other kids hang around a pool hall. As he related in the book he wrote in 1978 with John Rousmaniere, "No Excuse to Lose," that experience nurtured two things: an

inferiority complex and the need to overcome it by winning sailboat races.

The warm climate and the frantic hedonism of the Southern California lifestyle make West Coast yacht racing a year-round thing, less clubby, more competitive and more intense than the Eastern variety. It was an ideal place for an ambitious kid like Dennis Conner to find his niche.

Going into the 1980 campaign, he had won an Olympic bronze medal, two Congressional Cups, two Star Class world championships, and two Class A victories in the Southern Ocean Racing Circuit. And he had seen America's Cup competition up close in 1974 as a kind of journeyman helmsman, standing in the very spots where Ted Turner sailed to both his greatest disaster and triumph, at the helms of *Mariner* and *Courageous.*

It would be difficult to find a better candidate than Conner for the title of Ted Turner's direct opposite. He is as cool as Turner is hot, as organized as he is chaotic, as private as Turner is public. Screw up aboard Turner's boat during a race and his wrath is swift, loud and brutal, and just as quickly forgotten. Conner "keeps his anger inside," according to Edward du Moulin, his 1980 campaign chairman. Men who've sailed with him for years swear they have never seen him lose his temper. Turner demands assurance, Conner asks for suggestions. Turner needs public adulation, regardless of his performance. Conner only needs to know that he is the best.

John Bertrand sailed with Conner in the 1978 SORC off Miami aboard *Williwaw*, a 46-foot ocean racer. In "Born to Win" he recalled the start of one race in particular:

"We were to leeward of three or four boats, all reaching down to the line on an off-the-wind start. Dennis was at the wheel, talking quietly and calmly, assessing the speed of *Williwaw* compared to the competition. Checking the watch, judging his time-on-distance ratios, computing all the variables, and finally making his move. Two fast tacks, the sails suddenly full, *Williwaw* heeling over into the line — a start almost breathtaking in its perfection....

"As we hit the line, I glanced at his face. He had a strange, faraway look in his eyes and just a little smile — a private smile, introspective, aimed only at himself. He had just done it again. I realized at that moment that Dennis is a man who has to prove himself to himself all of the time, and he has to have his ego fed, although only he can really feed it."

In Newport, on off days during the early going in 1980, Turner might be down at the dock, signing autographs or holding forth to a circle of admirers. Conner, meanwhile, would be at Handy's Lunch, an unprepossessing luncheonette on Thames Street, hunched over an electronic game called Space Invaders.

"The highest score you can get is 10,000. He runs it up to 9,999 just to show me he can do it," Gary Hooks, Handy's owner, told a reporter in 1980. "He's very down-to-earth. He came in here every day last spring and never told me who he was. I'd known him four or five months before I knew he was THE Dennis Conner. I just thought of him as the Space Invaders king."

As usual, Conner had an edge. Back home in San Diego, there was a Space Invaders game in his recreation room. But more to the point, his gratification came from mastering a box of electronic circuitry, lonely, anonymous, passionless battles that required no arena, no spectators, no applause. And when the score was high enough, the little private smile.

During his long apprenticeship on other people's boats, Conner learned a lot about sailing and sailors. He decided early that he didn't have an abundance of natural talent, but that he could overcome that with hard work, long hours and meticulous preparation. As a student at San Diego College in the 1960s, he said he stayed up nights going over the hull of the Lightning Class boat he was racing with a microscope, looking for pinprick holes that might or might not create an infinitesimal drag as it went through the water. When he found them, he filled them. Even earlier, when he was 17 or 18, he found that organizing and leading a crew on someone else's boat was as much of a thrill as steering in a race. "It makes me feel important, I suppose."

By 1974, he was ready for a run at the Cup. And it was ready for him. "Suddenly, America's Cup sailing had, like the SORC and the Olympics, ceased being a pastime and started being serious business. I enjoyed the pressure and responsibility that summer, and I think I did pretty well under it," he wrote.

Conner said he felt like an outsider at that first *Mariner* meeting in a diner near Derecktor's Shipyard. Nearly everyone there had sailed with Ted, and he hadn't. They were the happy warriors and he was the hired gunslinger from the far West. But they were the ones doing it wrong, not he.

"I myself would not organize a crew simply by inviting my friends, as Ted did," he wrote. "I would select the best man for each job whether or not I knew him." The pressure of an America's Cup campaign, he said, "is so intense it can strain personal relationships. This is one of the best reasons why friendship and serious sailing should not mix."

When he sailed with Conner, Bertrand was impressed by the way he involved members of his crew in the decision making — by asking inappropriate people for their advice, for example. Conner might ask a tailer what he thought of the mainsail's shape, or the port trimmer whether they were going fast enough. It was a way of keeping them all on their toes, making them feel important. However, Bertrand wrote, he was surprised to see Conner completely ignore his crew once he got ashore. He just hopped off the boat, walked up to the bar, and had a drink with the boat's owner and other skippers.

Bertrand seemed equally surprised that the rest of the crew just laughed it off. "That's Dennis," they said. "The race is over, so now he has to hold court. That's what he does." And even if friendship and sailing don't mix, as Conner claims, his crews are invariably a loyal bunch, many of whom follow him from boat to boat like a team of hired mercenaries — "my guys," Conner calls them proudly.

By 1980, he had earned a reputation as a very tough, very aggressive helmsman who would do anything within the rules to win. Soon he had a chance to apply those same characteristics to building a campaign, one unlike any that had gone before.

NO STONE UNTURNED

Conner had not taken part in the 1977 match, but shortly after it was over The Maritime College at Fort Schuyler Foundation asked him to be its skipper in 1980. The foundation had acquired *Enterprise*, the Sparkman & Stephens boat eliminated by *Courageous* in 1977, and planned to enter it, with either *Intrepid* or *Independence* as a trial horse. As it turned out, they couldn't get either boat. Conner had other ideas, anyway. He said he would be their man, but only if they agreed to build a new boat, give him a free hand in picking a crew, and assure him he would not be fired. He would sail *Enterprise* against the new boat and decide for himself which he would choose. The syndicate agreed.

The new boat, *Freedom*, hit the water in May of 1979 and Conner started tuning both boats in June, almost a full year before his competitors. First, he restored *Enterprise* to her 1977 configuration, brought her up to top condition, and brought back her entire 1977 crew to sail her against *Freedom* for 10 days. That was just to get baseline data.

Then he started improving the boats, first one and then the other. He moved them from Newport to California so he could keep sailing all winter. "We tried to change one thing at a time so we'd know if it was a better solution," Conner explained. "And sometimes we changed things back to avoid confusion." He hired a physical trainer to put his men through grueling daily calisthenics before they went out onto the water to test their inventory of more than 80 sails, one by one. It was a long, slow, painstaking and thoroughly professional process.

Conner is not, strictly speaking, a professional. He ran a drapery manufacturing company in San Diego that somehow stayed in business when he was off sailing, which was most of the time. But when he completed his crew selection, choosing 21 men for his two boats from a pool of 120 applicants, it was clear that the "new professionals" of the America's Cup had consolidated their hegemony. The crew was not paid for sailing as in the old days, but nine of them were sailmakers, suppliers, or other boating professionals who had more than a sporting interest in the outcome.

Meanwhile, four challengers arrived from abroad. *Sverige*, the Swedish entry that bowed in 1977 despite impressive corporate backing, returned with Pelle Petterson again at the helm. Britisher Tony Boyden, having taken 16 years to get over his humiliation with *Sovereign* in 1964, formed a new syndicate with a new boat, *Lionheart*. Baron Bich, back for his fourth and final attempt, also had a new boat, *France III*. And Alan Bond returned with an improved *Australia*. They went through a series of trial races to choose the challenger while the NYYC's selection committee ran a less formal elimination process to choose a defender.

For the first time, the club faced four veterans. But in the end, none of them could match Conner's dedication. By the time *Freedom* reached the starting line against *Australia*, Conner and company had logged more than 300 days of sailing. In almost any category you could name, they put in at least twice as much time and effort as their competitors, foreign and domestic.

In pacing, style, intensity, professionalism and by-the-numbers organization, the Conner-style campaign was remarkably like a modern presidential race, with trial races in place of primaries. And like that process, it evolved into a continual thing, first stretching to year-round, then two years, finally almost from one contest to the next.

In truth, Conner did not invent the endless campaign. He correctly confers that distinction on another San Diegan, Gerry Driscoll, who sailed *Intrepid* in 1974. "He took *Intrepid* to California and started practicing during the winter and came back here with an old boat that no one gave any chance to do anything. He came within two minutes of defending the America's Cup. I was there. I know how close it was. He showed what extra effort and preparation can do.... All we've done is refine what others did before us."

But he was the first to carry it out with ruthless precision, and the first to win with it.

He finally chose the new boat, *Freedom*, over *Enterprise*. She had been drawn by Olin Stephens, without tank testing, as a conservative 12-meter, a refinement of his previous successes. She stayed even with *Enterprise* in light and medium winds, sailed a shade faster in a blow. She was fast, but she was no *Intrepid*, the breakthrough design that won all but one of her 19 trials races in 1967. Yet Conner's 1980 record was almost as impressive: 42 victories in 47 trial races.

True, those victories were over relatively weak opponents. Turner, who was spending $2 million a month to keep his satellite TV station afloat, had scheduled a low-budget, three-month campaign. *Clipper,* the only other boat for the defense, was led by 24-year-old Russell Long, with a crew of equally young newcomers. They came on fast toward the end, but they, too, had gotten a late start and there was no substitute for experience. The Conner juggernaut rolled over both of them.

It was the magnitude of victory, the devastating inevitability of it, that convinced observers Conner would have won in 1977 had he been there, and would keep on winning until someone beat him at his own game. And already he was being attacked as a spoilsport, a workaholic who was turning the world's most glamorous amateur yachting event into a professional grind.

He had a ready answer:

"In any other sport, no one ever has to make any apologies for trying hard. You never hear any criticism for gymnasts practicing for three years, eight hours a day. I don't think you have to make any apologies when you're at the pinnacle of your sport." Herreshoff, Connor's navigator, added, "You can't criticize winning.... So much of what you do in life is half-hearted. There's a tremendous satisfaction in going all-out."

SOUR GRAPES

Who could argue with that? Certainly the men they defeated couldn't. When Ted Turner's boat was eliminated August 25, he spoke his mind, as always, and what he said was worth some attention. But under the circumstances it sounded like sour grapes:

"The complexities of mounting a campaign today, with all the thousands of hours of testing that it requires, don't appeal to me. It's too much like working in a science laboratory.... It's great to win and it's not as much fun to lose. But it's not that big a deal. Christ, this is a sailboat race. It's the biggest one there is, but it's still a sailboat race."

When the selection committee made its fateful visit to *Clipper*'s dock four days later, her crew had no complaints. "We were trying in six weeks to catch up with what Dennis had done in two years. We did the best we could but it wasn't quite enough," said assistant helmsman Tom Blackaller — who would be far more vocal three years later.

But away from the microphones and TV cameras, there were grumblings and mutterings about Conner's single-minded run for the Cup. In some respects, it had been a little TOO single-minded, the critics were saying.

One criticism surfaced briefly in May, when Turner let it be known he was thinking of boycotting the upcoming trials unless Conner entered both his boats. Conner refused. Russell Long's *Clipper* campaign had started as a trial horse for Turner and the two were still working together to develop their boats. But Conner had announced he would drop either *Enterprise* or *Freedom* in June.

Turner said having four boats out there would sharpen the defense all around. It would give the selection committee another choice, Turner and Long would have another yardstick to measure themselves against, and above all it would permit continual trial racing, whereas a three-boat field meant one had to sit out each race. And the

Fort Schuyler foundation had a responsibility to train American crews for the future, he said.

Conner responded that a one-boat campaign was more likely to win and therefore better for the Cup. Ed du Moulin, syndicate chairman, said they didn't have the resources to develop two boats with Conner-like intensity, and a divided campaign would lead to internal rivalries and frictions that would hamper the effort — a point that was borne out three years later within the Defender/Courageous camp.

Both arguments had merit, but Conner's critics suspected he was more concerned about weighting the odds in his favor than he was about the good of the Cup. He wasn't going to let what happened to Ted Hood in 1977 happen to him. It seemed consistent with one of the other complaints often heard about Dennis Conner, that he tries to monopolize all the available resources, whether he can use them or not, simply to deny them to others.

Under close examination, most such charges seem born of frustration.

Norris Hoyt, a veteran America's Cup commentator both in print and on the air, was involved in Long's 1980 campaign for a time. Five years later he was still bitter about what he described as Conner's efforts to corner the market on the best sailcloth available in 1980, the new and exotic Kevlar/Mylar material. "We couldn't buy any Kevlar or Mylar because Dennis had bought the entire product for the year," Hoyt asserted. "He didn't want anyone else to get it. That's Dennis. We finally got our first Kevlar/Mylar mainsail when Dennis' contract ran out in mid-August, when it was too late. We were eliminated the next day."

David Pedrick, who was Long's designer in 1980 and was part of the team designing Conner's boats for his 1987 challenge, says that's mostly sour grapes. The *Clipper* campaign, he said, didn't turn to Kevlar/Mylar sails until after the June trials. "By that time Dennis was so far along in developing the sails and he knew there was a shortage of material, so he did the smart thing and made sure he bought enough material to cover his own needs. I don't think Dennis can be blamed because other people were not as aggressive."

Conner did try to sign people up with exclusive contracts, Pedrick said. "I'm sure it was true with Sobstad. We tried to buy some Sobstad spinnakers for *Clipper* in the August trials, and Sobstad said fine, we'll deliver them to you in October. But Dennis is not the only one who makes these deals. He's the one who probably makes the most deals and has the most success and obtains the notoriety, but it's pretty commonplace when you're playing a high-stakes game to try to lock somebody up. He's smart enough to get there first...."

Hoyt also complained that Conner had sewed up the best sailmakers for the year by using Hood sails on one boat, North sails on the other, and naming John Marshall, who was about to become president of North, to his crew. He asked Ted Hood to come down to Newport to help trim the Hood sails, by testing them against North's, recutting them, and racing North's again until Hood's were clearly superior. Then when Hood went back to Marblehead, Marshall used his changes as a basis for recutting HIS sails. "Again, I think that's pretty seedy," Hoyt said. "It's opportunistic. You get both of the good sailmakers on your side, and you hold them for a bit."

Others, including Ted Hood, think that's all part of the game. "That's pretty common," Hood said. "I may have been upset at the time, but that's just one of the things that happen. Dennis is a tough customer and he makes good deals. He'll get stuff out of you and use it to his advantage like that."

Even Hoyt, who is seldom at a loss for an opinion, has trouble coming to grips with Conner. "He's too remote," he says. "He lives absolutely in his own world. I don't know that anyone ever knows what Dennis is thinking. He's an arch manipulator. I have a feeling Dennis can get people to do things they don't want to without knowing they're doing it until it's too late. You really don't know whether he's living a life of quiet desperation, or whether he's enjoying himself."

Conner had every reason to be enjoying himself in 1980. "My way of relaxing is dreaming about what can we do next, the winning of it, the competition. That's my fun," he said. "I enjoy putting the effort together....I don't know how to explain it. I don't seek the publicity. That isn't important."

What he didn't enjoy was verbal sparring with the undisputed champion, Ted Turner. Conner wrote that he liked Turner when they first got to know each other before the 1974 *Mariner* campaign. But the relationship deteriorated later. Turner once punched Conner, at the Congressional Cup in 1976, after Conner had "persistently harrassed him" with protests, according to Roger Vaughan.

Those who were waiting for the seemingly inevitable fireworks between those two during the 1980 campaign were disappointed. Turner was on his best behavior most of the summer, and Conner openly admitted he was ducking any off-the-water confrontations because he knew he would lose.

Hoyt recalls one exception:

"I remember when a Japanese firm was giving away binoculars to various people. Turner got an enormous pair, on a stand, for his back porch. Dennis, who got a smaller pair, said, 'Gee, Ted, I didn't know you were going to be that far behind.' And Ted said, 'Dennis, I feel much safer behind you than having you behind my back.' "

That was Conner's last attempt at public repartee.

Relations between the two could not have been improved by the incidents of July 28, when Turner was "dismissed" from the last two races of the July trials for what the NYYC's selection committee regarded as "a serious indiscretion."

Turner asked the committee for permisssion to have a 12th man aboard *Courageous* during her race against *Freedom* that day, as a "sail consultant." The committee granted his request. What Turner hadn't told them was that his consultant was none other than Ben Lexcen, the Australians' designer and tactician. When Conner recognized Lexcen aboard the other boat, he got on the radio right away to protest to the committee. After the race, Turner was summoned and given his punishent.

Turner brushed past reporters with an uncharacteristic "No comment" after the meeting, but other sources explained he and Lexcen were old buddies who had sailed together and that Turner had asked help him aboard to see if he could help him solve some problems with *Courageous* ' rig. Conner reportedly was concerned that this would give the Australian a close-up look at *Freedom* during a race.

In any case, it was clearly against the rules. In response to the Australians' use of an American as a key crewman in 1977, the NYYC had written a provision into the 1980 race conditions that prohibited anyone from the defending country sailing with any of the challengers, and vice-versa. Turner offered to resign, was talked out of it, and flew off to Atlanta for a few days to attend to business. He was back in time for the all-important August trials.

Public reaction to that incident proved how firmly Conner's deadly earnest approach to defending the Cup had become institutionalized.

Hardly anyone sympathized with Turner, or found it curious that the NYYC had decided "friendly competition between foreign countries" would be best served by barring that sort of assistance. It might have been okay in the 1930s, but now the Cup was serious business!

Earlier in the summer Turner had annoyed the selection committee by engaging in a brief and impromptu race with the Australian boat. The NYYC had warned the defenders against the practice in 1977, on the grounds that showing their hand to the enemy that early was a dangerous thing. But Turner could no more resist matching himself against another boat than he could walk away from an open microphone. It happened on July 4, America's Independence Day.

"It was very light air, and you really couldn't tell anything," one of *Australia*'s crew said later. "But I think he'd be the only one to come over like that. I think Ted Turner is a true sportsman. The America's Cup is really a race of nation against nation, but Turner is treating it like a sporting event."

'OUR TIME IS GONE'

After being excused from the last of the June trials, Turner hoped for a comeback in July. But a series of accidents put him further behind. On August 25, after an aborted race in a dying breeze, the selection committee paid its call at the *Courageous* dock. With that visit the last faint hope of the Rhett Butler of the America's Cup, and amateur sailors everywhere, was gone with the wind.

It was late August, always the cruelest time on the America's Cup course. The remaining amateurs fell away in rapid succession. The Swedes and the British were counted out the same day as Turner. Russell Long was excused four days later, leaving Conner to await the outcome of the final elimination races between the Australians and the French, who were finally beginning to win some races for Baron Bich after a decade-long quest. But in the final series they salvaged only one out of five against the Australians, who won the right to challenge.

Only one thing stood in the way of Conner's triumph — the Australians' new "bendy" mast. They had been working on it secretly for weeks, copying the idea from the British who had introduced it aboard *Lionheart*. And now it was ready. The mast had a flexible tip which could be bent back to increase sail area by about 100 square feet without exceeding the measurement rule's limits. The French had protested *Lionheart*'s version, but the international race committee gave it its blessings. The consensus was that it had a significant effect on boat speed.

Could it be that two years of grueling training, meticulous preparation and the expenditure of $2 million would be overturned by a last-minute technological trick?

Not this time. Conner beat the Aussies 4-1 in a series of close races that could have gone either way. The general view was that he prevailed by some unorthodox sailing (playing the wind shifts rather than covering) and because the Australians hadn't had time enough to test the sails they had recut to fit the bendy mast.

The Aussies' only victory, by a mere 28 seconds in the second race, was a seesaw thriller sailed in light air. Bill Ficker, the 1970 defender, described it as "the best 12-meter match race in the history of the event." It might also have been one of the most scandalous, however. By the time the boats crossed the finish line, dusk had fallen and Conner was flying a protest flag. It turned out he was protesting the challengers' failure to turn on their navigation lights!

In the long history of America's Cup protests, this was probably the pettiest. Wiser heads prevailed and it was withdrawn the next day, a move that Conner's sail trimmer, John Marshall, described as "one of the most sporting things I've seen in all my years of sailing." But, he acknowledged, "it was a hard decision made under heavy pressure from a lot of people."

It was gratifying to know that the NYYC was still willing, and able, to exert that kind of pressure. But the signal that some Americans, at least, were willing to go to almost any lengths to secure a victory had been raised and seen throughout the world.

In that context, Jim Hardy's comments at the Australians' final press conference were more portentous than anyone knew. Alan Bond had already announced he would be back in 1983, with a new skipper. Hardy, who had steered during his three previous challenges, would be replaced by Olympic medallist John Bertrand.

"I'm just a winemaker and a weekend sailor," said "Gentleman Jim" Hardy. "Our time is gone. Dennis Conner has just proved that."

12

THE PRESS AND THE SIEGE OF WEST 44TH STREET

While successfully defending the America's Cup off Newport during the summer of 1980, the New York Yacht Club faced a different kind of assault back home. Welfare clients were dropping garbage onto the roof of its clubhouse.

It wasn't a protest, it was just that the clubhouse happens to be sandwiched between taller tenement buildings on West 44th Street and, well, garbage disposal is never easy in Manhattan. When it started hitting the glass dome over the trophy room, the house committee ordered the glass painted over. When that wasn't enough, they erected a steel cover over the dome. That shut out the daylight, but at least members were spared the unpleasant sight of rotten tomatoes hitting their fortress.

In a symbolic sense, it was all very familiar. The NYYC has been under siege of one sort or another for most of its 142 years, and more often than not its response has been passive, defensive, and ineffective. Toward the end of its America's Cup reign, the cumulative strain was beginning to show. Cracks were appearing in its once-solid foundation of gentlemanly civility.

In 1983, these fissures were skillfully exploited by an antipodal battering ram named Alan Bond. Ironically, he had a major assist from the one outside agency that might have saved the day for the club, the Cup, and for sportsmanship — the press.

WHAT IF . . . ?

This gets ahead of the story a bit, but imagine for a moment a different scenario for the summer of '83....

Dennis Conner comes to Newport with a new boat, which he keeps shrouded under a red-white-and-blue canvas. There are rumors of wings on its keel, but there's no confirmation. The NYYC posts armed guards at the dock to prevent anyone from getting a peek. In the trials, Connor's boat moves faster than any 12-meter ever has, annihilating the other defense candidates.

The Australians, bluffed out of the only opportunity provided by the rules to gaze upon the keel, begin to piece together the shape of Conner's secret weapon an be illegal. They ask the NYYC to take the wraps off. It refuses. They seek a ruling from higher authorities. The New Yorkers block every move.

Meanwhile, the Aussies hear rumors that the keel was designed by a non-American citizen, which is strictly against the rules. They send emissaries and get a verbal confession from the architect. But the Americans get to him and he refuses to put it in writing.

Countered at every step by the wily old yacht club with its battery of lawyers and skillful public relations experts, unable to gain official or public support in this unfriendly country, the Aussies decide to abandon the legal battle and fight it out like men, on the water. The Australian crew sails magnificently, heroically, but the secret keel is too much. They bow, gracefully, after seven races. The NYYC holds the Cup once again....

Can you imagine the public outcry, the torrent of abuse that would be aimed at the NYYC? And can you, therefore, understand the bitterness that lingers within the upper echelons of that organization? Because that is precisely what DID happen in 1983, but with the roles reversed. It was the Australians who were cheered as they carried off the Cup, while the New Yorkers, who had merely tried to get an impartial ruling, were vilified by their own countrymen.

WHOSE CUP WAS IT, ANYWAY?

The roots of the antipathy that led to that miscarriage run deep in the American psyche, as well as back into the history of the NYYC itself, which, as we have seen, has not always been above reproach.

Start with the gut-level impulse to support the underdog, a national trait that is not peculiarly American, nor Australian, but is probably stronger in those countries than elsewhere. In part it's an atavistic response to the tyranny of the British Empire from which both countries rebelled — an upper-class imperialism whose visible counterpart is the NYYC.

Probably it was the club that was the underdog as the summer began, but that could be seen only in retrospect. Its 132-year dominance of a single event was a powerful counterargument. The Australians played their role to the hilt through the press, appealing early and often to the American sense of fair play. Look, they said, we don't hold the NYYC against you because we know they don't represent average Americans, who are decent, honest, ordinary folks like ourselves.

By the end of the summer, bumper-stickers had appeared in Newport that read: "I love New York — it's the club I hate."

The Australians also exploited the old, old conflict of interest between the club's role as impartial steward and highly partisan defender of its trophy. They remembered the charges of "home-town justice" levelled by Sir Frank Packer in 1970, when club members measured the boats and ruled on protests and there was no appeal. Since then, of course, the New Yorkers had turned those roles over to impartial committees, but the memory lingered. And the basic conflict of interest was still there.

Perhaps all of that could have been overcome if the club had explained itself, and the press had listened. But that kind of dialogue was not within the nature of either group. Their differences in goals and perceptions made mutual suspicion inevitable. One of those differences was over the question of who owned the Cup, and how accountable its stewards should be.

The NYYC is an intensely, deliberately, even militantly private association, which exists to foster yachting, the chief pleasure of its members, and is otherwise utterly without redeeming social purpose. It is peopled by individuals of wealth, privilege and power. In its private and public dealings, it tries to maintain standards of gentlemanly conduct which have been so eroded elsewhere as to appear pompous and affected by comparison.

The American sense of fair play, embodied in the press, generally tolerates such organizations, but only if they refrain from operating in the public arena. The New Yorkers did not choose a public role; indeed they have often shunned it. But their stewardship of the Cup thrust increasing notoriety upon them as the contests for the prize grew more intense.

There was a certain ambiguity in the original deed of gift as to whether the Cup was the private property of the club that held it, or a truly national symbol of yachting supremacy. The club saw it as its own, the public as the nation's. Most of the attacks against the keepers of the Cup have stemmed from that basic identity crisis. And the club's chief antagonist in this seldom-stated and never-resolved conflict was the press.

The mere suspicion that the club might be tinkering with part of our national sporting heritage was enough to prompt outraged editorials whenever it arose. And as we have seen, it arose often, thanks in part to the club's possessiveness about the Cup, its obsessively private deliberations, and its Victorian code of dignified silence in the face of criticism. All of this stirred dark suspicions among journalists, trained as they are to equate secrecy with skullduggery. During the early years of the club's reign, the suspicions were justified — at least as viewed from the more enlightened perspective of a later time. Over the course of more than a century, the club amassed a small litany of sins, the repeated recitation of which has obscured its far more numerous acts of sportsmanship.

But often the suspicions were entirely unjustified, from any perspective. Nevertheless, once voiced, they found their way onto the same litany, perpetuated from one Cup challenge to the next by a succession of journalists who limited their research to the yellowing clip files of their predecessors. Many of these baseless charges originated with challengers, such as Lord Dunraven and Alan Bond. But one of the most outrageous and enduring was invented by a would-be defender.

Some of the story of Thomas W. Lawson's 1901 assault on the NYYC has been told in an earlier chapter. He was the Boston stock broker and speculator whose private and public feuds with club members inspired him to build a $200,000 yacht, then insist upon the right to enter her in the trials to pick a Cup defender even though he refused to join the club or give any of its members even titular authority over his boat. After all efforts at compromise failed, exasperated club representatives rightly concluded that Lawson's campaign was merely an elaborate scheme to embarrass them, and broke off the correspondence.

But that was only half of Lawson's revenge. The other half was a remarkable volume titled "The Lawson History of the America's Cup," published the following year in a limited edition (3,000 copies) paid for entirely by Lawson himself. It combines a detailed and objective history of the Cup's first 50 years, written by Winfield Thompson, a yachting historian commissioned by Lawson, with what must rank as the most scurrilous attack on the NYYC ever printed.

Thompson's part of the book is an invaluable resource for any student of Cup history. Lawson's, which begins with a chapter headed "Economic Conditions Produce a Vicious Class in American Yachting: 1870-1901," is pure venom. It may have been malice aforethought that led him to link the two, thus assuring that his blusterings would survive long after his campaign was forgotten.

Lawson set forth an elaborate theory of American social structure, tracing five distinct classes, all more-or-less admirable. But then: "In the early '70s the worst elements, — the weaknesses, the defects, the poison, — of these five classes generated a sixth class, as in Nature the mixing and stirring of certain elements, each in itself useful in its sphere, produces an insidious, noxious poison which, as it generates, spreads until it strangles and kills not only the foreign substances with which it comes in contact, but also the ingredients that generated it."

Warming to his task, he began to zero in on his target:

"In only one phase of life did this class find itself balked and powerless — sports. Natural cowards, queer in body and perverted in mind because of a vicious or low order of ancestry and habit, they could not take active part in those things which have for their foundation courage, manliness and well-proportioned bodies, and their wealth could not buy, their cunning steal nor their power seize these things, which Nature alone can give.... If they could not take active part in sport, if they could not appreciate its true merits, they would pretend to and they would, by taking possession of those associations which controlled sports, make it well-nigh impossible to distinguish between the pretence and reality."

It came as no surprise when Lawson eventually disclosed that the "most prominent" such association was none other than the NYYC.

But what is surprising was the vigorous support for Lawson and his spurious campaign expressed by editorial writers and columnists of the day. Lawson's book includes page after page of reprinted clippings, lauding him and damning the club. No doubt Lawson selected them carefully, but the sheer volume attests to the depth and breadth of anti-NYYC feeling among the press. Even "Mr. Dooley," the fictional social commentator invented by Peter Finley Dunne, had a comment:

> *No more gallant sailor rides th' waves thin hearty Jack Larsen iv th' Amalgamated Copper Yacht Club. 'What ho?' says he, 'If we're goin' to have a race,' he says, 'shiver me timbers if I don't look up th' law,' he says. So he becomes a yachtsman. 'But,' says th' Noo York la-ads, thim that has th' Cup on their mantel-piece, 'Ye can race on'y on two conditions.' 'What ar-re?' says Larsen. 'Th' first is that ye become a mimber iv our club.' 'With pleasure,' says he. 'Ye can't,' says they. 'An' havin' complied with this first condition, ye must give us ye'er boat,' says they. 'We don't want it,' they says.... 'Yachtin' is a gintlemans' spoort,' (Larsen) says, 'an' in dalin' with gintlemen,' he says, 'ye can't be too careful,' he says.*

It mattered not at all that the NYYC had not refused membership to Lawson, nor demanded that he give them his boat, nor refused it. (It wasn't offered.) The New Yorkers were "gintlemen," after all, and therefore fair game.

The more sober-sided press commentaries asserted that the Cup was a national emblem and its defense should be open to all, a reasonable if debatable position. But nearly all of them distorted the yacht club's stance and embraced Lawson's flagrant misrepresentations — doubtless because he made sure the press heard his side, whereas the club maintained its usual silence.

NATURAL ENEMIES

Aside from the question of who really owned the Cup, the press and the yacht club always were natural enemies. Someone once defined the role of the press as comforting the afflicted and afflicting the comfortable, and for all their protestations of detachment, hardly a journalist breathes who doesn't yearn to do both when the opportunity presents itself. And there are few more conspicuously comfortable targets than the NYYC.

A less lofty explanation of the same impulse simply might be envy of those with great wealth by those without, a category that includes most journalists — and most of their readers. Skewering yacht-clubbers is not only easy and satisfying, it guarantees an approving readership in most precincts. Sometimes the temptation is irresistible, even when the facts are unknown or contrary to the writer's biases, or his national allegiance. An often-quoted example is an article by a British writer after the postponement of the fifth and deciding race in 1920, between *Shamrock IV* and *Resolute*, because of high winds:

"The Yankees," he wrote, "have the frankness to ask the sporting world to be fooled by the calling off of the race because their cockleshell was unable to stand up against a summer squall in a sheltered bay, while the sturdy British challenger that had stoutly weathered Atlantic storms was not allowed to sail the course."

In fact, the course was laid out on the open sea, the race committee had asked both skippers if they wished to abandon the race, and it was the challenger who first said yes. No member of the press was anywhere near the course at the time; the Navy destroyer carrying the press corps had turned back to New York.

A more recent example occurred in 1974, when some Australian newspapers went so far as to hint that a near-collision on Rhode Island Sound between their challenger, *Southern Cross,* and a U.S. Navy destroyer might have been an unsuccessful American plot to sink the competition. That sort of suspicion feeds on itself, of course, especially when the accused maintains an aloof silence.

Then there's the additional problem that yacht racing is not meant to be a spectator sport — certainly not a mass-spectator sport. America's Cup races are held far from shore, and even if you can afford a spectator boat you're still too far away to tell what's going on. The races are long (roughly three to five hours, depending on the wind) and often tedious affairs. More often than not they are mere processions in which the winner gets an early lead and keeps it. In close races, the boats are so widely separated most of the time that even their crews don't know who's ahead. Furthermore, the whole exercise is hedged about by arcane rules that seem designed to discourage the uninitiated. Even the participants find them confusing at times, sparking disputes no one west of Oyster Bay could be expected to fathom.

Aside from boating magazines, few publications can justify the expense of a full-time yachting writer. And yet, every three or four years there's another America's Cup to be covered. The result is an ad-hoc press corps ("baseball writers in sneakers," Damon Runyan called them in the 1930s), who can't tell a jib from a jibe, never mind understand the countless nuances on which races and protests are won or lost. Some of them, like Runyan — who declared America's Cup racing "as exciting as watching grass grow" — react to these mysteries with ridicule and scorn. Others rely on press releases, media events and what their confreres have written. Of the two, they may be the more dangerous.

Even for yachting journalists, it's a damnably difficult assignment, and the press generally does not perform it well. After all, like Ted Turner, it has better things to do. But the volume of misinformation and misperceptions, along with the smart-aleck sneering, that gets into print or out over the airwaves every America's Cup summer is staggering. And that just feeds the club's natural antipathy toward the media, which causes it to close the portcullis even more firmly, which deepens the mystery ... and so on, in a vicious circle that results in mutual paranoia.

There was a time, early in the modern era, when the America's Cup was covered primarily by a small group of yachting writers who knew what they were talking about. Commodore Mosbacher, who knew all the great ones, mentions Bill Taylor, Ev Morris and Dave Philips among others. Then he noted that Philips, yachting writer for the Providence Journal-Bulletin, is one of the few survivors from that era.

"They were open-minded enough to try to learn from their elders who knew the game. Now it's being covered by 200 fellas who've never seen a sailboat close to, and they're comparing this with baseball or football. But it isn't baseball or football. The average salary of the guys on the boat is not $330,000 a year. If you're getting that kind of salary, you damn well owe it to whoever's paying it to make yourself available. That's a little different from the guy who's taking a leave from work, giving up his salary, laying out a lot of money to participate in a sport that he loves."

In part, Mosbacher was restating the old question: Who's Cup was it? The club had always recognized a national interest in its trophy, but it was club property, after all. The press, and by extension the public, were welcome to attend the matches and would be treated with civility as long as they behaved like ladies and gentlemen. But the club and its defenders were under no obligations beyond that.

Furthermore, Mosbacher said he and other defending skippers were not taught to expect "a lot of rude questions," especially when they were tired, aching, and they'd been licked. "I don't think we have always understood that we have to make ourselves available. And particularly when the questions show that there's no real understanding whatsoever of what went wrong or what went right. Even if the mast went over the side half of (the reporters) probably wouldn't see it."

Mosbacher found dealing with the press so burdensome when he was defending skipper that he appointed another syndicate member to be his spokesman.

Since then the demand for America's Cup news, like almost everything else about the event, has skyrocketed. Len Panaggio, in charge of the care and feeding of the America's Cup press corps in Newport since the 1958 race, recalls that a couple of reporters approached him that year and asked if he knew of a place they could set up their typewriters. He found them a hotel room, and that was that. In 1983, he issued more than 1,300 press credentials and the National Guard Armory on Thames Street was barely large enough to hold everyone during the post-race press conferences.

If you had removed all the veteran yachting writers from that assemblage, it still would have been a large crowd. The demand for news had far outstripped the supply of knowledgeable reporters just as they were needed most, when the 132-year siege of the NYYC entered its final phase. As the Keelgate drama began to unfold, the truth was often obscured in a blizzard of self-serving press releases, most of them issued by the Australians, who were only too willing to explain their side.

Unfortunately, by then the press and the NYYC were barely on speaking terms. Bus Mosbacher, a key member of the club's America's Cup Committee, revealed that only three journalists approached him for comment all summer. On the other hand, the committee made no real effort to publicize its side of the Keelgate story until it was far too late.

That failure to communicate was one of the great tragedies of the summer. Had they talked, both sides might have discovered they had more in common than either knew. Each sincerely believed it was upholding the best traditions of the America's Cup — honest inquiry, fair play, sportsmanship and that elusive spirit of friendly competition between foreign countries.

Because of the ancient antagonisms, a lack of preparedness and wholesale errors on both sides — all skillfully exploited by the Australians — that didn't happen. Instead, each side spent part of the summer trying to outwit the other, while Australia walked away with America's Cup.

PART THREE

The Fall

1983

In 1983, for the third time in the NYYC's 132-year reign, challengers outnumbered defenders in the trials. It had happened in 1977 and 1980, but then the margin was only four-to-three. This time the Americans again fielded three boats, but the foreigners numbered seven. Never was the Cup more vulnerable.

As the trials began, the beleaguered NYYC seemed ready, however. It had the best defense money could buy and a 132-year winning tradition. But no one, least of all the NYYC, was prepared for the audacity of the Australians' secret keel.

When it refused to go away, the New Yorkers were finally drawn into the kind of gutter fighting they had shunned for 132 years — and bungled it so badly they emerged looking like the villains the Aussies had always claimed they were. Knowing their cause was just, but unable to convince anyone else, they abandoned their legal challenge and chose to fight it out on the water, where they lost the Holy Grail in one final, glorious joust.

In the bitter aftermath, it was clear that more than a trophy had been lost.

13
BLOOD ON THE WATER

Of the ten challenges submitted to the NYYC after the 1980 race, seven materialized. Australia sent three and one each came from Britain, France, Canada and Italy.

What inspired this record turnout? By the score sheet alone, the quest for the Cup was surely the most quixotic of sporting ventures. In 24 matches, the Americans had won 78 races and lost only nine. No challenger had ever won more than two. An America's Cup challenge, as Samuel Johnson said of second marriages, was a triumph of optimism over experience.

But some very real reasons for hope existed after the 1980 match, in which the Australians won one race, almost won another and stayed in contention until the end. Theirs had been a relatively lackluster, underfunded challenge matched against the most determined defense ever mounted. The myth of American invincibility was crumbling.

Furthermore, the foreigners were closing the design gap. If there was blood on the water in 1983, it was partly because American sailing technology had been hemorrhaging for years.

That hadn't been a serious problem in the past. Challengers had always been able to copy American boats after they were built — by buying them outright, studying their photographs, or hiring designers who had worked on them. But by the time the copies were ready to race, the defenders had built a new generation. For 132 years, America managed to stay that one step ahead. Even the one known case of outright theft, when *Courageous'* plans were stolen from Minneford's Shipyard while she was being built in 1974, came too late to affect the '74 races. But when the purloined lines appeared in an Australian publication, everyone who cared to had a chance to copy the boat that ultimately was chosen to defend again in '77.

Meanwhile, American yacht design had become fixated on the basic Sparkman & Stephens line, of which *Courageous* was the prime exemplar. Robert N. Bavier Jr., former Cup skipper and publisher of *Yachting* magazine, was reflecting the experts' consensus when he wrote in 1979: "The International Rule has been explored so fully that the chance of a breakthrough is remote, if not nonexistent." He was dead wrong about that, but he was making the right point: American designers had reached a plateau, and the challengers were catching up.

But the biggest hemorrhage was through the growing internationalization of marine suppliers. North Sails had lofts in Sydney and Melbourne, for example, as well as in San Diego. In fact, John Bertrand was manager of North's Melbourne loft when he was named *Australia II*'s helmsman. North's sail technology was developed in the United States, but its sails were available everywhere.

It became impossible to police, so the NYYC simply threw in the towel by issuing a new interpretation of the deed of gift shortly after the 1980 series. Henceforth, challengers were no longer limited to equipment and facilities from their own countries. They still had to design and build their boats in their homelands — a key provision in the later controversy over the Australians' keel — but now they could shop for materials anywhere, including the United States, which turned out the world's best sailcloth.

Thus the club formally renounced the most constant ingredient in its winning streak — extending from 1851, when *America* won the Cup with state-of-the-art sails of Egyptian cotton, to 1980, when *Freedom* defended with state-of-the-art Mylar/Kevlar sails. From then on, challengers didn't have to wait for the next match to buy or copy America's latest technology, they could use it right away. A 132-year gap had closed.

There were other inducements in 1983. Despite rising costs, challenges had become almost irresistible from a publicity point of view. Every syndicate had at least some backing from national and international corporations that wanted to associate their names or products with a high-profile event.

The America's Cup profile had never been higher, thanks to the likes of Sir Frank Packer, Alan Bond and Ted Turner, who had drawn non-sailing journalists to Newport by the sheer force of their personalities. The press corps for the 1937 race numbered 192. In 1962, the year the Aussies came, 700 journalists showed up. In 1983, there were nearly twice that number. The event was on an upward, self-generating spiral, fueled by dollars and that even more precious currency, media exposure.

SEVEN CHALLENGERS

And so they came to duel in the wind, seven challengers from five countries. They were a diverse group, to say the least.

The Italians, first-time challengers from the Costa Smeralda Yacht Club, were backed by 18 blue-chip corporations and led by the Aga Khan. Their effort combined Old World grace with a surprising level of performance, considering their total lack of experience.

The French syndicate was headed by a soft-porn film producer ("Emmanuelle") named Yves Rousset-Rouard. It was heir to Bich's boat, *France 3,* but to none of the Baron's wealth or panache. It arrived in Newport *sans* Bich, *sans* trial horse, *sans* cash, and *sans* any real hope of winning.

The British mounted their largest invasion of Newport since the unpleasantness of 1776. It was headed by a 38-year-old prep school dropout and multi-millionaire businessman named Peter de Savary, a man with a fondness for expensive champagne, huge Havana cigars, headlines, fast cars, fast boats, his own opinions and winning — not necessarily in that order. At least one other syndicate had a faster boat, but no one left a larger wake.

The Canadians left one of the smallest. Their entry, the first since 1881, was launched by a lawyer named Marvin McDill and a group of businessmen from inland Calgary. When the NYYC received their challenge on April Fool's Day, 1981, it was a bit skeptical. Not only did the sponsors lack a yacht, a crew and even a yacht club, they lacked an ocean. Eventually they remedied all those problems, but they kept running out of money and breaking their boat.

So did one of the three Australian entries, the Advance syndicate. It had the slowest boat, which led to some jokes. At least one writer called her the Down Underdog. Someone else made an appointment for her at the local vet's. In July, heartened somewhat by her first victory in 20 tries, her crew undertook to paint the face of a dog on her bow, adding one feature at a time after each subsequent win. They never got much further than the whiskers.

Alan Bond, challenging through the Royal Perth Yacht Club, originally planned a two-boat campaign, both designed by Ben Lexcen. But when that became cumbersome, he sold plans for the conventional one, *Challenge 12*, to a syndicate in Melbourne. Typically, he tied enough strings to the deal so he could use her as a trial horse and a fallback in case his unconventional boat, *Australia II*, didn't work out. After the Melbourne group ran into some initial financial problems, Bond bailed them out. Then the syndicate was taken over by Richard Pratt, a wealthy box manufacturer.

There were times during the early going when people shook their heads over Bond's decision to turn a stablemate into a competitor. When the two boats practiced against each other in Australia they were said to be very even. As the trials began in Newport, they were rated almost equal. But Bond and Lexcen, who stayed with Bond's syndicate after the *Challenge 12* spinoff, knew better. They knew *Australia II* had wings.

And so the sharks had gathered. As if that weren't peril enough, the Americans meanwhile were engaging in some further bloodletting of their own.

14
THE DEFENSE: WITH FRIENDS LIKE THESE...

As always, in 1983 the Americans put up a bold front. Both syndicates strove to maintain a public image of deliberate, calculated, controlled movement toward another successful defense, the 25th. But a closeup look behind the scenes, denied the press at the time, reveals a very different picture.

The Freedom syndicate was a study in the arrogance of power, and the ruthlessness of the corporate campaign under stress. The Defender/Courageous camp generated its own stress. It showed what can happen when men with enormous egos try to adapt to the impersonal demands of the corporate campaign, and fail. Both camps showed the strains that result when a yacht race becomes more important than the racers.

As the 1983 campaign lurched toward open warfare, there were casualties on all sides — abstractions mostly, and therefore expendable. Things like sportsmanship, honor, truth, loyalty within the ranks, and that spirit of friendly competition that inspired the contest in the first place.

Loyalty was the first to fall.

UNCIVIL WARS

The Americans sent forth three boats, sponsored by two syndicates: Dennis Conner's Freedom syndicate and the Defender/Courageous group, formed by Tom Blackaller and Gary Jobson after the 1980 race. The NYYC would spend the summer putting them through their paces before selecting one to defend the Cup.

Right from the start there was a certain pursed-lip grimness about the defense campaigns. Some of the reasons were obvious, but what wasn't generally known at the time was that each group was also undergoing internal upheavals — civil war might be a better description in the Defender/Courageous camp — which drained energies and resources that might better have been spent against the challenger.

The inherent strains were daunting enough. For one thing, the endless campaign, developed by Conner but now followed by everyone, was a grind. Sailors who wanted nothing more than to get behind the helm of a fast boat found themselves bogged down in a two-year fund-raising and organizational process — an exhausting round of speech-making, arm-twisting, flow charts and transcontinental travel. And no matter how many hours they worked or how many calls they made, there was never enough time or money.

And 1983 brought its own special worries and distractions. The defenders were badly outnumbered this time, seven to three; their designers had failed to come up with a single boat significantly faster than the 1980 standard-bearer, *Freedom* (see next chapter), and two of the skippers, Dennis Conner and Tom Blackaller, were old and bitter rivals whose public bickering contributed to the general acrimony. When the trials got underway, the Australians' secret keel caused fear and loathing along the waterfront; for the first time in 132 years there was a growing conviction that whoever won the right to defend would lose the Cup — while the whole world watched. If all this weren't bad enough, it was clear by midsummer that many Americans were rooting for the enemy.

Onto this somber stage sailed Tom Blackaller, skipper of *Defender*, the Defender/Courageous syndicate's new boat. Under the circumstances what he had to say as the summer began was unusual enough to make headlines:

"We hope we'll be having a lot of fun doing this."

Some people thought he was whistling in the dark, trying to summon up the carefree spirit that belonged to chapters in Cup history forever closed. If so, it didn't work. Blackaller was destined to have less fun than anyone that summer, with the possible exception of the man who ultimately lost the Cup.

But there was more to it than that. It was a subtle bit of Conner-baiting, the opening salvo in the resumption of a feud Blackaller and

Conner had begun a decade earlier when both Californians were struggling to reach the top of the heap in Star class racing. Conner took himself too seriously, Blackaller said, and was spoiling the sport.

They were studies in contrasts. Tom Blackaller was the 43-year-old divorced sailmaker from San Francisco with the movie-star looks, a lion's mane of white hair that turned heads in Newport even when the turning heads had no idea who he was. He was an impatient extrovert whose shoot-from-the-hip verbal style, hearty laughter and less-than-fanatic training program reminded some of Ted Turner, the R-rated 1977 defender. If you were the casting director for a movie about the America's Cup, you'd want Blackaller for the leading role, Conner for a supporting part.

Conner was a demon behind the helm, the sailor's sailor, the man to beat. But off the water he was a somewhat paunchy 40-year-old drapery manufacturer and family man from San Diego, who seemed vaguely uncomfortable in the spotlight. He was the consummate organization man, backed to the hilt by a gilt-edged syndicate. Conner worshipped at the altars of dedication and training rather than at the dias of talent — though he possessed plenty of that. He placed great stress on the importance of maintaining self-confidence, but often seemed distracted and ill at ease, as if awed by the responsibility he bore as defending champion.

Their public bickering highlighted their differences:

"We don't go at it as doggedly as they (the Freedom group) do," Blackaller said in June. "We think in order for a campaign to be successful, you have to take the dogmatism, the militaristic things out of it.... You don't have to work seven days a week, 24 hours a day for 18 months. He's led everybody to believe that's what you have to do."

It was a theme Blackaller would hammer away at whenever he spotted an open microphone or poised pad and pencil. His secondary theme was that Conner could be psyched out, rattled to the point of making mistakes, and he, Blackaller, was just the guy to do it. Conner seldom replied, but when he did he generally stood on his record:

BLACKALLER: "Dennis is afraid of entering a contest where there is a chance of losing. He is afraid of sport. How can you be interested in sport if the idea of losing sends you into two years of boring, stupid, preparation? His fear has completely warped the nature of the America's Cup."

CONNER: "I'm pretty tough to psych out. I didn't win all those trophies in my office with rhetoric."

BLACKALLER: "He approaches competition as the Pentagon would approach designing a weapons system. You know, no stone unturned, billions of dollars thrown at it, years of testing and everyone going around saying 'Yes sir' and 'No sir.' That's abhorrent to me."

CONNER: "The answer to the scathing personal criticism that Tom keeps coming up with is that he and I have agreed to disagree on the concept of how to produce the best defense. It's a compliment that everyone is doing it our way; even Tom, the man who hates to practice, is following in our wake."

Blackaller had other complaints, particularly about Conner's refusal to race both of his boats, *Freedom* and *Liberty*, in the trials. It was the 1980 argument all over again, with Blackaller replacing Turner for the prosecution, Conner again making his own defense. Only this time he had an even better argument, one that Conner tended to find conclusive regardless of the topic: It worked, didn't it? Once again he waited until the last minute to choose one boat and relegate the other to trial horse status. He chose *Liberty*.

Blackaller was not alone in thinking that withholding *Freedom* — still a highly competitive boat — weakened the whole defense. But Conner was unmoved. He was not a team player, unless it was *his* team. He believed in competition, not cooperation. He never gave an opponent an even break if he could help it and left nothing to chance. He ran his campaign by the book — the book he wrote with John Rousmaniere in 1978 called "No Excuse to Lose." In it he wrote, "Once you get to the point where you honestly feel inside that you have done everything within your power to win and have given yourself no excuse to lose, you're really going to be hard to beat."

He proved unbeatable in 1980, so the Maritime College at Fort Schuyler Foundation, which backed his 1980 campaign and held onto *Freedom* when it was over, was delighted when he signed on again for 1983. This was the foundation's fourth campaign, the first having been in 1974 with *Mariner*, a losing campaign despite a portentous change at the helm, Conner replacing Turner. In 1977 its *Enterprise*, steered by Lowell North, was beaten by Turner's *Courageous*. Then it came back in 1980 with Conner and *Freedom* and won it all. Not surprisingly, when the 1983 Freedom Campaign was launched Conner got more-or-less whatever he wanted, including what amounted to a no-cut contract and an open checkbook for expenses.

Those who thought Conner had gone all-out in preparing his 1980 defense marvelled at the 1983 version of the endless campaign. This time he started three years in advance, not two. He spent $4 million, not $2 million. He commissioned two new boats, not one. And when those two weren't satisfactory, he calmly ordered a third. He tested an incredible 180 sails from North and Sobstad and paid the development costs for new and more exotic Kevlar/Mylar laminates — a reported $70,000 for one experimental mainsail alone.

The Freedom syndicate's internal battles developed more or less directly out of its leader's scorched-earth approach to campaign-building: First you grab every resource in sight, or tie it down with an exclusive contract to keep it out of the hands of your competitors. Then you double-team every problem, explore every avenue, throw enough money around, maintain an autocratic control to keep the whole thing from getting out of hand, and eventually the cream will rise to the top. Except that the cream nearly curdled in 1982 when a bitter feud erupted between Conner's competing designers.

That battle, described in the following chapter, resulted in a parting of the ways — probably permanent — between two America's Cup giants: Sparkman & Stephens and Dennis Conner, arguably the best 12-meter designers and the best 12-meter skipper in the world. It had been a bloody but mainly private fight, and if the resolution was ruthless, it was also quick and relatively clean. As 1983 began, Conner's internal problems appeared to be largely behind him.

Those of the Defender/Courageous camp, however, were just beginning.

TWO BOATS, SORT OF

Their campaign was conceived by Blackaller and Jobson toward the end of the 1980 Cup trials, in which they both sailed as tacticians aboard losing boats, Blackaller on Russell Long's *Clipper*, Jobson on Ted Turner's *Courageous*. Later they joined forces with David Vietor of Horizon Sails, who had crewed with Long in 1980, and Leonard Greene, an aerodynamics engineer and owner of a company called Safe Flight Instruments, who had bought *Courageous* from Turner with an eye toward a 1983 campaign, with Vietor at the helm. The deal — much like Turner's in 1977 — was to lease *Courageous* to the fledgling syndicate (which couldn't afford to buy her), with the understanding that she would be entered in the trials as a contender, not serve as a mere trial horse for the syndicate's new boat. Vietor, it was understood, would be at her helm.

Blackaller and Jobson were predisposed to a two-boat campaign anyway, and weren't terribly worried about being sidelined by their stablemate; *Courageous* was nearly 10 years old, after all, an antique by Cup standards. Even if she did well in the trials, they believed, the club's America's Cup Committee (which also functioned as the selection committee) would never choose her to defend the Cup. Meanwhile, she'd be available to tune the new boat, *Defender,* already commissioned from designer David Pedrick. So everything seemed to be falling into place. The combined syndicate started building an organization that included several Turner alumni, and set about lining up backers to pay for a $4-million campaign, roughly what the Freedom/Liberty syndicate said it would be spending.

And it might have worked — if *Defender* had been a faster boat, if Vietor had been replaced earlier, if the syndicate had raised more money, if Blackaller had controlled his temper, if Blackaller and Vietor's replacement, John Kolius, hadn't come from such very different sailing schools, if the egos involved had been of normal dimensions, if they could have agreed on who was in charge, if....

Long before the trials, the buoyant optimism evident at the start of the campaign sank without a trace in a sea of recriminations.

Money was the first problem: there wasn't enough. Blackaller later acknowledged he had underestimated the syndicate's needs until it was almost too late; when *Defender* was launched in June, 1982, it was $500,000 in debt. The original budget provided for building a second contender if the first didn't fly, but that proved a pipe dream: *Defender* would be their one and only chance at a new boat.

Making a virtue of their poverty, they called *Defender* "the people's boat" and described themselves as "the sailors" as opposed to "the coupon-clippers" in Conner's camp — even though much of their backing came from Texas oil men. Meanwhile, Blackaller said he tried to convince himself he could win even with a slow boat if he had to. As it turned out, he would have to, and he couldn't.

Blackaller's early complacency over the budget and the boat were two of the syndicate's major errors, he said in an article he wrote for Sports Illustrated (March 12, 1984). A third was not buying *Courageous* outright; had they done so, Vietor would not have remained at the helm through 1982. In his opinion, Blackaller wrote,

Vietor "wasn't able to realize *Courageous'* full potential, and that masked, for much too long, the fact that *Courageous* was a lot faster than she looked. That, in turn, masked the fact that *Defender* was slower than we thought she was."

When Vietor finally relinquished *Courageous'* helm in December, during the syndicate's winter training in California, it was turned over to John Kolius, a 31-year-old Texan with no 12-meter experience but impressive racing credentials in other classes, including two J-24 world championships. It took Kolius a few months to learn how to handle the old boat, but when he did she pulled even with the new one, then passed her. Blackaller and Jobson began to get nervous.

Kolius, like Conner in 1974, was the new kid on the block who soon had everyone talking. Before the summer was over, it had become a journalistic ritual to follow his name with the phrase, "the rising star of the America's Cup." A lot of that had to do with his sailing ability, of course. But part of it was his coolness under pressure, his just-one-of-the-boys style (you wouldn't find Conner or Blackaller carrying sails off the boat after a race), his sense of perspective ("I think you can sail against someone and still be friends — you don't have to be a jerk about it."), and even that rarest of commodities on a 12-meter dock, a touch of modesty. Asked why he had been picked to steer *Courageous,* he said it was because Blackaller wanted someone low-key whom he could get along with — which was probably partly true.

SHOUTING MATCHES

Blackaller wasn't getting along at all well with his syndicate management just then. By January of '83, he and the syndicate chairman, Chuck Kirsch — whom he and Jobson had brought in — were having frequent shouting matches. The subjects ranged from fund-raising, which was lagging, to Blackaller's girlfriend, of whom Kirsch disapproved, to who was in charge — which never was completely resolved. Blackaller said all this took a heavy toll on his psyche, interferring with his sailing ability.

Gary Jobson explained that when he and Blackaller realized they'd need some business expertise, they called Martin "Max" O'Meara, veteran of four previous Cup campaigns and an insurance executive from Hartford with a no-nonsense, businesslike manner. He joined as operations manager in September, 1981.

"Max O'Meara made the whole thing happen," Jobson said. "Without him there wouldn't have been a Defender/Courageous syndicate. His thinking was we really needed a chairman, and right around that time Kirsch had come to me, then to Blackaller, saying he'd really like to help. So Tom got Kirsch and O'Meara together." O'Meara apparently liked what he saw and urged the two sailors, who didn't know Kirsch, to bring him aboard. They agreed, Jobson said, despite advice against the move from a number of sources:

"We didn't listen to anybody. We wanted to get going. In the enthusiasm to make it all happen, you know, you kind of agree to things quickly. Here's O'Meara really being a tremendous help, saying I need Kirsch as kind of our figurehead, and everybody quickly agreeing to it.... It was probably good to have Chuck there. It's just that he and Tom didn't get along later."

That's an understatement.

Charles "Chuck" Kirsch, then 56, is a wealthy businessman from Michigan with a respectable racing record aboard his yacht *Scaramouche* and a history of effective volunteer service to the sport, as vice president of the United States Yacht Racing Union and deputy chairman of the Offshore Racing Council. His drapery hardware and window covering company was sold about the same time Blackaller and Jobson were gearing up for their run at the Cup.

Kirsch, who says he is not the sort of guy who enjoys name-calling contests, says he still likes and respects Jobson and Blackaller, though he knows the sentiment isn't reciprocated. He is no wimp — you don't get to be a chief executive or a top-ranking yachtsman by avoiding fights — but he's no shouter, either. Pitting him against Blackaller was a little like matching a tall Michigan pine against a buzz saw.

"Tom can get very — vociferous," Jobson said, pausing to find the right word. "He wasn't diplomatic in the early going. When Tom would start yelling, that would upset Kirsch. So Kirsch's reaction was to get back at him quietly in the back rooms. Or, every now and then - - several times this happened — Kirsch had in his pocket a letter of resignation from Blackaller. That was at O'Meara's insistence; in case the skipper of either boat did something really bad or they needed to get his resignation, he had it. And Kirsch would rattle this letter at Blackaller every now and then. It was very unsettling. 'If you're not nice to me, I'm going to pull out your letter of resignation.' You know, it's kind of ridiculous, isn't it?"

Blackaller confirmed Jobson's recollection about the letter, but Kirsch denied it. "I never even saw it," Kirsch said. (Jobson later said he never saw it, either. He said all he knew about it was what Black-aller told him.) Kirsch said he threatened to use it just once, and then only obliquely: "What I said was, 'Tom, you and I had better get to-gether on what we're doing, or one or the other of us isn't going to be here.' "

That turned out to be an idle threat; they didn't get together, and neither one left.

"We had a big shit fight in March of '83," Jobson said. "We had this prospectus that Tom and I had put together, and Kirsch had gone and gotten the thing reprinted without telling us, and changed it around in a way that eliminated both Blackaller's and my names." He and Blackaller said this precipitated a big fight over who actually controlled the syndicate — the founders, or the guy they had brought in as chairman.

Kirsch said he barely remembers the incident. "Their names weren't left off," he said. "It was a matter of who was taking responsibility for what. They wanted to be vice presidents, if you want to call it that. And we felt there was a different structure that would be required to work, and I can't even remember what it was now. As I recall, we changed it to make them feel better about it, and still make it work. It (the prospectus) was never a major issue, it was resolved, and it never came up again."

In any event, another issue, one both sides see as central, did keep coming up: Were the two boats actually getting equal treatment, as the syndicate's promotional material claimed? And if so, should they have been?

According to Jobson, Kirsch and Kolius had formed an alliance as early as April, and were doing their best to stab Blackaller in the back. Kirsch maintains the syndicate management tried to give the two boats and crews an equal opportunity, but in fact *Defender* ended up getting more attention because she needed more. Blackaller complains that this even-handed policy was "a fatal error" because the NYYC's selection committee would never have picked an old boat to defend the Cup.

When asked about Jobson's backstabbing charge, Kirsch said he didn't want to get into that argument. "But I can tell you facts, and the fact was that Kolius and *Courageous* did not have a fair shake un-til I insisted we give them a fair shake. We didn't have the sails for them in June and July we should have had. I won't go into the arguments as to why that happened, but we had to insist that we break out of the existing sailmaker relationship that we had, even though it was within the same company (North Sails). Instead of all of the sails coming from the California loft, which is Blackaller's loft, we were able to break it down so we could then get sails that were made in North's Connecticut loft, because they (the *Courageous* crew) weren't getting them from California."

"That's bullshit. Total bullshit," said Blackaller, who was and is owner and manager of North Sails' loft in Alameda, California. "Kolius got paranoid. In fact, he went and got some sails from North Sails East so he could have more control over his own sail program, and that was okay. There was no problem. But he was not having any problem getting sails out of our California loft at all. It was just totally paranoid. He felt that our California loft might have been building better sails for *Defender* than we were for *Courageous*, which they weren't." Jobson said both boats were getting the same sails, from three different lofts, not just North. The problem with *Courageous* was her crew used the same few sails every day, and they wore out.

On the other hand, Blackaller acknowledges he and Jobson were constantly arguing that *Defender* SHOULD get preferential treatment. That led to a lot of shouting matches, he said, and listening to him more than two years later, you can believe it:

"Jobson and I never ever believed that *Courageous* could be selected, because she was an old boat. The New York Yacht Club wouldn't do it. If you stood back and looked at it, you HAD to put all your effort into *Defender*. You just had to. If you're suggesting a political thing, that Jobson and I were slanting the thing toward *Defender* — of COURSE we were! It was the only fucking way you could win the goddamn thing! Some people would say, 'Oh, gee, that's not fair. Think of the poor guys on *Courageous*...' that's a bunch of bullshit. The guys on *Courageous* got a great shake out of that thing. They got a terrific boat, they got money lavished on that boat, they had every opportunity. They weren't shorted at all.

"But that's exactly what the executives of the whole thing got to thinking: Blackaller and Jobson are trying to rig it for *Defender* — you're fucking right we were! It was our deal, we raised all the goddamn money — why shouldn't we do that?"

Jobson disassociated himself from Blackaller's comments. He said he believed in the two-boat approach from the start, still believes in it, and always thought *Courageous* had a chance to win.

In any case, as Kirsch pointed out, the record would show that far more time and money was spent on *Defender* in a losing effort to correct several flaws, than on *Courageous* — including four major and expensive modifications. But it is equally clear that Kolius enjoyed more personal favor. Blackaller says he even uncovered a syndicate plot to replace him with Ted Turner at one point (Turner wasn't interested). On the other hand, even before the 1983 series ended, Kirsch and Kolius announced they would be joining forces again for the next campaign, whether defense or challenge.

SCORPIONS IN A BOTTLE

There were other disputes, each recalled in equally divergent ways. But one thing all parties agree on is that by the middle of the summer the once united syndicate was a camp divided:

"At the end of July, after there had been a number of things that were not working out — one of which, of course, was Blackaller's temper — we finally got to the point where the crew, not me but the crew, were starting to fight with each other," Kirsch said. "Once we selected which crew was on which boat, then they stopped communicating and sharing information, and they started becoming adversaries."

The crew selection took place in December of 1982, Blackaller recalled, right after they got Vietor off the helm of *Courageous*. That had been delayed because they couldn't pay Vietor's charter fee until then. Vietor had been letting them use the boat for free, and "we were afraid he would take his boat and go home, and that would have really fucked us up."

The selection process itself was a tipoff, if any were needed, that Blackaller intended to make his boat first among equals: "Jobson and I decided who we wanted, and we gave the other guys to Kolius," Blackaller explained. That was okay with Kolius, he said; after all, Blackaller and Jobson had recruited all 22 crew members, including Kolius himself, and they had just appointed him skipper of *Courageous*. He was in no position to complain. Furthermore, they were all first-rate sailors.

But the lines were clearly drawn: There was a No. 1 boat and a No. 2 boat. The problem was the No. 2 guys reacted by trying harder. The low-key Kolius and his men — young, united and gung-ho — were up by 6:30 every morning for a team meeting followed by calisthenics. If the boat needed any work, they would do it themselves — sometimes long into the night. "The *Defender* crowd," Kolius' tactician remarked at the time, "kind of gets up whenever they feel like it." Or as Kirsch put it, "The *Defender* crew wanted to do it in what I call the Blackaller style, where you appear at 10 o'clock at the dock, jump behind the wheel and go out and sail around for a few hours, then get back off again and go out and do something else that you like to do with your personal life."

Kirsch said the conflict had reached the point in July where he wondered whether the syndicate should formally divide into two groups, the *Defender* syndicate and the *Courageous* syndicate. The executive committee felt that would be unwise so they struggled on, like scorpions in a bottle.

One result, according to Jobson, was that the two boats no longer tuned up against each other — to the detriment of both. As any sailor knows, there's no way to measure adequately a boat's performance except to race against another boat. And it's especially important to have such a yardstick when major changes are being made, as they were to *Defender* in the intervals between the June and July trials and the July and August trials.

Jobson maintains that Kolius deliberately shut down *Defender*'s testing program between the trials by refusing to sail *Courageous* against her. "It was all subtle, you know: 'Well, we're going in early today,' or, 'We're coming out late,' or, 'We want to try this jib,' or, 'We're not available to race,' or, 'This guy's got to go off and see his mother....' Every day it was something else. But it was a very well calculated campaign to shut down our testing. And it destroyed the Defender/Courageous group. *Courageous* was winning a small battle against us, but losing a big war against Conner. We had a lot of arguments over this. We were looking to our leadership, Chuck Kirsch, to handle it for us, but he was spineless," he said.

Blackaller thinks that's an overstatement. "I believe that Kolius just exercised his right to be as competitive as he could be in that situation," he said. He agreed Kirsch should have done something about it, however — that he should have insisted Kolius cooperate the way the skipper of a trial horse would.

"I can't tell you specifically what Kolius did or didn't do, or Blackaller did or didn't do," Kirsch said. "When the communication broke down, then anything that anybody did was always going to be argued about."

Jobson's personal campaign ended rather abruptly one day shortly after *Defender* was excused from the trials. According to Jobson, Kirsch simply kicked him out of the camp: "He said, 'I don't want you down here anymore,' " Jobson said. "I tried to tell 'em I had some really good tricks sailing-wise that *Courageous* could have used tactically against Conner, because I'd learned a lot sailing against him. But they didn't want to hear them. If they'd used them, they probably could have won a few races."

Kirsch's recollection is a little different:

"I don't think we ever kept him off the dock. There was a point after they were eliminated when he was not being constructive.... He had a tendency to be the first guy (after a race) to run and talk to the press, whether he was on the boat or not. Gary likes that role, but we didn't think it was appropriate for Gary, who was on the team that was eliminated, to be the spokesman for the guys who were still sailing. Frankly, there's no love lost between Jobson and Kolius, and that was where the problem was."

HIDDEN AGENDAS

Clearly there was more involved in the syndicate's civil war than a clash of personalities. In retrospect, it's fairly easy to trace the seeds of the problem right back to the initial concept.

Jobson and Blackaller were committed to a new boat. Jobson apparently believed in the idea of a two-boat campaign, and Blackaller gave it lip-service because he saw it as the best way to develop their own boat's competitive edge. In February, for example, at the height of the shouting matches, Blackaller was blandly telling a Los Angeles Times reporter: "I honestly don't care which one wins out when we pick a boat. I'm like the father of twins — I hope both get an equal chance." But in his heart he KNEW *Defender* would come out on top.

Things started to fall apart when the new boat proved slow. What made it worse was that Jobson and Blackaller had brought in Kirsch, who listened to what they said about two equal boats — and believed it, at least at first. That belief hardened into a solid commitment once Kirsch went out and lined up backers on the basis that *Courageous*, still a sentimental favorite and sure-fire money-raiser, would get an equal chance to enter the trials.

Jobson accused Kirsch of having a "hidden agenda" — i.e.,

favoring Kolius. But in fact, it was Blackaller and Jobson who had the hidden agenda — perhaps hidden even from themselves:

"While we really only wanted (*Courageous*) for a trial horse, we knew that we had to let those boys do everything they wanted to make that boat as fast as possible, or we wouldn't have a viable trial horse. And it split the camp right down the middle," Blackaller said. "I felt the two-boat approach would work because I didn't realize how strongly the competitive urges of the guys on the other boat, if left to their own devices, could divide the efforts. I couldn't bear to make them second-class citizens — which I could have done. We couldn't bring ourselves to do that. I think in the end that was a mistake."

Both Jobson and Kirsch recognize another serious flaw in the Defender/Courageous syndicate: the fact that the guys who started it brought in someone else — worse yet, someone they didn't even know — to take charge.

Says Kirsch: "It was a little bit bass-ackwards to start with. You can't have the sergeants going out and hiring the generals." Presumably Blackaller and Jobson saw Kirsch's role initially as limited to running the non-sailing aspects of the campaign. But as soon as the sailors started butting heads they needed someone with unquestioned authority. And that they didn't have.

Kirsch said he would never be part of a two-boat campaign again: "You know, the egos get so involved. That's one of the things that happen to the guys that sail, that's what motivates them. You have to recognize that.... Believe me, there is no one person who can knock their heads together and say, hey, you guys, act like men instead of kids."

But it was Blackaller, the sailor, who came closest to defining the source of the problem for his campaign, and for the America's Cup:

"The basic problem is that the goddamn America's Cup campaigns are so long, so drawn out, so political and there are so many people involved, that it just gets everybody all screwed up. You know, it isn't really the personalities involved: individually they're all nice guys. Kirsch is a nice guy, me, Jobson — but when you throw all these people together for years on end, with no racing going on, it's dynamite. If we had races every day it would be a different matter. Nobody would have time for that shit.

"The America's Cup, as it is now constituted, is no goddamn fun."

15
HOW NOT TO BUILD
A 12-METER YACHT

If the public and private battles among the sailors and managers weren't enough, both of the would-be 1983 defenders also had problems with boat design, and dealing with the sensitivities of those who designed them. Before the 1983 defense was over, each of the three naval architects involved would charge he had been stabbed in the back. These conflicts, too, were largely hidden but equally devastating — not only to the individual campaigns but to the increasingly quaint notion that America's Cup racing is a sporting activity.

1983 was not a good time to be a designer of 12-meter yachts in America. Their problems were rooted in the complacency that had developed during the 1970s over the supremacy of American design — and the panic that replaced it as the 1983 campaign evolved.

There hadn't been a real breakthrough boat since Olin Stephens' *Intrepid* in 1967, and there were those who felt she would be the last. Every successful design since then had been a refinement of *Intrepid*'s lines, including the 1980 defender *Freedom*. For nearly a decade, since the *Mariner* disaster of 1974, yachtsmen had regarded any attempt at innovative design with dark suspicion. The 12-Meter Rule, in existence since 1906, imposed stringent limits on what designers could and could not do, leaving them a finite number of variables to play around with. By the 1980s a number of people believed the optimum combination had been found, that further experimentation would be a waste of time and money, both of which are in chronic short supply in a modern Cup campaign.

Olin Stephens was not among them. Long after the dust of 1983 had settled, he looked back on that period:

"The bad tank results and the coming of aluminum boats, which are easier to alter than wooden ones, led to the generally accepted feeling, which I think was pushed by the sailmakers and the sailors, that if you just get any good 12-meter, tune it up very well, get the sails right, get to know the boat and get a good crew, this was about the most you could do. Of course as a designer I couldn't be expected to subscribe to that point of view, and I always thought there was some possibility of some kind of a breakthrough, maybe bigger, maybe smaller. There was less and less chance to demonstrate that possibility during the two or three matches of the 1970s, however."

David Pedrick, designer for the *Defender/Courageous* syndicate, put it in more personal terms:

"The attitudes in the United States were that we were better, we had these good boats, we were making them a little bit better every time, which was enough to keep winning by one- or two-minute margins. The basic complacency of the United States syndicates made it kind of a stagnant condition for the defense efforts. It was very frustrating for designers to try to deal with that. I don't think any of the designers for the past couple of times have had fun. We've had our hands tied and were afraid to do our best."

Meanwhile, the sailors were flying high. Bus Mosbacher had proven in 1962 that a good helmsman and crew could win with a slower boat. But it wasn't until Ted Turner came along that the cult of The Skipper As Demigod reached full flower. He had sprung onto yachting's center stage in one breathtaking leap by buying a Cal 40 in the early 1960s, entering it in the Southern Ocean Racing Circuit — and winning by the biggest margin ever. As a Sports Illustrated story commented: "Winning the SORC in a stock boat is like a guy buying a Buick and winning an auto race."

Turner, the upstart from inland Atlanta, then outraged a number of people by celebrating his victory in typical Turner fashion: He got drunk and he talked to the press. The Turner Manifesto was stated succinctly in his conversation with the New York Times:

"The elements of success in ocean racing are, in order of importance, a great crew, and in particular great helmsmanship. You've got to be able to steer the boat right. Second is competent navigation, and third is good equipment."

When he steered *Mariner* into oblivion in 1974, no one held it against him; nobody could have won with such an obvious dog. And Turner's blistering and quotable criticism of her hapless designer, Britton Chance, did nothing to improve the designers' image. (See Chapter 10.)

After his easy win with *Courageous* in 1977, Terrible Ted was downright insufferable. When he came back in 1980, he said, he wouldn't change a thing. He had the perfect boat, the perfect crew, and HE was perfect.

As we have seen, Turner did come back 1980 — and went down to resounding defeat. Dennis Conner had ushered in the era of the endless campaign that year, changing many things. At least two things did not change: The winning boat was yet another Sparkman & Stephens refinement of its *Intrepid/Courageous* line, and the sailors were still in control. Conner, although as different from Turner in personality as water and whiskey, represented the next step in the Skipper As Demigod tradition. He wanted to control everything, even the design of the boat. In 1983, he almost succeeded.

CONNER'S ARMADA

Everyone assumed S&S would be Conner's designer. Under the guidance of Olin Stephens, who had retired five years earlier at the age of 70 but still kept his hand in, the firm had built five of the six defenders since 1958, including *Intrepid* and her successors. Conner's temperament, his success with *Freedom*, the weight of responsiblity — everything seemed to impel him toward a cautious, conservative course and a continuing partnership with a proven winner. But an excess of caution, and perhaps his penchant for tying up talent, dictated a slightly different course: He would retain Sparkman & Stephens, but he would also commission another boat from another designer, Johan Valentijn.

Conner believed in experience, in proven performance, but he also believed in competition. He was said to have put some 120 recruits through their paces before choosing his final 1983 crew, ending up where another skipper might have begun: with nine Cup veterans out of 11 positions. Having designers compete was an unusual idea but not unprecedented; it had worked in 1937, when Starling Burgess and Olin Stephens both drew designs for Harold Vanderbilt. Conner, like Vanderbilt, bclicvcd in leaving no stone unturned. And also like him, he had good reasons for running scared.

So he asked both Valentijn and Bill Langan, chief designer at Sparkman & Stephens after Stephens' retirement, to take their best shots at a breakthrough. Each was kept in the dark about what the other was doing. The results were *Spirit of America*, the S&S design, and Valentijn's *Magic*, both christened on April 17, 1982. *Spirit* was a very long, deep boat designed for superior stability; *Magic* on the other hand was the smallest 12-meter ever built, weighing in at about 45,000 pounds — more than 10,000 pounds lighter than the norm. Each was, in a sense, a full-size test-tank model.

When they were sailed against each other, in what amounted to the first round of an informal, intramural defense trials by the Freedom syndicate, it was *Spirit* that won the right to advance to round two, sailing against the benchmark *Freedom* off San Diego. *Magic*, deemed hopeless, stayed behind in Newport, where she suffered the cruel fate of ending up high and dry beside the America's Cup Expo Center as a tourist attraction; for a couple of dollars anyone could take her helm and be photographed sailing her into the parking lot.

In San Diego, *Spirit* proved to be slower — devastatingly slower — than *Freedom*. The new boat simply couldn't beat the old warhorse.

Those were dark days for the Freedom syndicate. Her *Magic* was gone, her *Spirit* was flagging, and the prospect of facing Alan Bond again with the same old boat looked more like Bondage than *Freedom*. A blither spirit than Conner might have assessed the situation differently; a Blackaller or Turner might have said something like, "Well, we've tested the limits in two directions and neither one works. Looks like no one's going to beat ol' *Freedom*. Let's race her." It wouldn't have been the first time a 12-meter had defended more than once — *Intrepid* had done it in 1967 and '70. *Courageous* had done it in '74 and '77 and was back for a third go in '83, though she had been so extensively modified as to be virtually a new boat. And *Freedom* was fast, fast enough to win 32 of her 35 trial races on the way to retaining the Cup in 1980, when she beat the Aussies 4-1.

But Conner, predictably, wasn't satisfied. He had asked his designers to come up with a boat faster than *Freedom*, and they had failed. He knew he would be facing seven challengers who had given their designers roughly the same orders — not to mention the other U.S. syndicate's two entries. So he commissioned yet another boat, the one that would be named *Liberty*. He also demanded that

Sparkman & Stephens work on modifications to *Spirit*; the new drawings had to be done within three weeks.

EXIT SPARKMAN & STEPHENS

Accounts differ somewhat on what happened next, but there's agreement on the main outlines: Both designers wanted to do the new boat. Sparkman & Stephens thought it had the inside track because the boat would be an evolution of its *Freedom* design. Conner, on the other hand, had been leaning toward Valentijn, whose office was right on the scene in Newport and who was prepared to work full time on the project, which the larger S&S was not. Also, Conner was not given to dealing comfortably with dissension, and he had already had some sharp disagreements with Bill Langan over how *Spirit* should be altered. A compromise was worked out in which the designers would collaborate, with Valentijn as project manager. Neither was happy with the deal. Just how unhappy Valentijn was can be gauged from his version of how it collapsed:

"Dennis had this wonderful idea that the boat should be designed by committee of Sparkman & Stephens, Johan Valentijn and Halsey Herreshoff. I agreed, but then Bill Langan was trying to outmaneuver me and trying to be smart about it and suddenly he came up with this design and said we are ready to build, this is it.... So I told Dennis I was going to resign, which I did. I learned there the hard way that, hey, there's somebody always pushing the knife in your back and then turning it around a few times, and that was Sparkman & Stephens. Then they told everybody I had screwed them, which is not true...."

Langan's version, as quoted in "Upset: Australia Wins The America's Cup," by Michael Levitt and Barbara Lloyd (1983; Nautical Quarterly/Workman Publishing, New York), differed:

"I had to do the modifications to *Spirit* on the loft floor at Newport Offshore, because of the constraints of time. At one point Johan, as project manager, came up to the loft floor and said, 'What you are drawing is not what we asked for.' I responded that we had the final say.... That turned into a big mess.... Things happened so fast; it got out of control, what with all the people involved — all these people trying to come up with two boats that were sufficiently compromised that everyone could feel happy. It was a pretty nasty situation."

Halsey Herreshoff, grandson of the legendary Nathaniel Herreshoff and a naval architect in his own right, a veteran of six Cup defenses and designated navigator for Conner's 1983 campaign, may have had the most dispassionate inside view:

"We felt that at that late stage, in September of '82, the best thing to do was a moderate approach — to try to make something a little bit better than *Freedom*, but not too far off, because as far as we knew that was about the best type of boat there was. They (Valentijn and S&S) agreed to collaborate, but the actual physical drawing of the hull lines would be done in the Sparkman & Stephens office in New York by their draftsman, Mario Tarabocchia, who had drafted most of these boats over the years. Johan tried to have input through meetings with Langan. That's a very difficult thing, because whoever puts the pencil to paper is the one really doing it.

"When they (S&S) were left to their own devices down there, they made this drawing of a boat that was very like *Freedom* in the bow and very different in the stern. When I saw that my reaction was, 'Wait a minute here; this may or may not be what we want to have, but Johan should have an input in this.' I think Johan had some kind of session with Mario about it, and a couple of days later Johan said, 'I quit.' "

Clearly the collaboration wasn't going to work. The syndicate's inner circle met to decide what to do. When the conversation turned to rejecting Valentijn's resignation and firing Sparkman & Stephens instead, Herreshoff was troubled.

"I right away had a lot of questions about the ethics of this," he said, "because after all, if the plan was to develop the boat based on *Freedom*, the ethical thing was to do that with the people who had designed *Freedom*. So that was an element in the deliberations. But, of course, with such a vital thing, you have to do what you think is going to work."

The time had long since passed, apparently, when anyone who had a boat on the line would even question whether the America's Cup, a yacht race, was "such a vital thing." By 1983 it was clearly understood, at least among the sailors, that when the Cup was at stake such abstractions as personal loyalties, professional ethics and gentlemen's agreements were simply expendable in the face of that great Twentieth Century imperative: You have to do what you think is going to work. In the end they left it up to Conner, and he picked Valentijn.

Langan and Stephens were furious. Stephens had been involved in Cup defenses before Conner and Valentijn were born, starting with

Ranger in 1937. They had turned over the closely guarded lines of all their recent 12-meter designs to Valentijn and Herreshoff during their brief collaboration — an act equivalent to Coca-Cola turning over its secret formula to Pepsi in anticipation of a merger — only to be told, in effect, thank you very much for your work and your plans, we'll take it from here. Dennis Conner and company had not simply turned over another stone, they had kicked over a monument.

"I've never seen Olin so mad," Langan was quoted as saying in late 1983. "The entire time I've known him, I don't think I've seen him mad more than a couple of times.... I mean, that someone could do that to Olin Stephens, after all the years he has put into the sport. Everyone was acting in good faith, and Olin had gone a long way to make the compromise work, and then they had essentially kicked him in the teeth.... We considered going to the America's Cup Committee and saying, This isn't cricket; this is not the way the game should be played. It is supposed to be a sport.... I felt so bad that I strongly considered quitting. If these are the lengths you have to go to win, who needs it?... Why were we beating our brains out to satisfy the ego of this one guy (Conner) on debatable speed differences? Dennis is good. That's the one thing you can't argue about; but I don't think you have to attain greatness the way he goes about it. I sure hope he's an oddity, not the rule, because I'd like to stay in this business." ("Upset," pages 73-74.)

"Maybe if we had all been a little more reasonable and a little more patient with each other, (the collaboration) could have continued," Herreshoff reflected long afterwards. "If Johan had been a little more patient and persuasive, it could have continued. But it was a bad arrangement. Obviously there was bad blood. The truth of the matter is both had performed badly (i.e., designed slow boats), and there was no way everybody was going to feel good afterwards. Maybe neither one of them should have gotten that second job, because they failed the first one. They both had opportunities to design an *Australia II* that year, but they didn't succeed in doing it. I don't really think either one of them should feel he can blame somebody else."

As if to rub salt in the wound, the Freedom syndicate refused to let Sparkman & Stephens out of its agreement of exclusivity. Not only would Conner not use them, he wouldn't let them design a new 12-meter for anyone else, either. But nothing could prevent S&S from working on existing boats of their own design, and they quickly entered into a contract to do just that with Conner's U.S. competitor, the Defender/Courageous syndicate. They went to work on modifying the old warhorse *Courageous* — with a vengeance. Meanwhile, Valentijn started drawing the Freedom syndicate's fourth and final boat.

VALENTIJN'S DAY

Johan Valentijn should have been a happy man. The Dutch-born designer was at the very summit of his field after a relatively brief and restless career. Valentijn, nicknamed "The Flying Dutchman" because of his rapid switches of allegiance, had been working on Cup contenders since 1977 when he collaborated with none other than Ben Lexcen on Alan Bond's *Australia.* He then designed *France 3* for Baron Marcel Bich's fourth and final challenge in 1980. By the following year he had taken up permanent residence in Newport and become a naturalized American citizen, making him eligible to work for an American syndicate under the NYYC's new (and stiffer) residency rules — and earn the unlikely distinction of being the first man to design both a challenger and defender. And now the onetime S&S apprentice had beaten out the masters and won yacht designing's biggest plum: drawing the final boat for the odds-on favorites to defend the America's Cup.

But happiness was an elusive commodity in the 1983 campaign, especially among the defenders. Although it remained largely behind closed doors, the bitterness generated by the split with S&S would continue to haunt him. And there were other problems. Time was growing terribly short. He would have to draw the lines for the new boat in a mere 10 days, then go immediately into the lofting stage. There was no time for models, tank tests, extensive computer analyses or any of the other standard preliminaries. Given enough time and freedom to experiment, he had produced a dismal failure. Now he would have to draw a winner in a hurry, and get it right the first time. Not only that, he said, he also had to deal with "heavy input from both Dennis and Halsey, but there was no way of getting around it. I didn't have the free hand that I like to have."

Herreshoff disputes that. Early on he and Conner had laid down a number of parameters having to do with length, weight, sail plan, etc. (all of which were very similar to *Freedom*'s). But once Valentijn was given sole responsibility, "he was pretty free to do whatever he wanted to" within those limits, Herreshoff said. (Whether Valentijn would have been so quick to share the glory and Herreshoff to disclaim it had *Liberty* won, will never be known.)

With the lines of *Freedom* and other S&S boats available to him, Valentijn designed a conventional boat that borrowed features from several older 12-meters. Andrew McGowan of Newport Offshore, *Liberty*'s builder, called her a "family boat" with a "bow like *Freedom*, a keel like *Enterprise*, a deckplan like *Magic*'s, a long counter like *Courageous*, and a radius transom like almost everyone else." She was a good, solid, competitive 12-meter, probably a shade faster than *Freedom*. If she wasn't destined to be a superboat, at least she would be satisfactory — and safe. The corporate boat for the organization man. In any other Cup year she would have been good enough.

MAGIC'S WINGS ARE CLIPPED

Valentijn had another preoccupation in the middle of the summer of '83, one that few people knew about at the time. While he was doing his best to help tune *Liberty* before and during the trials, he was also experimenting with keel wings.

By mid-July, Valentijn claims he had worked out the design of a keel similar to *Australia II*'s, "with modifications, even," based on "early information" about it and with the help of Boeing engineers. He also had *Magic*, which happened to be ideally suited to such a keel. Then along came Russell Long, who steered *Clipper* in the 1980 defense trials, eager to mount a last-minute challenge with an *Australia II*-type keel — that is, if he could borrow a boat, have a keel made, and be handed at least the nucleus of a crew.

There's considerable confusion, even among the partcipants, over the intense three days of discussions that followed. Valentijn said the whole idea originated with Long, Long said it came from Robert McCulloch, chairman of the NYYC's America's Cup Committee, and McCulloch attributed it to Dennis Conner. On one thing all accounts agree: Valentijn was optimistic at first, then reversed himself, saying the keel probably wouldn't work. Long, assuming Valentijn's pessimism was based on an objective string of numbers spewed from a computer somewhere, threw in the towel. "I like longshots," he said, "but that one was a little too long, even for me."

The real story, according to Valentijn, is that when viewed strictly as an engineering problem, the whole plan looked promising. It died for reasons that had more to do with group dynamics than hydrodynamics:

"What was happening there was very simple. Dennis had his campaign with *Liberty*, then Russell Long was trying to maneuver the New York Yacht Club so that he could enter at the last moment with a boat with a winged keel. It was two groups trying to pull strings. The deal with Long was that I would have to spend a lot of my time toward *Magic*. The Freedom syndicate didn't feel it was warranted, that I was more valuable toward their camp. I had to keep working on *Liberty*, for example, to get the most out of her.

"I was asked by the New York Yacht Club and Dennis Conner's group and Russell Long what I felt about doing it. So I made some studies, and I felt there was quite a large chance that we could improve the boat — the chance was quite good that we could get the boat up to par, or slightly better than *Liberty*. We sat down and figured out the whole logistics, and it was all possible, really, because it doesn't take very long when you are under pressure to do a lot of things.

"In the end I was asked again, and I was being pulled around like a yoyo, so I told Russell I felt there was only a five-percent chance of succeeding, and I didn't think it was worth it anymore. But it was really politics that made me do it. It just became too complicated. I felt at that time that there was more than a fifty-percent chance that we would be able to improve and to prepare the boat.

"It would have been embarrassing to the Freedom Syndicate if they would take *Magic*, do this job, give it to Russell Long, and Russell beat Dennis — and the whole political game was based around that."

Edward du Moulin, the syndicate's executive director, strongly disputes this version. Syndicate politics, he said, had nothing to do with it. "It was a logistical thing. We just couldn't have supported a third crew at that late stage. I have never met a naval architect who didn't believe he could improve upon one of his own designs, but it just wouldn't have worked. You couldn't just slap a winged keel on a boat that wasn't designed for it and expect it to succeed."

But Valentijn, long after the event, was still plagued by the conviction that he had been deprived of the chance to work his *Magic:*

"If people's egos were not involved, then I think *Magic* would have happened," he said. "And, you know, maybe we would have won. Maybe we still would have lost. Who knows?"

RUDE TREATMENT

If Valentijn was unhappy, his counterpart with the Defender /Courageous syndicate sounded downright miserable, at least in retrospect: "I have never been treated as rudely personally, certainly by a 12-meter client, as I was by the syndicate management," David Pedrick declared in the summer of 1985.

Pedrick, a slight figure with sandy hair and an engaging smile that contrasted jarringly with his bitter words, is another S&S alumnus now on his own; his Pedrick Yacht Designs is a few blocks away from Valentijn's office in Newport. He had been asked by syndicate founders Tom Blackaller and Gary Jobson to design their new boat, *Defender*. Both sailors had been aboard *Clipper*, a Pedrick design, during her failed campaign in 1980. They were convinced she was potentially the fastest 12-meter that summer, despite the outcome. They wanted something very much like her for '83.

The syndicate's operations manager, Max O'Meara, put a somewhat different slant on it. He said the syndicate was just getting off the ground when he joined in September of 1981. "There was very real doubt as to whether we could get any kind of campaign put together. With the lack of time, the questionability of funds, our decision was, we don't have the ability or the wherewithal or the time to do anything other than a conventional boat in the mold of the *Courageous-Clipper-Freedom* proven hull forms. We knew, absolutely knew, that if somebody — Dennis Conner, Alan Bond or anyone else — came through with a breakthrough boat, our efforts would be for naught."

Pedrick gave them what they wanted, no dispute about that. The troubles began when *Defender* hit the water and proved to be disappointingly slow, too slow even to beat her nine-year-old stablemate, *Courageous*. What happened next — or did not happen — is a matter of sharp disagreenment between Pedrick and the syndicate managers:

"The syndicate was not well set up to understand and evaluate *(Defender's)* weaknesses and then do something about them," Pedrick said. "There was no on-board data processing capability that might

have shown some problems. The use of *Courageous* as a trial horse
was not very effective; they went for many months not properly
identifying weaknesses in the trial horse and therefore failed to reveal
weaknesses in *Defender*.... When we measured the boat out in
California, they didn't bother to spend the money to weigh it and
therefore it didn't reveal a problem that showed up later in June. And
once we started to do the corrective work on the boat in June and
July, it was too late. So there was a very complacent attitude about
the role of technology in design even by conventional standards —
and outright cheapness.... they didn't even use my (follow-up) services
for the first six or eight months."

Pedrick felt he should be paid for any follow-up design work he did
after *Defender* was launched, as his contract specified. The syndicate
management — O'Meara and Chuck Kirsch, chairman — agreed,
but only if they had authorized the work in advance:

"David Pedrick is a fine young man, a wonderful naval architect,
perhaps brilliant," O'Meara said. "It was unfortunate for him, and
twice as unfortunate for us, that his design didn't do what we all
hoped and prayed that it would do, which was successfully defend the
America's Cup." In fact, he said he has recommended Pedrick to a
number of other people looking for 12-meter designers for the 1987
campaign, and wouldn't hesitate to hire him again himself. (Pedrick
ended up with Dennis Conner's '87 syndicate.)

That said, he acknowledged there had been some disputes over
Pedrick's 1983 contract:

"My attitude as a businessman is, if the owner of the boat elected
to hire the design firm for specific purposes, they should bill us and
expect to be paid with reasonable promptness. I did not feel, nor do I
feel now or would ever feel, that when anybody from the design firm
came out on a social occasion as our guest, and partook of our tenders
and so forth, that the clock should run. David Pedrick and the people
in that firm had a standing invitation, on a social basis, to come out
and even entertain their clients or prospective clients on a reasonable
basis, at our expense. But I didn't expect that Pedrick, whenever
things were slow at the office, for example, overstating the case,
would simply march down onto the dock, without a work order or an
authorization, and have a pleasant day out on the water, eating
sandwiches and drinking pop — and then bill us at $200 an hour or
whatever the design fee would be. That became a bit of an issue."

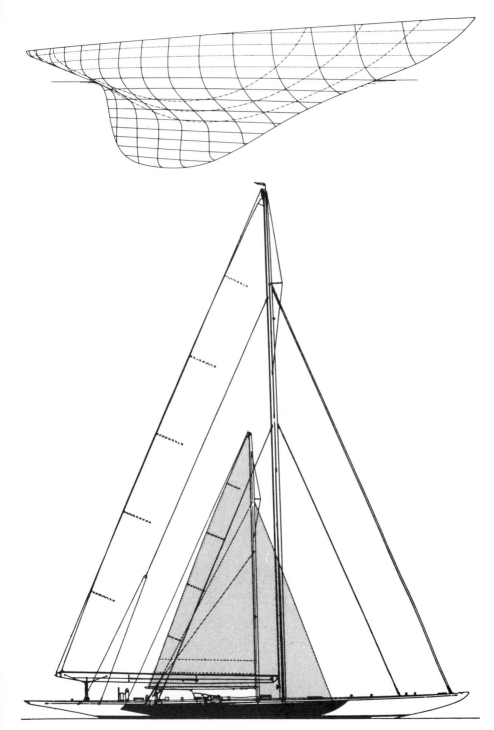

These Sparkman & Stephens drawings show the evolution of America's Cup yachts between *Ranger* in 1937 and the next defender, *Columbia* in 1958. The lines here belong to the 12-meter *Vim,* built by Harold Vanderbilt in 1939 (she raced in England that year, where she won 21 of 27 starts and nearly was named defender in the new America's Cup era).

The generous publicity lavished on the Cup and its personnae helped change the event. Although participants were barred from commercializing the event — until 1977, when the rules started to change — corporate America was quick to appreciate the rising media attention the America's Cup was stimulating. (Providence Journal)

Gretel's famous foul against the defender *Intrepid* in 1974. *Gretel*, to leeward, luffs up after the starting gun, almost forcing *Intrepid* into the committee boat. Although clearly in the wrong, *Gretel* pressed her protest and threat-ened diplomatic relations between the U.S. and Australia. (Rosenfeld Collection, Mystic Seaport Museum)

Ted Turner's victory in 1977 aboard *Courageous* ended the era of "happy warriors." From now on, organizations, rather than individuals, would dominate the America's Cup scene. Bill Ficker, at right, was skipper of Cup winner *Intrepid* in 1970. At left is Gary Jobson, Turner's tactician, who would sail again as a tactician in both 1980 and 1983.

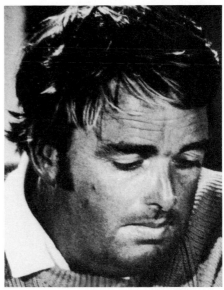

A study in contrasts. Brash and brassy Ted Turner, left, dominated the America's Cup scene in the late 70's with skill and the sheer force of his personality. All-American Dennis Conner, shown above with NYYC Chairman Robert McCullough following Conner's 1980 victory, backed his sailing abilities with meticulous and rigid organization. The combination, he said, gave him "no excuse to lose." There were no excuses (below) when Conner lost the Cup in 1983. (Providence Journal)

Other headliners in 1983 included Ben Lexcen (top), *Australia II*'s controversial designer, and John Bertrand (left), the winning skipper. Reactions to his outspoken 1985 book "Born To Win" gave Australians their first real taste of disharmony within the ranks. John Kolius (right) became the upstart of 1983, ousting brand-new *Defender* from the defenders' trials aboard old warhorse *Courageous*. The parentage of *Australia II*'s winged keel (far right) is still in question. (Lexcen: AP; Kolius, Bertrand: Providence Journal)

Perhaps relieved that the burden of defense was no longer theirs following the tempestuous 1983 running of the America's Cup race, the New York Yacht Club committee (facing page, above) cheered *Australia II* as she crossed the finish line, ending 132 years of U.S. domination. At the same moment a half a world away in Sydney, Australia (above), *Australia II*'s victory gave rise to emotions of a different sort. At last the grandeur was as real as the alcohol. Many Americans at the time found themselves rooting for the underdog Australians; many more were saddened. Almost immediately, syndicates began forming — an unprecedented 10 at one time — in a flag-waving, all-out effort to bring the Cup back to U.S. shores. (NYYC, rowboat: Providence Journal; Sydney Crowd: AP)

Alan Bond gleefully accepted the America's Cup from the New York Yacht Club at ceremonies in Newport at a mansion previously owned by Harold Vanderbilt. The jubilation of 1983, however, shown by the massive crowd that greeted *Australia II*'s crew on arrival in Perth, below, quickly soured. Australians soon learned it was far easier — and much more fun — to play the role of underdog. (Bond: Providence Journal; crowd: AP)

Bertrand sails into storm

JOHN BERTRAND m
sailed a ~~~~~~~~

America's Cup goes corporate

s cites 'syndicate politics'

~~~ billed   hoped Kolius would st
~~~ America II can

THE PROVIDENCE JOURNAL-BULLETIN

Aussie 'Cup wars' sin

Keel scam uncovered

book hurts: Lexcen

world he believes is probably
undiscovered."

But Bertrand's criticism is
~~~~~ Austra-

The following passage fr
the book, describing how F
trand felt as he crossed
finish line, has been descri
~~~~~esentative of the ton

MARK RYAN

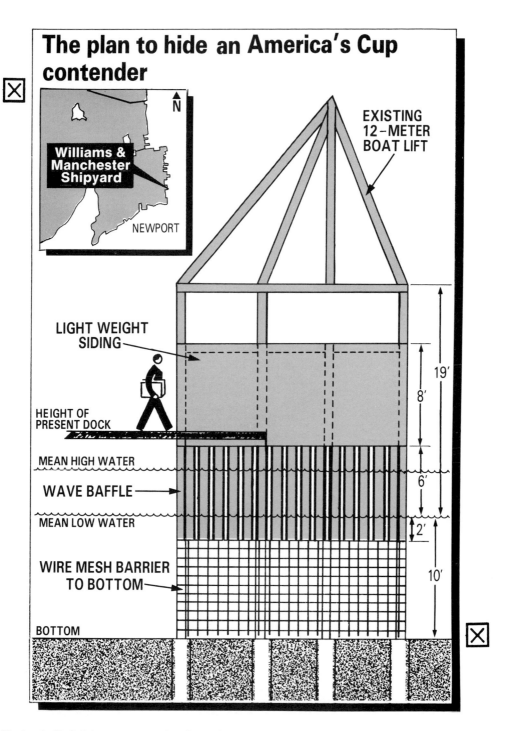

The plan to hide an America's Cup contender

Williams & Manchester Shipyard

NEWPORT

EXISTING 12-METER BOAT LIFT

LIGHT WEIGHT SIDING

HEIGHT OF PRESENT DOCK

MEAN HIGH WATER

WAVE BAFFLE

MEAN LOW WATER

WIRE MESH BARRIER TO BOTTOM

BOTTOM

19'

8'

6'

2'

10'

The level of infighting, secrecy and spying and general poor sportsmanship reached in 1983 have continued apace. Here was one 12-meter builder's recent solution to the rampant "sporting espionage" that is now the hallmark of America's Cup competition. (Providence Journal)

In America, the drive to recover the America's Cup in 1987 resulted in sponsorship participation by numerous corporations, including Newsweek, Cadillac and, as shown in this photo, Amway, which hedged its bets by contributing both to the Australian defense and to the *America II* challenge.

French Kiss was launched, with keel under wraps, in October of 1985. Her name reflects one additional step forward in the inevitable progression toward overt commercial sponsorship. The money behind the *French Kiss* challenge was donated by the multinational KIS photo processing company. Baron Bich (insert) was the first, and most persistent, French challenger. (*French Kiss:* Marie Lesure; Bich: Providence Journal)

Pedrick's version of the impasse is that his frequent observation trips were part of his effort to do "everything I could to help the boat and the crew." All he wanted in exchange, he said, was reasonable compensation and permission to make the alterations he felt were needed.

"I finally renegotiated some terms to help out during the summer of '83, and even that — it was crazy how it was received when I presented it to Chuck Kirsch. I said I wanted to help, but I couldn't do it for free.... I ended up working, with the office, for less than $10 an hour in 1983. I mean that was a gift to them. But when I presented that to Chuck, his attitude was, you know, I am the junior one, they're the boss, and they ought to be telling me what the terms are. I said fine, let's talk. But nobody's doing anything.... I would try to do things, and they would have the high and mighty type of attitude that I didn't count and they ought to be calling the shots. But they didn't call them."

The problems with *Defender* were substantial. After she was built at Newport Offshore she was trucked overland to California for a series of winter trials, then back to Newport. When she arrived she was measured — and failed. She wasn't a legal 12-meter! Furthermore, it was discovered she was sagging at both ends — possibly the result of her cross-country trips aboard a flatbed truck.

Having finally struck a deal, Pedrick and his office got to work making alterations, including an expensive "tummy tuck" which had the effect of raising both ends. These brought her into conformity with the 12-Meter Rule and improved her performance. Before the campaign was over, she would go under the welder's torch four times. The operations may have helped, but not enough. Meanwhile, *Courageous*, against all expectations, was doing surprisingly well in the trials.

In view of all that, it's not surprising that O'Meara would react emphatically to Pedrick's charge of complacency:

"We went the last mile to equip this boat with the very best that was available," he said. "We assembled a team of championship sailors. But the best jockey in the world can't win on a slow horse, and unfortunately (*Defender*) just did not cut the mustard. With Pedrick's design team cooperation, we did four major design modifications during the campaign to try to improve its performance. We spent hundreds upon hundreds of thousands of dollars. When push came to shove and it became obvious something had to be done, it was done — not once, not twice, not three times — four times! We cut that boat apart four times! Name anybody else in the history of the America's Cup that has gone into major surgery four times to try to improve their boat. The answer is nobody. So you cannot make the case that the Defender/Courageous syndicate did anything less than everything that their abilities and their financial resources and their emotional levels would permit them to do."

O'Meara thinks Pedrick's bitterness might be the result of a combination of his (O'Meara's) rather blunt style, the fact that Pedrick had been pushed hard to get the boat right, and above all the deep disappointment everyone felt over *Defender*'s performance. If so, he says, Pedrick should realize that everyone else was pushed just as hard, everyone was disappointed, and no one has any complaints against him because of the way the boat sailed.

"It is not unknown for a brilliant designer to do his very best and produce a turkey," O'Meara said. "In no way do we say anything disparaging about the Pedrick design team. Maybe David is still brokenhearted and hasn't matured in this situation to the point where he can look at it objectively, and maybe he's trying to find fault when he would be better advised to say he gave it his best shot, he aimed for the fences, but he happened to swing and strike out. But the next time he's going to stand up there and hit a home run for us. Nobody feels bad about David Pedrick; we think he is one of the naval architects that all Americans can take pride in."

ENTER SPARKMAN & STEPHENS

But there was another source of conflict, the fact that Pedrick, like Johan Valentijn before him, had to share design responsibilities within the syndicate with S&S. And nothing was likely to mollify the anger and hurt he felt over the final and almost farcical indignity that led to, in late August of 1983.

Pedrick had an exclusive contract with the syndicate, he said, but when John Kolius came aboard as the new skipper for *Courageous* in 1982, he decided he wanted his own designer rather than sharing one with the *Defender* crew. This, Pedrick said, "was a legitimate point of view," especially considering that S&S had designed *Courageous* originally. "However, it was in breach of the agreement I had made with the syndicate prior to that. They wanted exclusivity with me, and

I wrote to them that that was to be mutual. Contracts don't mean very much in the sailing world; it's unfortunate, but that's the way things are.

"John Kolius when I called him said it wasn't his decision; Max O'Meara said they were just doing what the skipper wanted. So it was the kind of thing where I thought it was a pretty unethical and gutless maneuver on their part. They had a legitimate reason for wanting to do it that way, but it was a case where they stomped on me and I think breached the contract with me."

But the crowning blow came on August 29. The NYYC had abandoned its protests against the Australians, declared winged keels eligible to race, and had been quietly urging the potential defenders to give them a try. Pedrick's mood that morning was not improved by the fact that his boat had been eliminated from the trials two days earlier while the old S&S-designed *Courageous* was still racing. And then he learned, quite by accident, that Bill Langan of Sparkman & Stephens had secretly installed keel wings on *Defender*!

When he rushed off to Cove Haven Marina in Barrington, Rhode Island, to see for himself, he was stopped by Chuck Wilson, the syndicate's project manager. Wilson told him he had orders to keep everyone out of *Defender*'s shed, "including you." When the story hit the press, Pedrick confined himself to the comment that he was "out of the 12-meter business for 1983." But he was seething. Not only had they let another designer tamper with his boat, they hadn't even let him know about it!

Pedrick may not have known it at the time, but he was not the only one kept in the dark: Thanks to the split between the *Defender* and *Courageous* crews and the almost paranoiac compulsion to hide anything having to do with keel wings at that point, the syndicate management decided not to tell ANYONE connected with *Defender*, and only one member of the *Courageous* crew, John Kolius.

Max O'Meara makes no apologies:

"We entered into a contract with this guy (Pedrick), we didn't marry him," he said. "At the time this was done, *Defender* had already been eliminated from the competition. The so-called wings that were designed by Sparkman & Stephens were designed for installation on *Courageous*. It was not widely known, because the nature of the America's Cup game is you don't broadcast these things. So we were certainly under no obligation to tell David Pedrick that the

Courageous people were interested in wings. Nobody in his right mind is going to take a boat that is still in competition and slam some experimental wings on it. We had only one other 12-meter available to us, *Defender*, so we put the wings on it.

"As a businessman, I'm not concerned about the fragility or sensitivity of naval architects. We bought and paid for *Defender*. It was our bloody boat, it wasn't his bloody boat. When you buy something and you've got all right, title and interest to it, you can do anything you damn well please under the law of the land. I really don't understand (his unhappiness). I suppose it's pride of authorship or something else. But if he can claim pride of authorship, I think we all can claim pride of ownership."

The keel wings, to no one's surprise, proved to be worthless and were never installed on *Courageous*, which was eliminated a few days later. It was a desperate maneuver, awkwardly carried out; just one more example of the extent to which the defense had unraveled by the end of the summer.

EPILOGUE

The postscript to all this came about a year and a half later, during an interview in which Dennis Conner was defending the team-design approach to his 1987 challenge. There's a long and dishonorable tradition among America's Cup losers: The skippers blame the designers, and the designers blame the skippers. In that respect, at least, Conner is very traditional.

"Don't forget," he said, "I had two of the best designers in the world last time, and they fucked up."

In one short and graceless sentence, the man who lost the Cup managed to combine debatable facts, betrayal, and insulting language that would have been gratuitous were it not so self-serving.

Probably he didn't mean it to convey any of those things. It was simply the dispassionate appraisal of a mechanical failure at the heart of a corporate campaign. People were cogs in the wheel and sometimes they fucked up. It happened. His comment probably wasn't intended to offend. But it served as a perfect epitaph for the defense of 1983.

16
SECRECY, SPYING AND DIRTY TRICKS

What would you call an international conflict that includes enemy surveillance, secret weapons, coded messages, underwater espionage by navy frogmen, covert activities, attempted sabotage, disinformation campaigns and psychological warfare? In the summer of 1983, some people called it a yacht race.

The hostilities opened in the summer of '82 with a cannon shot and a ramming at sea.

EARLY SKIRMISHES

The British were the first challengers to arrive in Newport, a full year before the others. Theirs was a major amphibious assault involving four 12-meters, 50 personnel occupying four rented houses, a seaplane, a helicopter, a floating command center (*Kalizma*, a 140-foot luxury yacht that once belonged to Elizabeth Taylor and Richard Burton) and a small fleet of support craft. It didn't take them long to start scouting the enemy.

Both American crews were in Newport at the time, tuning their boats for next year's campaign. But Peter de Savary, the cigar-smoking British commander, quickly zeroed in on Dennis Conner, knowing he likely could learn more from watching Conner, the defending champion, than from spying on the Defender/Courageous group. Or he may have picked Conner when he learned his tactics rattled Conner more than Tom Blackaller, et al. Or maybe it was just that Conner was the only one who fought back.

In any case, whenever Conner took one of his boats for a sail, a small British surveillance craft, usually an outboard-powered 13-foot rubber inflatable called "Rubber Duck," left port to shadow him. Manning it were two or three men with a video camera who recorded his every move. Reportedly sometimes put themselves directly between Conner's boat and his trial horse.

Conner tried evasive action. Once he sailed 20 miles to the other side of Block Island in rough seas in an effort to shake the Brits. When that didn't work, the Americans trailed invisible monofiliment fishing lines behind their boat to snag the enemy's propeller. One day someone on *Defender*'s tender fired a mock "warning shot," a blank round from a starting cannon. That was just for fun, but when one of the Freedom syndicate's support boats deliberately (albeit gently) rammed Rubber Duck, the Brits took it seriously.

The Americans complained they had caught British crewmen snooping around their workshed. The Brits spread rumors that a series of engine problems on their support boats might have been the result of sabotage. They charged that the Freedom syndicate was trying to get their immigration cards suspended and that the FBI had been called in. Before the summer tune-ups ended the air was filled with more charges and countercharges than even the most contentious Cup matches generate — and the match was still a year away.

Secrecy and spying have been part of the Cup scene since 1887, when the Scottish challengers built *Thistle* under wraps and an American newspaper sent a diver down to check out her keel. That attempt failed; New York water was murky even then. But in 1937 the defenders got a leg up when they copied a revolutionary sail from the British challenger, *Endeavour*. A member of *Ranger*'s afterguard had studied the new quadrilateral jib through binoculars while *Endeavour* was still in England. The kind of overt scouting practiced by de Savary's men had been going on between the Americans and the Australians at least since 1962 and was generally accepted — at least when done from a discreet distance.

But charges of outright harassment, especially this early in the campaign, were something new. Even if unproven they indicated an escalation of the conflict that needed to be nipped early.

Robert McCullough, former commodore of the NYYC and head of its America's Cup Committee, tried to intervene. He got nowhere. McCullough asked de Savary to stay away from Conner. De Savary replied that he intended to do anything within the rules to win the Cup, and that was that. McCullough, not for the last time in this campaign, left the meeting empty-handed and with no real recourse.

The harassment ended when both crews moved their boats to warmer waters for the winter. But the whole episode highlighted the grim determination of both the challengers and the defenders, and the ease with which the latter could be rattled. It was an ominous prologue to 1983, when the Australians arrived with a secret keel.

THE KEEL CAPER

Alan Bond's syndicate had gone to great pains to keep *Australia II*'s keel hidden, even in Australia. They kept it shrouded while she was carried to Newport aboard a container ship. According to an Australian source, their precautions were justified; American spies tried to get a peek while the ship was still en route. When she put in at New Orleans, for example, the Aussies were warned about a ship's agent whose employer had a son with the Freedom syndicate. Sure enough, when he came aboard he asked for a quick look. Needless to say, he didn't get it.

Just when the first photographs of *Australia II*'s keel were taken may never be known. Representatives of several of the syndicates claimed to have seen photos taken as early as May, when *Australia II* first arrived. But none had been published. Enough information had leaked out to whet public curiosity, but not satisfy it. By mid-July, the keel was Topic A along the waterfront, thanks in part to *Australia II*'s 21-3 record at that point. Even de Savary, the irrepressible head of the British syndicate, paid homage to the keel after a fashion.

De Savary decided to celebrate his 39th birthday on July 13 by easing one of his support boats into the dock right next to *Australia II*, where he leaned on his boat's air horn, made a great show of trying to peek under the shroud, and shouted to the armed guards, "Please give Mr. Bond our regards, and suggest he tighten up on his security." And with that he roared off in a cloud of cigar and diesel fumes.

So many people had been snooping around, in fact, that Warren Jones, *Australia II*'s executive director, was getting testy:

"They're driving us bananas. I can't believe it," he complained. "It's our boat. Why don't they leave us alone and let us get on with our job?" He promised that any outsiders caught inside the modesty skirt would be hauled off to court.

Ten days later he made good on the threat. A member of the Canadian syndicate's support team, James W. Johnston, and another man had been spotted swimming under the keel in wetsuits shortly after dawn. The guards nabbed Johnson and turned him over to police, who confiscated his underwater camera. The other diver got away. A spokesman for the Canadians later said Johnston, identified as a driver for one of the syndicate's support boats but actually the team photographer, had been acting on his own, that he had been reprimanded, and that the whole thing was a practical joke.

The Australians were not amused. They pressed trespassing charges, quickly sought a court order to prevent the film from being developed, and increased their security precautions around the boat. When Newport's city solicitor said he would have to develop the film and introduce the photos as evidence to prove trespassing, the Aussies dropped the charge in exchange for the undeveloped film and a formal apology. They said they now knew the identity of the other diver and had been assured he wasn't carrying a camera.

The real story didn't emerge until after the races. As told by Jeff Boyd, *Canada I*'s tactician, and Canadian journalist Doug Hunter in "Trials: *Canada I* and the 1983 America's Cup" (1984, Macmillan of Canada), the Canadians made not one but two attempts to photograph the keel. The second was successful, but the first was more startling from one point of view: It marked the first known attempt in America's Cup history at covert activities by active-duty military personnel.

Bruce Kirby, the Canadian's yacht designer, was anxious to know more about *Australia II*'s undersides. Others in the camp took that as a signal to get serious about an underwater spy mission, something they previously had merely toyed with as a prank. As it happened, a Canadian Navy launch was due in Newport about that same time, to carry spectators and patrol the challengers' race course. It carried navy frogmen among its crew.

The naval commander, appalled by the consequences if word got out, vetoed the idea immediately. But a member of the syndicate approached the divers privately and they agreed to the mission. Using Kirby's waterproof camera, they slipped into the water one early morning in July, photographed the keel, and returned undetected. Unfortunately, they were better frogmen than they were photographers. The pictures were worthless.

Emboldened by the frogmens' success in avoiding the Aussie guards, Johnston and a young member of the support crew named Brook Hamilton decided to try it themselves. At 5:30 a.m. on July 23, they entered the water wearing wetsuits and carrying cameras.

Johnston proved to be a better photographer than frogman. He made enough noise in the water to arouse a guard and after a Keystone Cops chase among the boats and docks, he was caught and surrendered his camera. Hamilton got away. But he still had his camera, containing pictures of the keel.

The syndicate's official position was that Johnston had acted on his own, that it had been a lark, and that they knew nothing about a second diver. But as soon as Johnston was released from jail, he developed Hamilton's film. He made one set of 15 prints — which were stolen on July 28 at a party after Johnston, who was rather enjoying his sudden celebrity, got roaring drunk and showed the photos to everyone present. Eventually two prints found their way to the Toronto Globe and Mail, which published them on the front page the day of the final race.

According to another source, Ben Lexcen, *Australia II*'s designer, visited the Canadian crewhouse in mid-summer. When he went to the men's room, he was startled to see a photograph of his own keel tacked up behind the door.

Aside from the Australians, whose humor had deserted them, most people in Newport treated the keel caper as good fun, which it was. It was too late to copy the keel, so the photos wouldn't give anyone an unfair advantage. But rumors abounded that summer about other covert activities that could change the course of history. And some of them were true.

MULTIPLE CERTIFICATES

Aside from the Aussies' keel the most celebrated secret weapon surfaced about the same time Johnston and Hamilton went swimming. *Liberty*, after a medicore performance in the June trials, was on a hot streak that included nine straight wins between July 23 and 29. But Conner's opponents on *Defender* and *Courageous* were puzzled by her inconsistent behavior — incredible downwind speed one day, followed by a poor showing the next. She almost seemed to be a different boat from day to day. It turned out she was.

The *Liberty* people had been secretly juggling her ballast and sail area, depending on the weather conditions. On the face of it, that appeared to be a gross violation of the rules — the same violation Lord Dunraven charged almost a century earlier. But in fact Conner had found a way to beat the system: Multiple rating certificates.

They tried a number of different combinations of ballast weight and sail area (if you add to one, the 12-meter measurement rule forces you to reduce the other) and settled on three configurations, one for light wind, one for a heavy breeze and one for intermediate conditions. They asked for, and received, the selection committee's permission to have the boat officially measured and rated in each of the three modes, and to switch from one certificate to another from time to time.

It wasn't quite the same situation that greeted James Ashbury's second challenge in 1871, when the NYYC claimed the right to choose its defender each day from among four candidates, each designed for a different wind strength. But it was close. Each change required only that a measurer inspect the boat's flotation marks and sign the new certificate, as opposed to making a complete remeasurement, which took a day and a half. The committee agreed not to tell anyone else about the trick — not even the other defense candidates.

When someone from the Defender/Courageous syndicate noticed an extra flotation mark on *Liberty*'s hull, the secret was out.

Conner first tried to put reporters off the scent. "We have one certificate," he said. "If you read the rule you'll see that it's illegal to have more than one." That was literally true, of course. *Liberty* did have only one certificate — at any given time. But Conner was using a verbal loophole to conceal an actual one, and it didn't fool anyone for very long. Johan Valentijn, *Liberty*'s designer, and syndicate manager Edward du Moulin tried to convince a reporter that the whole idea was to allow *Liberty*'s crew to find her best overall trim during the July trials, not adjust for daily wind conditions. That didn't fly either.

But it wasn't Conner's manipulation of the rules or even his attempted coverup that enraged Blackaller and his outspoken tactician Gary Jobson the most. The time had long since passed when anyone would seriously object to an America's Cup competitor secretly taking advantage of a soft spot in the rules. What really infuriated them — besides not thinking of it first — was that the selection committee hadn't cut them in on the deal.

McCullough claimed the committee members intended to do just that. First they wanted to see if the ploy would work, then they planned to tell the Defender/Courageous group about it to prevent the challengers from copying the idea. But Blackaller and Jobson blew the whistle before the committee had a chance.

Blackaller remains skeptical of McCullough's explanation. He attributes the secrecy to favoritism toward Conner's group — a favoritism he says Conner and others in his syndicate actively curried.

"They were kissing the ass of the committee 24 hours a day, and we never even talked to them," Blackaller said. "That whole thing was so repulsive to me right from the start that I just never could get with it — which was a mistake on my part. You can't play the game without catering to the politics of the straw hats."

It isn't strictly true that Blackaller never spoke to the committee. He did at least once, and that time he was highly critical of the way it was conducting its investigation of the Australians' secret keel — a very tender subject for the men in the straw hats, as we shall see. Blackaller is convinced that discussion speeded his demise as a contender. "That was just a stupid thing for me to do. I should have kept my mouth shut," he says.

No one denies the committee had a closer relationship with Conner's syndicate than with the Defender/Courageous people, but McCullough and others adamantly reject the favoritism charge. Furthermore, McCullough said *Liberty*'s multiple-certificate advantage didn't enter into her selection, either. It's just that she was sailing faster than the other two boats in September, when it counted.

The whole episode did nothing to improve relations between the NYYC and two of its three potential defenders, not to mention the club's growing list of detractors outside the defense camps.

RUMORS

Two mighty and uncontrollable forces drive an America's Cup campaign, wind and rumors. Every match from 1851 on has had its share of the latter — remember *America*'s propeller? The 1983 match had more than most. Like the wind, many of them came from nowhere, ruffled the waters for a time, and died. But some lingered.

One of the more persistent rumors had to do with sandbagging, or deliberately holding your boat back to gain some real or imagined tactical advantage. It isn't illegal, but it isn't exactly sporting, either. The June trials were not yet a week old when Blackaller levelled that charge against Conner, who had lost his first three races. Blackaller's theory was that Conner would rather lose a few meaningless races at the beginning than provide his opponents with the tough competition they needed to tune their own boats. Conner said he hadn't planned on losing. When pressed on the question of sandbagging, he replied: "That's my business."

Meanwhile, members of the Freedom syndicate were spreading a similar rumor about *Australia II*. That boat's only weakness seemed to be on the downwind legs, where many of the other challengers were able to gain on her during the trials. The story was that Bertrand, the Aussie skipper, didn't want to let his competitors know just how fast his winged flier really was. So he deliberately reined her in downwind by cocking the trim tab, turning it counter to the rudder. *Liberty*'s navigator Halsey Herreshoff, among others, said the Americans had heard that from a reliable source, whom he declined to identify.

Given the prevailing ethical climate — Social Darwinism would be a charitable term for it — this was a plausible charge. Indeed, in what was rapidly becoming the summer of the Big Psych, the only shrewder move would have been NOT to slow the boat and encourage the story that they were doing so. And that, as we shall see in a later chapter, is exactly what Bertrand claimed he did.

"IT MAY BE ILLEGAL, BUT WHAT THE HELL?"

The sixth race — the one *Australia II* won to tie the score at three-all and set the stage for "the race of the century" — was a kind of watershed in America's Cup sporting ethics. The day began with attempted sabotage and the discovery of a theft. But those were minor distractions compared to what happened, and what was rumored to have happened, on the race course.

The excitement began about 2 a.m., when *Australia II*'s guards spotted a diver in the water near the entrance toher dock. He escaped, but when the guards checked the area they found a rope, hung with plastic garbage bags, across the entrance to the berth. The rope was intended to snare the boat's winged keel and slow her down substantially. The saboteur's identity was never learned.

The race started without further incident. *Australia II* got off to an early lead, thanks to a huge, favorable windshift. She had already rounded the fourth mark as *Liberty* approached it. Then, as the two boats were about to pass each other heading in opposite directions, Conner deliberately sailed a collision course toward *Australia II*. He was close-hauled on starboard tack so he had the right of way. Therefore, it was *Australia II*'s responsibility to avoid collision or a foul by altering course. Bertrand did so and went on to win easily.

"The only chance we had to beat them was to foul them out," Tom

Whidden, *Liberty*'s tactician, said later. "I have a feeling they thought it was illegal, but it's not, as long as you don't alter course to seek them out. There is a rule against that."

No one argued the legality of it, but the sportsmanship involved was another matter. "There are some things you do in yachting, and some things you do not do," Alan Bond said at the post-race press conference. "This was one thing you definitely do not do." If there was a Pecksniffian quality about his indignation, it was lost on most of his listeners. Bond had seized the high ground so adroitly and held it for so long he seemed to belong there.

Along with the attempted sabotage, the Aussies had discovered another unsettling crime before the boats left the docks that morning. Two of their walkie-talkies were missing. The theft might have occurred during the night, or perhaps when Bond had opened the dock to the press for the first time after the fifth race the day before, creating a huge mob scene.

The radios were replaced immediately. The culprit was never identified, so it may never be known whether there was a connection between the theft and another persistent and nasty little rumor: that the Aussies were getting illegal wind data. It is known that the radios were used to communicate between *Australia II* and people in her support boats — "our spies up the course," Bertrand called them. The main topic of these coded conversations was wind direction.

That's perfectly legal and standard procedure — providing it ends with the warning gun 10 minutes before the start. Thereafter, competitors are strictly forbidden to receive any outside information on wind or sea conditions. In 1983, whispers came from both camps that the other was getting secret data after that time, from boats strategically placed upwind. After the races, each side flatly denied doing any such thing, but each continued to suspect the other.

For the Americans, these suspicions reached their zenith during the sixth race. At the post-race press conference, Bertrand expressed surprise that Conner had let him steer off to the west alone rather than covering him when *Australia II* headed toward the first shift.

"Dennis was obviously playing the wind shifts, as we were, and he figured, I assume, that they were going in the right direction," Bertrand said.

"If he could see the shift, he must have had X-ray eyes," Conner replied icily.

Long after the series, Johan Valentijn, *Liberty*'s designer, revealed what no one in the syndicate said publicly at the time: They suspected Bertrand had a little help predicting the shifts from one of their support boats stationed off Block Island. They had no proof, he said. But the suspicions were so strong that some of the *Liberty* people tried to borrow a special scanner from the Navy that could pick up radio transmissions on nonstandard frequencies. They couldn't get it in time, however.

"So what we did when we were remeasuring the boat for the last race and Lexcen was there," Valentijn said, "is set it up that somebody would come up and ask me about the frequency scanner while I was talking to him. And Lexcen just looked and turned away as if he was ignoring the whole issue. But we did it deliberately to make them understand, that, hey, we're onto your game, if you are playing your game. The way he looked and the way he walked away we felt that they were really — that they probably did it. I mean, I have no proof of it. But we very strongly suspected."

Pressed for the root of those suspicions, Valentijn offered no evidence beyond Bertrand's success in predicting the wind direction. It was on just such fragile wings that most rumors flew around the docks that summer, strewing paranoia in their wake.

But one other persistent rumor — that both skippers used their trial horses as gigantic, upwind weather vanes — was partially confirmed by none other than John Bertrand himself.

Both men regularly brought their trial horses out to the course with them each morning, ostensibly for some last-minute practice before the race. *Challenge 12* had filled that role for the Australians since her elimination as a contender in August. In "Born to Win," Bertrand described parting company with her before the second race:

"They would be on a hard starboard tack as soon as the midday gun fired, and would thus give us a guide, way up the racecourse, as we set off. This may be illegal, but what the hell? We would know nothing about it, of course."

In those three sentences, Bertrand managed to encapsulate the moral Zeitgeist the year America lost the Cup. Not only was it acceptable to engage in borderline cheating, and to deny it if caught, it was okay to BOAST about it afterward.

It was the perfect setting for a secret keel controversy, and for the end of an era.

17
KEELGATE I —
WAR DECLARED

By late July, *Australia II*'s score in the trials stood at 25-3. To the Americans, her hidden keel had taken on the menace of an invisible Great White Shark prowling the waters just off a crowded beach, which the NYYC had guarded for 132 years without a single fatality. Something needed to be done.

But when the defenders finally went into action, they raised howls of outrage in the Australian camp and triggered cries of "Foul!" around the world. The keepers of the Cup were branded as trying every sneaky, legalistic maneuver they knew to get *Australia II* disqualified. What else could you expect? Hadn't the New Yorkers always bent the rules to give themselves an edge?

The real story is far more complicated.

OPENING GUN

When the Aussies brought their hidden keel to Newport on May 26, people treated it almost as a joke, a harmless eccentricity. Asked about the green shroud draped around it, John Longley, *Australia II*'s manager, said, "We call it a modesty skirt. We like to keep our lady's private parts hidden." Halsey Herreshoff, Dennis Conner's navigator, shrugged it off: "We understand it's a bulb keel with some fins. It's different, but they've got nothing to lose."

But after the Aussies sailed to 10 victories in their first 10 starts, the joking stopped. "It certainly looks like it works," said Johan Valentijn, *Liberty*'s designer. "I wouldn't put any money on anyone right now." His caution, of course, was justified. It worked. It worked as no keel had worked before. There is little doubt that it made *Aus-*

tralia II the fastest 12-meter ever built.

Part of its secret was that its revolutionary wings minimized turbulence underwater. But on shore they had the opposite effect. Questions swirled around the keel: What did it look like? What made it work? Was it legal? Did Ben Lexcen really design it, or was it the illicit brainchild of Dutch engineers?

Answers to the first two questions unfolded gradually, with no help whatsoever from Lexcen, Alan Bond or anyone else in *Australia II 's* camp. They kept the keel's secrets carefully hidden. Lexcen claimed they kept a shark swimming under the boat to keep intruders away. That was a typical Lexcen flight of fancy, but the two armed guards standing watch at the dock were very real. They even barred the way, briefly, to Australian Prime Minister Robert Hawke in June.

As interest intensified, however, sketches of the keel began to appear in the yachting press, some of them supposedly based on inside information. Gradually yacht designers began piecing together what made *Australia II* fly. By concentrating weight at the bottom and cancelling out the extra drag that imposes, they decided, the wings made *Australia II* the yacht-racing version of a free lunch. It could carry at least as much sail as the best of the conventional designs, but was significantly lighter AND more stable. And because the keel was shorter than most, fore-and-aft, the boat was more maneuverable.

The result of all this was a 12-meter that could turn within her own length, gain a couple of seconds with each tack, accelerate quickly, stand up straight and go fast upwind and down, in light or heavy air. She could also sail closer to the wind than her competitors. In short, everything a boat needs to do to win races she could do better. And almost all of that superiority could be attributed, directly or indirectly, to those wings on her keel.

As *Australia II* chewed up the foreign fleet, the NYYC and its defenders watched with interest, then concern, and finally with something close to panic. Meanwhile, they had been getting information from shadowy sources that suggested the keel was vulnerable on legal grounds.

As steward of the Cup, the club was obligated to mount an impartial investigation of these charges. As defender, it desperately hoped to prove them. It was the age-old conflict of interest, made more acute by the fact that the responsibilities for enforcing the rules and mounting the best possible defense resided in the same committee

— the America's Cup Committee, also known informally as the selection committee, chaired by Robert McCullough.

But maybe it could avoid that conflict this time by getting one of the other challengers to protest.

Thus it was that Doug Keary, one of the managers of the Canadian syndicate, got a last-minute invitation on July 24 for dinner that evening aboard *Fox Hunter,* the NYYC's official launch, with McCullough and other committee members. Bruce Kirby, the Canadians' designer and a member of the club, was also invited. It was the day after their photographer, Jimmy Johnston, had been caught swimming under the Aussies' keel.

As told in "Trials," it was a pleasant evening, with the Canadians getting what Keary later referred to as "lots of encouragement" from the New Yorkers on the Johnston caper. As they were leaving, Kirby was handed some papers. One of them was a copy of a letter from McCullough to Mark H. Vinbury, a member of the measurement committee that had given *Australia II* a clean bill of health earlier in the summer, attacking the legality of the keel. Another was a note suggesting the Canadians consider filing a protest.

The letter to Vinbury was the yacht club's opening gun in the international imbroglio that came to be called "Keelgate," a reference to the infamous Watergate conspiracy a decade earlier. The letter alleged that *Australia II* had not been fairly rated under the rating rule and measurement instructions of the 12-meter class, as established by the International Yacht Racing Union (IYRU). It said the keel was a "peculiarity" as defined in Rule 27, which meant that the measurement committee should have referred the design to the "National Authority" (in America, the United States Yacht Racing Union). Until that was done, it alleged, the measurement was incomplete according to the rule and hence no rating could be given.

The memo also asserted that the keel's downward-sloping fins increased its draft when the boat was heeled, as it would be when racing, and alleged that this added depth — up to 10 1/2 inches — meant the boat exceeded the limits of the 12-meter measurement formula. (How the yacht club acquired the keel's dimensions wasn't disclosed at the time. Long after the races were over McCullough said they came from a member of one of the other Australian syndicates. He said he couldn't remember who or which one. "There wasn't a lot of love lost between them," he commented.)

The Canadians decided not to do anything about it. They were still negotiating with the Aussies' lawyers over the delicate matter of trespassing under their boat and had no desire to open a second can of worms. But, meanwhile, the letter found its way onto the doorsteps of the other challengers and into the press.

It was an immediate sensation. The possible consequences of such a challenge were staggering: *Australia II* could be knocked out of the race. By protesting every prior defeat at her hands, each of the other challengers could revive its own sunken, or rapidly sinking, hope of being selected.

THE RANKS ARE DRAWN

Having thrown that particular hand grenade into the enemy tent, McCullough and other committee members temporarily escaped its reverberations by setting out to sea on the club's annual regatta, thus leaving the Australians a clear field for righteous indignation in the next day's papers. That was the first of what became a very long string of public relations disasters.

Warren Jones, the Australians' chief spokesman and strategist throughout the keel episode, pointed out that the boat had been unanimously approved by the three-man measurement committee, and said that should be the end of it. "Australians are brought up in sport to accept the referee's decision," he said. "Obviously, certain members of the New York Yacht Club went to a different school."

He asserted that the keel was perfectly legal ("The only unfair advantage is that we thought of it first"), and that the club's protest would have been more creditable if it had acted earlier in the summer, not waited until *Australia II* had established herself as a clear and present danger. He also suggested that circulation of the memo among the challengers was dirty pool — an obvious attempt to encourage one of them to break ranks and protest the keel, so the club could keep its own hands clean.

If that was the intention, and it apparently was, it backfired. Within hours, representatives of all six syndicates emerged from a 90-minute meeting with a statement unanimously backing *Australia II*. Whether their action was motivated by good sportsmanship, a shared distaste for the NYYC's tactics, a conviction that the keel was if fact legal, or all three considerations is a moot point: By signing the statement, each syndicate head almost certainly wrote *finis* to his own America's Cup dream. The public perception was that the ranks had been drawn, with the good sports on one side and the NYYC, as usual, on the other.

It was the timing more than anything else that brought a hail of ridicule and contempt down about the patrician shoulders of the New Yorkers. If the keel was questionable now, with the trials more than half over and *Australia II* way out in front, why hadn't it been just as questionable back in June, when the score was 0-0? Rather than acknowledge the obvious — that the club hadn't acted until *Australia II* proved herself a real threat — McCullough and the others, after they returned from their cruise, hewed to the line that they were simply pursuing their duty to see that all contenders played by the rules.

First they explained the delay on the grounds that *Australia II* had to have sailed "a representative number of races" before a protest would be justified. Then McCullough said the Aussies themselves were responsible: "Their efforts to keep this secret didn't give us enough data to present to anybody," he said. "It wasn't until we could put all the pieces together two or three weeks ago that we had an idea what we were up against. Then our 12-meter experts told us they didn't think it was legal and should be tested." Left unspoken was the fact that the club had fervently hoped one of the other challengers would protest first. Not only would that have relieved it of its obvious conflict of interest, it would have avoided the jurisdictional problems that later developed.

Rubbish, said the Aussies, responding to the published explanations. "Do you think they would have brought this up if we hadn't been fast?" Jones asked. It was meant as a rhetorical question and was treated as such in the press, many of whose members harbored dark suspicions about the integrity of those aloof and powerful men who held the Cup, suspicions that rapidly hardened into conviction.

BLUFF OR SLIP-UP?

It didn't come out until weeks later that the New Yorkers had either missed — or been bluffed out of — a golden opportunity early in the summer to view the keel first-hand.

At a press conference in August, McCullough acknowledged that under the rules the club could have sent an official observer when *Australia II* was formally measured shortly after she arrived in Newport, "but we missed the date." Later, after checking into the matter further, he said, he found out the Australians had arrived a day late, throwing off the measurement schedule. They were supposed to notify the club and other interested parties a day in advance of the new date, but they failed to do so.

Nevertheless, Johan Valentijn, *Liberty's* designer, was on hand for the measurement — but was barred from the shed by *Australia II*'s armed guards, who demanded written credentials. Thus the measurement was conducted without outside observers.

According to McCullough, Warren Jones boasted about that afterward: "We bluffed you out," Jones reportedly chortled. If anyone had shown up with the necessary credentials, the Aussies would have been forced to let him in, he would have seen the keel, it could have been challenged then, and the course of America's Cup history might have been very different. McCullough said not getting a witness there was "a dumb slip-up." But he described the charge that the club didn't think of moving against the keel until it looked unbeatable as "a bum rap."

While editorial writers and cartoonists were having a field day at the club's expense, the New Yorkers a few days later suffered what must have seemed the unkindest cut of all. Olin Stephens, dean of American naval architects and designer of all but one U.S. 12-meter defender up to that point — the same Olin Stephens who had been rebuffed by *Liberty's* syndicate the year before — said the keel was within the rules. His comment had no legal weight, but so great was his preeminence in design circles, so respected his views, that Ben Lexcen seemed to be merely stating the obvious when he commented, "It was like being blessed by God."

In a wide-ranging interview long after the dust of 1983 had settled, Stephens, a softspoken man more at home in front of a computer terminal than a podium, said his off-the-cuff comments during a 12-Meter Association meeting had been intended simply to congratulate Lexcen for solving a technical problem that had plagued designers for years. He had no desire to become embroiled in the dispute, which affronted his sense of sportsmanship. When Lexcen tried to get him to put his remarks in writing, he said, he declined.

Meanwhile, McCullough's memo had gained a more sympathetic reading from its addressee, Mark Vinbury, the U.S. member of the three-man international measurement committee. (The others were Jack Savage of Australia and committee chairman Tony Watts of Britain, the official measurer of the International Yacht Racing Union.) Why Vinbury? Because unless the club could persuade the committee to reconsider its unanimous approval of the keel, there seemed no legal way to proceed further. Vinbury was not its chairman, but he was a member of the NYYC and its official measurer. He also lived in North Kingstown, Rhode Island, just across Narragansett Bay from Newport, which put him within convenient arm-twisting range.

Within 24 hours of receiving the NYYC memo, Vinbury was having second thoughts. He fired off a letter to chairman Watts: "I have no question that our committee measured *Australia II*'s keel according to the rule," he wrote. "I am concerned, however, that the rule as it is currently written is not able to assess the unusual shape of this keel and thereby fairly rate the yacht." He suggested the measurement committee ask the IYRU's Keel Boat Technical Committee to rule on it.

That was all the encouragement the NYYC would get from that quarter — Watts and Savage declined to reconsider — but it was enough to prompt the club's next move, which must have been in the works for weeks. On August 3 it sent a 34-page memo directly to George Andreadis, chairman of the Keel Boat Technical Committee (which normally meets once a year, in November, to discuss rules changes and interpretations) at the IYRU's London office. It asked for an immediate ruling on whether *Australia II* had been fairly rated. It set forth various legal interpretations and technical assessments of the keel from four U.S. yacht designers, which essentially amplified on the arguments in its first memo to Vinbury. Vinbury's letter to Watts was labelled Exhibit One.

But when this weighty document was released to the press, it was Exhibit Two that caught public attention — a memo dated July 29 to the NYYC's America's Cup Committee from Halsey Herreshoff, *Liberty*'s navigator. No technical knowledge was required to follow the meaning of its first sentence:

"If the closely guarded peculiar keel design of *Australia II* is allowed to remain in competition or is allowed to continue to be rated without penalty, the yacht will likely win the foreign trials and will likely win the America's Cup in September."

The Australians were dumbfounded. Defeatism in the *Liberty* camp! And right out there in public! Not only did it expose the consternation in Conner's camp, it also seemed to confirm the Aussies' charge that the club was acting only out of a desperate fear of losing rather than its oft-professed regard for its responsibilities under the deed of gift. "Desperate men do desperate things," Warren Jones commented in one of those typical one-liners calculated to demolish 34 pages of carefully reasoned argument.

After the races, Herreshoff downplayed the whole thing. He said he had no regrets about making public the syndicate's private fears. He had written the memo at the request of James Michael, who as legal counsel to the NYYC's America's Cup Committee was gathering documentation for that 34-page brief. He sent it directly to Michael, Herreshoff said, "but I've been around long enough, in politics and so forth (he's on the Bristol, R.I., town council), to know that it would probably get into the public eye." In fact, when Michael asked his permission to release it to the foreign syndicates, Herreshoff said he readily agreed, knowing it would quickly reach the press. Michael confirmed Herreshoff's account.

But this version is at odds with the simpler explanation offered by McCullough, the principal architect of the NYYC's keel protest:

"It wasn't supposed to be released," McCullough said in a post-Cup interview during which he acknowledged a number of public relations gaffes: "Jim Michael's secretary included it in the batch of stuff that went out and we didn't catch it. Halsey was upset about it, and I don't blame him."

While McCullough's committee was losing the public relations war, it wasn't doing much better on the legal front. Its appeal to the Keel Boat Technical Committee precipitated a convoluted jurisdictional dispute. Among other things, the patrician gentlemen in the blue blazers and straw hats suffered the further indignity of being informed by Nigel Hacking, secretary-general of the IYRU, that they had no standing: Not only was the NYYC not a member of the IYRU, not only had it bypassed the measurement committee and its own "National Authority," the United States Yacht Racing Union (USYRU), it also had no interest in the dispute because it had never faced *Australia II* on the water.

The club solved one of those defects by enlisting the USYRU to take up its cause. The union's executive director did so with enthusiasm, firing a mortar round right across the Aussies' bow. The smoke from that was still hanging in the air, however, when Warren Jones answered with a cannon. It was aimed directly at the Freedom Campaign, and it nearly blew them out of the water.

18
KEELGATE II — THE DUTCH CONNECTION

August 13 dawned with gusty winds and steep seas, too stormy for racing. It was just as stormy on shore. "Aussies accused of keel hush-up," said a headline in the morning paper.

The story reported on a three-page letter sent by Thomas F. Ehman Jr., then USYRU's executive director, to Nigel Hacking, secretary-general of the IYRU in London. In it, Ehman charged for the first time that an Australian measurer had raised questions about the legality of the keel when *Australia II* was measured in her homeland eight months previously. He said the measurer, acting under the same Rule 27 later cited by the NYYC, "evidently had doubts about the peculiarity of her keel appendages" and reported them to the Australian Yachting Federation.

The AYF, Ehman alleged, convened a special committee to study the matter, one of whose members was Jack Savage, who later certified *Australia II* in Newport as a member of the International Measurement Committee. The special committee unanimously recommended that Ben Lexcen seek a ruling on the "appendages" from IYRU's Keel Boat Technical Committee — the same action the NYYC was now urging. But Lexcen declined, Ehman charged, and the AYF "was persuaded not to make the report. Ever since, the keel and its appendages have been shrouded in the utmost secrecy."

Those were the strongest words yet from an American source, hinting broadly of dereliction of duty, improper influence and a deliberate coverup Down Under.

USYRU, based in Newport, had (and still has) close ties to the

NYYC. When Ehman left the organization after the 1983 match, it was to manage the *America II* syndicate, the club's 1987 America's Cup challenger. In this instance, his advocacy went well beyond the intermediate appellate-court role apparently envisioned by the IYRU, which acts as yachting's supreme court. The letter was drafted with the help of James Michael, the NYYC's counsel.

Months later, Ehman acknowledged the wording "may have been a little looser than it should have been." He said the facts, as explained to him by two reliable sources, were that the measurer had referred the keel wings to the AYF as a possible "peculiarity," and that Anthony Mooney, Ehman's counterpart in the AYF, had then personally looked at the keel and decided it was not peculiar after all. "Our feeling was, and still is, that the AYF should have gone to the IYRU, but they simply signed off on it instead," Ehman said.

In any case, it was inflammatory enough to prompt Warren Jones to let fire with both barrels. The first was a strongly worded denial of Ehman's allegations, backed by statements from the measurers involved. There was no such special committee, he said in a press release, and any suggestion that either the measurer or the AYF had been influenced in their decisions was "a gross distortion of the fact."

But it was the second barrel that got the headlines. Jones charged that the Freedom syndicate secretly tried to buy a copy of *Australia II*'s keel from the Dutch testing tank where Lexcen developed it — a clear violation of the NYYC's 1980 resolutions regarding country of origin. Furthermore, it acted with the full knowledge of the club's America's Cup Committee, which is responsible for enforcing those same resolutions!

It was the most sensational charge against the Americans since Lord Dunraven accused them of cheating in 1895. And, unlike Dunraven, the Aussies had proof — a copy of the secret telex from Edward du Moulin, the Freedom syndicate's general manager, to Peter van Oossanen, head of the Netherlands Ship Model Basin (NSMB) in Wageningen:

> ATTN.: DR. VAN OOSSANEN
> UNDERSTAND THAT YOU AND YOUR TEAM ARE RESPONSIBLE FOR DEVELOPMENT AND DESIGN OF SPECIAL KEEL FOR AUSTRALIA II.
> WE ARE FINALLY CONVINCED OF HER POTENTIAL

AND WOULD THEREFORE LIKE TO BUILD SAME
DESIGN UNDER ONE OF OUR BOATS.

WE WILL KEEP THIS CONFIDENTIAL AS NOT TO
JEOPARDIZE YOUR AGREEMENT WITH ALAN
BOND.... PLEASE TELEX US YOUR DESIGN AND CON-
SULTANCY FEES AND ANY OTHER CONDITIONS
WHICH MIGHT APPLY....

KIND REGARDS.

EDWARD DU MOULIN

MANAGER, FREEDOM CAMPAIGN

Jones said the NYYC was directly implicated through McCullough, who knew about the syndicate's attempt to buy the keel design but "didn't seem concerned about it." McCullough later
denied knowing about the telex in advance: "I certainly wouldn't
have written it that way," he commented. But he acknowledged the
club and the syndicate had been plotting strategy together.

Whatever the Americans hoped to gain from this was dashed by
the response from the NSMB, in a telex to du Moulin two days later. Jones thoughtfully enclosed a copy of that in his press release:

WE ... WOULD ASK YOU TO NOTE FIRSTLY THAT
WE WERE ASSOCIATED WITH THE AUSTRALIA II
CAMPAIGN BY WAY OF A TANK TESTING CON-
TRACT. THEIR DESIGNER MR BEN LEXCEN RESIDED
AT WAGENINGEN FOR FOUR MONTHS WHILST HE
COMPLETED DESIGNS FOR BOTH AUSTRALIA II AND
CHALLENGE 12.

AS WE ARE CONTRACTED TO THEM NOT TO TEST
12M MODELS FOR ANY OTHER 12 METRE SYNDICATE
UNTIL THE COMPLETION OF THE 1983 CAMPAIGN
WE HAVE TODAY ADVISED THEM OF YOUR QUERY
AND REQUESTED THEIR PERMISSION TO UNDER-
TAKE WORK FOR YOU. BUT UNFORTUNATELY THEY
HAVE ADVISED US THAT THEY ARE NOT PREPARED
TO ALLOW SUCH DISPENSATION.

THANK YOU FOR YOUR ENQUIRY AND WOULD BE
ONLY TOO DELIGHTED TO DISCUSS WORK FOR YOU
RELATED TO ANY CAMPAIGN IN 1986....

On the face of it, du Moulin's telex was simply staggering. The NYYC had been accused often of bending the rules in its favor, but never before had it been caught cheating. The revelation seemed to make a mockery of the club's public protestations that it was challenging the keel only because it had a responsibility to enforce the rules. Not to mention the relatively minor malfeasance of inviting the Dutch engineers to violate their contract with Alan Bond.

Once again, however, appearances were deceiving. It turned out the telex was a trick, part of a clandestine effort on the part of the club to prove their well-founded suspicions that Dutch engineers had had more to do with developing *Australia II*'s keel than the country-of-origin rules allowed. It took weeks for the real story to emerge, however, piece by piece. When it finally did, the NYYC no longer stood accused of cheating. That suspicion shifted to the Australians — where it lingers still.

But the club was under indictment for having practiced the most incredibly inept detective work, coupled with the most self-destructive public relations, in the entire history of the America's Cup. To this day many of its own members find it guilty of being an accessory to the loss — some would say theft — of its own trophy.

JOOP SLOOFF'S STORY

After the 1980 series, the NYYC issued new interpretations of the deed of gift relaxing the country-of-origin restrictions on equipment and materials. This move was hailed by Warren Jones and Alan Bond, among others, as a big step toward removing the defenders' monopoly on the best sailing technology. The club drew the line at allowing challengers to build their boats anywhere except within their own countries — a reasonable restriction if "competition between foreign countries" was to mean anything at all. One of the footnotes to these resolutions reads as follows:

"A foreign designer — however he is designated — participating in the design of a boat or a sail would violate both the letter and the spirit of the above Resolution, and any boat or sail so designed would be ineligible for use in America's Cup competition...."

Because Australia lacked a suitable tank-testing facility of its own, the club granted Bond's syndicate permission to use the Netherlands Ship Model Basin in developing its 1983 challengers. NSMB is one of the most sophisticated yachting research centers in the world. It was understood, however — at least by the NYYC — that the restrictions outlined above would still apply; the Aussies would use it only to test models Lexcen had designed.

When Bond's syndicate asked for clarification, the club's America's Cup Committee responded with a letter from Victor A. Romagna, its secretary. It set very general limits:

"Officially your tank tests in the Netherlands Ship Model Basin are entirely within the rules if:

1. They were under the sole supervision of Australian nationals.

2. The designs were from the drawing board of Australian nationals.

3. Results are used in the design of that Australian challenger only."

Ben Lexcen spent four months at NSMB, beginning in March, 1981, during which the design of both *Australia II* and *Challenge 12* evolved. Lexcen has acknowledged that his work at Wageningen went far beyond merely testing designs he had already drawn. He went there, he said, with "a blank sheet of paper" and worked with a team of six to eight Dutch engineers. He needed their knowledge of computer programs and other high-tech aspects of design. Lexcen, who quit school at age 14, admitted these areas were *terra incognita* to him.

He also acknowledges there was a constant give-and-take of ideas between himself and the engineers at Wageningen. Van Oossanen, for one, was well qualified to offer advice. He has written papers and given lectures on yacht design and 12-meter boats.

At one point, van Oossanen called in Joop W. Slooff, an aerodynamicist with the Dutch National Aerospace Laboratory (NLR). Slooff had been toying with the idea of adapting aerodynamic shapes to hydrodynamics — especially keel wings. Furthermore, his lab had a computer program that could be adapted to test the results.

Who first suggested adding wings to the keel became a highly charged question once the yacht club's investigation began. If it wasn't Lexcen, the keel could be declared ineligible.

Lexcen himself, in several interviews published after *Australia II* won the Cup, has maintained what seems to be a studied imprecision on the subject. For example, in "Ben Lexcen, the Man, the Keel and the Cup," a biography by Bruce Stannard, he is quoted as follows: "The process of design is so complex. It's hard to say where one person's ideas start and another's take over."

Stannard said Lexcen had tried fins or wings on smaller boats —
5.5s and dinghies — and either they didn't work or he couldn't see
any improvement. He concluded winged keels wouldn't work on 12-
meters; the extra wetted surface would exact too severe a penalty. But
in talking with van Oossanen and Slooff, Lexcen told Stannard, the
idea "came up and just grew from there."

Slooff's version is less ambiguous. He says the idea was his. Indeed,
it was he who innocently supplied the NYYC with its first lead to the
Dutch connection.

Slooff was in the United States in May, 1983, lecturing in Dayton,
Ohio. On his way home, he decided to stop off in Newport. He knew
little about the event at the time, and apparently nothing at all about
the country-of-origin rule.

When he approached the docks, he encountered Johan Valentijn,
whom he recognized from yachting magazine photographs as
Liberty's designer. Slooff started talking to him in Dutch, Valentijn's
native tongue, about his involvement with *Australia II*'s keel.
Valentijn says flatly that Slooff took complete credit for the design —
boasted about it, in fact.

When the controversy got into print and Slooff was made aware of
the implications, he backpedaled. He acknowledged talking with
Valentijn about the keel, but denied taking credit for it. Lexcen, he
told reporters, was the team leader and therefore the design was his.
But later, with the Cup match in the history books and the heat off,
Slooff confirmed Valentijn's version. Angered by the Australians'
attempt to patent the keel and their refusal to give him proper credit
after they won the Cup, Slooff spoke out in a New York Times interview with yachting writer Barbara Lloyd.

According to the Times and Nautical Quarterly (spring, 1985),
Slooff said he not only suggested the wings, he also proposed the
keel's revolutionary upside-down shape. When Lexcen and van
Oossanen told him to go ahead and test his ideas, he worked for about
a week turning the concepts into computer-generated line drawings
— apparently the same drawings that accompanied Lexcen's international patent applications. (Lexcen was never granted a patent.
Accounts differ as to whether he withdrew the applications or was denied because of prior claims. A number of people unrelated to the
Keelgate controversy came out of the woodwork after the keel was described in the press to say they had invented it first.)

CONTACT

Valentijn said he told Dennis Conner about the dockside conversation in May, but Conner didn't want to make an issue of it. At that point *Australia II* hadn't even arrived in Newport and no one knew what a threat she would prove to be. Accounts differ as to whether Slooff's claim was even reported at the time to members of the America's Cup Committee. But after *Australia II* made her mark, Valentijn recounted the conversation in detail. The committee asked him to find out whatever he could.

It was then that Valentijn hatched the plan to have du Moulin ask for the keel design, strictly as a ploy to find out how much NSMB had to do with it. Valentijn said he drafted the telex himself and du Moulin signed it. If the Dutch agreed to the proposal, it would have been a confession that they had designed *Australia II*'s keel. He said they felt the plot had a good chance of succeeding, because they knew the Dutch were ignorant of the country-of-origin rule and therefore had nothing to hide.

Did anyone involved anticipate that the Dutch would get on the phone to the Aussies as soon as they got the telex?

"No," Valentijn said. "I thought we would catch them by surprise. I guess we were very wrong. We didn't know they were so closely related to Warren Jones. We found out the hard way."

Van Oossanen, in fact, grew up in Australia, near Sydney Harbor, and still spends part of every year there. He was an old friend of Ben Lexcen's. But even if that connection had not existed, the success of the plot depended on the NSMB management being willing to get new business by secretly breaching their contract with Alan Bond. It is a telling commentary on the fragility of yachting ethics (and perhaps those of the NYYC) in 1983 that Valentijn, du Moulin and anyone else in on the ploy apparently just assumed they would.

Du Moulin's telex was dated July 20. Van Oossanen's response, in which he told the Americans he had reported their request to Bond's syndicate, came two days later. Why had Jones waited more than three weeks, until August 13, to detonate this devastating bombshell?

Asked about that a year after the match, Jones said he spent the interval worrying and puzzling over what the Americans were REALLY up to. He said the Australians saw through the ostensible purpose of the telex immediately: The Cup defenders weren't looking for a keel, they were trying to gather evidence. But he simply could not bring himself to believe they would be so naive as to expect the ploy to work. He kept thinking there must be some far subtler, more devious intention, but he couldn't figure out what. So he waited. When Ehman's unproven charges against the AYF surfaced, Jones decided the time was right for a counterattack.

But there's another possible explanation. "We have to make sure we have our high ground guarded," Jones told Stannard, outlining his Keelgate strategy. "And when we get on the high ground, those on the low ground are going to be in big trouble." Perhaps Jones wasn't as sure of his elevation as his August 13 press release conveyed.

According to this scenario, he would have been just as happy as the NYYC to keep the telexes secret forever.

By July 22, both sides knew the ploy had failed, and each side knew the other side knew. But Jones also knew, by this theory, that if the club pursued the matter with even a modicum of intelligence, sooner or later it was likely to come up with a smoking gun. Too many people in Wageningen knew too much. Furthermore, the Dutch had never been made co-conspirators. The Australians, unlike Valentijn and du Moulin, apparently had a healthy respect for the integrity of the NSMB engineers and had not told them about the country-of-origin clause.

So each side knew it was vulnerable to disclosure by the other. A tacit understanding developed: If the New Yorkers quit snooping around in The Netherlands, Jones would keep du Moulin's incriminating telex to himself. According to this scenario, the standoff continued until the Australians got word from Wageningen that the Americans had broken the unspoken agreement by sending a couple of emissaries to NSMB.

That visit was on August 10. The emissaries were Antoon van Rijn, an old friend of Valentijn's then living in North Carolina, and Valentijn's uncle, Wil Valentijn, who joined van Rijn in The Netherlands. They were sent in response to a Dutch newspaper story, in which NSMB spokesmen were taking credit for *Australia II*'s keel design. They said the results of their meeting were highly encouraging. Van Oossanen, apparently still unaware of the legal implications for his Australian clients and friends, had spoken freely.

Jones counterattacked three days later. That would have given him time enough to learn of the meeting from van Oossanen — in fact, Jones had been tipped off about it in advance — and prepare his press release. If the Americans were going to bring the Dutch connection out into the open anyway, why not beat them to the punch? And while he was at it, he might as well make it LOOK as if he was on high ground, even if he was up to his elbows in swamp water.

The press release, in fact, was positively Olympian:

"Notwithstanding the practice of the New York Yacht Club and now the USYRU in making public its rhetoric relating to the *Australia II* keel," it read, "it had been our intention not to issue publicly copies of correspondence relating to this matter. We now feel compelled, however, to make sure that people are aware of the extent to which some Americans have been prepared to go to hold the Cup. We now reveal...."

Even in his wildest fantasies, Jones could not have imagined the extent to which the Americans would self-destruct after this hit the press. Rather than contain the public relations damage by explaining the true purpose of the telex, the NYYC compounded it. It still hoped to find a smoking gun, apparently, and for that reason decided to keep its investigation into the Dutch connection under wraps.

That left du Moulin a limited number of options in trying to explain his telex. He made the best of them: It was never the Freedom syndicate's intention to enter a winged keel in competition, he said in a press release. He said the syndicate really hoped to put wings on its retired boat, *Magic*, which it still owned.

Not surprisingly, this fanciful explanation was greeted with public skepticism. Furthermore, when the real motive began to surface 10 days later, the club still maintained a stony silence — and again was made to look desperate and foolish.

When the Providence Journal-Bulletin reached him by telephone on August 24, van Oossanen disclosed that he had been visited earlier that day by Richard S. Latham, a representative of the NYYC's Cup Committee, who had asked him to sign a statement that NSMB employees were largely responsible for the winged keel. He refused, he said, because he realized the statement could disqualify *Australia II* and because it gave him too much credit for the design.

He also disclosed the August 10 meeting with Wil Valentijn and van Rijn, in which he said they tried to "coerce" him into taking credit for the keel. Having failed, van Oossanen said, the two men then went to the Dutch Ministry for Public Works (which provided 10 percent of NSMB's financing), and told its director NSMB had designed the keel, and The Netherlands really ought to take credit for it. The result, van Oossanen said, was a call from the minister in which he "strongly voiced the opinion that it would be good for Holland to take credit for the keel."

Once again, so it appeared, the NYYC had been caught in an underhanded attempt to knock *Australia II* out of the race without ever having to face her on the water, and once again it had been rebuffed. Worse yet, it was falsely accusing the Australians of doing precisely what the Americans had been caught red-handed trying to do earlier: use a foreign design, in violation of the club's own rules.

But once again, it wasn't that simple. As had happened so often throughout the summer, the NYYC had pursued what sounded like solid evidence of Australian foul play only to be finessed by its own bad timing, clumsy detective work and plain bad luck — not to mention the Aussies' ability to create a smoke screen with their smoldering indignation.

After their August 10 meeting, Valentijn and van Rijn drew up an "affidavit" they said reflected van Oossanen's version of the keel design. Among other things it gave Slooff credit for the idea of using wings, and confirmed that the "assistance" Lexcen received in Holland went well beyond what the club's resolutions permitted.

On August 24 the NYYC sent Latham and Wil Valentijn to Wageningen to get van Oossanen to sign it. Latham was chosen, he said later, because he is familiar with yachting rules (he's a chief judge for the USYRU) and the design process, being an industrial designer. "Jim Michael was the logical person," Latham added, "but he's a lawyer. They thought that would tense people up over there."

Latham was a member of the America's Cup Committee but had been on the periphery of the Keelgate investigation thus far. He was given a four-day crash course by Michael, Johan Valentijn, Halsey Herreshoff and others. Then he and Wil Valentijn were sent off, with a copy of the affidavit in Latham's briefcase.

LATHAM'S STORY

Latham's vivid recollection of their meeting with van Oossanen and his boss, M.W.C. Oosterveld, is a fascinating vignette, almost a microcosm of what has happened to the America's Cup itself. The picture that emerges is of two honorable men and two observers, caught up in a nasty subterfuge they neither fully understood nor had any taste for:

"When I came to the table in Holland," Latham recalled, "I learned that Peter (van Oossanen) had spent the summer in Newport. Just by accident, almost, he had come back to Holland for a week at the time when we asked for the interview. And that, of course, was a bit of a shocker."

It was even more of a shocker, Latham said, when van Oossanen told him what he was doing in Newport: He said he had designed the computer program *Australia II* was using to measure its performance on the water during the trials, and in fact had been running it himself — another apparent violation of the rules against foreign assistance.

"Peter was quite open because he felt very proud of himself and what they had accomplished," Latham recalled. "He was coming off of a real high at that moment (because of the boat's performance). So he really laid it all out, no problem. I was very curious about the theory and all that. Being an engineer, I could talk his language." Van Oossanen gave him a complete rundown on how the keel evolved. It was clear that Slooff had played "a very key role in that whole thing," Latham said.

"Anyway, it wasn't a bad meeting at all. And at one point I handed him the (America's Cup) rules and said, 'I wonder if you are aware of this.' I don't think he was, quite frankly. He looked at it, and then he said, 'Will you excuse us?' He and his boss went off for about a half an hour. Then they came back and said, 'Well, let's just put it this way: We're not going to say anything more.'

"I said, 'Well, I don't think you need to say anything more. You've already said enough.'

"We all were sort of wondering, what do we do next? We all sat and stared at each other, and I said, 'Gee, I don't know, why don't we leave, because I can see from this point on you would feel that you were endangering the Bond syndicate and yourself if you even talked any more.'

"Peter kind of cracked up. He became very emotional, and I really felt for him. He talked about how this had all come about, that he had had these theories for a hell of a long time, that he'd tried to get Bond to do it before, to really come and give him a shot at this, and he never did it. And finally, almost through a series of accidental circumstances, he'd been able to do it. He'd managed to make this whole damn thing work and had proven it to himself and to all his colleagues — you know, he'd given papers on this thing for the past five years.

And here he'd managed to achieve this success, and he just simply wasn't going to see it blown away. What could I do but sit there and empathize with the guy? So we just left."

DISCONNECTION

That empathy, the unspoken link between two men of science, was broken by the time Latham returned to Newport, the unsigned affidavit still in his briefcase. And so was the Dutch connection. As usual, it was Warren Jones who wielded the cutting tools.

On August 25, Jones issued a press release containing the text of a telex he said was sent to him by van Oossanen. The telex alleged Latham's affidavit "contained many incorrect statements which attempted to suggest that Ben Lexcen was not solely responsible for the design of *Australia II*," and that van Oossanen had refused to sign it.

"I find the New York Yacht Club's position and efforts on this matter to be deeply disturbing and offensive," the telex continued. "I hope they will have the good sense to desist from further untrue charges attributing the design of *Australia II* to anyone other than Ben Lexcen. In this regard, I am prepared to have my comments on this matter made public."

That last sentence was an unnecessary bit of window-dressing. Jones later acknowledged he had drafted the telex himself, with publication very much in mind. Latham said he found out later no one at NSMB even knew anything about it.

The NYYC made no reply. Once again the Cup's defenders left the high ground vacant, and once again Jones seized it:

"It is unfortunate that the America's Cup Committee, which is an arm of the prestigious New York Yacht Club, has chosen to conduct this reprehensible campaign of harassment and false claims...." he thundered. He said the Australians were especially upset that the club hadn't confronted them directly: "Why didn't someone say, 'Look, we've had a lot of disturbing, scurrilous statements, dockside scuttlebutt. What is your response to it?' New York Yacht Club, please come and talk to us.... Stop attacking us behind our backs. Or stop taking dockside rumor and trying to turn it into fact.... This transcends what is acceptable."

Latham, who assumed the telex had in fact come from van Oossanen, felt angry and betrayed by what he knew to be a complete distortion. He was mad enough to write a blistering counterattack to

Oosterveld, van Oossanen's boss, and release it to the press, along with the unsigned affidavit.

The letter said he had asked van Oossanen to read the affidavit carefully and make any changes he wished. Van Oossanen agreed it was basically accurate and needed only minor corrections. "He (van Oossanen) went on to add, however, that he was a close personal friend of Ben Lexcen and would not sign any statement, even if true, which might be of harm to Lexcen," Latham's letter continued. "At that point you, Dr. Oosterveld, intervened and prevented Dr. van Oossanen from indicating the innaccuracies in the draft. Notwithstanding this restraint upon (him) he repeated several more times that the draft was substantially correct in reporting the part NSMB and NLR played in the research and design work that produced the plans and keel of *Australia II*."

Latham told Oosterveld he could understand van Oossanen's reluctance to implicate his friend Lexcen and jeopardize future contracts with Bond by signing the affidavit. "I cannot, however, comprehend how you, as Dr. van Oossanen's superier, and as a senior official in NSMB, an institution with an international reputation, would suppress the truth and at the same time seek to conceal the important contributions by NSMB and NLR to the conception of the keel design . . . of *Australia II*."

To those who were still paying attention, Latham's letter made the most fascinating reading of the summer. But it wasn't released until September 5, the day *Australia II* won the right to challenge. By then, Keelgate had been resolved and everyone's attention was once more drawn to the battle at sea. The story got little play in the press. Latham's letter, in fact, was couched in the form of a demand for personal vindication rather than an official rebuttal. It asked for a public retraction of what he described as van Oossanen's "completely false" and potentially libelous telex.

Oosterveld responded within a week or so, in the form of a two-page letter which didn't reach Latham, who has an industrial design firm in Chicago, until after the races were over. Latham declined to reveal his exact words, but "the gist of it was that you can't ask a man (referring to van Oossanen) to testify against himself. He expressed the wish that the whole thing be put to bed, and I answered that the New York Yacht Club had done just that by dropping all protests."

And so the inquiry into the Dutch connection, which began so explosively with du Moulin's ill-conceived telex, just petered out. In the end, the New Yorkers allowed solid evidence of Aussie cheating to slip through their fingers.

Things might have turned out differently if Valentijn had gotten Slooff to sign a statement back in May, or if his uncle and van Rijn had brought a tape recorder with them on August 10. Even as late as his August 24 meeting at NSMB Latham might have pulled it off — if he had been just a little more devious, if he hadn't shown his Dutch colleagues a copy of the rules, if he had been a little less empathetic.

Why did the NYYC keep coming up empty-handed?

"Everyone seems to think we knew all about what was going on," Latham said. "We didn't. We were just trying to get some information. None of us was thinking like the CIA at that moment; we were still looking at it as a gentleman's game. Maybe it's fair to say we were all a little naive."

POSTSCRIPT

Perhaps the Dutch were a little naive, too. But as the 1987 contest approached, that seemed to have vanished. We know now that Peter van Oossanen had a special reason to celebrate the victory of *Australia II.* But he also faced a dilemma: How could he capitalize on his and NSMB's role in winged keel design without jeopardizing future relations with the Aussies by claiming credit?

He solved that very neatly in January, 1985, in a talk titled "The Development of the Twelve-Meter Class Yacht *Australia II,*" which he delivered to a group of sailors and naval architects at the U.S. Naval Academy in Annapolis.

Big test tank facilities like NSMB have several very knowledgable scientists on their staffs who customarily "make available this knowledge on specific topics when working together with designers," van Oossanen said, as quoted in Sailor magazine's April issue.

"This, however, does not make them responsible for the final design, and any suggestion in this direction is incorrect. Ben Lexcen alone was responsible for the design of *Australia II.* It is likely, however, that if he had not worked at NSMB but somewhere else on the *Australia II* project, the yacht would have looked quite different and probably not have a winged keel."

At last count, nine Cup syndicates — all four Australian defenders and five challengers from Europe and Canada — had gotten the message and were testing their 1987 designs at NSMB.

19
KEELGATE III —
CAPITULATION

The NYYC's capitulation, like its transfer of the Cup a month later, was handled with a public grace that concealed deep bitterness. But nothing could conceal the almost farcical way the final act unfolded.

On August 20 the normally voluble Peter de Savary, head of the British syndicate whose *Victory '83* was within one day of nailing down the right to face *Australia II* in the challenge finals, called a press conference to reveal a secret he said he'd been keeping for more than a year: The British had asked the IYRU the previous summer for a confidential ruling on winged keels. Both the IYRU and Anthony Watts, its chief measurer and later chairman of the International Measurement Committee for the Cup races, had ruled they were permitted, he said. Furthermore, Watts had written later to Ian Howlett, *Victory '83*'s designer, saying his previous ruling appeared to apply to *Australia II* as well.

If that was so, that part of the controversy apparently had been settled before all the fuss began!

De Savary explained the British had asked for the ruling because they had been considering wings for their own keel, an idea he said they later abandoned. He said he had asked for confidentially because he, like the Aussies, didn't want anyone else copying the idea. That presumably explained why the IYRU had said nothing about it.

But de Savary's own silence after the British decided against wings was harder to understand, especially as he and Alan Bond were known to be good friends. "We wanted to see if the Australians could sort out the matter by themselves with the authorities and the challengers," he said. "Now it seems to us the matter has gone on far too long. It's time to get back to boat racing."

It was a strange explanation. But then, it was a strange press conference. Bond shared the podium with de Savary, but was unusually tight-lipped. And two of the most intriguing questions were asked not by members of the press but by a couple of interlopers.

Bond said his syndicate agreed with de Savary, and that he would answer no more questions about it. Nonetheless, a question was posed to him by Kenneth B. Weller, offshore director of the USYRU. When, Weller wanted to know, did the Australians learn of the British correspondence?

"Today," Bond snapped.

"Then your keel was entered in the competition without any knowledge of the IYRU opinion?" Weller persisted. Bond reminded him that he intended to answer no more questions.

Then Gary Mull stood up and identified himself as one of two Americans on the IYRU's Keel Boat Technical Committee.

"It is the policy of the Keel Boat Technical Committee to announce all rule interpretations each November to the public," he said. "My question to Mr. de Savary is, does he know of any reason why this interpretation was not made public last November?" De Savary said he did not.

Bond then grabbed the microphone and, referring to an interview Mull had given the Providence Journal-Bulletin earlier in the week, said, "I think, Mr. Mull, that you have demonstrated that you are biased on this question. It is therefore improper that you should be here. I request that you leave." Mull did so.

Outside, he expressed his puzzlement that he and other members of the keel boat committee, which he said has a policy against secret rulings, had not been informed — especially as he had specifically asked Watts for all 12-meter interpretations and had received nothing on the British wings.

Two days after de Savary's press conference, a possible reason for his earlier silence was revealed: It turned out Victory '83 had wings after all — or at least "winglets" — installed earlier behind a "modesty skirt" resembling Australia II's.

This revelation came from none other than Mark Vinbury, the measurement committee's U.S. member. The British asked him to come to their dock August 22, to look at Victory '83's winglets and give them a confidential opinion on whether she would have to be re-measured with them attached. Vinbury looked at the keel and told them the wings were okay since they were of neutral buoyancy and therefore didn't add to displacement. The yacht would not have to be remeasured.

Victory '83 then sailed off to meet *Australia II* in a semifinal race. (*Australia II* won by 1:21. Aside from being the first known test of wings against wings, the race had little meaning; both boats had already qualified for the challenger finals.)

Vinbury agreed to keep quiet about the wings, de Savary said later. But an hour after *Victory '83* left the dock, Vinbury was back with a copy of a letter he had written to USYRU, saying he believed the wings were a "peculiarity" and questioning whether the yacht could be "fairly rated" under the existing rule — the same caveat he had belatedly expressed about *Australia II* earlier in the summer. He also had a copy of a letter to the IYRU written by Weller, USYRU's off-shore director, in which Weller cited Vinbury's doubts and called for an inquiry.

De Savary was furious. He regarded Vinbury's letter as a breach of confidentiality. He also said the USYRU, which was the "National Authority" only for U.S. boats, had no business butting in. (The Australians had raised the same objection about USYRU's role earlier. Like many of the summer's jurisdictional battles, that one ended inconclusively.)

But the secret was out. De Savary disclosed the British had been working on horizontal fins for 18 months, for possible use in the finals against *Australia II*, and had been using them on and off all summer under *Victory '83*'s trial horse, *Australia*. He pointed again to IYRU's sanction of the previous summer and said that should settle the matter of their legality.

Meanwhile, members of the America's Cup Committee were looking for confirmation of the IYRU's winged-keel sanction. First they learned that neither the two American members of the Keel Boat Technical Committee nor Beppe Croce, president of the IYRU, knew anything about such a ruling. The committee's chairman in 1982 had died.

After the races were over and the Cup was on its way to Perth, they searched through the IYRU's files. Nothing. Eventually, they were told the ruling was an informal one, made by the three British members of the Keel Boat Technical Committee and the secretary-general of the IYRU, Nigel Hacking, also a Britisher — not even a majority of the 14-member committee. No evidence of a formal ruling has ever been found.

At least some Cup committee members still harbor resentment over the "stonewalling" they say they got from the IYRU, and the suspicion that the entire episode was an ex-post-facto fabrication by de Savary and Bond. According to that theory, the whole thing was cooked up by the Aussies to abort a meeting called by the IYRU for August 30, at which the union planned to look into all the questions surrounding the legality of *Australia II*'s keel. That meeting was in fact cancelled in the wake of the NYYC's capitulation four days before it was to be held. (The IYRU's Keel Boat Technical Committee took up the question of keel wings at its regular November meeting after the races — and ruled they were legal. The discussion lasted only ten minutes.)

To add to the intrigue, about a year after he won the Cup Bond told a journalist that he had known about the IYRU's sanction of wings for *Victory '83* back in 1982, shortly after it was issued. He declined to reveal his source. Later, de Savary was asked if that were true.

"I don't know," he said. "He might have known about it. He's a very clever man, you know."

THE FINAL ACT

Things moved rapidly after de Savary's August 20 press conference. First Vinbury blew the whistle on *Victory '83*'s wings. Next, Warren Jones gave the NYYC a copy of the 1982 letter from Watts to Howlett, containing the opinion that *Australia II*'s wings were legal. Then Latham came away empty-handed from his meeting at NSMB.

On August 26, with the challenge finals starting the following day and the Cup series itself less than three weeks away, the NYYC found itself losing on all fronts. Bowing to the inevitable, Robert G. Stone Jr., the club's commodore, and Robert McCullough, chairman of its America's Cup Committee, made the long walk to the podium in the National Guard Armory on Thames Street and announced to the world that the NYYC was dropping all protests against winged keels, whether Australian or British.

They said their decision was based on the IYRU ruling on *Victory '83* and its subsequent opinion that it applied to *Australia II* as well. "For reasons unknown to us, neither the British challengers nor the International Yacht Racing Union saw fit to advise...us of it," Commodore Stone said in a prepared statement. "Regrettably, this omission has resulted in unnecessary controversy.... If we had known about it, this whole controversy would have been over before it began."

They also acknowledged their failure to establish a Dutch connection. McCullough said the club had pursued it because of a story in a Dutch newspaper, not rumors. He categorically denied that Latham had tried to coerce anyone into signing false statements. "We were there to find facts, not to light fires," he said. He also denied the Aussies' charge that the club had obtained information on the exact measurements of the keel illegally: "We didn't go after it; it was given to us from more than one source.

"I think that our conduct has been absolutely straightforward. We have tried not to push our weight around at all or make any wild public statements," McCullough said.

Stone's statement ended on an upbeat note: "With these matters resolved we can now all focus on the match itself to be settled on the water, and may the better yacht win."

Keelgate finally was over — or so everyone thought at the time. But then the Cup committee heard more rumors, including one that the Aussies had used an American-designed mast. They decided on one last counteroffensive. On September 11, two days before the racing was to start, McCullough handed Alan Bond a three-page "certificate of compliance" and asked him to sign it, "under penalty of perjury."

The 10-point document asked Bond to swear to detailed statements such as the following:

"Neither the *Australia II* syndicate nor Ben Lexcen contracted with or retained the Netherlands Ship Model Basin to perform consulting and research services to assist in the design of *Australia II*. Neither the Netherlands Ship Model Basin nor the Netherlands National Aerospace Laboratory, or any employee or representative of either of said organizations, contributed any inventions or design concepts which led to or were incorporated in the design of the keel, hull and/or rig of *Australia II*."

The committee was asking Bond to deny the whole laundry list of allegations it had heard about the parentage of the keel. It was customary to ask challengers to sign a simple statement that they had complied with the race conditions, and Bond did so the following day. But this document went far beyond that. Bond refused to sign it.

McCullough then went to William Fesq, former commodore of the Royal Sydney Yacht Squadron and liaison chairman for all the challengers, told him the story, and said, "Find another challenger." Fesq refused to consider it.

The next day the America's Cup Committee met in private two hours before the pre-race captains' meeting (see Prologue). They gathered aboard *Summertime*, the luxury cabin cruiser owned by Emil "Bus" Mosbacher Jr., vice commodore of the NYYC and a member of the Cup committee. Mosbacher thinks there were 18 in all, including several past and present flag officers and the America's Cup committee, some of whose nine members were absent.

The question before them was whether to disqualify *Australia II*.

Almost everyone present had followed the committee's keel investigation at close range and was convinced the Australians had violated the conditions of the match. But they had no tangible proof — certainly nothing that would stand up in the court of public opinion, where they already stood all-but-convicted of shrinking from a fair fight. If they barred *Australia II* at this late date, they would be branded as history's greatest spoilsports.

Afterward, there was disagreement over the vote, or even whether any vote was taken. There is general agreement that it wasn't close, however. After everyone had had a chance to say his piece, there was a clear consensus: The club had no choice but to go ahead with the match.

Two or three people argued strenuously for the other side. Among them were Victor Romagna, the committee's secretary, and James Michael, its legal counsel. They saw Bond's refusal to sign as a clear admission of guilt. And they felt the club had a duty, as trustee under the deed of gift, to see that the rules were upheld. If they were vilified for that, so be it.

It was Romagna who first disclosed the meeting, in the pages of "Upset," by Michael Levitt and Barbara Lloyd. "We were in a tight spot," Romagna was quoted. "We didn't want to appear to be spoiling it for the sake of spoiling it, but we were convinced the Australians had overlooked nearly every rule. We went around the room and everyone said their piece. Then all of a sudden, the discussion came to a shuddering halt.... We didn't have the guts to stand up and say we won't race...and so we just folded our tents and went off into oblivion."

After "Upset" appeared in December, 1983, McCullough offered a far less dramatic version. As committee chairman, he emphasized the practical problems:

"We asked (the Australians) to sign a document, which they refused to sign. A couple of members made it clear they thought that was an admission of guilt, but others said they wouldn't have signed it, either. Only one or two members spoke in favor of cancelling. After all, at that point what could you do about it? As long as we decided we couldn't get proof, we had to live with it. Almost all of our people felt that way: You've got to go ahead."

Robert Bavier, a former Cup defender, looked at the implications for the sport:

"To me, it would have been terribly unfair. These Australians had done a great job, they were sailing well. To me the America's Cup is a great thing, and cancelling would have been the end of the America's Cup."

But it was Arthur J. Santry Jr. who was described as the most forceful advocate for the majority. Santry, who became commodore in 1986 and will therefore preside over the club's first Cup challenge in 1987, emphasized the public relations aspects:

"When you have a world event of this sort, with thousands of people having come from all over, with all the money that had been spent in preparation, you can't say, 'Well, gee, tomorrow's the day of the game, boys, but we don't like what you're doing, so there's not going to be any game tomorrow.' You can't conduct yourself in that manner."

Minutes after the meeting broke up, Michael learned their suspicions about the Australians' American-designed mast were true.

"As I walked into the Vanderbilt mansion for the 5 o'clock captains' meeting," he said, "I was handed a telegram, which gave me confirmation of the fact that they had simply used all of the American know-how and applied it to this spar. So they had an illegal spar. I handed that to Bob McCullough as we walked into the meeting room. He glanced at it and put it in his pocket, and that was the end of that."

Looking back on it, Mosbacher said the decision stemmed from "the almost overpowering dedication of those trustees and flag officers and members of the club present to the fact that the club is made up of men who are sportsmen and gentlemen, and should deport themselves as such even if they knew they were being cheated or had."

Michael saw it a little differently: "The officers of the club, led principally by Arthur Santry's very strong position in the matter, decided that the public relations aspect of the situation overrode all the other considerations, and therefore we should go forward," he said.

There is no question cancelling the race would have provoked a firestorm of criticism such as the club had not seen in the entire 132-year history of the Cup. To those who were following events through the press, the Keelgate pattern seemed obvious: The NYYC had been grasping at straws all summer, in a desperate attempt to avoid a fair fight on the water. Most of its maneuvering was done in secret — a tacit confession that its tactics couldn't stand the light of day. Whenever one of those sneaky moves was exposed by the Aussies or their friends, the club either said nothing or tried to lie its way out of it. Cancelling the races would have been the crowning, unforgivable outrage.

To those on the American side who had an inside view of events and a big stake in the outcome, the decision NOT to cancel was the real outrage. In "Upset," Fritz Jewett, Freedom syndicate chairman, put it this way: "They put expediency ahead of principle. We were counting on the New York Yacht Club to represent us in these issues, and as far as we were concerned, the New York Yacht Club let us down."

Johan Valentijn, who designed the boat that lost the Cup, has an even more pungent view: "I think they deserved to lose the Cup, really. They played so stupidly all summer long. I mean, I'm a member of the New York Yacht Club, but I think they're a real dumb bunch of horse's asses."

20
THE BIG PSYCH

America's Cup battles are fought on land as well as at sea, as we have seen. But there is a third front, the shadowy, ill-defined realm of the mind, where fear and reality can collide and alter each other in unpredictable ways. In this arena of psychological warfare, races can be won or lost before the boats leave their docks. In 1983, it may have been the most crucial battleground of all.

TURNING POINTS

As Cup competition stiffened during the 1960s and '70s, the campaigners gradually learned how to bring every aspect of their assaults to the razor edge of fine-tuned perfection. The boats and sails were stripped down and trimmed almost to the breaking point, sometimes beyond it. Then the crews' skills were honed through months of daily calisthenics and repetitive training until they responded automatically and as a unit, like a well oiled machine. As these workups stretched from months to years, only one variable remained largely untapped and uncontrolled — the innermost thoughts and emotions of the competitors.

The 1983 campaign changed that. It brought to the fore two men who passionately believed in the power of psychological motivation, mental visualization, expanded "comfort zones," and other tricks from the sports psychologist's grab bag. Now, as the 1987 contest looms, these professional mind-tuners have become standard fixtures of each campaign.

Sports psychology was still in its infancy, still the butt of jokes and ridicule, when Dennis Conner used some of its techniques in his 1980 victory. It was part of his repertoire again in 1983, though no one talked about it very much.

Meanwhile, John Bertrand became skipper of *Australia II.* Bertrand not only embraced sports psychology as an essential discipline for his own crew, he turned its lessons in positive thinking upside down and used them against his opponents. In Newport, he developed a psychological weapon that not only was a perversion of the power of positivism, it was also a deliberate fraud, founded upon secrecy and lies. But as Bertrand himself might have said, what the hell? It worked, didn't it?

Conner set the stage in 1978 with his book, "No Excuse to Lose," which addresses mental attitude as one of a number of keys to winning yacht races.

The Conner philosophy is that everyone has a psychological "comfort zone," a level of performance in which he feels comfortable. If an athlete finds himself in competition over his head, he will do fine as long as he's behind, where he knows he belongs. But once he gets ahead, he starts feeling uncomfortable. Subconsciously but almost inevitably, he will look for a way to blow it, to get back where he feels safe.

Winners are people whose comfort zone has been expanded to the limit. For Conner, that happened in 1971, when he won his first major sailing championship, the Star Worlds. He hadn't expected to win. In fact, he had a number of psychological excuses all prepared for NOT winning. But when he won anyway, his self-image changed dramatically.

"My image of a Star champion was of somebody who very rarely lost any races at all, anywhere, so all of a sudden that image became my self-image, and my comfort zone changed radically.... I had to be serious and win all the time. From then on, I couldn't give myself any excuse to lose. There are some sailors who don't work hard on their boats and gear, and I think it's because they are looking for excuses to lose."

John Bertrand read Conner's book, of course. He said he found it "very illuminating." While others read it for its pages and pages of practical advice on winning races, Bertrand was looking for Conner's psychological Achilles heel. He found it, right there in that statement of his basic beliefs. But he didn't realize how powerful a weapon it was until he got to Newport.

Bertrand's psychological turning point came in 1976, in the

Montreal Olympics. He was racing for the gold medal in the decisive race, hotly pursued by an East German. Suddenly he began to have self-doubts. He had gone beyond his comfort zone. He felt the need to make a quick, positive move, so he took a risk — and capsized. The gold was lost, but the lesson remained, along with the image of the East German's face, a mask of cold, impassive, controlled determination.

Bertrand began his study of sports psychology right after the games. He learned that it was a highly developed science in East Germany and other Eastern Bloc countries, where mind-control is more acceptable than in the West. He learned about comfort zones and mental visualization and all the rest. He learned why he had tipped his boat over. And he began to understand one reason the Australians' past Cup campaigns had failed. They simply hadn't thought of themselves as winners.

Now, in 1980, he was the designated skipper for Alan Bond's 1983 assault. Bond, predictably, had no use for sports psychology, Bertrand wrote. Neither did the syndicate's manager and chief strategist, Warren Jones. Bertrand brought sports psychologist Laurie Hayden aboard anyway, over Bond's objections ("This guy's just excess baggage"), and Hayden went to work developing a diverse bunch of sailors into a crew with a winning attitude.

They concentrated on building self-confidence and on stress management, especially the unaccustomed stress of being ahead in an America's Cup race against an American crew. Bertrand read them passages from his own source of inspiration, Richard Bach's "Jonathan Livingston Seagull." They even listened to American voices, and the sound of a following 12-meter bow wave, just to get used to the experience. The whole idea, Bertrand wrote, was to expand their comfort zone to an area where no Australian had ever gone before, crossing the finish line in the final America's Cup race as the victory gun fires.

It was only after they got to Newport that the Aussies discovered the enormous potential of the flip side to all this — of the terrible insecurity a secret weapon like their winged keel could inspire among the enemy. If Bertrand's version of events is to be trusted, when they found that out they launched what turned into the biggest and most spectacularly successful con job in the history of sports.

THE SUPERBOAT MYTH

To hear Bertrand tell it, it wasn't Ben Lexcen's keel that won the Cup. That made *Australia II* go fast, probably as fast as the best of her rivals. But it certainly didn't make her unbeatable. Under some conditions, he said, she simply could not win against the best of the other challengers, let alone the Americans. During the early training in Australia, he even considered switching to her trial horse, the conventional *Challenge 12.* And had he done so, he believes he and his crew still would have won the America's Cup.

They won, he claims, partly because of more rigorous crew training, better psychological preparation and a more thorough sail-development program than any previous challenger. But that merely made them competitive. What gave them a clear and perhaps decisive edge was the Superboat Myth, the carefully nurtured panic among the Americans that the winged keel made *Australia II* invincible.

Bertrand insists the Australians did nothing to promote that idea. It began as speculation in the press, then rapidly hardened into journalistic dogma as *Australia II* won her first 10 trial races. They sensed the advantage: "From all my previous experience," Bertrand wrote, "I knew there is nothing quite as offputting in a big race as to be up against an opponent whose boat was a bit of a mystery."

So the Aussies quietly dropped their original plan, to take the wraps off the keel as soon as they judged it was too late for anyone to copy it. And Bertrand decided to perpetuate the myth any way he could. His chief ally in that "glorious lie," he said, was the press. Whenever the boat was beaten, he would either blame himself or claim they were testing sails — anything to obscure the fact that *Australia II* was shaky downwind and in a chop.

It worked marvelously. The press bought it, all of it. Not only was the myth enhanced, but Bertrand's smiling self-effacement, his willingness to acknowledge errors and praise the skill of his opponents, created another myth. He became the darling of the press corps and the public, in contrast to Dennis Conner, who often seemed aloof, condescending or downright sulky. And all the time he was lying through his teeth! Chances are Bertrand's press image would have been very different had its members known at the time what he really thought of them:

The Superboat Myth, he wrote, "was a lovely story for the newspapers, possessing the three advantages many sports journalists prize above everything: (1) It was dead easy to understand (not like the real issue, sails, which are wildly complicated and scientific and full of difficult connotations like aerodynamics); (2) It might even be true; and (3) Even if it was not true, it was the type of thing we probably would not deny. Perfect."

Once launched, the myth took on a life of its own. For example, *Australia II* usually climbed out to a huge lead on the first, upwind, leg, but lost ground downwind. Somehow, the word went out that Bertrand was cocking the trim tab one way, the rudder the other — the nautical equivalent of stepping on the brakes — to mislead his opponents about his real boat speed.

Not true, says Bertrand. He said the fact is the boat was slow downwind, at least early in the summer before they perfected their sail trim. "We didn't plant the rumor, intentionally, but we never quelled it. In hindsight, we SHOULD have planted it. That type of rumor was absolutely fantastic for our push to win the America's Cup."

A QUESTION OF CREDIBILITY

The problem with Bertrand's fascinating, readable and revealing book is — how much of it should one believe? Was Bertrand lying in 1983, when he gave full credit to the secret keel? Or is he lying now, when he gives full credit to his crew, with an extra large portion for himself? When a self-confessed liar writes a self-serving account, in which he reveals his delight in misleading the public, any reasonable man would read with caution. When his book is about a subject as fraught with deception as the America's Cup, a reasonable man might be expected to toss it out unread.

As we will see in Part IV, that's exactly what Alan Bond was reported to have done after he read a few pages. The big problem he and Ben Lexcen and the rest of the *Australia II* camp reportedly had with Bertrand's account is that it is a little TOO self-serving. They regarded Bertrand as a member of the crew. Bertrand portrays himself as their leader, their inspiration, and one of the campaign's chief strategists.

On the other hand, published reports of the Aussies' angry reactions included no denials that they had invented the Superboat Myth. They just thought their skipper had taken too much credit for it. There is no doubt that everyone in the syndicate, from Alan Bond on down, saw the secret keel as a psychological weapon of enormous potential. Who saw it first, and when, is academic.

The problem of credibility goes far beyond Bertrand's book. Now that psychological warfare, secrecy, disinformation, media manipulation and other lies by whatever name are accepted as legitimate weapons in the Cup campaigner's arsenal, every statement must be greeted with suspicion, sifted for hidden motivations.

One year after he masterminded the Aussies' victory, Warren Jones took time out during the 12-Meter Worlds in Sardinia to answer a reporter's questions. Among other things, he said he and his syndicate had expected the NYYC to protest their keel, and had prepared their legal defense even before they left Australia. He said they drew up detailed briefing papers on four points they thought the club might challenge them on, not necessarily all related to the keel. They noted where they might be vulnerable, the outlines of the probable attack, and the appropriate response.

As it developed, Jones said, the NYYC behaved exactly as predicted on three of the four issues, but never brought up the fourth -- the one on which the Aussies felt they were most vulnerable! Jones declined to say what that was, "because we have a regatta to race in 1987."

Jones knew his comments were likely to appear in print before the 1987 match. Was he simply boasting about the thoroughness of their preparations in 1983? Or was that fourth point a red herring, meant to bedevil and distract any challengers who might read about it?

Similarly, what was behind Alan Bond's comment, made to the same reporter the day before, that he had known about the IYRU's sanction of *Victory '83*'s keel wings (see previous chapter) back in 1982? Was it true? Or was it a land-based version of the Superboat Myth, designed to convince his 1987 opponents that any attempt at secrecy would be futile against the omniscient Aussie spy network?

By contrast, certain members of the NYYC claim to have heard reliable stories of panic and disarray in the Aussie camp at the height of the Keelgate investigation. According to these rumors, Jones and his compatriots thought the jig was up more than once, that it would be only a matter of time before their keel was exposed and their boat was disqualified. Supposedly, they were prepared to substitute *Challenge 12* for *Australia II* when that happened.

But the New Yorkers had their own axes to grind. And after 1983, no one can safely assume their honor as gentlemen would prevent them from passing on unverified rumors as gospel truth — or worse.

We may never know whether the tactical and psychological warfare waged by the Aussies was a carefully planned campaign, or an ad hoc, day-by-day response to changing circumstances. Either way it was remarkably effective, even brilliant — though a big assist must be given to the NYYC's tendency to shoot itself in the foot.

PREOCCUPATIONS

As far as Bertrand was concerned, the biggest psychological advantage he had was that Dennis Conner would be his opponent. Bertrand believed that if anyone could be psyched out by a piece of equipment he couldn't match or even see, it would be Conner. "He is just about as sensitive as anyone to those twin allies of the match racers — boat speed and bullshit," Bertrand wrote. "I am quite certain that *Australia II* was on his mind, more than it should have been and more than was good for him."

It shouldn't have been on Conner's mind at all early in the summer. He had enough to worry about. While *Australia II* sailed to a 11-1 record in the challengers' June trials, the defenders were all bunched up, *Liberty* and *Courageous* with 6-5 records each, *Defender* at 5-7. It was only June and already Conner had lost as many races as he had in all of 1980. But even at that early stage, there was a growing preoccupation in *Liberty*'s camp with *Australia II* and her secret keel. Syndicate members soon were shadowing virtually every move Bertrand made on the water from a support boat.

"I've been in international sports in the past, and I know guys like Conner," Bertrand said in an interview while on tour promoting his new book. "They rely so much on their equipment. And if they don't believe in their equipment, they can really start to become undone. It's all mystical, and if you don't have the magic, forget it."

Conner, whose syndicate had paid for an unprecedented four boats, no longer had his *Magic*, nor his *Spirit*. Worse yet, though few people knew it at the time, after the June trials he also lost his *Freedom*.

His original plan was to sail *Liberty* in June, make some extensive modifications to *Freedom*, the 1980 winner, between the trials, and sail her in July while *Liberty* was upgraded. Then he would sail *Liberty* in the August trials and into the Cup match, thus continuing the methodical leapfrogging approach he announced at the beginning of the campaign. But the syndicate made a basic error. They forgot about the consequences of a recent change in the 12-meter rules. When the official measurer was called to recertify the modified *Freedom*, he told the dismayed syndicate heads he could not. She had been exempted from the new rules by a grandfather clause, but the changes made to her hull nullified the clause. She was no longer a legal 12-meter! Conner, who prided himself on his equipment and his preparations, who liked to keep his options open until the last minute, was down to his last boat.

One thing that concerned many people about Dennis Conner was that he took on too much responsibility. Unlike Bertrand, who left everything that didn't bear directly on sailing in the capable hands of Warren Jones and other syndicate members, Conner involved himself in every aspect of the campaign. In fact, he seemed obsessed by details.

"I think Dennis had too much on his plate," said Norris Hoyt, a veteran America's Cup observer and radio commentator. "You watched Dennis, and all through the campaign he got fatter, and he got tired. Back at home they had this giant computer. Everything the boat did every day was on the tapes. Dennis would sail the boat all day, go home, and while everyone else was exercising, he would sit there and go over the tapes.... He'd have half the crew down there wet-sanding (*Liberty*'s hull) through the dark of the night, under floodlights. After he finished with the tapes, he'd go down and mess with that, check them out, feel the hull with his fingers. And I don't think you can do that for two years and keep focus."

Conner also had worries that had nothing to do with sailing. Back home in San Diego his drapery business was unravelling. Conner had entered the business in partnership with Alan Raffee, a sailor who took a tolerant attitude toward his partner's sailing pursuits. When Raffee died in a plane crash in 1979, the company went to his children, whose approach was clearly more businesslike. In October, 1983, Kim Raffee disclosed that a legal battle had been going on all summer. Among other things, Conner was being sued for salary he allegedly collected for three months during which he was in fulltime training for the Cup.

SIGNS OF STRAIN

But the major distraction in Conner's camp, as in everyone else's, was the secret keel. Just how worried they were about it became obvious when Halsey Herreshoff's famous memo — the one in which he said *Australia II* would likely win the Cup unless something could be done about the keel — surfaced early in August.

Only once before had any defender or would-be defender expressed the unthinkable thought. That was in 1934, when *Rainbow* had lost the first two races and was trailing by six minutes in the third. Her skipper, Mike Vanderbilt, turned the wheel over to Sherman Hoyt and went below to mourn the impending loss of the Cup. But to talk about losing even before being selected as defender, after 132 years of victories, was blasphemy bordering on hysteria.

Herreshoff said later he wrote that provocative first sentence to get the attention of the NYYC's America's Cup Committee — to shake the gentlemanly reserve from the men in the Brenton-red trousers and blue blazers and get them to DO something. Conner hadn't seen the memo before its release, Herreshoff said, but he had agreed with the contents. Everyone in the syndicate felt the same way, he added.

Despite Herreshoff's later denials, he almost certainly intended the memo to remain private. When it slipped out, it was obvious to anyone who had read Conner's book that the psychological war was already over. The man most likely to defend the longest winning streak in sports history, the man who lived or died according to the images in his own mind, had given himself an excuse to lose!

Herreshoff, not surprisingly, rejects that interpretation. Certainly it wasn't meant as "an excuse to lose," he said, and neither the memo nor the concern it expressed had any effect on the crew's performance against the Australians. But no one really believed that. To the Aussies — indeed, to observers of any allegiance — his memo amounted to unilateral disarmament just as the psychological war was heating up. Even Bertrand, who had sewn the seeds of this defeatism with the Superboat Myth, could hardly believe the extent of his victory. "I was staggered. The Americans were clearly terrified," he wrote.

Later, when the tensions between Blackaller and Conner boiled over, Gary Jobson, Blackaller's tactician, joined the psychological salvo. When Australia lost a semifinal race against the British and Conner accused them of sandbagging in order to divert attention from their keel — an absurd charge, given the importance of every race at that stage — Jobson said Conner was cracking under the strain. "I think subconsciously (Conner) doesn't want to win the trials because he's afraid of losing the Cup," he said at the time.

Conner's counterargument to Jobson's foray into amateur psychology was delivered two weeks later. It was his usual, and favorite, rebuttal: He won the trials, convincingly.

But meanwhile the NYYC had abandoned its efforts to outlaw *Australia II*'s keel. *Liberty*'s crew would have to enter the most important series of their lives knowing their skipper and syndicate leaders expected to lose.

PSYCHED OUT

A year and a half later, Johan Valentijn, *Liberty*'s designer, was still furious at the selection committee for having released Herreshoff's memo:

"That was a bad deal. That was schtupid, I mean plain schtupid!" he said, his thick Dutch accent thickening a bit more with emotion. "Halsey was pretty mad, I remember that. I mean he wrote it as a little note to the NYYC, that's all, telling them what the feeling was, because Halsey and Dennis were very down about the psychological aspects of this whole thing. I mean they were psyched out. And when that went around, they (the Australians) played it to their advantage. It was just plain dumb."

Did worrying about the keel affect Conner's performance?

"Yes, definitely," Valentijn said. "It was an excuse to lose." He said the syndicate held almost daily meetings about the keel issue, and that these sessions distracted Conner. "And if you get distracted, you just don't perform as well. I knew when Dennis had a good day and a bad day. If we had a problem and we talked about it, he would go out and not do very well because it was on his mind.... In the end he got very upset and very worried about it, and suddenly he was afraid of losing. Suddenly he felt they were going to lose the Cup. And he lost the Cup because it was on his mind, every day all day."

Valentijn's assessment should be taken with several grains of salt. First, one should note "The Flying Dutchman" had switched allegiances once again; now he was speaking as designer of the California-based Eagle Syndicate's 1987 challenger — a direct rival to Conner's 1987 group. Second, he is better known as a designer than a helmsman or tactician. And finally, as we have seen, he had more than a few axes to grind after his unhappy experiences in Conner's camp, and Conner's later blunt criticisms of his design.

But the question hung in the air long after the 1983 race was history: Had Dennis Conner been psyched out?

"Who can really tell?" John Bertrand replied. "In the final race, mistakes were made that some people found surprising. But under the environment and the pressure, it's not surprising. You see it all the time. They took a gamble by jibing away — this is all in hindsight — and they made a series of mistakes thereafter that went from bad to worse. Part of that is the so-called psych and the myth of our ultimate potential. We were sailing close to perfection. And I believe the *Liberty* afterguard made a series of mistakes which were partially a result of the aura of the *Australia II* image."

In his book, Bertrand said *Liberty*'s afterguard seemed rattled during the critical fifth leg of that last race, which the Americans began with a 57-second lead and ended 21 seconds behind. They were sailing too low, their spinnaker wasn't properly trimmed, and their heads were swivelling around, staring back at the Aussies as the distance between them rapidly narrowed. They jibed 11 times as opposed to the Australians' six, losing about 30 feet with each jibe. Bertrand ascribed that to panic. "We bided our time and they made the mistakes."

But Bertrand isn't exactly an unbiased witness, either. Nor was he really in any better position to judge the American skipper's state of mind. Only one man on earth could do that.

Dennis Conner, about 40 pounds lighter and looking far more relaxed, was back in Newport in the spring of '85 to participate in the Admiral's Cup trials. He sat on the deck of a boat before one of the races and contemplated the question, his eyes masked by dark sunglasses.

He started with a statement straight out of the sports psychologist's arsenal: There are two realities, he said — what's really going on, and the psychological reality. "And the psychological reality was that we were going to win. What you do is imagine yourself crossing the finish line, coming back to the dock a winner. You hold that image...."

Had he been able to do that throughout the 1983 series?

"Yes. Absolutely. We believed we were going to win. That was our psychological reality." On the other hand, he acknowledged that the keel, the conviction that the Aussies had a faster boat, made things "very difficult."

Did it affect the way he sailed?

"Well, sure it did. I mean we knew we had a slower boat, so we had to take chances. We took enormous chances. Maybe we should have taken even more. In that last race, for example, we had only three sails aboard; we did everything we could to lighten the boat. If it had blown over 12 knots we wouldn't have been able to finish."

Yes, but did the psychological stress over the keel affect his performance?

Conner thought for a long time before responding.

"I guess the answer is I have no way of telling. You'll have to ask other people. But I don't think anyone could have done better."

Thus the question was still hanging in the air as Conner and a host of others began psyching themselves up for the next campaign.

21
THE RACE
OF THE CENTURY

After more than two years of nonstop planning, organizing and training, after $50 million had been spent, after the long summer of scheming, psyching and protesting, it finally came down to a battle between two boats and their crews. For two weeks the America's Cup became a yacht race once again — and what a race! The New York Yacht Club could not save its Cup, but after this bitterest of summers the racing itself went a long way toward redeeming the event.

A dramatist could hardly have written a more exciting script. Tension built through the first two races, which the Australians lost because of breakdowns. The first was on the fifth leg of the first race, when John Bertrand was forced to throw the wheel over hard as Conner made a sudden jibe in front of him. The strain was too much for *Australia II*'s steering gear; a pulley collapsed and the boat broached out of control. *Liberty* won by 1:10.

The second happened the next day, before the start. The headboard car that carries the mainsail to the top of *Australia II*'s mast broke during a sudden wind gust, dropping the mainsail 18 inches. The Aussies retrimmed their sails as best they could and actually outsailed *Liberty*. Then the wind began to fall and the sail sagged even further. Conner regained the lead on the fourth leg and went on to win by 1:33. The Americans were up by two, but everyone knew it hadn't been a real test.

The third race was abandoned when the wind died and the time limit ran out, but it gave the Americans a chilling taste of the speed of an uncrippled *Australia II*. The Aussies crossed the starting line first and just pulled away from there. They were six minutes ahead when the clock ran out.

Both skippers seemed unusually relaxed as they joked their way

through the press conference that followed, Bertrand apparently happy
that his boat had performed so well, Conner that the race didn't count.
"God must be an American," Conner remarked. But in fact, the non-race
was the psychological turning point of the whole series, as both skippers
later acknowledged. Finally *Australia II* had been given a chance to show
her real speed. She plainly had enough to win the Cup, and there didn't
seem to be much the Americans could do about it, except pray that God
kept his citizenship.

The "real" third race began almost as a repeat of the day before, with
the Australians climbing out to an early lead in light air and smooth seas.
They sailed a flawless race and defeated the Americans by a larger margin than any previous 12-meter challenger, 3:14. At the press conference
someone asked Conner if God took Sundays off. "No," he said, "but even
He couldn't cope with *Australia II* today."

It had been the second light-air day in a row and more of the same was
predicted for the morrow. *Liberty* had little chance in those conditions, so
Conner exercised his right to call a lay day, to wait for wind. How much
wind? "About 40 knots," he said with a wry smile.

Asked later how he had spent the lay day, Conner had a one-word answer: "Worrying." The Aussies spent it testing sails. If the results of the
fourth race are any indication, worrying was better preparation than sail-
testing: Conner jumped *Australia II* at the start with an audacious move
that required perfect timing, sailed a perfect race, and came in first by 43
seconds.

Now the score was 3-1; the Aussies would have to win every one of the
last three races. Even with a demonstrably faster boat, it was a daunting
prospect. Many of the several hundred Australians who had come to
Newport to cheer on the home team, having spent up to $10,000 for the
trip, made return flight reservations. Keel or no keel, it appeared history
was about to repeat itself.

"Don't count us out," warned Alan Bond at the post-race press
conference. "We had our backs to the wall at the battle of Gallipoli and
we won that one." Reminded that the Australians had been slaughtered
by the Turks in that battle, Bond struggled to recoup: "The point I meant
to emphasize is that Australians hate to give up," he said. Dennis Conner
wasn't gloating: "I guess God works on Tuesdays," he remarked. He
looked a little more relaxed than he had after the previous race, but far
from jubilant. He knew his opponent better than anyone. Against a boat
that fast, a 3-1 advantage had perhaps evened the odds, but no more.

There was another breakdown just before the fifth race, and this time
it was *Liberty*'s turn. Her portside jumper extender collapsed when a

large wave hit the boat in the middle of a jibe as she was tuning up with *Freedom*. After a support boat raced back to the dock for a replacement, repairs were made. But the new jumper was the wrong size and it, too, failed four minutes into the race. *Liberty* lost by 1:47. It was the first time since 1934 a challenger had won two races, and the Australians and their partisans celebrated as if they had won the Cup itself. On *Liberty's* dock a few hundred yards away, the sirens, horns, whistles and cannon fire that greeted *Australia II's* triumphant return sounded more like a distant battle than a victory celebration. Conner stood for a long time, staring up at the broken extender.

Conner won the start of the sixth race, for the third time in a row.He forced Bertrand to tack away to port before the gun, covered him, and hit the line at top speed a full seven seconds before *Australia II*. He covered two Aussie tacks, matched their speed and seemed in full control.

But then he allowed Bertrand to sail off to the left for a long time before turning back to cover. By then it was too late: *Australia II* had found her own wind over there, one that was both faster and blowing in a more favorable direction than the air around *Liberty*. The next time the boats converged the Aussies crossed in front by a comfortable margin. Then they got another lift and opened up a lead of 20 boat lengths. They romped to a 3:25 win, adding 11 seconds to the record they had set the previous Sunday.

Once *Australia II* got way out in front it became a dull race. But the result could hardly have been more exciting: For the first time in history the series was tied 3-3! Everything hinged on the last race, and the challengers, having come from behind, had the momentum. The America's Cup teetered on the brink, after 132 years.

At the press conference someone asked Conner how it felt to be the first skipper ever to be pushed to a seventh and final race.

"Well, it's going to be very exciting to be involved in the race of the century," he said. "I think my crew is a group of winners and they know how to come back from a couple of tough defeats and I'm counting on them to pull us through on Saturday."

Meanwhile down at *Liberty's* dock, away from the microphones, TV cameras and tape recorders, someone shouted across to one of those crew members:

"Hey, Kyle, you going to go out and get those guys?"

Kyle Smith, one of *Liberty's* grinders, shook his head and replied: "I wish I knew. I wish I knew."

COUNTDOWN

With two decisive victories under their belts, the score tied and the momentum clearly going their way, the Aussies surprised everyone after the sixth race by calling a lay day. As Providence Journal-Bulletin yachting writer Dave Philips wrote, "It was like having a groggy opponent on the ropes and stepping back to give him a chance to clear his head."

"We called (it) for two reasons," Bond explained. "Principally to allow us to check the boat from stem to stern and to give our crew some relaxation after two very testing days."

The call may have been shrewder than it seemed at the time: All other things being equal, the crew with the faster boat has the advantage when both are given time to reduce the element of chance — equipment breakdowns or mistakes brought on by fatigue or overexcitement. Psychologically, it gave the Aussies a chance to calm down and the Americans another day to worry.

But it also gave the *Liberty* crew a chance to play their ace in the hole: their multiple certificates. With light winds expected on Saturday, they towed *Liberty* up to Cove Haven Marina where they switched to their light-air configuration by removing a reported 924 pounds of lead and adding to the sail area. Then they had the yacht recertified. The whole process had been carefully rehearsed and tested, but even so it was so time-consuming that they couldn't have done it without a day off.

While that was going on Conner, presumably feeling he had left no stone unturned, went off to play golf at the Newport Country Club with Bus Mosbacher. John Bertrand, who had lost more starts than he had won since the series began, practiced starts with *Australia II* against *Challenge 12.*

Meanwhile, excursion boat operators were ecstatic. Not only would there be a history-making seventh race, it would be on the weekend and people would have an extra day to sign up — which they did by the hundreds. Bob Dahmer, manager of Rentacruise, had only seven reservations for a possible seventh race before the Aussies won the sixth on Thursday. By Thursday night he had 270 more takers and was heading for a complete sellout. He did hold back one ticket, though, for a man who called from Detroit to say he would hop into his car and drive all night to get to Newport if Dahmer would reserve a space.

Saturday dawned warm and sunny. The spectator fleet churned out of Newport like a mammoth, man-made tidal surge and reassembled 7.5 miles off Point Judith. Then they waited, engines idled and sails furled, looking from a distance like a large floating city. A Goodyear blimp flew overhead with TV cameras that would feed live coverage of the race worldwide, while dozens of planes and helicopters carrying news photographers circled around her like drones around a queen bee.

The yachts approached the starting line, 132 years of history in the balance. Then, with two minutes to go, the postponement flag went up aboard *Black Knight*, the race committee boat. The wind had shifted too much for a start. The committee tried again two hours later, but by then the breeze had fallen to less than four knots. The race was abandoned for the day.

Back in Newport, where the streets and sidewalks were clogged even before the estimated 2,000 spectator boats returned to disgorge their multitudes, the postponement was taken in stride. "It's a conspiracy by the bar owners!" shouted one bearded tourist at a waterfront restaurant. Then he laughed and took another drink. In Perth, Australia, where it was nearly 2 a.m. when the race was called, the Royal Perth Yacht Club had obtained a special liquor license so it could keep its bar open throughout the night. "This could go on all week," said one supporter amiably, downing another beer.

Alan Bond was equally philosophical about the abandonment, but his humor deserted him after Dennis Conner called a lay day, to give his crew a chance to juggle the ballast again if the weather forecast called for stronger winds. Bond knew there was nothing against that in the rules, but he didn't like it:

"I've never heard of (a yacht) anywhere being changed like this, on a daily basis," he told a packed press conference after the abandonment. "We're not satisfied. We're not happy.... We came here to race one yacht, not three yachts." He suggested, in a voice dripping with sarcasm, that the Americans paint their boat different colors "so we'd know which one we're racing." He suggested red, pink and green. He also vowed *Australia II* would start the next race flying a protest flag because the rule "needs to be tested."

These were rather strong words for a man who had spent a reported $50,000 to $75,000 in legal fees, hired armed guards and kept a portion of his yacht under wraps to prevent several other rules from being tested, or even applied. But Bond knew his audience. By that time vast portions of the public, and not a few members of the press, were disposed to see his complaints as merely turning the tables on the New York Yacht Club, which had tried so desperately to have the Aussies' keel outlawed. As usual there was no public response from either the club or the *Liberty* syndicate. They might well have replied with the words used by Warren Jones when the keel protest began: "The only unfair advantage is that we thought of it first."

On Sunday, the forecast for Monday's race remained the same: light winds. *Liberty*'s crew decided to leave her ballast alone and the Aussies decided not to protest the original change. *Liberty* spent most of the day up at Cove Haven Marina, awaiting the latest forecast, but Bertrand and his crew took *Australia II* out for more practice, especially starting maneuvers. Conner, waving a telegram from President Reagan wishing him good luck on the morrow, said it was symbolic of American support generally. Bertrand said his crew was "very calm, very confident, very much in control, and looking forward to a great day tomorrow."

THE RACE OF THE CENTURY

Monday, September 26, 1983. Dennis Conner looked relaxed as he supervised preparations at the dock that morning, sipping coffee from a Styrofoam cup, chatting with syndicate members and other well-wishers. The Liberty Belles, made up of wives and other syndicate insiders, were there in their American-flag shorts and Liberty T-shirts, shouting out ragged cheers (*"Liberty! Liberty!* That's for me!") like high school cheerleaders reassembled for their 20th reunion. Someone had lugged a high-power sound system onto the next dock, aimed the speakers at *Liberty*, and blasted everyone with a loud, scratchy recording of Kate Smith singing "God Bless America." Cup Committee Chairman Robert McCullough and NYYC Commodore Robert Stone made an unusual dockside appearance to shake hands with Conner and wish him well, underscoring the club's enormous stake in the events of the next few hours. Then *Liberty* was towed slowly from the dock to meet *Australia II* and her destiny: to extend or close the longest chapter in sports history.

Recorded music blared from both tenders as they entered the harbor, *Fire Three* pulling *Liberty* and *Black Swan* (named for Alan Bond's brewing company) towing *Australia II*. *Liberty*'s instrumental themes, from the sound track of the contemporary movies "Chariots of Fire" and "The Empire Strikes Back," seemed especially appropriate, otherworldly calls to arms for a battle to be fought in slow motion by men and high technology in graceful warships of incongruous beauty. *Australia II*'s theme was almost jarringly down-to-earth, defiant lyrics from Australia's hard-rock group, Men At Work: "Do you come from a land Down Under / Where women glow and men plunder." That, too, seemed appropriate.

Once again the yachts approached the starting line and once again the postponement flag went up due to a last-minute wind shift. But this time the breeze settled down, blowing at 8-12 knots from the south-southwest. After more than three months of hard racing, almost three years of preparation and 132 years of American domination, the boats finally got away at 1:05 p.m.

Neither was aggressive during the starting sequence, both wanting to avoid any possibility of fouling out. The start itself was a trade-off: Conner got across first by eight seconds, but Bertrand's end of the line was a little closer to the first mark. *Liberty*, as usual, sailed toward the right while the Aussies went left. When they tacked back toward each other Bertrand got a lift that propelled him out in front as they crossed. It began to look like a repeat of the 3:25 rout of the previous Thursday.

Then, to the surprise of veteran yachtsmen among the spectators, *Liberty* tacked and Bertrand failed to cover. This time *Liberty* got the lift. When the two yachts converged a second time, Conner was out in front. *Liberty* rounded the first mark 29 seconds ahead amid a deafening blast of horns from her partisans. She gained some more distance on the second leg (a reaching leg, her best point of sail), turning the mark 45 seconds in front. But then the Aussies changed spinnakers and cut her lead to 23 seconds on the third leg, which had been turned from a reach into almost a dead run by a wind shift. On the next leg *Liberty* was the first to catch a couple of good lifts and rounded the fourth mark 57 seconds in front.

Nearly a full minute ahead with only two legs left to sail! Conner was going to pull it out after all!

At Christie's, a Newport restaurant that had become a hangout for Australians, the standing-room-only crowd fell quiet as they stared at the TV set. Out on the course Ben Lexcen couldn't bear to watch; he and Tom Schnackenberg, *Australia II*'s sail coordinator, left *Black Swan*'s rail and went below. On the press boat a number of sportswriters retired to the cabin to begin their stories about how *Liberty* retained the Cup. Photographers in the bow turned their lenses on Senator Edward Kennedy in a nearby boat.

Seemingly the only places the issue was still in doubt were the cockpits of *Liberty* and *Australia II*. Conner and company knew the Aussies would gain on the run. The question was, how much? "We all knew what *Australia* could do on the downwind leg," navigator Halsey Herreshoff said later. "That was the one thing we were afraid of. When we led by 57 seconds, I never thought we had it."

As the world now knows, they didn't have it. As soon as the Aussies rounded the mark and hoisted their spinnaker for the 4.5-mile run down the fifth leg, they started gaining, though no one outside of the boats knew it at first. Both began the run on starboard tack at a slight angle to the wind. *Liberty* was about seven boat lengths in front. As they sailed away from the mark and each other, their only reference points, it became impossible for spectators to tell who was gaining or by how much.

Realization came slowly and by different signs. The men in the boats knew it first. Aboard *Liberty*, Herreshoff took ranges on their opponent and Conner, the human computer, digested the results: The Aussies were gaining at a rate that would put them ahead at the next mark. Halfway down the leg the boats were spread well apart in light and shifty winds. Many spectators believed the Americans were still comfortably ahead. But Conner knew otherwise; the Aussies were only 15 seconds behind, and gaining fast.

On the press boat, the alarm was given by Gary Jobson, who had signed on as a commentator after his losing effort as tactician aboard *Defender*. He saw *Liberty* jibe over suddenly, back toward *Australia II*. He grabbed a microphone from an Australian commentator, who was beginning an explanation of the Aussies' impending defeat. "He must be behind," Jobson said urgently. "Conner must think he's falling behind or he would never have jibed over like that."

Indeed, the Aussies had caught two isolated wind shifts that boosted their speed. Conner was trying desperately to sail back across the course in time to cover *Australia II* while he still could. Meanwhile, aboard *Black Swan*, Lexcen and Schnackenberg were still below, still unable to watch. They were staring glumly through a porthole at the New York Yacht Club's committee boat. Suddenly, their attention was riveted. "We could tell by the expressions on their faces that we were catching up," Lexcen said later. They scrambled for the deck in time to see the boats converge.

Conner managed to get in front of the Aussies, but Bertrand simply bore off, sailed right through *Liberty*'s cover and crossed in front of her by 10 or 15 feet.

For several seconds no one spoke aboard *Liberty*. "Does anyone here have any ideas?" Conner finally asked, breaking the silence. No one did. A 12-meter boat simply isn't supposed to be able to do what *Australia II* did — sail both lower (more directly in front of the wind) and faster, and pass another boat to leeward despite its wind shadow. "It was very frustrating for us, of course, but there wasn't much we could do at that point," Conner said later.

Bertrand rounded the mark with a 27-second lead and pointed his boat toward the finish line and destiny. Conner tried desperately to break through on that last upwind leg, using every trick in the book and some that weren't. He tacked his 55,000-pound boat a gut-wrenching 47 times, a record for Cup competition. Bertrand matched him tack for tack, maintaining his cover. Lexcen, aboard *Black Swan*, remembers praying: "Please God, little boat, hold together. Please hold together."

Conner tried to wriggle loose with false tacks, in which he turned up into the wind as if to change course, only to fall back on the original heading. He tried tacking with a long hold in the middle, making Bertrand guess which way the boat would flop over. At one point he drew Bertrand far off course, almost into the spectator fleet, hoping desperately for a wind shift that would save him. It was an exhausting workout for both crews, during which Conner gained slightly — leading some critics to suggest he should have kept tacking duels in his repertoire right along, despite *Australia II*'s vaunted superiority.

But it was too late. Bertrand sailed into history at 5:20 p.m., crossing the line 41 seconds ahead of the Americans. The America's Cup belonged to the Australians.

"SOMETHING REALLY WONDERFUL"

Oh, how sweet it was! When the cannon fired as *Australia II* crossed the line, her crew, to a man, raised their arms in jubilation. Within seconds the spectator fleet, happily oblivious to personal safety, converged on the suddenly tiny and fragile 12-meter from Down Under, eager to share the moment regardless of nationality. The air was filled with spray (a blend of salt water, champagne and tears), green-and-yellow balloons and the sounds of horns, sirens, fireworks, revving engines and incoherent shouts.

Somehow in the midst of all this a rubber dingy filled with Swan lager and champagne managed to speed alongside the Aussie boat. First Alan Bond scrambled aboard, then Ben Lexcen and Warren Jones. There were bear hugs all around. "We beat 'em! We beat 'em!" Jones shouted. Eventually *Australia II* was hooked up to her tender for the long tow back to Newport and the whole madcap parade lurched toward home in the rosy glow of a setting sun, a grinning Lexcen at the wheel of his magic boat.

The crowd around *Australia II*'s dock, meanwhile, was setting a new America's Cup record for consecutive choruses of "Waltzing Matilda," heedless of the evening chill. Some of them — those with the Australian accents — had spent several thousand dollars to be there. No one knows how many Australians were in Newport for the Cup, but a reasonable guess, based on spectator boat bookings, would run into the thousands. Many of them had been living or touring in this country temporarily and traveled only a few hundred miles to get there, but many others had come halfway around the world just for this moment. Barbara Bosich of Perth, who drove up from her temporary home in New York to see the last race, explained it best:

"We're not such a big country, and we've just done something really wonderful," she said.

Back home in Perth it was 5:20 a.m. when *Australia II* crossed the line, but it may as well have been midnight on New Year's Eve. Some 2,000 people were crowded into the Royal Perth Yacht Club for a champagne breakfast victory party. Prime Minister Robert Hawke stopped in unexpectedly and was drenched with champagne. He declared the day a national day of celebration: "Any boss who fires his staff for not turning up today is a bum," he said. In Melbourne, a street party involving 5,000 roistering fans developed into a brawl, with 25 arrests and one death.

On the dock in Newport it was turning into a long wait. Darkness fell and *Australia II* was still somewhere out there in the gloom. The truth is both 12-meters and their crews were within a few hundred yards for many minutes, stuck in a logjam of boats. Eventually their Coast Guard escorts bullhorned their way through and suddenly there they were. Only it wasn't *Australia II* that appeared first but the American boats, *Liberty* and *Freedom*, lashed to either side of their tender, *Fire Three*. Each was flying a large American flag illuminated by Coast Guard searchlights. "The Stars and Stripes Forever" blared from *Fire Three*'s sound system while Dennis Conner stood at the bow waving his arms back and forth. At first it appeared he was saluting the victors but he was really urging the boats blocking his path to get out of the way. He had come to congratulate the winners and he wanted to get it over with quickly.

Finally *Australia II* entered the circle of light surrounding the dock. *Liberty*'s crew climbed aboard and shook hands all around. When Conner got to Bertrand, tears were streaming down his face. "I did my best, John," he said. "I could not do any more than that." Then he followed Bond, Bertrand, Lexcen and other Aussies to the deck of *Black Swan*. When the tender eased into the dock, the Americans made their escape as quickly as possible through the surging crowd.

For Conner, probably the world's best 12-meter sailor but who now most certainly would be known as the man who lost the Cup, it was an especially poignant and awkward moment. With his wife Judy at his side, he hung back at *Black Swan*'s stern, dabbing at his eyes with a handkerchief. Rather than push through the dockside crowd, he and Judy chose to flee over the waterside rail into a dinghy. From there they scrambled and stumbled through a thicket of helping hands from the deck of one small boat to another, dependent at the end on the kindness of strangers. Finally they made it to shore and the welcome darkness beyond the TV lights. Only the ordeal of the final press conference remained.

For Bond, the high school dropout and onetime sign painter, it was an exquisite moment, the climax of a 13-year, $16-million effort. Shortly after reaching the dock, he was handed a telegram announcing that an unofficial national holiday had been declared back home. That news seemed to cause as much excitement and jubilation among the crew as had winning the Cup.

By common and unspoken consent, no one was thrown into the water, the traditional victory rite. Even if a large enough patch of water could have been found among the jam of boats, which was doubtful, it was too late, too dark, too cold. Anyway, the crowd had something else on its mind: "Let's see the keel! Let's see the keel!" they chanted, egged on by *Australia II* crewmen.

A few days earlier Warren Jones had said the Aussies might not take the wraps off their keel until some days after the last race, win or lose. The motivation behind such a monstrous anti-climax became clear when a reporter asked if it would be a sponsored event. "I hope so," Jones had replied. "We need the money." The Aussies were prepared to sell their moment in history to the highest bidder.

But now, whether carried away by euphoria or because no sponsor had been found, Bond, who had been distracted by the telegram, finally acknowledged the plea. He faced *Australia II* and in an almost Biblical gesture slowly raised both arms to signal that the boat should be lifted, without her skirt. As Ben Lexcen stood on her bow, clutching a bottle of champagne, *Australia II* rose slowly in her hoist. As soon as the keel came into view, the crowd roared its approval. Bond acknowledged it with a flourish, grinning broadly as dozens of photographers swooped in for a closer look and several people in small boats scurried under the hull to reach out and touch it, kiss it, as if it were a holy relic.

Bertrand stood quietly on *Black Swan*'s afterdeck, hugging his wife Rasa. For him, too, it was the realization of an impossible dream. If he was not the world's best 12-meter skipper, he had at least beaten the best, and that may have been even sweeter.

After about 40 minutes, the Aussies began edging their way through the crowd, and a steady rain of champagne, toward the Armory where the world's press awaited them. Outside the locked gates, where uncredentialed fans had been waiting for hours, the rain turned to beer as they passed. As they approached the Armory the crowd waiting out front, jamming Thames Street from curb to curb, caused what police later described as a "mini-riot." First they closed in so tightly that the Aussies couldn't move. Then, with Bertrand just a few feet from the entrance, the crowd surged forward, pushing over a guard's table and slightly injuring a couple of policemen, leading them to slam the heavy front door almost in Bertrand's face. When reporters told them what they had done, they opened the door and let him in. Then they closed it again — this time on Alan Bond and his wife Eileen. Eventually everyone got inside, but in the melee someone stole a $50,000 watch from Mrs. Bond's left arm, the last part of her to get through the door. (It was recovered later.)

The Aussies had the conference to themselves — Conner, du Moulin and others from the American camp had already come and gone — and it became more a continuation of the celebration than a news event. Ben Lexcen, beaming with euphoria and perhaps an overdose of bubbly, said he was "stunned" by the victory. He hadn't had enough confidence, he said, and was worried right up to the end that Conner would somehow pull it off. Bond, asked about the future of the Cup now that the Aussies owned it, settled one question: It would not, as some had suggested, be renamed the Australia's Cup: "It would be a great break with tradition if it wasn't continued to be called the America's Cup." Mostly it was a time for the entire crew to be introduced, bathed in TV lights and glory, before they all pushed through the crowds once again and retired to a private celebration at Bond's Newport home.

There had been huge crowds around *Liberty*'s dock, too. But there the long wait had been more of a vigil than a celebration.

As the boats headed back toward the harbor, three people bobbed gently up and down in a tiny dinghy just below the press dock beside Liberty's compound — a man, a woman and a boy who appeared to be about nine years old. A single red balloon was tied to the dinghy. The boy was holding a small American flag. They sat there patiently, not smiling, speaking among themselves in hushed tones, paying no attention to the milling press corps just above them. Few people noticed their arrival, even fewer their departure. But they must have been there for hours, shivering slightly in the chilly breeze as day turned to night.

When *Liberty* finally picked her way through the darkness and mass of small boats to her dock after her longest day, her crew seemed still in shock, oblivious to the sporadic cheers and applause of the hundreds, perhaps thousands of sympathizers who occupied every dock, deck and rooftop in sight. They went through the motions of securing the boat for the night like sleepwalkers, seldom glancing up. They didn't seem to notice the crowd of reporters and photographers barely 20 feet away on the adjacent dock, or the little dinghy just beneath it with the sad faces and the American flag clutched in a small fist. There were embraces from wives and girlfriends, condolences from syndicate members, a few bottles of champagne, quiet, private conversations.

When Halsey Herreshoff stepped off the dock, heading for the Armory to help Conner through the press conference, he was surrounded by reporters. He chose his words carefully at first: "This is a great moment, one of the greatest moments in sports history...the end of an era," he said. "The unthinkable has now happened.... We're sad we lost, but we're not embarrassed. We all feel we did all we could.... We did all that could be done." Then he excused himself and walked toward the Armory. A reporter followed, asked him what the crew planned to do next:

"We'll all get together back at the house. Nothing has been planned. We'll just let it happen," he replied. He walked a few more paces, head down. "We'll probably get very drunk," he said.

Conner, meanwhile, had pushed his way through the crowds surrounding the victorious camp and made it to the Armory. Clearly it was a duty he wanted to be done with as quickly as possible. He started right in with a statement of his own, saying this night and this conference belonged to the Australians. "Today *Australia II* was a better boat. They beat us and we have no excuses." He paid tribute to his own crew, then he described the race as he had seen it.

When he got to the fifth leg — "the critical fifth leg," as he put it — his voice began to catch, his eyes filled. He paused for a moment. The press corps waited. Finally he finished the sentence: "...and that was the turning point." He tried to keep talking then, but his words began to waver. He summoned up one more sentence — something to the effect that America had nothing to be ashamed of — and then he stopped, 10 minutes after he had begun, thanked the press and pushed his chair back to leave. One reporter reached for a microphone and opened his mouth to ask a question, then closed it again as he watched Conner struggling for control. There were no questions as he made his escape.

Now all that remained was the long walk back to the security of the dock. With his wife Judy on his arm he started out quickly, walking under a huge hand-lettered banner over the Armory's front entrance that proclaimed "Australia's Cup." Then they strode along lower Thames Street, which had been closed to traffic, glancing to neither the right nor the left as they plunged through the throngs of people waiting for the Aussies to appear. Conner, never breaking stride or looking up, alternately shoved people gently out of the way and mumbled thanks as well-wishers shouted after him: "Dennis, good luck to ya!... You want a beer, Dennis?... We'll get 'em again, Dennis... Three cheers for Dennis Conner! No one else could have brought it as close as you did, Dennis...."

After a couple of blocks Dennis Conner, the human computer, the man who could find the invisible layline to the next mark in a fog, turned down a side street toward the water, looked around, and stopped.

"Excuse me," said the man who by now must consider Newport as his second home, "I'm lost." He had turned one street too soon. "I'd better get out of here while the getting is good," he said with a wry smile as he walked back to Thames Street.

Ahead of him the lights were still burning at *Liberty*'s dock, even though most of the crew had dispersed, but the press dock beside it was dark and deserted. The place occupied by the little dinghy with the red balloon and the flag held tightly in a small fist was now just a murky patch of water. The small group of people who had followed Conner from the press conference had vanished, peeling off one by one to get back in time to greet the victors. Only one reporter was still in his wake as he turned down the dimly lighted street toward the compound.

"Where are you going next, Dennis?" the reporter asked.

"Home," Conner said without looking back or breaking stride, his arm still around his wife.

132 years of sports history were over. But the endless campaign would go on.

PART FOUR

Transition

1983-1987

After 1983, many observers were ready to close the book on the America's Cup. Amateurism and sportsmanship had been all but ruled out, the campaigns were too long, too expensive, too exhausting — and now that the longest winning streak in sports history had been broken, who would want to go halfway around the world for what was bound to be an anticlimax?

But nothing succeeds like excess, as veteran Cup-watchers should have known. As the buildup toward Australia's first defense in January, 1987 (Australia's summer) gathered momentum, it became obvious that 1983 had been a mere prelude, a shakedown cruise along the Cup's new and beguiling course as an international media event. Its full potential for free-enterprise, free-spending and self-generating insanity had yet to be reached.

Corporate exploitation, media hype, skyrocketing costs, psychological warfare, political infighting, litigation, secrecy, spying, lying — every malaise ever cited in Newport as spelling doom to the America's Cup was reappearing in Fremantle, often in new and more toward a new level of prosperity and notoriety beyond the wildest imaginings of anyone who knew it as a mere sporting contest.

At times, it seemed to be totally out of control. But there were hopeful signs, too — some suggestions, at least, that it might survive its painful transition from genteel amateurism to ultra-competitive professionalism with at least some of its sporting traditions intact. It might even pick up some new ones — eventually.

But first it would have to survive the onslaught of boats and crews heading toward Perth in '87, most of whom seemed bent on mayhem rather than sport. Only one thing seemed certain; the next match would be anything but dull.

22
THE UNTHINKABLE
HAS NOW HAPPENED

On the morning of September 27, 1983, the City by the Sea — awash throughout the night in beer, champagne and the special, sentimental good fellowship that follows any titanic and prolonged contest — awoke with an enormous hangover and the feeling that it had been mugged: The America's Cup, crown jewel of her proud yachting tradition for 50 years, was gone!

All that remained was to turn it over to the winners. But that was such an unthinkable prospect that no one, in fact, had thought of how to do it until the last minute. After the Aussies tied the score 3-3, the New York Yacht Club tentatively decided the presentation should be made in Newport if, heaven forbid, that should be necessary. But the Cup remained securely bolted to its stand in the club's Manhattan mansion for more than two hours after the Aussies won it. Most of the members were in Newport and those left behind, listening in the bar to the final race over the club's only radio, seemed uncertain of what to do. They hadn't even been able to watch the race on television. "We don't have a TV in this place," a doorman said. "It's hard to believe in this day and age, but we don't."

Lois Muessel, head of the America's Cup office in Newport, finally radioed *Black Knight*, the race committee boat, which was still out on the course. Worried about people listening in on the open channel, she asked, "Will Mr. Foulk keep his appointment tomorrow?" William H. Foulk Jr., chairman of the NYYC's house committee, had been put in charge of transporting the Cup to Newport, if necessary. "I believe he will," came the answer. She then called the club with the news: The Cup would be shipped to Newport that night.

It was about 8 p.m. when the Holy Grail of yachting was unbolted and carried out the front door of the club's six-story granite and marble building to a waiting Brinks truck, through a small crowd that had gathered to witness. As the black box containing the Cup was carried down the steps, the onlookers, unmoved by the solemn and tear-stained faces of the mourners, broke into a chorus of "Waltzing Matilda."

The club's officers had decided to get the awful moment over with as quickly as possible: The Cup would be turned over at noon the next day, on the veranda of Marble House, whose broad expanse of lawn could accommodate the expected crowd. There was a certain fitness about the choice of Harold Vanderbilt's onetime home: Vanderbilt, who led the three Cup defenses during the J-boat era, had come closer than anyone else to losing the Cup, in 1934.

To the surprise of some, the New Yorkers proved to be good losers. The presentation was made with grace, style, and even a bit of humor. The freshly polished Cup, making its Newport debut, gleamed in the bright sun as Commodore Stone first handed Alan Bond the 40-inch bolt that had secured it to its table. "We don't want Alan to keep this for 132 years, but we thought he ought to have it," Stone said. Then he recalled that Ben Lexcen had once remarked that if the Aussies won the Cup they would hire a steamroller, squash it flat, and create the Australian Plate. No need to do that, Stone said; the NYYC had done it for them. With that he held up a battered Plymouth hubcap, suggesting it had great historical significance in this country, commemorating the landing of the Pilgrims. He handed it to a grinning Lexcen.

Mercifully, there were no long-winded speeches, no attempts to enshrine the event in oratory. When Commodore Stone finally turned the Cup itself over to Peter Dalziell, commodore of the Royal Perth Yacht Club, Dalziell thanked him simply: "The Cup will have pride of place in our clubhouse, and I welcome any challengers to the summer of 1987," he said. Commodore Stone assured him the NYYC would be there.

And with that it was done. The sun was still shining. The world had not turned upside down. A chapter had ended, but the book continued on. In the end, as the participants sipped champagne or quietly answered reporters' questions on that sun-drenched lawn, the informality of the transfer and the elegant languor of the surroundings seemed to impose upon some observers a sense of perspective that had been lacking through most of the summer: It had been a long, contentious campaign with a supremely dramatic finish, but the America's Cup was, after all, just a yacht race.

As we shall see, that was only a passing fancy.

FRUITS OF VICTORY . . .

For the winners, any sort of rational perspective would take some time. They held a very un-Australian celebration after their victory: a relatively quiet, subdued and private party at Alan Bond's rented mansion. "We're not professional party-goers," Bertrand explained after the ceremony the next day. In fact, they would need time to make the transition from sailors to national heroes. The crew had sailed the Cup series "with blinkers on," Bertrand said, because of the intense pressure. "I think we're going to start loosening up now and enjoying the fruits of victory," he added.

Indeed they would, and the fruits were heady: President Reagan held a reception for both crews in the White House Rose Garden the following day. Five weeks later, when all 41 members of the crew and syndicate had reassembled in Perth, the Aussies staged the greatest party in their country's history. An estimated 200,000 fans turned out to cheer their 10-mile motorcade.

As we shall see, Bertrand found his personal fruits of victory in the corporate spoils of the corporate campaign. Turning his back on both sailing and sailmaking, he stepped adroitly from cockpit to board room, with stops along the way to promote his book, endorse various products and represent the Western Australia Tourism Commission (for $50,000) as a roving ambassador.

. . . AND DEFEAT

For the losers, a proper perspective would take even longer. Especially for the two men whose absence at the presentation ceremony was most conspicuous: Dennis Conner and Robert McCullough.

Conner, after gamely congratulating the winners and facing the press, spent part of the evening with his crew, offering what condolence he could. But it was clear to anyone who saw him that night that he desperately wanted to get out of town. There were urgent personal reasons for both he and his wife to get back to San Diego; Judy, a teacher, had missed the opening of school and Dennis' business problems were mounting. But mainly, he just wanted to get away. On the morning of September 27, while other members of the crew were donning jackets and ties for the noon ceremony at Marble House, the Conners were at Green Airport, waiting for a flight home.

McCullough, the tall, imperious-looking former NYYC commodore who led its disastrous keel investigation, returned to New York almost immediately after the last race. He was heading for a pressing business meeting in Europe that he had already postponed once. (Now retired, he was then chairman of the executive committee of Collins & Aikman, a large textile manufacturer.) He was criticised in some quarters for his abrupt departure, despite the fact that he had explained the circumstances to both crews in advance and had congratulated the winners and consoled the losers immediately after the race, while they were all still on the water.

Certainly he was not the happiest of warriors at that point. Even months later he spoke with some feeling about the accusations of poor sportsmanship, the "rubbish" that was written about the keel campaign, and the Aussies' brazen misconduct: "There's no question in my mind that they broke the rules," he said.

WHICH IMAGE NEEDS FIXING?

It was that certainty, shared by the rest of the cup committee and the club's flag officers, that made the succession of tactical defeats and the steady drumbeat of public criticism throughout the summer seem so damnably unfair. For Commodore Stone, the frustration reached its peak in the week before the first race, prompting a highly uncharacteristic act: He wrote an open letter to the NYYC membership, blasting the press.

"There has been a great amount of misinformation and slanted comment in the press," he wrote, "most of it uninformed, and, as always seems to happen, from James Ashbury in 1870 on through Lord Dunraven, and to the present day, the New York Yacht Club has taken a considerable amount of abuse...."

McCullough returned to the theme a few months later:

"I think that the press, with a few exceptions, really didn't do its homework," McCullough said. "Too many reporters took the rantings and ravings of Alan Bond and the others at face value. What most people didn't realize was that Bond was in it for the publicity. He admitted it himself. They were just playing games with us.

"Probably the dumb thing we did was not have a high-powered public relations firm to uphold our side," he added. "Every time something came up and the Aussies held a press conference, we should have come back instead of not answering. There's always the big question: Are you going to get into a pissing contest with these guys, or aren't you? We decided not to." If he had it to do over again, he said, he would have responded, but tried to keep it "on a high plane."

Many of the other club members bloodied in the '83 campaign share McCullough's lament. If only they had hired a sharp PR man, the Cup — or at least their dignity — might have been saved. That sentiment led the club to take what some observers, at least, see as a fateful step after the 1983 debacle. It hired a public relations firm to help restore its image. (Now, presumably, if the club finds itself embroiled in something like Keelgate in 1987, we can look forward to pissing contests on a high plane.)

But as it readies its first-ever America's Cup challenge, there are those who wonder if such a quick fix is the appropriate response: Is it the club's image or the America's Cup that needs fixing? Is the introduction of corporate image-making a necessary countermeasure in the era of media overkill, or a pandering to the very forces that have devalued the event? If the club cannot win back the Cup by being true to its own image, should it even try?

Clearly the club in 1983 was victimized, in part, by a too-clever challenger and a too-credulous press. But some observers see those as scapegoats designed to conceal the real flaw in the NYYC's 1983 defense: The club was not true to itself.

"The New York Yacht Club is baffled by people who won't play by the rules. They're absolutely baffled," says Norris Hoyt, a longtime Cup watcher. "Their response is the response of gentlemen to gentlemen."

In 1983, their response was that of a street-fighter to a street-fighter — but they were too gentlemanly to fight well. They were willing to engage in clandestine counterspying, but when Richard Latham was sent to The Netherlands, he ended up empathizing with the man from whom he was supposed to be getting a signed confession. When they were falsely accused in the press, gentlemanly reserve — and perhaps a consciousness of their own ethical vulnerability — restrained them from counterattacking. Unlike the Australians, they were willing to engage in private deception but balked at lying in public.

There were several points during the summer of '83 when the club had a choice between standing on principle and trying to outmaneuver the Australians at their own game. The choices were never as clearcut as they look in retrospect, but they were there. The NYYC could have confronted the Australians about its suspicions from the beginning. It could have halted the trials until the Aussies unveiled their keel or provided satisfactory answers. It could have postponed the race until Bond agreed to sign the certificate of compliance. Above all, it could have explained its suspicions to the press and public in a simple, straightforward way, without any assistance from a public relations expert. Instead, it tried to subvert its own better instincts — and was betrayed by them in the end.

If that is to measure the NYYC by a higher standard than the Australians — and it is — that is because gentlemanly conduct had been the standard by which the New Yorkers themselves judged every controversy for more than a century, even when they honored it in the breach. "You can do business with anybody, but you can sail only with gentlemen," said J.P. Morgan, who served as the club's commodore in 1919-1921.

The Australians' view of all that was on the record for everyone to see more than a decade ago: "Sentimental nonsense." It should have been a warning.

Now that the Cup has become big business, where does that leave the gentlemen of the New York Yacht Club? It leaves them hiring a public relations firm and doing business with almost anybody in an all-out, $12-million effort to recapture their trophy in 1987.

23
MALICE IN UNDERLAND

The transfer of the Cup, and the rapid transformation of the event, posed several questions requiring deep thought. But first, after the long, contentious summer of '83, everyone seemed to be in the mood for comic relief. In any case, that's what we got:

• The stage was set back in April, 1984, when the Royal Perth Yacht Club received 24 challenges by the filing deadline. (The number has dwindled since then to 14.) There might have been 25 on that initial list, but for a slight technical problem: "We got a call from Saudi Arabia," a club spokesman said. "They were interested in challenging, but they didn't have a yacht club. They thought they could buy one of ours."

• The French, whose hapless 1983 effort was led by a soft-porn film producer, were back with two syndicates. One of them was backed by the Kis Group, an international photographic supplier. When the time came to name their boat, skipper Marc Pajot and his syndicate shrugged their shoulders with Gallic insouciance and did the obvious. Voila! *French Kiss* was born. Alan Crewe, commodore of Royal Perth, got into the spirit of the thing at once: "I hope they're tongue-in-cheek about the name," he remarked. First, the club decided the French had to change it, as it violated the rule against corporate identification, but finally they relented.

• Canada's 1983 campaign, its first in a century, had been mounted with the announced intention of uniting the country, torn by East-West rivalries. This time it had two syndicates, one from the East, one from the West. Said the Halifax chairman about the Vancouver group: "I wish they'd do one of three things: get the money and do it professionally and not embarrass Canada; stop and just get out of it, or join us." Said Vancouver about Halifax: "It's going to be fun to whip his ass, I'll tell you."

• One of the most deadly serious challenges was mounted by Dennis Conner, the man who lost the Cup. Naval architect Gary Mull recalls a design team meeting at a California laboratory also involved in Star Wars research: "It was held in a soundproofed lead-lined room, built for the sole purpose of discussing the nation's military secrets. It was swept for electronic bugs before every meeting. We were talking about putting scramblers on our telephones. I looked down the table and said, 'When are we going to hire Gordon Liddy for dirty tricks?' There wasn't a single smile. I thought to myself, 'Maybe they've already hired him.' "

● Meanwhile, the Royal Perth Yacht Club, in the awkward position (recently vacated by the NYYC) of having to run the races and mount a defense at the same time, was squabbling with both defenders and challengers on a subject of paramount importance. Racing rules? Conditions of the match? Nope. Television rights.

From these brief glimpses alone, it is obvious the America's Cup has undergone a sea change at least as dramatic as the 1958 shift to 12-meter boats. But as the players in this new high-stakes game jet around the world, lining up their bases as well as the cash (up to $12 million each) and other resources they need, there is little evidence that any of them paused long enough to count the less tangible costs.

Here and there, however, a few disillusioned voices were being heard from the sidelines. Many of them were yachtsmen who wondered what had happened to their sport. And for the first time, some of them had Australian accents.

At first, all was joyous Down Under. The America's Cup was never a mere yacht race there, it was a national cause. The victory touched off a wave of jubilation and nationalistic fervor such as no American — and perhaps no Australian — had experienced since the day World War II ended. Royal Perth put the Cup on public display, at an art gallery in Perth. Within weeks it was seen by more people than had viewed it during its entire 132-year history within the cloistered NYYC.

Royal Perth assumed its new responsibilities under the deed of gift in a magnanimous and statesmanlike way. Peter Dalziell, its commodore at the time, told the Australian press he thought reports of the disputes in Newport had been blown out of proportion. "If we were in the same position, I'd have done the same thing," he said of the NYYC's keel investigation. He said the New Yorkers had gotten a bum rap over the years, that the history of their stewardship had been one of steady movement toward greater fairness toward challengers. "The Americans ran things superbly and we have to match them when it comes to Perth," said Stan Reid, a former RPYC commodore.

Perth, capital of Western Australia, has been described as one of the most entrepreneurial cities on Earth, a city of hustlers. Like the rest of the country, it takes its sports seriously, especially those involving water; there is said to be one boat for every nine residents. For generations it has chafed under its geographical and cultural remoteness and the scorn of its more cosmopolitan compatriots, who used to say the best thing about Perth was the road to Adelaide.

The Western Australia Tourism Commission got on the bandwagon early. First, it hired John Bertrand to a three-year term as a part-time "roving ambassador," at an annual salary of $50,000. A few malcontents attacked the erstwhile skipper for exploiting his status, and berated the commission for its extravagance. But the commissioners stuck to their guns. With proper promotion, they estimated, a million visitors and a billion dollars could be drawn to Perth between 1986 and 1987.

Next, an announcement by a Western Australian tourism minister demonstrated the Aussies had a firm grasp of what the "new" America's Cup was all about. The federal and state governments, he said, would jointly finance the construction in Perth of a large convention center, including "the biggest and best gambling casino in the world."

By early 1986, seven major new hotels, two new marinas and hundreds of other tourist-related projects were being built in the Perth/Fremantle area. All told, the federal government kicked in $30 million. Private entrepreneurs were busy, too. At least 10 luxury cruise ships signed up for the races, to serve as floating hotels and observation platforms.

Alan Bond, who had seen the Cup's potential earlier than anyone else, was planning a new luxury hotel in Perth and a 45-unit townhouse development in Fremantle. He commissioned a new flagship for the Bond Corporation, a $10-million luxury yacht with a helipad on the top deck. To top it all off, he bought another brewery, thereby cornering 45 percent of the Aussie beer supply. In Australia, that's about as close to a national stranglehold as the law allows.

The Cup was brimming over with promises of limitless largess. The cheering had barely died before nine would-be defenders identified themselves. Eventually four of them dropped out and two merged, leaving four syndicates — America's Cup Defence 1987 (Alan Bond), Taskforce 87 (Kevin Parry), South Australian Challenge (Sir James Hardy), and Eastern Australia Defence Syndicate (Syd Fischer).

But even before that happened, to the surprise of no one in the New York Yacht Club, they discovered that the resources they needed all came from the same fairly small pie. Then they started bickering over who would get the biggest slices.

Some of the disputes were between Royal Perth and its potential defenders. One of the first developed when the club announced in 1984 that it had lined up a sponsorship deal with five major Aussie companies for $1.75 million, to help finance the running of the races. It said it was hoping to raise a similar amount from international corporations.

That stirred more than a little resentment among the would-be defenders, who were scrabbling to line up corporate backers themselves.

There aren't all that many major corporations in Australia (pop. 17 million), and the defenders felt they should have first crack. Besides, they said, RPYC didn't need that much; it was just being greedy.

But the big fight developed when the club hired an international marketing firm to sell overseas television rights for Cup coverage. Bond, whose syndicate was offering an exclusive TV package on its defense campaign to those same networks, was livid. Once again Warren Jones sounded the attack, this time against his own club: "All we want to do is defend the Cup," he said. "This will take a tremendous amount of money. The yacht club is prejudicing our chances of getting that money."

Commodore Dalziell responded, "Obviously, Mr. Bond is our senti-mental favorite and he has our complete support. But the event is bigger than the participants." How much bigger? A spokesman for the club's marketing trust estimated it would cost Royal Perth $1.5 million just to run the races, and that it would be expected to contribute a similar amount to a new marina being built by the government — more than television dollars alone could cover, surely, though in truth no one really knew how much the rights were worth.

The club asked the challengers to sign over their TV and logo marketing rights as well. Probably for the first time ever, Conner found himself in agreement with Bond and Jones. Conner's syndicate went even further, threatening to withdraw its challenge.

In the end the Royal Perth did what the NYYC had done so often. It backed down. It even abandoned a deal with the IYRU to have it participate in running the races, for which the IYRU would earn proceeds from marketing rights. At year-end, the question of who would profit from marketing and TV rights, and how much they were worth, was being negotiated by all sides.

As the NYYC could have told Dalziel, the Cup was more of a burden than any single yacht club should have to bear. But when the Royal Perth tried to shift part of the burden, there was hell to pay.

RPYC's plan was to strike a deal with the IYRU in London. The club and the IYRU would divide up responsibility for running the races—and the proceeds from marketing and TV rights.

That was a strange offer for the IYRU, which had always adopted an above-the-fray stance befitting its role as yachting's supreme court. "If the highest authority is running the challenger trials, where do we go for an appeal?" asked Sail America's project coordinator, Joanne Fishman. The RPYC insisted it only was trying to recoup some expenses. But, after 1983, Conner and the NYYC might have felt entitled to a few swipes. The shoe was on the other foot now, and if it pinched, so much the better.

But the biggest intramural battles Down Under were being waged among the would-be defenders, particularly between a couple of tough old multimillionaire business adversaries named Alan Bond and Kevin Parry, who headed the two syndicates given the best chance to defend. When last heard from, they claimed they were still friends. But there were times when even Perth, that old frontier town, didn't seem big enough for the both of them.

In another of his masterful deals, Bond once again set up another syndicate as a cooperative sparring partner by having Lexcen design its boat. This time it was the South Australian syndicate, headed by Bond's longtime friend and former skipper, Sir James Hardy. The deal was that Bond got the boat first, to race against the benchmark *Australia II*. That gave Bond's crew some valuable training, and allowed Lexcen to evaluate its design before drawing the plans for Bond's new boat, *Australia III*. Then Hardy would get his boat (which he named *South Australia*) and tune it up against *Australia II* while *Australia III* was being built.

It was a mutually beneficial deal; Hardy got a Lexcen design and a crack boat and crew to tune her up against. But to Kevin Parry and his skipper, Iain Murray, it seemed a little too cozy. They had a new boat named *Kookaburra I* (after Australia's best known native bird) and they needed a fast trial horse to tune against.

Parry made repeated overtures to Bond, asking for a series of races. "The sharper the competition, the more chance he has of keeping the Cup," he reasoned. Bond steadfastly refused. "By racing Kevin's best, we're giving away a lot of expertise, expertise we've gathered over many years," he said. Then, unable to resist a parting shot, he added, "And it would be wasting our time, too. His boat is dead dog slow."

The standoff continued until early April, 1985, when *Australia II* and *South Australia* went out for a trial race one morning — and found *Kookaburra* waiting in ambush. As the Bond and Hardy boats started their match race, Murray sailed alongside. According to Murray, and to some more impartial observers, *Kookaburra* outperformed both of the others. When Murray made sure the word got around, things got nasty.

Jones bitterly pointed out that the comparison was unfair. *Australia II* and *South Australia* were match-racing each other, using tactics that slowed both boats rather than going for flat-out speed, while *Kookaburra* sailed free. When Murray horned in on a second race and claimed his boat was an incredible 10 lengths ahead after 2.5 miles, Jones was absolutely furious.

At one point, Parry offered Bond a $50,000 wager, for a best-of-seven match race series. Bond reportedly agreed — if Parry put up $250,000 and Bond put up nothing. Parry found that unsatisfactory.

But Murray's piracy wasn't very satisfactory, either. You can't really evaluate a boat against an opponent who is doing his best to ignore you. So in June, Murray took a drastic step. He asked the America II syndicate, representing the New York Yacht Club, if it would be interested in some match races when its boat arrived in October. Not surprisingly, the answer was yes. In November *America II* and *Kookaburra* came to the line for the first competitive trial race between a potential challenger and defender in America's Cup history.

Bond and Jones were apoplectic. On television, Bond called Parry's syndicate "traitors" and accused them of "giving away the store."

"We have a responsibility to ourselves, the Royal Perth Yacht Club, and indeed to Australia not to help the opposition take the Cup away from us," Jones said, placing himself once again on the old, familiar high ground. But this time some members of the Australian press, who had learned a thing or two in Newport, pointed to what they saw as the real motive behind all the bluster: money.

It wasn't that Bond's syndicate was unwilling to waste its time on a boat that was "dead dog slow;" what really worried them was that it might be greyhound fast — and that the moneymen who controlled Australia's corporate purse strings were looking on with interest, waiting for a winner to emerge. Bond was the presumptive defender from the beginning, so it would be foolish to allow anyone to test him now, when even a single defeat could mean millions in corporate support.

The name-calling abated somewhat after the six-race *Kookaburra/America II* series. The Americans won it, 4-2. In mid-December, it was announced that Bond had agreed to compete against Parry, after all. By then each syndicate had a second new boat in the water, *Kookaburra II* and *Australia III*, and plans to build a third, if necessary.

Bond, meanwhile, was facing other problems. His syndicate was still $1.3 millioin debt from the campaign. Then, on October 17, 1985, the syndicate received an anonymous letter threatening to destroy its boats. A month later, fire destroyed several sails in a Bond loft.

The fire was traced to faulty wiring. But the letter was legit. "We're going to fix the local yacht. You can't stop us because if we can't get into the harbor, we'll get it when it's racing.... We've got boats or we can get a light plane.". Security at the Bond docks was tightened further. When *Australia III* was launched, Lexcen quipped: "She's bullet-proof."

Meantime, John Bertrand's book was published in Australia. To a disinterested reader, "Born to Win" is an often gripping, always fascinating inside story of *Australia II*'s triumph in Newport. But to

Bond, Lexcen and other members of the syndicate, it was an infernal outrage. Bertrand not only told all, he did it through his own rather egocentric vision.

Bond is portrayed as a brawler, occasionally devious, always cunning, and often extraordinarily generous. Lexcen comes through as a brilliant but childlike genius whose boats go like the wind but suffer frequent breakdowns — "Bennyurisms," the crew called them. And Bertrand's former crewmates, the men he said would have cut off their right arms for him if he asked, were more than a little annoyed that their skipper took such a large share of the credit for their collective victory, and at the same time managed to get some of their names wrong.

Some speculated over whether the book would cost Bertrand his $250,000 three-year contract as sailing consultant to Bond's '87 Cup campaign. Bond ended the speculation by declaring he and Bertrand were still friends despite the book, which he described as "a good novel," and that he could keep his job.

Although it was never stated, it may be that the angry reactions stemmed partly from the realization that Bertrand's alleged "novel" was actually an all-too-accurate depiction of the inner workings of a Bond-style Cup campaign. Bertrand laid bare the psychological warfare, intimidation and outright lies that underlay the Aussies' victory, heedless of the fact that the people he wrote about would have to face the NYYC, and the world, on the race course once again, while he escaped into the corporate corridors of power. Perhaps his crime was that his book provided the enemy a blueprint for taking advantage of the Cup's new rules — hard-won knowledge, almost as valuable as the line drawings of a competitor's new boat.

But by then, most insiders had a pretty good idea what the rules were anyway, on both sides of the world.

In the United States, the loss of the Cup failed to stir anything like the depth of emotion felt by the Aussies in winning it. Where feelings did run high, as in the New York Yacht Club, they were mixed. Good riddance, said some. But others, a majority, were determined to get it back.

To do so, they and nine other U.S. challengers had to learn the America's Cup game almost from scratch, so much had it changed. Four of them flunked the course and dropped out, leaving six syndicates — America II (NYYC), Sail America (San Diego Yacht Club), St. Francis (St. Francis Yacht Club, San Francisco), Eagle Syndicate (Newport Harbor Yacht Club, California), Heart of America (Chicago Yacht Club), and Courageous (Yale Corinthian Yacht Club).

But even for the survivors, the transition was a tough, perplexing, sometimes agonizing process. If the buildup in Australia seemed larger than sport, in America it was larger than life — and much stranger.

"We're not at war," Dennis Conner assured the Aussies when he visited Perth. But if war came, his Sail America Challenge '87 could acquit itself well against a small country. His $12-million campaign included experts in the space sciences and high-tech weaponry from NASA, Boeing and Grumman, coordinated by Science Applications International Corporation, a Defense Department contractor. His 19-member fund-raising committee had two former U.S. Secretaries of Defense, two former Chiefs of Naval Operations, and a former Chairman of the Joint Chiefs of Staff. The name of his foundation is the Sail America Foundation for International Understanding.

Tom Ehman, director of the NYYC's challenge, pooh-poohed the idea his syndicate was going overboard with security: "We haven't done anything extraordinary. The shipyard has a guard at the gate. You have to make an appointment to get through. Then there's a second security guard. The pen the boat is in is fenced to the bottom, to keep frogmen out. We've tried to be sure we have secure phone lines and secure facsimile lines back and forth. And if we're really worried about something being secure, we just don't write it down, and we don't say it face-to-face unless we're some place that's reasonably secure. But that's about it. It's not that big a deal." Maybe he should have tried harder. Australian sources in 1984 reported seeing several full-color snapshots of one of the New York boats, showing all her private parts, on the desk of Alan Bond's project manager.

The Chicago-based Heart of America Challenge succeeded in persuading the New York Supreme Court, which maintained jurisdiction over the deed of gift, that Lake Michigan is an arm of the sea. That must have taken some doing; it cost the Australians a reported $225,000 in legal fees and expenses just to get the same court to permit racing during Australia's summer, by changing two dates in the deed.

The Blue Dolphin Yacht Club of Newport Beach, California, dropped out after being sued by American Express over its slogan, "America's Cup, don't leave Perth without it." The corporation giveth and the corporation taketh away.

It also getteth. Corporate dollars are meeting 50% of the syndicates' budgets this time around, up from 5% in 1983. But along with this higher commitment comes a higher profile. *America II*'s first major sponsor was Cadillac; when Ehman pays a visit to one of the 33 yacht clubs affiliated with the challenge, a Cadillac representative generally tags along, handing out special *America II*/Cadillac key rings and urging club members to test drive one of his products.

The change wrought by *Australia II*'s victory was partly a matter of scale. Almost every significant number used in connection with the 1983 event had to be at least doubled for 1987 — twice as many challengers, three times as many boats, four times as many designers, etc. The NYYC's challenge calculated its boats would be in transit for a total of seven and a half months — more time than most of the club's defenders had spent on their entire training programs.

The figures with dollar signs attached had to be multiplied by even higher numbers. In 1983, all participants spent less than $18 million. The projection for 1987 was $150 million. Dennis Conner's syndicate budgetted $3 million for computer and tank-testing alone — about what he spent for his entire defense in 1980.

But it was also a matter of new and esoteric technologies, the fusion of aerodynamics, hydrodynamics and computer simulation. Those innocent-looking wings fashioned by the Australian/Dutch alliance had stunned and then galvanized the yachtsmen among America's high-tech community, prompting many of them to volunteer their evenings and weekends to the syndicates of their choice. The result was a moonlighting crash program in yacht design reminiscent of the post-Sputnik frenzy among space scientists a generation earlier.

"It has ceased to be a totally sporting event," asserted Alberto Calderon, a NASA physicist working on the St. Francis design. "It's not only sailing that brings us into this, we are seeking the frontiers of technology. It is a challenge that we regard as one of the most important."

"I think it's fair to say right now that there is more effort going into designing new 12-meters than the Navy spends on anything, except possibly a submarine," said Eugene Miller, technical director for a tank-testing center in Maryland.

Within months, nearly every syndicate announced a "breakthrough." How much of that progress was pure hype, calculated to pry more dollars from sponsors or strike fear into the hearts of the opposition, was an open and very murky question.

Warren Jones unleashed one of the first gusts in January, 1985, after most of the challengers had committed themselves to winged keels. They won't work in the sea conditions off Fremantle, Jones said flatly. "We were not at all surprised when we saw the American boat (*America II*) lifted from the water recently and saw it had no wings. We spent a million dollars learning the winged keel doesn't work off our coast, and now they've discovered it too."

Most likely translation: Wings work fine, and they both have 'em. Ehman, *America II*'s executive director, would neither confirm nor deny.

"Well, we know whether they work, so we know whether it's a ploy or not," he said. Which is it?

"Obviously I can't say," Ehman replied. "We kind of laugh about it, because we know. If they're saying the opposite of what they believe, and we know that's wrong and that they're trying to use it as psychological warfare, then we're just laughing at them because it's not effective."

Translation: Nice try, Warren, but forget it.

But wait a minute. Jones is a chess player, remember? Maybe he was just trying to get Ehman to say whether he had wings or not. Or maybe wings DON'T work, and he figured by saying so he would have everyone believing the opposite. Or maybe they DO work, but he figured everyone would say, "If he says they don't work, they probably do. No, wait a minute. He's too clever for that. I bet they don't."

This way lies madness — which is the whole point. "It's got to stick in people's minds. And they're saying, well, is that true or is it not true?" Ehman said. "I think they think we're trying to psych them out. I don't know that anybody's quite as sophisticated as people think they are, or we are, about some of the psychological stuff."

Keel-psych is going to be a little tougher in Fremantle. The water there is much clearer than off Newport; every time one of the boats heels sharply, her keel is clearly visible to anyone looking down from above. "We're getting the best advice from people in this country about how to paint the keels to disguise them, as *Australia II* did fairly successfully last time," Ehman said.

Arthur Wullschleger, 68, the syndicate's no-nonsense operations manager, sees the security measures as "an exercise in futility, but a necessary one. If you want to see what's on the boat, all you have to do is hop on a chopper. But psychologically, it's all very important. If it wasn't, we wouldn't be spending so much time and money on it."

Ehman has at least one other secret weapon, a trim, 29-year-old sports psychologist named Jane Kent, who is under orders not to talk to the press (presumably not even to Newsweek, one of the syndicate's major sponsors) until after the campaign.

Why all the secrecy? "I think after the series is over people will be able to point to some of the things she is doing and say, boy, that really had a big impact on their success," Ehman said. "Is that psyche? Sure it is. It depends on whether you think we're onto something or not. We think we're onto something, so we don't think it's psyche. We're just trying to tell people, look, we're making good progress here. We aren't going to tell them what it is. If that psyches them out, great."

A footnote: One of the books Kent included in a reading list following an article she wrote on psychological motivation was John Bertrand's old standby, "Jonathan Livingston Seagull."

Secrecy and psych are pretty stressful things, even if you have a secret weapon. In 1983, stress sent Ben Lexcen to the hospital with blinding headaches and chest pains. After being misdiagnosed as having had a massive heart attack. Lexcen was finally told he merely had high blood pressure. And stress doubtless contributed to an incident in late August that year, in which Commodore Mosbacher and his wife stalked out in the middle of an Australian dinner party. They were offended by something said by the after-dinner speaker, a professional satirist. Others thought the monologue was quite tame, as well as funny.

But this time around, stress was showing up early. With more than a year to go before the trials, rumors of intramural squabbling were supported by a spate of exits and entrances. From one end of the country to the other, skippers, designers, even syndicate chairmen were either stepping down or being pushed out. The move that sparked the biggest headlines was the resignation, and subsequent return, of John Kolius, skipper of the NYYC's front-running America II syndicate.

Kolius' resignation became known in September, 1985. A day or two later, he held a press conference, presumably to give his reasons and answer questions. He did neither. He read a prepared statement in which he made vague references to "syndicate politics," then, barely controlling his emotions, walked out before reporters could ask him anything.

Others involved were equally imprecise. There was talk of a communications breakdown, misunderstandings on both sides, and the suggestion of a power struggle. Kolius wanted to control too many aspects of the campaign, it was said, and was spreading himself too thin — especially as he was trying to run his sail company at the same time.

Clearly there was more to it than that. Chuck Kirsch, who founded the syndicate with Kolius back in 1983 when both were nearing the end of their Defender/Courageous campaign, had been replaced as chairman two months earlier, apparently at his own request. Arthur Santry, vice commodore of the NYYC, stepped in. Santry and Kolius did not see eye-to-eye about a number of things. Kolius resigned on September 19; three weeks later, Santry was out. A week after that, Kolius returned, saying any problems he may have had in the past could now be resolved. However, he also gave up both his position and other syndicate duties; from then on he would just drive the boat.

A few yachting writers found proof of their sport's corruption in these unattributed musings. An article in Motor Boating and Sailing described the "real story" as one of "politics vs. sailing, marketing vs. sport, managers vs. skippers" that proved "the 26th America's Cup challenge is more than a boat race, it's a multimillion-dollar international business."

But perhaps the REAL real story isn't to be found in the speculations themselves, but in the fact that so many people seemed so eager to make them. Even the Washington Post gave Kolius' resignation as much play as it might that of a minor Cabinet official. The America's Cup is a multimillion-dollar international business, surely. But it is also fast becoming one of the world's premier media events. If the trend continues, we will soon have endless coverage as well as endless campaigns.

Whether words like "sport" and "sportsmanship" will find a legitimate place in those stories once again remains to be seen.

24
REBIRTH IN PERTH?

After the events of 1983, it seems almost ludicrous to speak of sportsmanship and the America's Cup in the same breath. But perhaps future yachting historians will look back upon 1983 as the nadir of the America's Cup, the low point in a painful and tumultuous transition from amateurism to a new professionalism. That may be an overly optimistic view, but optimism and pursuit of the Cup have always gone hand-in-hand. Besides, there is some evidence:

The battles on shore that summer matched gentlemanly restraint against a cold-blooded determination to push the rules as far as they would stretch, or farther. It was an unequal fight, and it led to chaos, bitterness, and in the view of many, a miscarriage of justice. But the contest at sea matched two equally cold-blooded, equally determined and thoroughly professional crews — and produced the most magnificent racing in Cup history.

Maybe the lesson is that had the rules of the game been just as clear-cut on shore, or had both sides played by the SAME rules, the outcome would have been more sporting.

No one really expects 19th-century civility to reassert itself on the America's Cup course; the event has grown too big, too intense, too dependent on such 20th-century influences as the media and corporate sponsorship. But failing that, can we expect at least a return to sanity and some semblance of fair play?

Probably not in 1987. With less than a year to go, the madness seems too far advanced. If the summer of '83 was the death throes of amateurism, 1987 shapes up as the year the new professionalism will experience its birth pangs — and they may make the turmoil in Newport look like a tea party.

Tom Ehman thinks it will go more smoothly than that. He believes all sides made mistakes last time around, "and we all learned a lot from it, not only about each other but about how to go about these things in sport. I doubt you'll see any big controversies like that. I hope not. I think you'll see a real fine sporting event."

Ehman, as executive director of the United States Yacht Racing Union in 1983, had a close-up view of the imbroglio in Newport; now he is managing the NYYC's America II challenge. He combines an ingrained respect for the sporting traditions of yachting with a pragmatic acceptance of the new rules of the game. At age 32, he may represent the future of America's Cup management.

"We're also all pretty good friends," Ehman said, speaking of the main combatants in 1983. Doubtless there are those in Perth and New York who would find that statement a little too sweeping, but it is certainly true of the two yacht clubs. There are signs already that Royal Perth finds itself philosophically closer to the NYYC than to Alan Bond or Warren Jones.

But more to the point, it is probably true of the sailors in each country as well. Dennis Conner marvelled at the hero's welcome he got when he visited Perth, and Ehman says there's been a lot of socializing in Fremantle between the 1987 defenders and challengers. It is a camaraderie based in part on a shared understanding of the new intensity in America's Cup racing, and the new code of sportsmanship that goes with it.

Ehman says he is among those who believe *Australia II*'s keel was illegal. But ultimately, he said, it was legal because they managed to prevent it from being declared otherwise. "I don't want to be perceived as being critical of the Australians for doing what they did," Ehman said. "We will do the same thing. You have to go as far as you think you can go with the rule, because of the way this sport is administered. If it's not clear whether something is legal or not, you've got to go for it and see where the chips fall."

Preliminary reports suggest there will be a lot of chips falling all over Fremantle in 1987. But even now some people are thinking about reform. They may not be thinking of it in these terms, but what they are doing is trying to ease the transition, already well along, from the Cup's amateur era to a new professionalism. Their thoughts run to tightening the rules, reducing the appalling waste and duplication of resources, providing stronger management, and coming to grips with the rewards and pitfalls of corporate sponsorship. Some tentative steps have already been taken in those directions already, with mixed results.

Royal Perth has gotten high marks on its handling of the rules so far. Rather than draw up the conditions for the next match and send them out for approval, it asked for advice from the beginning and circulated working drafts among the challengers. "We all made suggestions and Royal Perth adopted most of them," Ehman said. "They've been very good about that."

RPYC also appointed Costa Smeralda Yacht Club, the Aga Khan's club and sponsor of *Azzurra* in 1983, as Challenger of Record — the club responsible for administration of the challenger elimination series and liaison between challenging and defending clubs. Some saw that as a slap in the face to the NYYC, but others thought it a wise move, like holding a summit conference in Geneva rather than Washington or Moscow. Besides, that put Comandante Gianfranco Alberini in charge, whose skill as a negotiator has turned several potential contretemps into acceptable compromises.

One result of this process is that the rules will be much more specific this time. For example, rather than a general prohibition against getting outside information on wind and weather conditions once the 10-minute warning gun sounds, there will be precise restrictions on what kind of radio equipment may be carried on the boats. "We even talked about the race committee giving each boat a hand-held walkie-talkie just before each race, so no one would have time to doctor it or change crystals," Ehman said.

On the other hand, all efforts toward pooling syndicates' resources and avoiding duplication of effort have come to naught so far. One of the first was aborted even before it was launched.

The launching was held anyway, on January 8, 1984, at the NYYC, and it seemed promising. A gathering of NYYC officers and several past and present Cup contenders heard a presentation from representatives of Science Applications International Corporation (SAIC), a major high-tech defense department contractor.

Their message was that all the syndicates needed the same information — precise weather data off Perth during the summer months — and they could provide it. They were saying, why don't you guys hire us jointly and save yourselves some money?

Johan Valentijn, Dennis Conner's designer in 1983, thought it was a plausible idea. The next morning he had breakfast with Conner. Conner asked him what he thought of the proposal. As Valentijn recalls it, he had barely responded when Conner said, "Well, let me tell you something. I've already got them lined up for me. They can't work for everybody like they're proposing here, because I signed them up a few days ago." Valentijn asked, "Why the meeting, then?" Conner said it had already been set up, so they just went ahead with it.

Valentijn thinks the NYYC was angered by his preemptive strike and that's why he isn't representing the club in 1987. In any case, Conner's wooing of the club was not reciprocated. Two weeks later, he announced he was forming a "national effort" to win back the Cup, based at the San Diego Yacht Club, of which he was commodore. "The New York Yacht Club deserves recognition for upholding the best traditions in yachting for more than a century, but because of the enthusiasm and support we have received for mounting a truly national effort, we feel this is the appropriate path to take," he said at his press conference.

The NYYC chose the syndicate put together by Chuck Kirsch and John Kolius toward the end of their Defender/Courageous campaign in 1983. But it, too, went the route of lining up several affiliated yacht clubs as co-sponsors — the first step in acknowledging what the club had never quite admitted before, that the Cup is indeed a national trophy, larger than any single club.

Almost from the start, when 10 U.S. challengers were struggling to raise the cash for a campaign, behind-the-scenes talks were going on among them about possible mergers. One startling revelation, in view of their mutually disparaging comments and Conner's insistence that his program is further advanced than anyone's, was confirmation early in 1986 that he had approached the America II challenge about merging. The two syndicates talked about it, more intensively after John Kolius' resignation (see previous chapter), but the discussions died when Kolius returned.

One obvious problem: Conner's Sail America Challenge is sponsored by Ford, America II by Cadillac. Similar conflicts apparently doomed similar overtures among other syndicates. Meanwhile, the U.S. challengers met in San Francisco in January, 1986, to talk about pooling corporate sponsorship, but it seemed hopeless that late in the game. One can be certain it is on several agendas for the post-1987 match, however, along with such suggestions as sail-offs within the challenging countries, so each would be represented by a single boat.

Management of the races has been a growing headache in recent years. Few members of the New York Yacht Club are willing to look at it this way, but it could be argued the Aussies' victory came just in time. Not only had the event outgrown its genteel traditions and its Newport playground, it had outstripped the ability of the NYYC — or perhaps any other club — to run it effectively.

It wasn't generally known at the time, but the NYYC was quietly trying to remove itself from the center of the storm even before the unpleasantries of 1983 began. Ehman, then director of the USYRU, disclosed long after the event that club representatives had approached him in June with the proposition that USYRU or some other agency take over the management of future Cup matches — providing, of course, that the Cup was still the property of the NYYC after September. The club desperately wanted to keep its trophy, but was almost as anxious to divest itself of the hassles involved in running the races, not to mention the inherent conflicts of interest its dual role involved.

There was talk of an Olympics-style organization and of keeping the match in Newport on a permanent basis. When the Aussies won, that was the end of that, of course. Now the shoe is on the other foot; Royal Perth faces an even more daunting logistical problem and, as we have seen, ran into some flak for the way it tried to shift some of its burden. It remains to be seen how well it will juggle up to 18 syndicates and their boats, as well as the conflict of interest that goes with the defender's territory. The betting is 1987 will be the last year a single yacht club tries to run the races unassisted, but what will take its place is unknown. Both Conner and Robert McCullough of the NYYC have said they favored the idea of turning the Cup over to an independent board of directors if they win it.

Corporate sponsorship has taken some bizarre twists, as we have seen. But one of the most bizarre was the photograph of Richard DeVos shaking hands with Alan Bond in Fremantle as DeVos became the second person (after Brian Burke, Western Australia's premier) to plunk down $10 and join Bond's America's Cup Defence Club. What made it startling was that the company DeVos heads, the Amway Corporation in Ada, Michigan, is a major corporate sponsor of the NYYC's America II challenge, and DeVos was the syndicate's finance chairman at the time! (Now he is its overall chairman.)

Amway is an international company involved in the direct marketing of housewares. The employees of its Australian branch wanted equal time, DeVos explained. So, with his blessings, they launched a grassroots campaign for Bond's syndicate. DeVos called it a "win-win" situation for the company. It's a startling thought for those who see commercial sponsorship as, at best, a necessary evil, but perhaps the key to restoring the spirit of "friendly competition between foreign countries" lies in the corporate connection!

But there are also potential conflicts in corporate support. One of the most glaring recent examples involved two major contributors to the America II syndicate, Perry Bass, a Texas billionaire who is honorary chairman of America II's board of directors, and Newsweek magazine. Newsweek did a cover story on Bass before it became a sponsor. But then, as if to make that presumably unintentional conflict as compromising as possible, the magazine built a two-page color ad for itself around its Bass profile — and placed it in, among other markets, a publication devoted exclusively to the America's Cup!

In time, the players will learn to avoid such growing pains. The real question is the future of sportsmanship and the America's Cup, whether the Cup itself stays in Perth or moves to New York, Halifax, or even to that newly discovered arm of the sea, Lake Michigan. The professionalization of the Cup is proceeding apace; already some syndicates reportedly are paying their skippers salaries into six figures. Will sportsmanship return?

It's an open question, but there was one hopeful straw in the wind early in December of '85. At a time when stories of secrecy, spying and clandestine activities by America's Cup syndicates were becoming routine, the NYYC's syndicate made news by moving in the opposite direction.

As Tom Ehman tells the story, he got a call from a foundryman in England who offered to sell the Americans copies of the secret plans for the British syndicate's new keel, for a mere $25,000. Ehman dismissed the caller as a crank. But just in case, he suggested the caller send him a corner of the alleged plans as proof. Ehman was surprised two weeks later when the incriminating piece of paper arrived in the mail. He immediately called the chairman of the English syndicate, then collaborated with a sting operation set up by the British police. The thief was arrested turning the purloined plans over to a policeman he thought was a member of the NYYC. The Brits kept their secrets and justice was done.

Justice has been a hallmark of the NYYC in recent years, but it was not always so. It took the club decades to ease the manifestly unfair conditions under which it ran its first several matches. Now the wheel has come full circle and many people will see justice — poetic justice — in the situation that faces the club as it launches its first challenge: To win back its precious Cup in the waters off Fremantle, it will have to defeat 17 other contenders.

Those are precisely the same odds the club offered its first challenger back in 1870.